WAR AT SEA

JAMES P. DELGADO

WAR AT SEA

A Shipwrecked History
from Antiquity to the Cold War

OXFORD
UNIVERSITY PRESS

OXFORD
UNIVERSITY PRESS

Oxford University Press is a department of the University of Oxford.
It furthers the University's objective of excellence in research, scholarship,
and education by publishing worldwide. Oxford is a registered trade mark of
Oxford University Press in the UK and certain other countries.

Published in the United States of America by Oxford University Press
198 Madison Avenue, New York, NY 10016, United States of America.

© Oxford University Press 2019

All rights reserved. No part of this publication may be reproduced,
stored in a retrieval system, or transmitted, in any form or by any means,
without the prior permission in writing of Oxford University Press,
or as expressly permitted by law, by license, or under terms agreed with
the appropriate reproduction rights organization. Inquiries concerning
reproduction outside the scope of the above should be sent to the
Rights Department, Oxford University Press, at the address above.

You must not circulate this work in any other form
and you must impose this same condition on any acquirer.

CIP data is on file at the Library of Congress

ISBN: 978-0-19-088801-5

9 8 7 6 5 4 3 2 1

Printed by Sheridan Books, Inc., United States of America

To all who sail in harm's way, and in remembrance of those who sleep in the deep, many in unmarked graves.
And for my granddaughter Kaleigh, who, like her mother, brings peace and love to my heart.

CONTENTS

MAPS

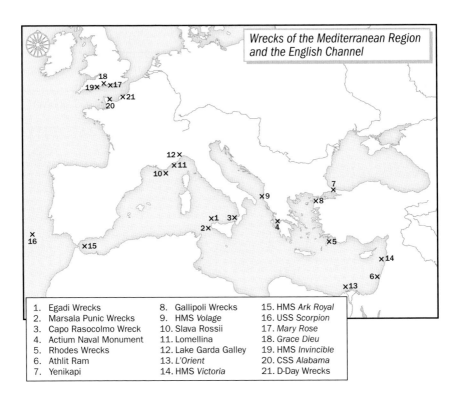

Wrecks of the Mediterranean Region
and the English Channel

1. Egadi Wrecks	8. Gallipoli Wrecks	15. HMS *Ark Royal*
2. Marsala Punic Wrecks	9. HMS *Volage*	16. USS *Scorpion*
3. Capo Rasocolmo Wreck	10. Slava Rossii	17. *Mary Rose*
4. Actium Naval Monument	11. Lomellina	18. *Grace Dieu*
5. Rhodes Wrecks	12. Lake Garda Galley	19. HMS *Invincible*
6. Athlit Ram	13. *L'Orient*	20. CSS *Alabama*
7. Yenikapi	14. HMS *Victoria*	21. D-Day Wrecks

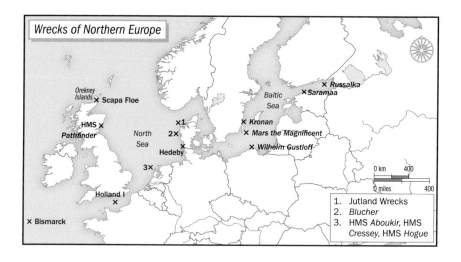

Wrecks of Northern Europe

Orekney Islands X Scapa Floe

HMS X
Pathfinder

North Sea

X 1
2 X
X Hedeby

3 X

Holland I
X

X Bismarck

Baltic Sea

X Russalka
X Saramaa

X Kronan
X Mars the Magnificent
X Wilhelm Gustloff

0 km 400

0 miles 400

1. Jutland Wrecks
2. *Blucher*
3. HMS *Aboukir*, HMS *Cressey*, HMS *Hogue*

Wrecks of the Gulf of Mexico/Caribbean and Central America

12 X

X 8
X 10

X 14
2 X

X 5

X 9

X 1

X 16
X 15

X 6

X 3
X 4

X 7

13 X

X 11

1. *La Trinité*
2. Monterrey Wrecks
3. Cortes's Fleet
4. USB *Somers*
5. USS *Massachusetts*
6. USS *Maine*
7. Battle of Santiago Wrecks
8. *La Belle*
9. *Maple Leaf*
10. USS *Hatteras*
11. *Satisfaction*
12. USS *Cairo*
13. Rockley Bay Fleet
14. U-166
15. Molasses Reef Wreck
16. Highbourne Cay Wreck

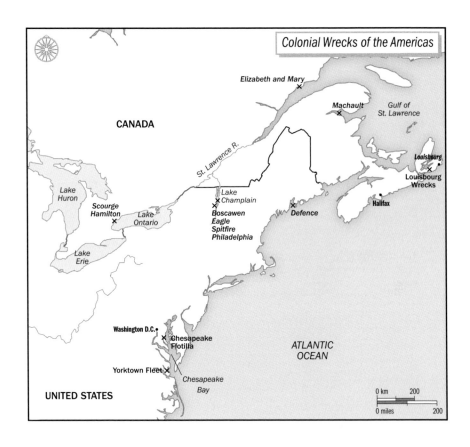

Colonial Wrecks of the Americas

CANADA

Elizabeth and Mary ✕

Machault ✕

Gulf of St. Lawrence

St. Lawrence R.

Lake Huron

Lake Ontario

Scourge ✕ Hamilton

Lake Erie

Lake ✕ Champlain
Boscawen
Eagle
Spitfire
Philadelphia

Defence ✕

Louisbourg •
✕
Louisbourg
Wrecks

Halifax •

ATLANTIC
OCEAN

Washington D.C. •
✕ Chesapeake
Flotilla

Yorktown Fleet ✕

Chesapeake
Bay

UNITED STATES

0 km   200

0 miles   200

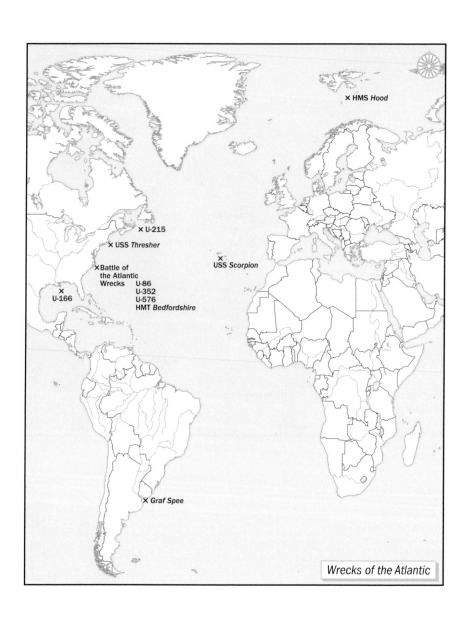

× HMS *Hood*

× U-215

× USS *Thresher*

× USS *Scorpion*

×Battle of
the Atlantic
Wrecks   U-86
           U-352
           U-576
           HMT *Bedfordshire*

×
U-166

× *Graf Spee*

Wrecks of the Atlantic

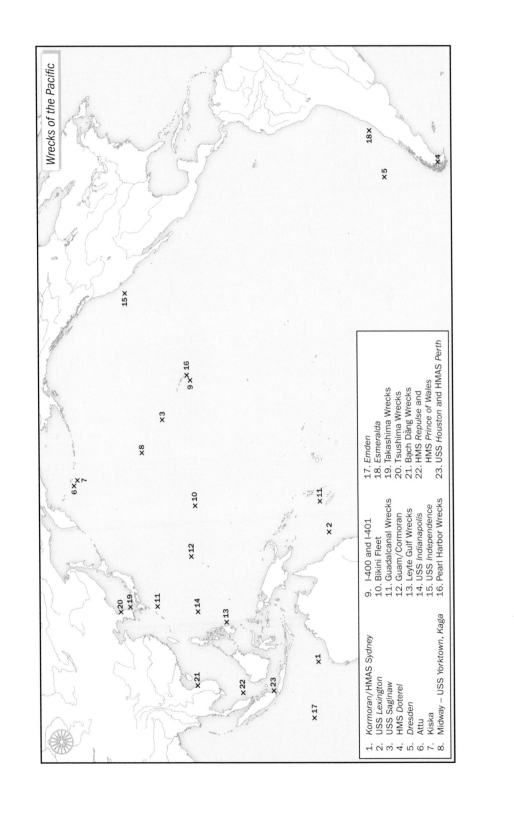

Wrecks of the Pacific

1. *Kormoran*/HMAS *Sydney*
2. USS *Lexington*
3. USS *Saginaw*
4. HMS *Doterel*
5. *Dresden*
6. Attu
7. Kiska
8. Midway – USS *Yorktown*, *Kaga*
9. I-400 and I-401
10. Bikini Fleet
11. Guadalcanal Wrecks
12. Guam/Cormoran
13. Leyte Gulf Wrecks
14. USS *Indianapolis*
15. USS *Independence*
16. Pearl Harbor Wrecks
17. *Emden*
18. *Esmeralda*
19. Takashima Wrecks
20. Tsushima Wrecks
21. Bạch Đằng Wrecks
22. HMS *Repulse* and HMS *Prince of Wales*
23. USS *Houston* and HMAS *Perth*

ACKNOWLEDGMENTS

I start with my editor, Stefan Vranka, and the incredible team at Oxford University Press. Stefan guided me with insightful review, edits, and questions as I prepared this book.

There are so many to whom I owe a debt of gratitude incurred in the field work, research, and analysis on the various projects I've been privileged to work on with you over the past decades. Equally, the same is true for the many of you who have collegially and helpfully shared the results of your own work, offered insights, and, on occasion, provided insightful review and helpful criticism. If I have forgotten, or not given due acknowledgment, I offer my apology in advance and my regret. Not one of us embarks on the journey of our careers, and indeed, in life, without the help and guidance of others. These include: Kathy Abbass, Steve Acheson, Jon Adams, Christian Ahlstrom, David Alberg, Chris Amer, Adrian Anastasi, J. Barto Arnold, Oguz Aydemir, Dan Bailey, Robert D. Ballard, Bradley Barr, George F. Bass, Daniel J. Basta, Kroum Batchvarov, David Beard, Edwin C. Bearss, the late George R. Belcher, Marc-Andre Bernier, Amy Borgens, Mensun Bound, Michael Brennan, Leslie Bright, John Broadwater, John Brooks, Ruth Brown, Burl Burlingame, Frank Cantelas, Pete Capelloti, Diego Carabias, Tane Casserley, Ken Cassavoy, Filipe V. Castro, Alexis Catsambis, Arne Emil Christensen, Robert Church, John Cloud, Art Cohn, David L. Conlin, Ed Cotham, Max Cramer, Kevin J. Crisman, the late Ole Crumlin Pederson, Clive Cussler, John B. Davis, the late Martin Dean, John DeBry, Kevin Denlay, Malcolm Dixilius, Christopher Dobbs, Chris Dostal, Carl Douglas, William Dudley, the late Claude Duthuit, Enis Edis, Lars Einarsson,

Andrew Elkerton, Dolores Elkin, Kelly Elliott, Pilar Luna Erreguerena, Gary Fabian, Rudolfo Fattovich, Larrie Feirrero, Antony Firth, the late George R. Fischer, Charles Fithian, Mike Fletcher, Ben Ford, Kevin J. Foster, Chelsea Freeland, the late Tom W. Freeman, Danijel Frka, the late Honor Frost, George Galasso, William H. Garzke Jr., Peter Gesner, Anna Gibson-Holloway, James Goold, Richard A. Gould, Rachel Grant, Jeremy Green, Robert Grenier, Captain Max Guerot, John R. Hale, Andy Hall, the late Wes Hall, Frederick "Fritz" Hanselmann, Edward C. Harris, Kenzo Hayashida, Alex Hildred, Fred Hocker, Olaf Hockmann, Robert Holcombe Jr., Keith Holland, Fred Hopkins Jr., Christopher Horrell, Joe Hoyt, James Hunter III, Gillian Hutchinson, Rebecca Ingram, Jack Irion, Maria Jacobsen, Stephen R. James, Bill Jeffrey, Paul F. Johnston, Michael Jones, Roberto Junco, David Jourdan, Savas Karakas, Donald Keith, Terry Kerby, Sean Kery, Jun Kimura, Roger Knight, Richie Kohler, Selçuk Kolay, the late Toshiharu Konada, Robert Kraft, Willi Kramer, Dave Krop, Lars Ake Kvarning, John Lambert, Harold Langley, Susan Langley, Richard Lawrence, Jonathan Leader, Daniel J. Lenihan, Megan Lickliter-Mundon, Le Thi Lien, Vu The Lo, Richard Lundgren, the late David J. Lyon, Bu The Mai, Mike Mair, Paul Mardikian, Peter Marsden, Colin J. M. Martin, Daniel J. Martinez, Rod Mather, Guy Matthias, Russ Matthews, Vello Mass, Michael "Mack" McCarthy, Innes McCartney, Bob Mealings, David Mearns, Captain Aurtur Meçollari, Chuck Meide, Tomas Mendizabal, Jonathan Moore, Julie Morgan, the late Torao Mozai, Larry Murphy, William Murray, Robert Neyland, Pam Orlando, Augustin Ortiz Jr., Ole Oskarsson, Sylvain Pascaud, Kaido Peremees, Brett Phaneuf, Robin Piercy, Steve Price, Cemal Pulak, Jim Reimer, Warren Reiss, Dominique Rissolo, George Robb, Johann Rönnby, Phillipe Rouja, Jeff Royal, the late Margaret Rule, Matt Russell, John Sands, Andy Sansom, Randall J. Sasaki, Michael Scafuri, Robert Schwemmer, Brett Seymour, Magdi Shalash, Donald G. Shomette, Russ Skowronek, Roger Smith, James Spirek, Mark Staniforth, the late J. Richard Steffy, William N. Still, the late David Switzer, Bruce Terrell, Sebastiano Tusa, Richard Unger, Frederick H. Van Doorninck Jr., Hans K. Van Tilburg, Ole Varmer, Nick Veronico, Andrew Viduka, Shelley Wachsmann, Ted Waitt, Joy Waldron, Cheryl Ward, Dan Warren, Glen

Watabayashi, Gordon P. Watts Jr., Peter Way, Ralph Wilbanks, Mark Wilde-Ramsing, Robyn Woodward, and Joe Zarzynski.

The field work that I was able to accomplish came through the auspices and support of my employers at the time, and I gratefully acknowledge the National Park Service, the National Oceanic and Atmospheric Administration, the Institute of Nautical Archaeology, and the Vancouver Maritime Museum. I also thank the National Geographic Society, Econova Productions, Ltd., the RPM Nautical Foundation, and the Waitt Institute for their support.

The following institutions and organizations were consulted and provided assistance, for which I am very grateful: Association CSS *Alabama*, Paris, France; USS *Arizona* Memorial, US National Park Service, Honolulu, Hawaii; Bateaux Below, Inc., Wilton, New York; the National Museum of Bermuda, Mangrove Bay; the British Museum, London; Confederate Naval Museum, Columbus, Georgia; the National Museum of the Civil War, Richmond, Virginia; Independence Seaport, Philadelphia, Pennsylvania; Institute of Nautical Archaeology, Texas A&M University, College Station; Kalmar Lans Museum, Kalmar, Sweden; Lake Champlain Maritime Museum, Basin Harbor, Vermont; the Mariners' Museum, Newport News, Virginia; the *Mary Rose* Trust, Portsmouth, England; Museum fur Antike Schiffahrt, Mainz, Germany; USS *Monitor* National Marine Sanctuary, Newport News, Virginia; National Museum of American History, Smithsonian Institution, Washington, DC; North Carolina Underwater Archaeology Unit, Kure Beach; the Imperial War Museum, London; the Western Australian Museum, Perth; the Imperial Palace Museum, Tokyo; Yashukan Museum and Yasakuni Shrine, Tokyo; the Istanbul Naval Museum, Istanbul, Turkey; the Royal British Columbia Museum, Victoria, Canada; the Museum of Hong Kong History, Hong Kong, China; the National Museum of Vietnamese History, Hanoi, Vietnam; Dier el Bahri, Egypt, Medinet Habu, Egypt; the Egyptian Museum, Cairo, Egypt; Akrotiri, Santorini, Greece; the Estonian National Maritime Museum, Tallinn, Estonia; the National Museum of Denmark, Copenhagen, Denmark; the Swedish National Maritime Museum, Stockholm, Sweden; the Maritime Museum of Finland, Kotka; Queensland Museum, South Brisbane, Australia;

Romish-Germanisches Zentralmuseum, Mainz, Germany; the Royal Naval Museum, Portsmouth, England; the Royal Navy Submarine Museum, Gosport, England; the Scottish Institute of Maritime Studies, University of St. Andrews, Scotland; Ships of Discovery/Corpus Christi Museum, Texas; South Carolina Institute of Archaeology and Anthropology, Columbia; Submerged Cultural Resources Center, US National Park Service, Santa Fe, New Mexico; US Naval Historical Center, Washington, DC; US Naval Historical Museum, Washington, DC; Underwater Archaeological Society of British Columbia, Vancouver, Canada; Vancouver Maritime Museum, Vancouver, British Columbia, Canada; *Vasa* Museum, Stockholm, Sweden; Vicksburg National Military Park, US National Park Service, Vicksburg, Mississippi; Viking Ship Museum, Roskilde, Denmark; and the Viking Ship Museum, Oslo, Norway.

I apologize to any and all who may have been forgotten in these acknowledgments. In the span of 40 years of working in the field and on many projects, sometimes it happens, and it does not mean that your support, help, and contributions went unappreciated.

Any errors and omissions in this book are my sole responsibility.

James Delgado

PREFACE

M y interest in archaeology began with a fascination of ancient people and how they lived. My earliest work, in my native California, was with the sites of the indigenous Ohlone culture in my hometown, and then the California Gold Rush and the role ships played in shaping San Francisco and my home state. As a young man coming of age during the Vietnam War, I'll also admit that I was wary of the military and did not have a powerful interest in military history. That changed when I served in the National Park Service (NPS) as maritime historian and worked for Chief Historian Edwin C. Bearss. A member of the 3rd Marine Raider Battalion, Ed fought at Guadalcanal, the Russell Islands, and New Britain, where he was grievously wounded. In 1954, he joined the NPS and began his decades-long career with the service, and when I joined his staff in 1987 it was to work on a then-new partnership between the NPS and the National Oceanic and Atmospheric Administration (NOAA) for the wreck of the Civil War ironclad USS *Monitor*.

As the maritime historian of the NPS, I also toured the United States to study ships, sites, and wrecks worthy of designation as national landmarks, and participated in maritime archaeological projects, which included work at Pearl Harbor. Over the course of four years, I toured every state and every maritime and naval museum, and dived on many wrecks, inspired and supported by Ed, who made it clear that I could not study, preserve, or understand unless I did these things. "You can't understand a battlefield unless you walk it," he said. So it came to pass that I spent those four years immersed in maritime and naval history, whether afloat or underwater. I explored sealed-off compartments, dark passageways, and cold boiler flats, and spent long hours in the archives or museum storerooms. All of these gave me a unique opportunity to explore frigates, submarines, battleships, destroyers, and carriers, as well as PT boats, tugs, and landing craft.

My experiences on land, in the archives and museums, and aboard the surviving warships made distant battles of the past more personal. But what made the connection, and made me focus increasingly on ships of war, was the time I spent with veterans. The first assignment that brought home this point was my interviews with veterans of the Pacific Theater of World War II, particularly American and Japanese survivors of Pearl Harbor. Logbooks, muster rolls, reminiscences, and faded photographs brought into focus battles from their memories rather than from physical remains. But by far my most intense experiences came beneath the sea as an archaeologist. Famous and forgotten ships, types of vessels and weapons otherwise glimpsed in photographs, paintings, or in models, and the physical reality of the battlefield added to my education and to my enthusiasm, and also revealed that archaeology can give voice to the dead in a way that even survivors cannot.

Diving on these ships and learning their stories carries a responsibility along with the privilege. The responsibility is to bring forth the images and stories and share them. I have been fortunate to meet and work with a large number of colleagues from around the world who have also explored lost warships. Many of us collaborated to create *The British Museum Encyclopaedia of Underwater and Maritime Archaeology*.

The exchanges with my colleagues as well as the undeniable fascination of simply seeing some of these submerged warriors and their battlefields were the inspiration for an earlier book, *Lost Warships*. *Lost Warships* was not intended to be a comprehensive review of war at sea, nor a detailed accounting of the development of the warship through history. It was neither full of the technical specifications for these ships, nor a blow-by-blow accounting of sea battles.

It was intended for a wider audience of divers, students of the past, and those interested in the saga of war at sea. Nearly two decades have passed since I wrote *Lost Warships*. *War at Sea* is much more than a rewrite of *Lost Warships*. The last two decades have seen an exponential growth in the number of warship discoveries, and even as I write this at the end of 2017, one of the last enduring mysteries of World War II at sea, the final resting place of the USS *Indianapolis*, the cruiser that delivered the atomic bomb to Tinian, and the famous carrier USS *Hornet* have been found. With colleagues, I am working on new expeditions that may imminently yield even more amazing finds in the deepest parts of the ocean.

After I wrote *Lost Warships* in 1999, I spent six years working as the traveling and diving archaeologist and host of National Geographic International's television show *The Sea Hunters*, in which I participated in and led expeditions to a number of lost warships, some of them only then recently discovered. None of those wrecks we dived, other than Kublai Khan's lost fleet, were featured in *Lost Warships*. Since then, archaeology has revealed a vastly larger site and hundreds of new finds. This is one example of many in which the archaeological study of warships has grown in the last two decades.

Adding to these new finds are amazing new developments that have emerged from ongoing excavations and laboratory analysis of finds from sites like the ongoing study of the massive collection of artifacts from the 1628 wreck of *Vasa*, the raised turret of the USS *Monitor*, or the interior of the raised Confederate Civil War submarine *H. L. Hunley*. *War at Sea* retains some of *Lost Warships*, but it is a substantially different, new book.

Since I wrote *Lost Warships*, another great shift in terms of the loss of living memory came as the last veterans of World War I passed away. What is now happening is the passing of the last generation to fight an extended war at sea during World War II. Those veterans who remain are in their nineties. They will soon all be gone, as distant to younger generations as those who fought in the Spanish American War were to mine. Also striking is the loss of shipwrecks, not only as these sites are trawled away as fishing grounds expand but also, shockingly, as artifacts are stolen off the seabed by modern salvagers who care nothing of these wrecks as graves or as historic and archaeological sites. This is highlighted not only off the coast of Europe with World War I wrecks, but in the Pacific.

The wrecks of the Battle of the Java Sea (1942)—the British heavy cruiser HMS *Exeter*, the Dutch light cruisers HNLMS *Java* and HNLMS *DeRuyter*, the Australian light cruiser HMAS *Perth*, the British destroyers

HMS *Electra*, HMS *Encounter*, HMS *Jupiter*, and the Dutch destroyer HNLMS *Kortenaer*—were discovered between 2002 and 2008, but subsequently were illegally salvaged. The US Navy's lost submarine USS *Perch*, also sunk in the Java Sea, has also been salvaged and destroyed. This is not the looting of a treasure ship for its gold; here, the illegal salvage is literally of entire ships for their bulk steel. Left behind are scant traces or nothing at all in one of the most shocking recent developments in the history of sunken warships.

I hope the pages that follow show you why we must preserve and study these wrecks. Through them, we have learned and can continue to learn the lessons they can teach us about war. This is true especially as these ships and the spaces within them provide eloquent physical testimony about not just the ships, but of life and death, and a sense of those who went down with them. Through the archaeology of lost warships, the dead can indeed tell tales.

James P. Delgado

WAR AT SEA

Earth's Greatest Battlefield

From space, the view of earth leaves no doubt that this is a water planet. Water dwarfs the landmasses, large as they seem to a landlubber's perspective. One great ocean washes all those shores, and though it bears many names—Mediterranean, Baltic, Indian, Pacific, and Atlantic, it covers most of the earth. The sea has defined our history since the beginning of human endeavor, when we first built ships. The sea is the source of our life and the connective thread of our commerce.

Millennia of war at sea have left a lasting trace in thousands of ships that in many cases are the graves of countless tens of thousands of men. Other than memory, how do we remember and commemorate these ships, these men, these battles? The battlefields of the ocean are a vast, unmarked grave. No monuments stand on patches of water marked only by coordinates on a chart. The sea rarely gives up the dead. To honor the living and the dead, we occasionally return to those battlefields, to speak of sacrifice and determination, or to silently toll the bell and toss wreaths into the dark sea. We erect monuments on land like Nelson's Column in Trafalgar Square, the

USS *Maine* Memorial at Arlington, and a score of other statues and ceno-
taphs around the world.

We save and memorialize surviving warships. By far the greatest number
of preserved historic ships in the world's museums are warships. For those
who did not serve, some sense of "what it was like" is conveyed by the reality of the armor, the guns, the cramped quarters, and the written word, the
oral history, the photographs, paintings, or films of those rapidly retreating
times—the stories behind the physical artifacts.

Some of those stories are reminiscences, as well as the analytical work of
historians. In more modern times, motion pictures have offered imagery of
row galleys at ramming speed, ships of the line hammering at each other
with broadsides, battleship salvos, carrier battles, World War II submarines
running silent and deep, and high-speed "cat-and-mouse" battles of skill by
Cold War submariners.

War at sea is a powerful subject rich in history, imagery, and emotion. It
should come as no surprise that all of these books, songs, and films; these
museum ships resting peacefully at the dock; or the displays of paintings
and memorabilia in galleries do not satisfy our need to remember, commemorate, and touch the past. That is why over the past several decades
divers, underwater explorers, and archaeologists have ventured into the
deep in search of lost warships. I personally know the allure, for I am one
of them.

History comes alive when you enter those dark compartments. I've felt
it, after sharing memories with survivors and then dropping down through
the water to see firsthand what they've talked about. I'm not alone. That is
why millions of viewers watch televised specials or live, Internet-based exploration of these wrecks. That is why archaeologists raise artifacts and
entire ships, like the Swedish galleon *Vasa* and Henry VIII's carrack *Mary
Rose*, to share with non-diving museum visitors.

This book is a review of what archaeologists have learned about lost warships, battles on the water, and the life and death of those caught up in those
conflicts—a tour, if you will, through an imaginary museum of underwater
archaeology. Many of these wrecks, and their stories, have been featured in
the popular media. The stories of *Vasa,* CSS *Hunley,* USS *Monitor,* USS

Arizona, Mary Rose, the Nydam ship, or the lost Mongol fleet of Kublai Khan are just some of the warships to "surface" in the public eye through television or in the pages of magazines like *Naval History* or *National Geographic.* For most people, the stories often end there, fading away into the background of our fast-paced digital world. But for archaeologists and other students of the past, archaeology is more than just the discovery.

Archaeology, the careful, scientific recovery and study of the past, is two centuries old. Archaeology beneath the sea dates only to the 1960s. Over the past few decades, thousands of shipwrecks have been discovered, and a few hundred have been documented, excavated, and recovered by archaeologists. Some sank in storms, or by accident. Others were sent deliberately to the bottom, blasted to a watery grave with their crews. They range in age from ancient row galleys that sank one another with huge bronze rams at their wooden bows to modern steel ships sunk by aircraft, missiles, or nuclear weapons. In studying these lost warships, archaeologists learn many things. Older wrecks may provide us with a detailed sense of what these ships actually looked like. Newer wrecks may provide a closer picture of an actual battle.

In the chapters that follow, I hope you see how little we actually know about many warships, from ancient times through the medieval period. In a number of cases, archaeologists and naval historians are "reconstructing" warships from paintings, sculptures, images on coins, models from tombs, and descriptions from ancient literature. Oftentimes, that is not enough. You need the actual wreck of the ship; otherwise, it's all a fair amount of guesswork. Many discussions, and occasional controversies, often dominate the field of nautical archaeology over the size of certain ships, the arrangement of oars, decks, and the construction of the hull—not to mention tactics and how battles actually would have unfolded.

Nautical archaeologists in particular are interested in how ships were built and worked, and specifically how different they were from merchant ships built to carry passengers or cargo. Changing technology of armament and propulsion influenced the design of warships, as did the availability of materials. Oftentimes changes did not happen progressively or uniformly around the world. Contrary to most history books, the Chinese adopted gunpowder weapons, the rudder, armor, and paddlewheels long before Europeans did. While the Mediterranean powers continued to focus on oar-powered warships, Northern Europeans were building larger, ocean-going sailing ships that developed into platforms for guns, which was the genesis of the famous galleon.

The physical evidence from the sea provides a better picture of when certain developments occurred such as the introduction of guns. It also gives us a better physical sense of the very sophisticated, often intricately developed methods of construction employed by the architects of war-ships. The carefully engineered bow of an ancient warship, built to with-stand the shock of ramming another ship, or the methodical reinforcing of an early multi-decked galleon to carry the weight of the guns remind us that our ancestors were at least as clever as we are today. Wrecks like the famous *Vasa* or *Mary Rose*, both of which capsized and sank, killing most of their crews, also remind us that some of those lessons of warship design were learned through harsh trial and error.

Archaeology is a tool used to study people and their behavior. Individuals and societies under stress often make choices that are revealing about themselves and their circumstances. The archaeology of warships often shows how ships can be built quickly, under exigent circumstances, to re-spond to a crisis. Years of tradition are discarded in times of strategic vul-nerability. Technology leaps forward. Certain types of ships are found to be more efficient, hence more construction of carriers, submarines, and de-stroyers during World War II than giant battleships. Shortcuts not accept-able in peacetime—such as ships built out of green, unseasoned timber, or the rapid "acceptance" of all-welded as opposed to riveted construction—arise from wartime emergencies. There are also examples of recycling. These are warships that are practically rebuilt under the guise of "repair" in fiscally strapped times. There is also the difficult and labor-intensive salvage of ships that would be "written off" in peacetime, while allowing them to be repaired and pressed back into service in wartime. All of these speak vol-umes about human nature.

Anthropologist Richard A. Gould has spent much of his career studying the social history of ships and what they reveal about us as a species.

The response to new technologies and the misapplication of those technologies is a particular interest of his. The 19th-century introduction of armor, steam engines, and shell-firing guns changed warships and naval warfare. But in some cases, such as the rise of the battleship, the efforts and energies expended were largely wasted. Battleships for the most part did not function, fight, or die as the tacticians and designers intended. In the hundred years that spanned the mid-19th and mid-20th centuries, 650 battleships were built. They were designed for ship-to-ship sea battles. But only 16 were sunk as a result of this type of action.

In this Gould sees a "consistent misapplication of new technologies to naval tactics." How this happened, and why, is a question he has examined. The answers are complex and perhaps debatable. Tactical indecision, confusion over what a new technology really means, the need to integrate a new technology even before all the implications are known or tested, the always fascinating difference between theory and practice, and the need to match a foe's developments, weapon for weapon, all play a part.

What is perhaps most important is how these wrecks speak to us about people. In the stories that follow, I hope that you, the reader, come away with a better understanding not only of the times and cultures that produced these ships of war, but of the people who built, lived in, fought in, and died in these ships. There are two themes in particular that I'd like to address. The first is our propensity, as humans, to use violence as a means to an end. In a number of these cases, the ships and sites you are about to visit speak to this problematic aspect of our nature. Some ships were built to project power and inflict violence, others were built to defend against those who would come by sea to take, to impose, or to harm. The second is that in many cases, and particularly in any future, in ages where empires, nations, rulers, or causes have faded into the history books, these shattered ships contain within them, whether figuratively or literally, those who were lost with them. While there are and will always be fervent adherents to an ideology, patriots who fight for love of country, and those who follow the drumbeats of war, there are others who go fight and die because like so many in history, they were caught up in something bigger than themselves, and in events over which they as individuals had no choice.

1

Beginnings

As for those assembled on the sea ... they were dragged, overturned, and laid on upon the beach, slain and made heaps from stern to bow of their galleys, while all their things were cast into the water.

—Ramesses III, pharaoh of Egypt, 1190 B.C.

Human civilization is only possible because of water. Water provides sustenance for people and crops and is a rich and diverse source of food when harvested. Even now, in the 21st century, more than half the world's food comes from the ocean. How long have humans turned to the sea for food? Archaeologists suggest that we began gathering near-shore shellfish as far back as 165,000 years ago. But when did humans build our first boats and take to the open water? When did organized warfare begin, and when did it take to the water?

Evolutionary biologist Eduardo Moreno of the University of Bern has proposed, based on DNA evidence, that a more belligerent group of people migrated out of Africa some 80,000 years ago, and that this "tribe of warriors," using weapons and big war canoes, traveled the coasts and up big rivers to expand and, if necessary, raid and conquer. It's a fascinating thought, and as Moreno notes, this "warfare culture may have given the out of Africa migrants a competitive advantage to colonize the world. But it could also have crucially influenced the subsequent history of The Earth."

Some of the oldest evidence of human seafaring comes from East Timor, off the north coast of Australia, where 42,000 years ago, we know ancient peoples took to the sea on voyages that took them offshore—and back to port. That's not so surprising when you consider that the ancestors of Australia's aboriginal people crossed the ocean to reach Australia 3,000 years earlier than that, although some scientists argue that those people, crossing about 18 miles of open water, may have simply drifted there on rafts.

Recently, the excavation of the cave known to locals as Jerimalai found solid evidence of "advanced maritime skills," lead archaeologist Susan O'Connor told *Science Magazine* in 2011. At least in terms of fishing, O'Connor said, people had these skills 42,000 years ago, because her team found the bones of deep-sea, fast fish, namely sharks and tuna, in the layers left inside the cave by generations of occupants. O'Connor's team also found a fish hook made from a mollusk shell that has been scientifically dated to 23,000 years ago.

Some archaeologists argue that the evidence is not conclusive enough to argue for ancient peoples taking to the sea in boats as far back as that. The oldest boats found by archaeologists go back some 10,000 years, and they are log boats and canoes. But canoes, lashed to outriggers, can become seafaring craft capable of crossing great distances and safely transporting people. The best-known example of that is the Polynesian voyaging canoe. Without getting much further down this rabbit hole, let's also remember that the human brain reached the level of "behavioral modernity," as paleoanthropologists term it, about 80,000 years ago, and by 60,000 years ago people were fanning out from Africa throughout the globe.

By 36,000 years ago, based on finds in caves, people were making musical instruments. We'd invented art that is striking, spiritual, and sophisticated. We were trading with one another, and we were burying our dead with ritual and care. Were we taking to the sea? I'm going to go out on a limb here and say yes. We just have not found those earliest sites because some 11,700 years ago, the most recent great ice ages ended, and over the next few thousand years, as the glaciers melted, the sea rose some 100 meters, drowning most of humanity's coastal settlements. The evidence of early human seafaring, for the most part, now lies beneath the sea.

In the place where people meet, trade, and work, especially in a quest for resources, conflict arises. Some of the earliest seafaring therefore had to involve sending warriors by water to fight, or encountering and fighting another group on the water. The earliest evidence of larger-scale human warfare excavated, dated, and analyzed by archaeologists, is a 10,000-year-old site called Nataruk near Lake Turkana, Kenya. There, at a coastal settlement on the edge of a now dried-up lagoon, at least 27 people, six of them children, and one of them a late-term pregnant woman, had been shot with arrows multiple times and beaten with enough force to break bone, and then left in the shallows, unburied.

■ The skeleton of a young, pregnant woman, one of the victims of the lakeside attack at Nataruk (Marta Mirazon Lahr. University of Cambridge) KNM-WT-71255b

Archaeologist Marta Mirazón Lahr, who co-led the excavation, noted that the attack appeared premeditated, and initiated from afar, based on the stone of the projectiles in the victims' wounds. Why were they massacred? Lahr believes the attackers were after the resources that the people of Naturuk had that were "valuable and worth fighting for," such as dried meat or fish, nuts, water, or women and children. There may be earlier sites, I will argue, that also lie at or near now-drowned Ice Age coastal settlements. War by and perhaps on water goes back a long way, whether you agree with Moreno, at 80,000 years, or with Lahr, at 10,000 years ago.

WAR CANOES

The oldest and the longest-lasting "warships" are war canoes. Canoes span the world's cultures. They include inland watercraft used on rivers and lakes, as well as on the ocean. This earliest form of watercraft goes back millennia. Canoes were ideal not only for transporting people and commodities but also for warfare. Whether or not canoes in the distant past included types specifically devoted to war probably varied with the beliefs of specific cultures. In the Americas, early European observers noted that larger canoes ordinarily used for transport could, when the time came for a raid or war, be specially blessed and painted with symbols for war. As humanity's oldest craft, it has perhaps been easy for later cultures and groups to deem canoes "primitive craft." They were nothing of the sort.

In West Africa, war canoes up to 25 meters long were used to fight battles on inland lakes, rivers, and along the coast. African accounts of fights on the water went back centuries, and continued through the 19th century. There are numerous European accounts of African war canoes, with African rulers amassing war fleets, and, in response to the arrival of the Europeans, adapting to new weapons. One account offers a vivid description of how eight canoes, armed with European guns, attacked two Dutch trading canoes on the Benin River in 1716. These canoes belonged to and were crewed by Ijo (Ijaw) people of the Niger River Delta. Reportedly, a Gatling gun mounted in a canoe was used by the Ijaw in the Kalabari Civil War of 1879–1883.

■ This image from the Daily Graphic of March 30, 1895, is titled "King Koko in His War Canoe on His Way Down River," and depicts a cannon-armed craft of King Frederick William Koko, Ming VII of Nembe, the ruler of the Nembe Kingdom on the Niger Delta. (Wikipedia Commons)

On the Northwest Coast of the United States and Canada, the intricate waterways of the Inside Passage and Puget Sound were home to diverse, and often warring groups of maritime peoples who used their canoes to raid one another for slaves and commodities, or for revenge, and to engage in wars of territorial expansion. These craft, according to ethnographer David Mitchell, ranged from 20 to 24 meters in length. They were formidable, especially when packed with up to a hundred armed warriors. Early European explorers and fur traders on the northwest coast respected, if not feared them, particularly when some of the early European and American ships on the coast were small and carried smaller crews. The islands of Haida Gwaii, on the British Columbia/Alaska border, were the setting for dozens of attacks on—and six seizures of—fur trading ships from 1789 to 1854.

The Haida, known to some as the "Vikings of the North Pacific," built some of the greatest of these canoes, carving each one from a single cedar log.

▪ "War Canoes," by Canadian artist Emily Carr, depicts First Nations canoes at Alert Bay, British Columbia, in 1912. (Wikipedia Commons)

With high prows, usually adorned with the crest of the chief who owned them, these "head canoes" were used for war. When that happened, the crests were removed as the canoes were stripped for battle. A bear crest from the prow of a Haida war canoe now in the collection of the Canadian Museum of Civilization is an evocative and powerful example. The museum also has a 17-meter-long Haida war canoe carved in 1904 by famed artist Charles Edenshaw. Another, 19-meter-long example, also probably carved by Edenshaw, is displayed at the American Museum of Natural History in New York. They are the only known survivors of a once vast and feared type of war craft.

By the same token, the oceanic canoes of the Pacific engaged in voyages of exploration, colonization and then interisland contact until about hundred years prior to the arrival of the Europeans in the 16th century. The decline of interisland trade did not mean an end to the canoe, and Europeans noted amazing examples of canoes, including war craft, in Tahiti, the

Society Islands, and the Cook Islands. Captain James Cook made detailed notes on 18- to 21-meter-long canoes, numbering into the hundreds, during his first visit to Tahiti in 1769. Cook described oblong platforms on the forepart of the largest canoes "about ten or twelve feet in length, and six or eight in breadth...supported about four feet by stout carved Pillars." "The use of these platforms," he noted, "are for Club Men to stand and fight upon in time of Battle, for the large Canoes, from what I could learn, are built most, if not wholly, for war." The battles speak to the earliest form of naval warfare: "their method of fighting is to Grapple one another and fight it out with Clubs, spears and stones."

The Maori of New Zealand built large *waka taua* (war canoes) that were as long as 39 meters, and carried by up to 80 warriors. In addition to fighting it out alongside one another, the Maori also propelled their craft at high speed to ram an enemy to capsize them, and then kill or capture the opposing crew. The Maori were not intimidated by early Europeans, from first contact on. In 1642, Dutch explorer Abel Tasman recounted how his ship's boat was rammed by a Maori *waka taua*, killing four of the

■ Maori War Canoe in the Auckland War Memorial Museum (Szilas, Wikipedia Commons)

Dutchman's crew. The power and size of these craft are matched by beauty. A stunning example in New Zealand's Otago Museum is the 1840-built *waka taua Te Paranihi*, which has been restored with elements from other *waka taua*. Intricately carved head and stern boards and sides adorn the 55-foot-long, powerfully built war canoe.

The Hawaiians' canoe culture also included war canoes (*kaua wa'a*), and like those of Tahiti, they were double-hulled. Perhaps the best-known use of them in war came with the conquest of the Hawaiian archipelago by Kamehameha the Great from 1795 to 1810. Kamehameha built a large fleet of more than a hundred canoes, and changed Hawaiian warfare at sea through the adoption of European muskets and swivel guns he placed on his canoes. In the 1795 Battle of Kepuwaha'uka'ula, canoe fought canoe with cannon and gunfire, while the king directed the battle from the deck of his sloop *Fair American*, which the Hawaiians had captured from traders.

ANCIENT WAR ON ASIAN WATERS

When civilization first emerged in China several thousand years ago, it took shape on the banks of the two great rivers that continue to dominate the land to this day. Falling out of the steppes, cutting through rocky gorges and then meandering across the muddy alluvial plains, the Yangtze and Huang (Yellow) Rivers have defined China's landscape and life since the beginnings of civilization. The two great rivers are the cradles of Chinese culture, flooding the rich plains to give birth to the rice farms, and connecting cities and markets across the landscape more effectively than paved roads.

It is those water links—rivers, streams, and lakes—along with an intricate system of canals, that dominate China. Both rivers figure prominently in China's history and economy, serving for millennia as highways for both trade and war. Because of their rivers, much like the Egyptians, the Chinese developed a number of rivercraft, and worked their internal waters with riverine merchant craft and an inland navy. Chinese endeavors onto the high seas took thousands of years to unfold.

War afloat is as old as Chinese civilization. The late G. R. G. Worcester, the principal English-language authority on Chinese watercraft, asserted that as early as Neolithic times wars between neighboring groups "were of constant occurrence, and the use of boats for fighting or moving troops must have begun very early in a country so well provided with natural waterways." Worcester believed that the earliest Chinese craft, for navigating the rivers and marshes, were rafts, then flat-bottomed riverine craft, and, in the final stages of development, ocean-going junks. Archaeologists have discovered inscriptions on bone and shell fragments from the Shang dynasty (1766 to 1122 B.C.) that depict simple, raft-like craft suited to the rivers and sheltered coastal waters of China.

What is most frustrating to those seeking to better understand ancient Chinese craft is that there are few representations, only epigraphic evidence and tomb models. Chinese literature, however, is full of references to watercraft and to war afloat before A.D. 1000. The first general history of China, *Shih Chi*, written around 90 B.C., reports on naval battles as early as 473 B.C., when the king of the Wu kingdom attacked the Ch'i kingdom from the water. Another state, the kingdom of Yueh (modern Chekiang), had a large navy of riverine craft and always fought on the water, including a prolonged 21-year war with Wu. Accounts of these wars also suggest some tactics. A 4th century B.C. history written by a Master Mo, the *Mo Tzu*, describes how the navy of Ch'u defeated Yueh's with a newly developed device known as the *ko-ch'iang* or "hook fender." Joseph Needham, analysing the account, believes this innovation was a T-shaped iron hook attached to the end of a long spar, "pivoted in derrick fashion at the base of the mast" that could be dropped quickly to pin an enemy's ship at a desired distance—or lowered to fend it off.

A 5th century B.C. bronze from the Warring States period shows what some scholars believe were large, decked canoes engaged in battle. While men below paddle, the fighters on deck, armed with halberds and swords, fight it out with their ships bow to bow. Two figures at the bow grapple, with one man grabbing the other's head and thrusting down into his neck with a sword. Behind the figure being stabbed, another warrior jabs down with his long-hafted dagger-axe to hack at the stabbing swordsman.

Three figures are in the water beneath the boats. They may be swimmers or the dead. Details of the boats and weapons are sketchy, but they show that naval combat was close in and personal in this age, much as it was at the beginnings of naval warfare in the Mediterranean.

But close in did not necessarily mean boarding. The use of the *ko-ch'iang*, and the evidence of another bronze vessel join literary accounts to describe warfare afloat in which opposing fleets approached only so far to fight close, but not aboard each other's ships. A flat bronze bowl, attributed to the Han dynasty and dated to around the 2nd or 1st century B.C., shows a two-decked ship or canoe, with rowers armed with daggers or swords in scabbards at their waists, rowing while standing up on deck, the warriors armed with halberds and bows and preparing to engage the enemy. At the stern, a single figure beats on a drum.

A later account of a king of Wu who reigned from 514 to 496 B.C. listed five types of ships and their tactics. "Nowadays [around 500 B.C.] in training we use the tactics of land forces for the best effect. Thus great-wing ships correspond to the army's heavy chariots, little-wing ships to light chariots, stomach-strikers to battering rams, castled ships to mobile assault towers and bridge ships to the light cavalry." The "great" and "light" wings probably referred to sails, while the stomach-strikers were probably rams, as were another type mentioned in later accounts, a "colliding swooper."

Needham, analyzing the literature, makes a compelling case for the strikers and swoopers as ships built to collide with enemy ships to capsize them. Among his citations is an A.D. 220 account by Chiang Chi, the *Wan Chi Lun* (The Myriad Stratagems) that talked of ships butting "into each other as if with horns. Whether handled bravely or timidly, all were overturned, whether blunt or sharp all capsized (and sank)." The bridge boats were small flat craft, probably sampans, that could be lashed together to build a pontoon bridge to cross a river, and then separated into small fighting units with armed crews.

The literary accounts therefore provide more evidence than epigraphic records or artifacts to suggest how war was waged afloat. The fleets approached to the sound of loud drumming and shouts, with brightly colored banners and painted decorations of animals or spirits to awe the enemy, or, as the *Chin Shun* suggests, to "overawe the river spirits." As the ships closed, some of them would ram the enemy to capsize them and send men into the water. On other occasions, the accounts talk of fire ships filled with burning material and oil to set the enemy fleet ablaze and destroy it without battle. As the ships closed, the *ko-ch'iang* was used to fend off or grapple an enemy. From opposing decks, spear and halberd thrusts, volleys of arrows, and a slash or stab with a sword as an enemy drew close defined battles on the water.

What the bronze reliefs do not show at all, but which the literature documents, is the different types of ships and boats used in war. One ancient account lists five different warship types. Some scholars debate whether Chinese warships were as diverse in design as this account might suggest, and believe that the text, which is referred to in later histories, might describe ships of a more recent vintage. This is one of the fundamental problems archaeologists face. Brief descriptions, colorful and wonderful to imagine, and boats and battles drawn to artistic conventions do not provide details of construction, types of ships, or maneuvers and tactics. The best way to reconstruct the past is an actual ship or the remains of a battle. Without them, we are left with a vague and foggy picture.

The beginning of ancient Chinese craft doubtless derived from more than one tradition, as skin and bamboo rafts and floats continued in use for millennia along with canoes and planked craft. Archaeologists suggest that the first Chinese craft may have been canoes, like those shown on the bronzes, which later gave way to planked craft. Others suggest the Chinese first used skin or bamboo rafts, and from these beginnings, plank boats gradually came into use. The late nautical archaeologist Paul Johnstone believed that "boat-coffins" discovered in caves in northern Szechuan dating back to the first millennium B.C. represented actual boats. While these craft were set high into cliff sides as repositories for the dead, they either were working craft or fresh, full-scale models of this culture's boats to convey the dead into the afterlife. About five meters long and a meter wide, these square-ended, nearly flattened "coffins" have considerable overhang at both ends. Their appearance suggested to Johnstone that they were an intermediate between a dugout and the sampan.

The Chinese word *sampan* comes from combining "san," or "three," and "pan," or "planks." It was these craft, not bamboo or skin rafts, that gradually evolved into larger boats and ships, although Needham suggests that the internal structure of bamboo is what probably suggested bulkheads and watertight compartments for wooden ships to the Chinese. The earliest rendition of a sampan used in war is found on a late Han dynasty carving on the stone walls of a funerary shrine for the Wu family (known as the Wu Liang Chi) in southwestern Shandong. The carving, one of several inscriptions on the shrine, dates to around A.D. 151 to 170. It shows two sampans, filled with men armed with swords and bows, engaged in combat beneath a river or canal bridge while chariots and men on foot battle on the land.

Other archaeological evidence documents more sophisticated and extensive naval forces. During the Han period (210 B.C.–A.D. 220), clay tomb models show that side oars for steering ships were replaced with the invention of the stern rudder. Larger ships were coming into existence, as shown by the archaeological excavation of an ancient Ch'in dockyard at Canton. The Canton dockyard's slipways for hauling ships show it was capable of handling vessels with a beam or width of some eight meters and more than 30 meters in length. Larger ships were able to accommodate heavier superstructures, including fighting towers on their decks. A 1st-century A.D. wooden model of a riverine patrol boat, recovered from a Han tomb at Ma-wang-tui in Ch'ang-sha was propelled by oars and carried a substantial deck structure with a stern castle and an elevated rampart amidships. Contemporary accounts talk of naval forces with thousands of ships and boats like these, as well as larger craft, engaged in battle.

ANCIENT NAVAL BATTLES IN THE MEDITERRANEAN

Despite thousands of years of often-intense naval combat in the Mediterranean and its surrounding waters, very little has come out of the sea from ancient warships. Why? Probably because the most ancient of these warships were for much of that time smaller, lighter craft that were pulled out of the water when not fighting. When they fought, they did so in

■ Assyrian bireme from the South-West Palace of Sennacherib at Nineveh,
700–692 B.C., now in the British Museum (Wikpedia Commons)

sight of land, close to shore. After a period of service, they were dismantled
and recycled. Ancient warships that fell in battle were usually captured or
disabled, drifted ashore, or broke up on the surface of the sea.

They were not always sent to the bottom. If destroyed, they were probably hauled onto the beach and burned, as the ancient historian Plutarch
suggested 1,900 years ago. Walking the beaches near the site of the battle of
Artemisium, where the Greeks clashed with a Persian fleet in 480 B.C.,
Plutarch described stone memorial tablets and "a place on the beach where
deep down, mingled with the thick sand, you can find a dark, ashy powder,
which seems to have been produced by fire, and it is believed that the
wrecks and dead bodies were burned there."

Whatever the reasons, archaeologists have extracted only tantalizing
clues from the water—a handful of wrecks and a few weapons. But from
the land, in combination with ancient texts, archaeologists, historians, and
other classical scholars have learned a great deal about ships of war from
thousands of years ago.

THE EARLIEST NAVY?

From skin, reed, and log boats, the ship slowly developed in the Mediterranean. From log boats and canoes to rafts—some made of bundled reeds—as well as skin boats stretched over a wooden framework, early seafaring took hold on the Nile, the Tigris, and Euphrates, and the open waters of the Adriatic, Black, and the Mediterranean Seas. By the early Bronze Age, some 5,000 years ago, more elaborate boats and ships made with wooden planks had emerged. The incredibly sophisticated form of Pharaoh Khufu's solar bark was disassembled and buried next to the Great Pyramid of Giza around 2500 B.C. and rediscovered in 1954, excavated, raised and reassembled. It is now housed in a museum alongside the pyramid.

Other finds from royal ship burials at Abydos, Dahshur, Abu Rawash, Saqqara, and Lisht have included more intact craft as well as fragments. While some archaeologists have argued that ceremonial boats and river craft did not necessarily translate into successful ocean-going ship designs, excavation of caves at Wadi Gawasis, an ancient harbor on Egypt's Red Sea coast, found cached rigging and hull planks and empty cargo boxes. The finds are the remains of both seagoing trade and ocean-going ships that sailed to and from the fabled African land of Punt. The excavations were led by the University of Naples's Rodolfo Fattovich. Nautical archaeologist Cheryl Ward led the analysis of the ship remains. The finds date from Egypt's 12th dynasty (roughly 1985 to 1773 B.C.) and continued through the 20th dynasty 600 to 700 years later.

The ships of the Punt trade are depicted on the walls of the mortuary temple of the female pharaoh Hatshepsut at Deir El Bahri, near the Valley of the Kings. What Ward has shown is that much of the form and methods of construction found in the royal boat burials—all craft capable of navigating the Nile and lakes—also translated into successful ocean-going craft. The painted reliefs carved into the walls of Hatshepsut's temple show armed soldiers who sailed on the ships to protect them, and with that, the question is, do the finds at Gawasis also provide the first hard evidence of a fleet that was part naval, part merchant?

BEYOND EGYPT

The evolution of the ship in the wider Mediterranean region gave rise to far-flung networks of trade, and, ultimately, to the use of the sea as a means to extend the boundaries of power and control. By the second millennium B.C., the world's first navies were created by Mediterranean states. Ancient historians credited the near-mythical ruler of Crete, Minos, with the creation of the first navy. "He made himself master of a great part of what is now termed the Hellenic Sea," according to Thucydides, writing in the 5th century B.C. "He conquered the isles of the Aegean and was the first colonizer of most of them."

Archaeologists excavating on land throughout the Mediterranean have proved the far-flung existence of Minoan trade by recovering Minoan artifacts in Egypt, the Levantine coast (today's Israel and Lebanon), the Aegean isles, Turkey, Greece, and Italy—including Sicily and Sardinia. Trade goods alone do not indicate an ancient Minoan empire, but their scattered presence is evidence of Minoan naval power strong enough to protect ships carrying trade goods to distant lands. The excavation of the center of Minoan power, at Knossos on Crete, starting in 1900, has revealed a vast palace and a series of settlements remarkable in that unlike other early settlements, walls did not protect the Minoan cities. As Lionel Casson, the dean of classical maritime studies, writes, Thucydides knew what he was talking about. "The people of Crete . . . had been daring and active traders and the possessors of a great navy; Minoan towns needed no stone walls, for wooden ones, their ships, protected the island."

Archaeological evidence—scant depictions on pottery, seals, and fragmentary murals from the ruins of Minoan towns and cities—indicates that these early warships were no different from merchant ships, except that they carried armed warriors to fight battles ashore instead of cargo. The well-preserved ruins of a buried Minoan city on the Greek island of Santorini have provided graphic clues. Beginning in 1967, Greek archaeologists slowly peeled back a thick layer of volcanic ash, exposing a complex of two- and three-story mud brick buildings and narrow streets. The site, known as Thera, was buried during a volcanic eruption sometime around

1628 B.C. at the height of the Minoan civilization. Archaeologists at Thera discovered a series of plaster wall paintings lying beneath layers of ash. Considered by scholars to be the greatest "treasure" at the site, they are a unique document of life from the distant past.

The ruins of one building, known as the "West House," or the "Admiral's House," included a series of scenes that had been painted on a plastered wall. The scenes show several ships, coastal towns, and a river—all of which suggested to archaeologist Christos Doumas, who led the excavations at Thera since 1974, that this is a scene of a significant overseas voyage. The long, sleek ships, filled with armed warriors with helmets, shields and spears, have been the subject of much analysis and scholarly debate. Is this a depiction of a naval campaign, a religious festival on the water, a symbolic view of Minoan shipping and trade, or scenes, as Doumas suggests, "inspired by the maritime ventures and overseas missions of the seafarer who lived in this building"?

Whatever they do show, these fragile images from a far-distant time, painstakingly recovered, piece by piece from an ancient disaster, are powerful images that meant a great deal to the person who owned the "West House." I have stood in the shade of the huge building that covers the excavation at Thera, on a dusty street laid bare after millennia of burial beneath volcanic ash, feeling the long progression of time. The Thera murals, and the ships they show, are an evocative message even if not fully understood, from across the gulf of time.

Whatever the message, the Thera frieze is our most vivid and tantalizing record of Minoan ships. Long and sleek, the ships are both rowed and paddled, although some carried a single mast and sail. Only one ship has its sail set. A simple cabin at the stern, with what could be a small deck in that area, supports the helmsman and what could be a timekeeper to synchronize the rowers' strokes. The warriors in the ships carry long spears or sea pikes, which also appear in the hands of warriors ashore. I would argue that these images we may be seeing the survival of the earliest ships—long, sleek canoes, not unlike Polynesian voyaging canoes, that could travel fast and far. They are a distant cry from the massive rowed galleys of the classical civilizations, and yet the Thera ships, at least until we find one of these as a wreck, give us a visual representation of what we could argue is the quintessential human ship, a type that in time would carry people throughout the world's largest ocean, the Pacific.

THE FIRST WARSHIPS AND BATTLES AFLOAT

By the second millennium, two distinct types of ships began to evolve— the merchant vessel and the warship. The Mycenaeans, a scattered group of peoples on the Greek mainland, took to the sea during the height of Minoan power, and by 1500 B.C. had conquered the Minoans. These fierce warriors developed the war galley, a long, oared ship suited only for raiding, piracy and war. These were the ships that carried the Greeks to Troy. Lionel Casson, drawing from Homer's descriptions of the Greek warships in *The Iliad* and *The Odyssey*, describes them as fast, slender, and graceful craft.

War galleys carried a single sail on a mast that could be raised to take advantage of the wind. When the wind did not blow, or in times of battle, the sail and mast were lowered and stowed and the men took to the oars. The smallest war galleys were about 10 meters long, carrying 20 oarsmen; they most commonly carried 50 oarsmen and may have been as long as 27 meters. And yet they were only three meters wide and with a low freeboard. Open, or as Homer termed them, "hollow ships," with only a small deck forward and aft, contained galleys that were probably very much like a modern rowing shell.

With such sleek hulls, the Mycenaean war galleys were easily beached. Casson notes that the *Odyssey* describes how Odysseus made a fast getaway from the island of the Cyclops by shoving his ship off the beach with one good heave on his boat pole. But the lightness of the galleys came with a price; they were not strong craft and working them was difficult and risky. Nonetheless these ships were the standard Mediterranean warships beginning around 1500 B.C. Amazingly, other than often-stylized depictions in art, and Homer's words, we know nothing definite about these ships because none has ever been discovered. What we do know, as the preeminent archaeologist and scholar of Greek rowed warfare, John R. Hale, writes, is that "actual naval battles were rare events in early Greek history." Using their small, light ships, they limited themselves to "seaborne assaults on coastal towns," of which, Hale notes, the Trojan War "was just a glorified example."

The power of Mycenae waned after 1250 B.C. when a major invasion of the Mediterranean by seafaring groups of Indo-Europeans occurred. Known as the "Peoples of the Sea," they destroyed Mycenaean cities and occupied the Levant. Their destructive arrival ushered in a "dark age" and the first recorded sea battle in history. Around 1176 B.C., Egyptian pharaoh Ramesses III and his large navy met the Sea Peoples in battle, probably in the Nile Delta.

What we know about the battle comes from a carved relief on the wall of Rameses's mortuary temple at Medinet Habu. Rising out of the desert, the imposing ruins tower above the sand. A wall several stories high, with traces of bright paint and deeply carved images, is an awe-inspiring sight. For maritime scholars, one series of scenes incised in stone is, as archaeologist Shelley Wachsmann notes, "the most important iconographic evidence" not only for the ships of the Sea Peoples but also for "ship-based warfare before the introduction of the ram as a nautical weapon." By carefully analyzing the relief, and making educated deductions from its artistic depictions, archaeologists have some sense of what the ships were like, and how the battle was fought.

Groups of decked galleys, with soldiers on board, fought a "land battle" at sea, not only from their decks, but from elevated crows' nests, with the Egyptians staying out of range of the Sea Peoples' spears and shooting down the invaders with archers. The reliefs at Medinet Habu show Egyptian ships closing with their opponents after a volley of arrows, tossing a four-armed grapnel from the bow into the rigging of the enemy, and capsizing the light, shallow Sea Peoples' ships. The enemy soldiers drowned, or were pulled out and captured, as were their ships. Once free of troops, and with nothing heavy on board to sink them, capsized Sea Peoples' ships are shown floating in the water.

Ancient war afloat was close, personal, and nasty. It is easy to imagine how two ships—maybe more—closed to within a few meters of each other. Muscled arms threw heavy spears that thudded into thick planks before

The Sea Peoples battle at Medinet Habu (from Dorothea Gray, Seewesen Archaeologica Homerica, 1974, Wikipedia Commons)

breaking off, while others hit flesh and bone, bringing oarsmen and sailors to a halt. The ships collided, the decks swarmed with armed men as blood ran thick into the scuppers and spread out in a cloud across the surface of the water. The dead and dying were thrown into the sea, and the living captured the surviving crew and their ship.

Without ships sinking, the only archaeological traces of the battle would be loose weapons scattered on the seabed. Buried and wrecked ships, along with tantalizing clues such as stone anchors and scattered traces of cargo, are our only physical links to the time of the first warships. As yet no direct archaeological evidence of Bronze Age war at sea has been found. There are tantalizing traces. An underwater discovery near Beit Yannai on Israel's Mediterranean coast of a Late Bronze Age dagger and a Canaanite sickle sword may be evidence of an early sea battle.

Finding even traces of massive battles and naval losses from antiquity has proved difficult. Greece's first underwater archaeological survey was a government-led search for the presumed site of the Battle of Salamis in 1884. While unsuccessful, it marks one of the earliest naval archaeology projects not only in Greece but in the world. More recently, a multi-national effort, The Persian War Shipwreck Survey, sought to find one or more of the ships lost during the Persian Wars. Focusing on areas where ancient sources said large numbers of ships had sunk either in battle or in storms, the three-year survey between 2003 and 2006, combed the waters off Cape Artemision, Euboea, Salamis, and near Mount Athos. Fishermen had pulled two ancient Corinthian helmets out of the sea off Mount Athos. The survey team sent a remotely operated vehicle (ROV) down 97 meters only to find an amphora and a ceramic jar. The jar, however, held a bronze spear's butt spike with some of its wooden shaft preserved with it. Some shipwrecks were located, but nothing that could definitely link to the Persian Wars was found.

RISE OF THE RAM

Egypt repelled the onslaught of the Sea Peoples. But it did not pursue naval control of the Mediterranean. Instead, a group of sea traders from Sidon, on the Levantine coast, expanded a commercial network of maritime trade west, establishing colonies in North Africa at Utica and Carthage. Controlling much of the western Mediterranean and trading out into the Atlantic as far north as Britain, these peoples, now known as the Phoenicians, ultimately came into conflict with a group of Greek city-states.

The Greek city-states rose out of the dark age that followed the onslaught of the Sea Peoples. By 800 B.C., Corinth, Athens, Miletus, Sparta, and other cities began to expand their trade, and over the next 200 years, the Greeks established overseas colonies to the east in the Dardanelles, north to the shores of the Black Sea, and west to Italy and Sicily. This brought Greece into conflict with the Persian Empire, the Phoenicians, and the Etruscans and inaugurated a series of wars on land and sea for control of the Mediterranean.

The first major change in war at sea comes from this time. In this age, the galley—propelled by oars but also carrying an auxiliary mast and sail—was the principal fighting ship. Around 850 B.C., the Greeks added a projecting, bronze-sheathed underwater ram to the bow of their galleys. Possibly adapted from a projecting beak at the bow of earlier warships that facilitated running the ship up on the beach, the ram changed the way ships fought at sea. While ships still grappled and men fought it out on deck, the ram, as Lionel Casson notes, shifted the emphasis "to the men who manned the oars." John R. Hale explains that in two early battles, the commanders' decisions to rely on their ships' rams "and the skill of their steersmen rather than man-on-man combat" brought about what he rightly calls a "seismic shift in naval warfare."

The rise of the ram was the ancient equivalent of introducing gunpowder, or in later terms, the tank or the airplane. With the ram, victory went to well-trained crews who responded instantly and accurately to orders to drive a ram into the enemy's ship. The ram, a game-changing weapon, started a naval arms race that lasted for a thousand years, as city-states and empires built successively larger ships with larger rams, as well as large fleets, to "out gun" one another.

By 800 B.C., the standard warship was the fifty-oared *pentekontoros* with a ram at the bow. But a change in the design of warships introduced a new

■ The Lenormant Relief, c. 410–400 B.C., depicting rowers inside a trireme, as displayed in the Acropolis Museum, Athens (Tilemahos fthimiadis, Wikipedia Commons)

type of vessel. While earlier warships had been open hulled, like a Viking ship, the Greeks added a deck to protect the oarsmen and to provide a platform for the fighting men. The addition of a deck level led to a second row of oars for greater speed. These new ships were known as *biremes*. This development, sometime around 775 B.C., in turn led to the design of a decked ship that carried three banks of oars, the Greek *trieres*, or trireme, around 725 B.C.

The trireme and the ram were the key inventions that gave the Greeks naval control of the Mediterranean for the next three centuries. The trireme, with a trained crew of citizen-volunteers (*Ben Hur* notwithstanding, the ancients, including the Romans, did not use galley slaves) was a fast, deadly ship. The use of the trireme dictated a change in tactics. Rather than closing and fighting with arrows, spears, and boarding ladders, triremes lined up in columns and maneuvered to ram the enemy, causing his ships to founder.

Triremes carried oars, masts, and sails. When sailing any distance, the triremes put in to shore at night, beaching so that the men could go ashore to forage for food and set up camp. To fight, the triremes removed their masts and sails to lighten ship, and then rowed out to meet the enemy. The Greek trireme carried three rows of banks of oars manned by 170 rowers, and a force of 30 marines and officers. The ships used three tactical maneuvers: the *diekplus*, the *periplus*, or the *kyklos*. The *diekplus* was used to break through an enemy's line of ships and ram them from behind. The *periplus* was used to circle around an enemy's ships and ram them. The *kyklos* was a defensive manoeuver. The ships would form a circle, sterns touching and the bow standing out like the hubs of a wheel.

Rather than individual ships fighting it out, the Greeks adopted fleet tactics, with groups of ships drilled to fight together, practicing fast manoeuvers to ram and then, if needed, close in, heaving grappling irons and then boarding for fierce, hand-to-hand combat on the decks. As the ancient historian Plutarch noted, for the Greeks in this age, the key to naval victory was simple. "They learned from their own behavior in the face of danger that men who know how to come to close quarters and are determined to give battle have nothing to fear...they have simply to show their contempt...engage the enemy hand to hand and fight it out to the bitter end." Thus was set the basic form of naval warfare for the next thousand years.

■ The Winged Victory of Samothrace, a naval victory monument, with Nike poised atop the prow of a warship, displayed at the Louvre Museum (SpirosK Photography, Wikipedia Commons)

The maneuverability and power of the new ships was proved in battle in or around 540 B.C., when Greek colonists in southern France and Corsica, with a fleet of 60 triremes, defeated a larger force of 100 Etruscan and Phoenician ships near Corsica. Between 540 and 525 B.C., most Mediterranean powers adopted the trireme, building large fleets of them.

Triremes fought the major sea battles between Greece and Persia—notably at the epic battle of Salamis, in 480 B.C., when a united Greek fleet defeated the navy of Xerxes. Triremes also fought in the bitter Peloponnesian War between Athens and Sparta that followed between 431–404 B.C. Amazingly, with dozens of battles and hundreds of ships lost, archaeologists have not discovered a single trireme shipwreck. The scant clues other than graphic depictions on pottery and in stone are the remains of the buildings they were housed in. When not in use, the triremes were housed ashore in large-roofed ship sheds with sloping ramps that led down to the water. Archaeological study of the ruins of these sheds, particularly those from the Athenian dockyard at the Bay of Zea in Piraeus, near Athens, provided the first direct physical evidence of the length and beam (width) of triremes—about 37 meters long and six meters wide. The ships were classified according to their age as "selects," "firsts," "seconds," and so on. The oldest ships were sold, usually for breaking up, according to one ancient Greek inscription listing the scrap value of discarded bronze rams.

The next phase in the development of ancient warships was the rise of the polyremes. A new series of wars, fought for the control of Sicily and the seas surrounding it, pitted Carthage, the Sicilian Greek colony of Syracuse, and the rising power of Rome against one another. New, larger versions of the trireme, mounting greater numbers of rowers, appeared around 400 B.C.

Quadriremes (fours) and quinqueremes (fives) were built, some ships reaching more than 60 meters in length. At one time, historians believed that these ships, and the "sixes," "nines," and "tens" that followed, might have referred to the number of banks of oars, one bank per level, so that a ten would be 10 levels high! But such ships—towering above the water— would have been impossible to build or sail. Instead, working with a three-level system like the trireme, scholars like John S. Morrison and John Coates

■ The modern replica trireme Olympias (Ionnis Houvardas, Wikipedia Commons)

have reconstructed these ships on paper with more than one man per oar, often staggering the number of men per oar on each level. A "five" would have two rows or levels of oars, three men per oar on the first level, and two men per oar on the next.

WARSHIPS FROM ALEXANDER TO CAESAR

The navies of the last three centuries B.C. were a varied lot, with ships of different sizes and classes, much like later navies with battleships, cruisers, and destroyers. The naval wars of this period saw contenders for control of the sea outbuilding one another both in sheer numbers of ships and in their size. Again, in comparison to a later time, the key to power was seen in the number of oarsmen—"tens," "sixteens," "twenties," and "forties" instead of 12-, 14- or 16-inch naval guns. These were the ships used by Alexander as he seized control of the Mediterranean, capturing island cities like Tyre with combined land and sea forces.

The death of Alexander the Great in 323 B.C. started a war between his generals for control of the far-flung Macedonian Empire. Antigonus, with his son Demetrius, held Greece, while Seleucus held Persia and Ptolemy dominated Egypt. Dionysus, the tyrant of Syracuse, is credited with the invention of the "five," Demetrius of Greece is credited by ancient historians with the invention of the larger ships—sixes, sevens, all the way up to a sixteen. As Demetrius built larger ships with more oarsmen and larger decks carrying not just armed men, but catapults, fire pots, and ballista that fired bolts and stone shot, his ships were matched and then surpassed by those built by other rulers. Ptolemy IV, it is said, built a gigantic "forty," perhaps an unwieldy marriage of two hulls into a massive catamaran.

In this age of the super-galley and varied fleets, sea battles were fierce melees as ships of different sizes closed with one another, firing missiles, bolts, and darts before ramming. Armed marines, standing on decks, or in wooden turreted towers at either end of the ships, fought with long spears, arrows, and swords. Grappling irons brought ships close in so boarding parties could spring on to the enemy's deck. In this, we see the gradual and then dramatic change in ships as weapons of war. For thousands, perhaps tens of thousands of years, boats and ships had carried warriors to invade and fight on other shores. Now, ships fought on the open water.

THE ATHLIT RAM

Discoveries beneath the sea provide us with a tantalizing hint of larger warships from this period and the sophistication of the ram. Archaeologist Yehoshua Ramon, snorkeling in shallow water offshore of Athlit, which lies near Haifa on Israel's northern coast, discovered a ram in 1980. Lying in the shallows of only three meters of water, the ram was raised for careful scientific study by archaeologists from Israel and the United States. Repeated surveys of the bay where Ramon discovered the ram yielded no additional traces of the warship that once carried it. It had apparently drifted close in to shore after being wrecked and disintegrated, leaving only the heavy ram with remains of the warship's bow inside it.

The "Athlit Ram," after cleaning and preservation, proved to be an exceptionally well-preserved, cast-bronze warship ram that weighs nearly 500 kilograms. This ship-killer held 16 timbers from the bow of the lost warship inside its socket. In a meticulous, painstaking process, J. Richard Steffy of the Institute of Nautical Archaeology carefully extracted the timbers, which were form-fitted inside the ram.

Steffy's analysis of the surviving wooden structure of the ram showed a well-designed series of strakes and timbers that distributed not just the weight of the ram but the forces and stresses of the act of ramming into a heavily constructed hull bottom. Steffy's analysis of the wooden remains inside the Athlit Ram suggests carefully and strongly built warships. The key, says Steffy, is that the "entire bottom of this ship was essentially the weapon," not just the bronze ram.

No other wooden remains of the ship at Athlit were discovered. There are only the sixteen timbers from inside the bronze ram to suggest how the original warship's hull was built. The ram timbers and wooden wales that

■ The Athlit Ram, as displayed at the National Maritime Museum, Haifa, Israel (Oren Rizen, Wikipedia Commons)

ran along each side of the keel suggested that the ship weighed as much as one metric ton per meter of length—a heavy ship indeed.

Fast and hard-hitting was not always a good combination. Steffy pointed out that a motorcycle hitting a brick wall at 100 kilometers an hour will destroy itself, while an 18-wheeled truck loaded with 20 metric tons of freight will knock the wall down at 10 kilometers an hour. "Our warship was more like the eighteen wheeler than the motorcycle," he says. Momentum was the key, as was remaining agile to "drive that ram home." The Athlit Ram suggests that the builders of that warship discovered the right balance between weight of the timbers and the good "punch" and the overall lightness of the vessel to enable the oarsmen to maneuver quickly.

The bronze ram itself was an amazingly sophisticated weapon. Made of a high-grade bronze (90 percent copper and 10 percent tin), the ram swept out from the bow to a reinforced head with three "narrow fins" that spread the force of ramming into a blunt impact in a concentrated area less than a half-meter square. This would break planks, crack frames, and flood the enemy ship without smashing a hole in the side and raising the possibility of the ram getting stuck. The Athlit Ram was firmly attached to its warship and could not break away without serious damage. It was not a bee-stinger, but a sophisticated, engineered "warhead" mounted on the ship.

How old is the Athlit Ram, and what else can we say about the warship it was mounted on and how it may have been lost? Symbols cast into the bronze indicate that it dates from 204 to 164 B.C., and that the ram probably came from a Cypriot warship, probably not a trireme, but a four-banked type known as a tetreres. Archaeologist William Murray, analyzing the symbols and pondering how the ship came to be lost near Athlit, feels it was a smaller warship based on the Levantine coast that may have been lost in a storm or during an unrecorded naval skirmish during dynastic struggles for control of Phoenicia. We will probably never know the exact circumstances of the ship's loss, but those answers are not as important as what archaeologists gleaned from the amazing bronze ram plucked from the sea.

Before the Athlit find, other ancient rams were known to archaeologists, including one sold by an antiquities dealer in 1987 and now in Bremerhaven, Germany, and others, all like the Bremerhaven ram, small castings, without wood inside. All of these earlier rams had been discovered privately so they were not excavated by archaeologists. While yielding information about various styles and sizes of rams in antiquity, none offered as much detail as the Athlit Ram.

As research continues in the region, and new technologies allow us to go deeper, the possibility, if not the hope, is that more ancient ships will be found and studied. These could be ships older than the earliest seagoing ship yet found and excavated, the Uluburun shipwreck, found off Turkey, which dates back 3,300 years. We may also find, at last, evidence of Bronze Age sea battles, if not earlier, not only in the depths, but perhaps buried in the mud off the mouth of the Nile. However, archaeologists finally did discover not only ancient warships but also the scattered remains of a naval battle in the sea from the age of Rome, which is where we shall go now.

2

Rome and Beyond

The assailants coming from many sides shot blazing missiles and with engines threw pots of flaming charcoal and pitch. The defendants tried to ward off these fiery projectiles and when one was lodged it was quenched with drinking water. When that was gone, they dipped up seawater, but...they were not always successful. Then they smothered the fires with their mantles and even with corpses. They hacked off burning parts of the ships and tried to grapple hostile ships to escape into them. Many were burned alive or jumped overboard or killed each other to avoid the flames.

—Cassius Dio, *The Roman History: The Reign of Augustus*, c. A.D. 220

Archaeologists working in the Mediterranean, the Aegean, the Adriatic, and the Black Sea have discovered and excavated more Roman shipwrecks than from any other civilization or empire. Divers, explorers, and archaeologists have documented hundreds of Roman wrecks, not just in the Mediterranean region, but off Northern Europe and Britain as well. These shipwrecks are direct physical evidence of Rome's command of the seas and oceanic trade that brought tin from Britain, lead from Spain, grain from Egypt, and goods such as wine, olives, and marble from all across the Mediterranean. Despite decades of maritime and underwater archaeological work, however, the sea has yielded scant traces of Roman warships or sea battles.

Rome's legions are better known than its fleets, not only because of archaeology but also because scholars and the public have paid more attention to the troops and land battles. This is not surprising. Even during the heyday of Rome, the Romans' links to the sea were ambiguous. The sea, with its capricious moods and risk of shipwreck and drowning never fully appealed to the land-spawned citizens of Rome. The sea was an efficient avenue for transporting goods. Once the initial wars were fought for control of the Mediterranean and Rome's civil wars ended, the Roman navy's principal tasks were the patrol of trade routes and frontiers, and the suppression of piracy. There was no tradition of recurrent sea battles, as had so indelibly marked the Greek consciousness, nor did most Romans ever venture to sea either for recreation or as passengers.

THE RISE OF ROME

As previously discussed, the Athlit Ram comes from a period when a series of smaller powers struggled to control the seas in the aftermath of the death of Alexander. No one power, save Carthage, was able to exercise authority over a large area. But the emerging power of Rome, as it expanded beyond the Italian peninsula, came into conflict with Carthage in Sicily. This struggle propelled Rome to change in less than two centuries into an imperial power that ruled the Mediterranean as a "Roman lake." To achieve that, Rome had to defeat the Carthaginians as its principal rival on the Mediterranean. The former Phoenician colony inherited Phoenicia's maritime trade routes and naval knowledge, and built a formidable fleet of hundreds of ships to patrol— and control—the sea. Archaeologists excavating a now-shallow circular lagoon outside of Tunis, the modern city atop ancient Carthage, have documented the remains of a massive naval harbor known as the Cothon. Three hundred meters in diameter, and surrounded by massive sandstone walls, the harbor had a 21-meter-wide entrance and housed 200 warships. A central, fortified tower, the Admiral's Island, guarded the entrance. The ring enclosed a series of ship sheds that allowed the Carthaginians to haul their warships out of the water for repair and storage. Excavations led by archaeologists Frank M. Cross and Lawrence E. Stager exposed the lower courses of the Cothon in the 1970s, finding a sophisticated structure that confirmed ancient accounts of its size. Archaeologist Henry Hurst of Cambridge led the study of the Cothon and notes that while it was impressive, it was "strategically ill-conceived, needlessly lavish" and that the emphasis was form over function—a decidedly modern and eminently human failing.

Archaeology also gives us insights into another aspect of Carthage's naval technology: building prefabricated ships. Between 1970 and 1974, pioneer maritime archaeologist Honor Frost excavated two Carthaginian wrecks off Marsala in Sicily. One of the ships was fairly well preserved and measured some 35 meters from bow to stern. Propelled by two rows of banks of oars, the ship was not only long but sleek, traits that show it was built for speed. Frost believed that this craft, as well as the well-preserved bow of the second ship, was a warship. Other archaeologists disagree, and based on restudy of the recovered wreck remains by nautical archaeologists Denise Averdung and Ralph Pedersen, we are looking at a Carthaginian merchant ship. Moving beyond the pros and cons of the warship argument, the significance of the find rests more in how it was built.

Phoenician symbols and letters painted onto the timbers showed Frost and her team that the ships had been built in prefabricated sections that allowed workers to quickly piece them together. That archaeological find, compared to ancient accounts of how rapidly Carthage could build a fleet is yet another ancient example of human ingenuity. Archaeology also can show us evidence of less desirable aspects of our humanity. Frost's excavation revealed carpenter's shavings lying inside the ship's bilges, as well as the leaves from a tree caught in the putty used to caulk the hull. "Built in haste" and sunk when new, the Marsala Punic Ship shows not only sophistication in shipbuilding but also rushed work. That's not surprising, as Frost's analysis of the wrecks suggests they were lost close to the end of Carthage's first war with Rome, at a time when the port these ships were headed to—or from—was under siege.

Rome waged a lengthy series of wars against Carthage between 264 and 146 B.C., discovering in the process that their land-based power was no match for an enemy who commanded the seas. The key to ultimate victory was to wrest control of the sea from Carthage. Rome embarked upon a hasty program to build warships and meet the Carthaginians on the water. Rome defeated Carthage only after gaining control of the sea lanes and sending a 30,000-man army across the water to lay siege to and destroy Carthage itself. The Punic Wars ended with the Romans in command of a fleet of some 200 ships and thousands of naval veterans. Rome would never be the same, and in the centuries that followed, was never again free of the need to control the seas.

Rome's assumption of naval power came as a result of its struggles with Carthage. Rome's three wars with Carthage saw the Romans copy the captured ships of their enemies to build large fleets. At the end of three successive Punic wars, Rome controlled the western Mediterranean and the Adriatic. Now the most powerful state in the region, Rome and its fleet

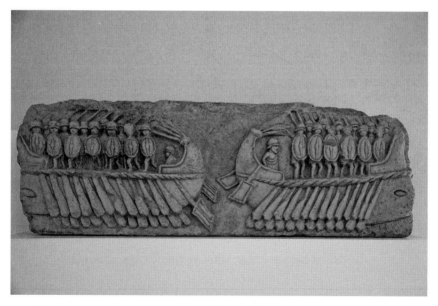

■ A Roman warship with troops on board, from the 1st century B.C. to the 1st century A.D., from a copy in the Museum für Antike Schiffahrt, Mainz. The original is in the National Museum in Naples. (Carole Raddato, Wikipedia Commons)

were drawn into various power struggles in the eastern Mediterranean for the next 200 years.

THE BATTLE OF EGADI, 241 B.C.

A fisherman's discovery of a bronze ram off Sicily's northwestern coast, near Trapani, led to what is now a decade-and-a-half-long project that has disproven the commonly held idea that ancient warships did not sink. The discovery of 16 bronze rams, weapons, helmets, and amphorae all come from sunken Carthaginian and Roman warships lost at the Battle of the Aegates Islands, now called the Egadis in modern Italian. It was not just any battle, but an epic final battle that essentially ended the First Punic War with a decisive victory by the Roman commander, Gaius Lutatus Catalus. It came after more than a decade of successive Carthaginian naval victories. The battle was essentially a Roman ambush of heavily laden Carthaginian warships that were ferrying supplies to besieged Lilybaeum (today's Marsala) on Sicily.

Several years earlier, in 249 B.C., another Roman fleet had met defeat at the hands of the Carthaginians in roughly the same waters, losing 93 out of 120 ships, some sunk, but most of them were captured at the Battle of Drepanum (modern Trapani). In the several years that followed, a lengthy land war dragged out in Sicily. Control of the seas was essential, and so patriotic Romans privately raised money to build a new fleet of some 200 ships, not only privately built but also privately crewed. Catalus had drilled his men carefully, mindful of the lessons of Drepanum. His blockade of both Lilybaeum and Drepanum cut off supplies from Carthage. Carthage responded by sending a fleet of some 250 ships under the command of Hanno, the son of Hannibal. On March 9, 241, the Carthaginian fleet approached Lilybaeum, heavily laden with supplies, arms, and men.

Hanno stopped in the lee of the Aegates to wait for the wind to change. The next morning, March 10, with the breeze heading toward shore, Hanno and his fleet set sail for what would have been a fast passage. Catalus, even with the wind facing him, decided to cut off Hanno and fight on the water rather than let them land, and ordered the ships to be stripped down for battle, as well as unstepping masts so that he had a light and maneuverable fleet. Surviving ancient sources, notably the historian Polybius, are silent on the actual battle, but the results were dramatic, with Hanno losing 120 ships, 50 of them sunk outright, while the Romans lost only 30 in a four-hour-long battle.

Facing even more prolonged war on land, Carthage decided to negotiate a peace with Rome in which Carthage had to abandon Sicily and Aegates and pay Rome a war indemnity of 145,000 pounds of silver each year for twenty years.

When a fisherman pulled a bronze ram from the sea off the Egadi Islands in 2004, it launched a collaborative project between Sicily's Soprintendenza Del Mare in Sicily and the RPM Nautical Foundation. Archaeologists have meticulously sonar mapped the seabed off Levanzo Island in the Egadis, investigating and recovering important artifacts to define and document the victors and the losers who sank in 249 B.C. when Rome and Carthage clashed here.

What the surveys have revealed, lying in waters some 79 to 103 meters deep and spreading out for nearly a hundred square miles, is the world's first ancient naval battlefield discovered by archaeologists. The finds include ballast from wrecked Carthaginian warships and scattered amphorae, some Roman, others Punic, and hence supplies perhaps not only for the warships, but for the besieged Carthaginian forces ashore in Sicily. There are also helmets, some perhaps lost when the warriors wearing them went down with their ships. There are also 16 bronze warship rams, a discovery that stunned archaeologists around the world. Until this project, only three ancient "waterline" rams had been found. That number, as of 2017, was exceeded, and the survey is not yet complete. The survey thus far has found smaller rams, for example, from the triremes, not the larger quinquiremes, and so the search continues for the area of the battlefield where the main line met in combat.

What has also excited archaeologists is the debunking of the assumption that ancient warships had not yet been found because they did not sink because they were lightly built. The clustering of some of the finds on the seabed includes helmets lying close together, and in one case next to the ram from a warship. However, after 2,000 years, and fishing nets snagging pieces out of the sea, it's difficult to say how they all came together—are these from men who went down with the ship, or loose helmets lost when it sank? Archaeologists who study ancient armor have carefully studied the helmets, which were a popular style of the time and one probably used on both sides. One helmet, and maybe a second, have what may be Punic letters inscribed on them. Are these graffiti, a unit designation, or a warrior's initials?

There are many questions left to be answered. But what is clear to the teams is that entire warships sank to the bottom, and presumably, some with their crews. It is there that the helmets take on a somber significance. They speak to the lives lost, which given the 80 ships that sank, would have numbered into the thousands, perhaps even within range of 10,000 men. As we will see later in this book, one of the most powerful aspects of the archaeology of war does not come from studying ships and weapons and

■ Egadi 2. The RPM Nautical Foundation discovered this ram among Greco-Italic amphorae in an area of rock outcroppings. Damage to its fins suggests it was broken, probably during combat, and wood from the enemy vessel was found still embedded in the surviving fins. (RPM Nautical Foundation)

■ Egadi 3. Also damaged in battle, this small ram was discovered in 2010; analysis suggests it may have been involved in a ram-to-ram collision. (RPM Nautical Foundation)

their effectiveness. The lesson, as shown even without visible or tangible human remains, is the terrible price of war. As I said in the introduction, the sea is our greatest battlefield, and as such, it is our largest graveyard.

Analysis of the rams themselves has yielded fascinating conclusions. The Egadi rams are smaller than the Athlit Ram, suggesting that the ships engaged in this battle were not behemoths but smaller, more easily handed warships. That makes sense, especially in line with accounts of the battle that stressed the need for both speed and maneuverability. In modern terms, the Battle of Egadi may have been more of a destroyer battle than battleships slugging it out. As well, some of the rams have stories to tell— inscriptions cast into them show both Roman and Carthaginian manufacture. Some of them firmly date the rams to the period of the battle.

It appears that some of the Roman rams came from ships captured in earlier battles by the Carthaginians and pressed into service by their new masters. The defaced head of a Roman deity (or a warrior) cast into one ram bears the scars of what Sebastiano Tusa and Jeffrey Royal see as deliberate defacement, while another Roman ram lies next to Punic pottery. Other ram inscriptions suggest that they were privately financed, as family names and rank appear on them. This nicely coincides with the ancient accounts that after the defeat of 249 B.C., and the loss of much of the fleet, Rome turned to private sponsorship to build a new navy.

One Carthaginian ram has a Punic inscription that seems to ask that divine power help it do its deadly work, with one possible translation being a prayer to Baal "that this ram will go into an enemy ship and make a big hole." Another reportedly brags that this ram "eats ships." When raised, it was found to still have fragments of a Roman hull wedged into its face. While we can only guess about the violent deaths of crews based on the helmets scattered across the seabed, there is no guessing when it comes to some of the rams. They bear the scars of battle. One is split and missing some of the fins that gave the ram its punch. There are V-shaped notches in a second, perhaps from a ram-to-ram collision, and a missing front corner on another. One ram has its fins bent from striking an enemy hull. These not-so-subtle traces again demonstrate how close up, personal, and brutal ancient war was, including battles at sea.

ROMAN SEA POWER, 201–50 B.C.

While Rome vied with Carthage for control of the western Mediterranean, one of the most powerful and organized navies in the eastern Mediterranean was that of the city-state of Rhodes. The Rhodians, an island people, built a strong navy to enforce freedom of trade on the sea. It emphasized smaller, lighter ships in fewer numbers. Rather than build a huge fleet of "super-galleys" like their neighbors, the Rhodians believed in an efficient, well-trained force that relied on allies from other nations to come to their aid if overwhelming force was needed. To even the odds, around 190 B.C. the clever naval tacticians of Rhodes invented a new naval weapon, which Lionel Casson points out was "the last one to be invented until the very end of the ancient world." Rhodian warships carried "fire pots," blazing containers suspended from long poles that were used to set an enemy on fire.

The Rhodians also invented the *triemiolia*, a stripped-down, fast trireme that used both sails and oars. The principal enemy of Rhodes were pirates who used a fast version of the two-level galley. Known as *hemiolia*, these "one and a half" banked ships also used both sail and oars to chase down merchant ships. Images on pottery of these craft give us a sense of what they were like, with some oarsmen replaced by sails. But the details of these two types of fast ships of war are unknown, as unfortunately no one has yet discovered a wreck of either type. Archaeologists working on Rhodes have documented the navy yard and hundreds of inscriptions from monuments and tombstones that provide a detailed sense of the Rhodian navy and the men who fought in it.

Rhodes appealed to Rome for help in 201 B.C. in response to the growing naval power of potential enemies and the decline of the Egyptian fleet, which was Rhodes's traditional ally. Rome, at the end of its second war with Carthage, then possessed the mightiest fleet in the western Mediterranean and was the logical place for the Rhodians to seek help. That help came with a price. Over the next few years, Rome moved to crush the naval powers of Macedon and Syria, and by 190 B.C. Roman power extended into the eastern Mediterranean.

Following these victories, Rome allowed its naval forces to decline, even as its armies advanced to distant frontiers. The decline of Roman sea power allowed piracy to flourish. Pirates roaming the seas not only attacked ships at sea but also raided coastal towns, including those on the Italian mainland. In 67 B.C., Rome struck back, building a fleet that swept the seas clean under the command of Pompeius Magnus (Pompey the Great). These fleets became the genesis of a renewed Roman navy.

■ A model of a Roman warship depicted on Trajan's Column, in the Museum für Antike Schiffahrt, Mainz (Carole Raddato, Wikipedia Commons)

Ships of various sizes comprised the Roman fleets of the last century B.C., including the larger "super galleys" that had first appeared a few centuries past. The range of these types of ships, and estimates of their sizes, as well as the nature of war at sea in this period are available through contemporary Roman accounts of the civil wars of 49 to 31 B.C., a rich artistic and written record on Roman sculpture and monuments, and a handful of maritime archaeological discoveries.

THE MARITIME ARCHAEOLOGY OF THE ROMAN CIVIL WARS

The Republic of Rome's rise to power and its wars of expansion ultimately led to a clash between two powerful military men who jockeyed with each other for control of the empire. Gaius Julius Caesar's assumption of power as dictator for life following his defeat of Pompeius Magnus ended the first period of that civil war. Renewed conflict followed Caesar's assassination in 44 B.C. Caesar's great-nephew Octavian was joined by Marc Antony to defeat Caesar's assassins, and then meet a challenge from Pompeius Sextus, son of the dead Pompeius Magnus.

A Roman warship wreck at Capo Rasocolmo, Sicily, dates to this period of the Roman civil wars. It may be a casualty of the Battle of Naulochus, which lies close to the site. There, off the Sicilian coast near modern Spadafora, Agrippa, one of Octavian's lieutenants, defeated the forces of Pompeius Sextus on September 3, 36 B.C. In that clash of equal-sized fleets of 300 ships each, Agrippa won, sinking 28 of Pompey's fleet, and capturing all but 17 warships that managed to flee. Agrippa lost only three ships. Is the Capo Rasocolmo wreck one of these casualties?

Unfortunately, very little of the ship has survived on an exposed reef in only eight meters of water. Italian archaeologists who examined the wreck site in 1991 discovered metal and stone artifacts, and no timber. The hints that it is a warship are thirteen *glandes*, or slingshot, and a lead seal that bears Pompeius Magnus's insignia. Broken and intact millstones lying on the wreck site may be ballast, not cargo, as none matched to make a functional pair.

Like the Egadi Carthaginian warships, this may be another example of an ancient warship that was carrying ballast. Based on these few clues, archaeologist Alice Freschi feels that the wreck may either be a storm-wrecked member of Pompeius Sextus's fleet or an actual battle casualty of Naulochus.

Another relic of ancient war at sea was a find close to the wreck in the Straits of Messina 17 years later. In September 2008, archaeologists discovered a bronze ship's ram in nine meters of water just 45 meters offshore. The Acqualadroni Ram (named for the bay in which it was found) is impressive; I was privileged to see it while it still in a freshwater storage tank in Sicily just after it was brought to shore. When you look at the complexity of the casting, and the amount of cost expended in terms of bronze and labor, as well as the engineering involved to make a ram, you see firsthand that this is no simple, blunt-force weapon, just as Richard Steffy pointed out in the study of the Athlit Ram.

Similar in size to the Athlit Ram more so than the Egadi rams, it also had preserved wooden timbers from the warship inside the hollow cast-bronze ram. The pine wood used to build the ship dated to the time of the First

Punic War and has suggested to archaeologists that it may have come from one of two battles north of Sicily off the Aeolian Islands in the Tyrrhenian Sea, the Battle of Mylae (260 B.C.) or the Battle of Tyndaris (257 B.C.). Mylae was the first naval battle of the Punic War, and the first time the Romans employed their famous *corvus* to spike and hold an enemy ship.

Under the command of Gaius Duilius, one of Rome's consuls, a fleet of about 100, maybe more, Roman ships clashed with a Carthaginian fleet of 130. Using the *corvus*, the Romans spiked and captured 31 enemy ships, and sank 13, while losing 11 of their own. Three years later, at Tyndaris, a Roman fleet ambushed a passing Carthaginian fleet, sinking eight and capturing 10, while losing nine of their own. If the Aqualadroni Ram is from either of these battles, archaeologists have suggested the ship, damaged in either battle, was lost while trying to reach Messana, the Roman naval base in the Straits of Messina. Coming at the same time as the Egadi ram discoveries, Aqualadroni was an exciting find and suggested that Egadi will not be a one-time discovery of a submerged ancient battlefield. As Sherlock Holmes would say, the game's afoot, and other ancient naval battle sites and warships with rams await discovery.

Archaeologists working at another archaeological site, this one on land, have learned more about rams and warships of the period. In western Greece, a large memorial on land overlooks the site of the Battle of Actium, the last major sea battle of antiquity. There, in 31 B.C., a Roman/Egyptian fleet of 500 ships loyal to Marc Antony and his consort and ally, Cleopatra, met Octavian's smaller fleet of 400 ships in battle. After defeating Caesar's assassins and Pompeius Sextus, the two rulers of the Roman Republic withdrew to respective power bases—Octavian in Rome, Antony in Alexandria. There Antony was joined by Cleopatra, queen of Egypt and a shrewd political manipulator, as both his lover and co-ruler of an eastern Roman/Egyptian empire. Roman support for Antony withered in the face of his Egyptian alliance. The Senate declared war on Cleopatra to halt her plans, and Octavian readied for combat to defeat his last rivals for domination of the Roman world.

Octavian's lieutenant Agrippa whittled away at Antony's naval forces, allowing Octavian to ferry an army across the Adriatic to meet Antony in combat on the Greek Peloponnese. At Actium, the narrow entrance to the Ambracian Gulf, the two armies faced each other while the fleets clashed offshore. Usually, Romans prevailed in a sea fight because their heavily armed ships closed with the enemy and the troops that poured onto the enemy's decks fought fiercely. Agrippa used these tactics to his advantage at Naulachos, inventing a grapnel called the *harpax* that was fired into the opposing ship's hull. With a thick iron and wood shaft that could neither easily be pulled out nor cut free, the *harpax* allowed Agrippa's troops to winch in the enemy vessel for close-in fighting and boarding.

At Actium, Antony and Cleopatra's fleet was not only greater in number but also included large ships—sixes, sevens, and tens—that dwarfed Agrippa and Octavian's smaller ships. Boarding and fighting was not an option, since Agrippa had roughly half the men his opponents did. In order to win, Agrippa had to change tactics—first by throwing fire from catapults to gain an advantage, and then by out maneuvering and ramming the heavier, slower Roman/Egyptian fleet.

Octavian's fleet won as the small ships darted in and out, quickly ramming the heavier enemy ships and then retreating from boarding range. Cleopatra fled the battle in her ship, followed by Antony. Disheartened, their fleet, now in disarray, was left to Octavian's mercy. It was not forthcoming. Agrippa closed and used incendiary weapons to set the enemy fleet ablaze. When the flames died out, Octavian was the victor. Pursuing Antony and Cleopatra, his conquering troops took Egypt in the aftermath of their suicides. Octavian assumed control of all of Rome and inaugurated the new Roman Empire in 27 B.C. as Augustus Caesar.

To commemorate his victory at Actium, Augustus erected a memorial on the hillside overlooking the site of the battle. Archaeologists discovered the ruins of the memorial in 1913, against the hillside of Mount Michalitsi near modern Preveza in western Greece. Excavations at the memorial have revealed a rectangular earthen podium, supported on three of its sides by a low, stone retaining wall, and topped by the foundations of a long, covered portico or stoa.

Archaeologist William M. Murray has searched the waters off Actium for the lost warships of the battle, but evidence of the ships remains elusive.

However, Murray has been able to learn a great deal about them by studying the memorial, whose low southern wall once supported a collection of bronze warship rams from the defeated fleet of Antony and Cleopatra placed there by Octavian as an offering to the gods. Murray identified odd shapes on the wall as the stone sockets used to mount the rams. Working from the marks and mounting sockets in the stone, Murray has found evidence of 23 separate rams of different sizes, representing a number of warships, large and small. About 10 meters of the wall no longer survives; given the spacing of the rams along the surviving section, Murray estimates that another 12 rams lined it, making a total display of 35 of the elaborate bronze weapons. This, he estimates, represents just one-tenth of the total of Antony and Cleopatra's warships that Octavian captured or destroyed.

The elaborate carving of the ram sockets in the stone correspond closely with the shape of the Athlit Ram, the only ancient ram found and available when Murray did his study. The shape of the stone sockets showed Murray that the bows of the lost ships of Actium were similar to that of the Athlit warship. The examples at Actium, however, says Murray, "were much more massive, and were designed to deliver and withstand ramming blows of much greater force." The evidence from Actium, even without the actual ships or their rams, suggests that Steffy's conclusions about the heavy nature of ancient warships of this period are correct. The bottoms of these ships were thick, heavily built structures. The entire ship was the weapon, and the ram merely the warhead. Based on the size of the sockets, Murray has determined that the ram sockets represent a number of large ships, including tens, sixes, and fives. The sheer number of rams dedicated to the gods at Actium "confirm the ferocity of the final battle and support the accounts that describe a great conflagration at the battle's close."

THE IMPERIAL ROMAN NAVY, A.D. 100–400

Following Augustus's victory at Actium, the naval forces of the empire underwent two significant changes. The first was the shift from larger warships to smaller vessels. Agrippa's experience at Actium led Rome to move to a standardized force of light, small ships, the *biremes* or *liburniae*. Just as the Romans had copied the Carthaginian warships to build a navy 200 years earlier, they now copied the small, fast ships of the Illyrian pirates of the Adriatic. Related to the earlier *hemiolia* of the Greek pirates, these new, small *liburniae* were, according to illustrations, one- or two-level, open-decked galleys. While larger warships remained part of the naval inventory, the *liburniae* became the standard Roman warship for the next four centuries.

The second Roman naval development was the concentration of the fleets in several naval bases throughout the Mediterranean, in Britannia, Gaul, Germania, and on the Black Sea. Major bases at Ravenna and Misenum guarded Italy's eastern and western shores, while the other bases occupied strategic positions that allowed the Romans to hold sway over important bodies of water and major sea routes.

From its bases, the imperial Roman navy patrolled the seas, but fought no major sea battles. The reason for this is simple: the Mediterranean had become a Roman lake known to them as *Mare Nostrum*, or "Our Sea." A late empire tract on warfare, written sometime around A.D. 400 by Publius Flavius Vegetius, discoursed at length on the politics and strategies of war on land. As for naval warfare, however, Vegetius wrote that "its arts require less to be said for the reason that the sea has been long pacified, and our struggle with the barbarian races is played out on land."

But a powerful naval force was needed, and the fleet even then played an important role. Vegetius reminded his readers that "the Roman people for the pomp and advantage of their empire used not to fit out the fleet on the spur of the moment in response to the needs of some crisis, but always kept it in readiness lest they should ever be in danger."

The imperial Roman navy during those centuries was an extension of the army afloat. Armored Roman marines, equipped with spears, swords, and arrows, formed the fighting force, while oarsmen maneuvered the ship into battle. By A.D. 100, the Romans began to abandon the heavy rams of earlier warships, emphasizing smaller, horn-like rams similar in drawings to those on the Marsala Punic warship wreck. As well, the Romans had earlier added large wooden towers to the decks of large warships. These carried siege weapons and artillery such as catapults and bolt-throwing ballistae. As Vegetius explained, "Land warfare requires many types of arms; but naval warfare demands more kinds of arms, including machines and torsion-engines as if the fighting were on walls and towers."

The popular image of Roman warfare at sea is huge ships with galley slaves struggling at the oars, the slaves whipped into "ramming speed," and the crashing of timbers as two galleys collide. Locked together, on fire, the decks are filled with swarms of armored men stabbing, spearing, and falling screaming into the sea. That's the way *Ben Hur* showed it, in vivid color on the movie screen, with Charlton Heston straining at the oars and Jack Hawkins, in armor, short sword at the ready, fighting on the deck above.

But that's not exactly how it was. The Romans did not use galley slaves; soldiers volunteered to take the oars. More soldiers, on the deck, stood by to board and seize an enemy ship. The objective was not to sink the other ship, but to take control of it by killing as many of the enemy crew as possible. Fire was a last resort, even at Actium. There, at the close of the battle, Octavian ordered fire "because he saw that it was impossible to win in any other way, and he believed that this was the only weapon which would help him," according to Roman historian Cassius Dio.

Cassius Dio, Vegetius, Appian, and other ancient historians say that Roman naval commanders used a variety of weapons at a distant range to kill as many men as possible before boarding and fighting it out hand-to-hand. Archaeologists have excavated an amazing array of Roman weapons from land sites—stone-throwing catapults, large and small; ballistae that shot small stone balls and iron bolts; as well as the weapons for close-in fighting. But none of these have been discovered underwater—except for the lead slingshot excavated from the warship wreck off Capo Rasocolmo, Sicily, that may be a casualty of the 36 B.C. Battle of Naulochus.

At Naulochus, modern historian E. W. Marsden, in his classic work on Greek and Roman artillery, notes that "the actual battle started with heavy shooting, some of this being done by artillery. When the fleets came to close quarters, some ships attempted to ram their opponents, while others sailed through the enemy line hurling stone shot and bolts as they passed."

Marsden goes on to say, "They were operating in fact, in the same way as Nelson's vessels at Trafalgar."

To fight at sea, Vegetius went on, "besides drags and grapnels and other naval kinds of weapons, there are arrows, javelins, slings, 'sling-staves,' lead-weighted darts, mangonels, catapults, and hand-catapults, shooting darts and stones at each other. More dangerously still, those confident of their courage move up their warships alongside, throw out bridges and cross over the enemies' ships to fight it out there hand to hand…on larger warships they even erect fortifications and towers, so that they may easily wound or kill their enemies from higher decks as if from a wall. Arrows wrapped in burning oil, tar, sulphur and bitumen are implanted blazing by catapults in the bellies of hostile ships." Vegetius concluded by asking, "What could be crueler than a naval battle, where men perish by water and fire?"

Unfortunately, neither archaeologists nor divers have discovered the wrecks of late Roman warships. No traces of a Roman sea battle—not even at Actium—have been spotted despite searching. The characteristics of the ships, the weapons carried aboard, and the tactics and strategy of Rome's extension of its power to the sea comes like that for so many other ancient navies, from inscriptions, the writings of ancient historians, and carvings and paintings on walls and monuments.

THE MAINZ BOATS

German archaeologists, however, have discovered the well-preserved wrecks of late empire Roman riverine warships at Mainz. Roman military operations, beginning with Julius Caesar's conquests into the heart of Europe and to Britain, heavily relied on the rivers as a means of transport and rapid movement. Rivers also served as important strategic frontiers. The key to Rome's command of the rivers were small light galleys known as *lusoriae*, which formed the naval fleets of the northern frontiers.

The fresh water and mud of the Rhine has preserved the remains of several Roman boats, including *lusoriae*, that date to the 4th century A.D. Archaeological excavations at Mainz, a Roman legion's camp and later the

■ The remains of one of the Roman warship wrecks from Mainz, Wreck 1, in the Museum für Antike Schiffahrt (Carole Raddato, Wikipedia Commons)

capital of Germania Superior, have recovered the remains of five boats in 1981–1982, providing the first detailed look at these Roman riverine warships. Archaeologist Olaf Hockmann describes the Mainz boats as "sleek, shallow-draught, and low-sided undecked river warships with fifteen oars per side." Reconstructions of the Mainz boats show they were about 19 meters long, with a 3-meter beam, and drew only a half meter of water. Archaeologist Peter Marsden, studying the form of the boats, estimates that they cruised at speeds of about seven knots, and could reach a maximum speed of 10 knots.

Built of oak and coated with pitch on the outside, the Mainz boats show a merging of Roman Mediterranean building practices with a Northern European Celtic tradition. They demonstrate again the Roman tendency to adopt local or regional vessels into their fleets. This is not surprising given the Roman enthusiasm for incorporating the traditions, gods, and customs of conquered peoples.

Also not surprising, given the Roman preference for standardization, the Mainz boats showed that they were assembled with the aid of temporary

■ A modern replica, based on archaeological remains and ancient depictions, of one of the Mainz Type B Roman riverine warships, a *navis actuaria*, in the Museum für Antike Schiffahrt (Carole Raddato, Wikipedia Commons)

"molds" or templates, which Hockmann points out "would have eased mass production by following standard plans, defined by the moulds." The reconstructions of these Roman riverine warships on the German frontier provide direct physical evidence of the appearance and form of the boats. They also show that archaeology can reveal, through the details, how people or empires reflect their nature and character.

RAIDERS AND WARRIORS OF THE SEA

Even as the Mainz boats were built, the Roman Empire was in chaos. Rival factions fought for control of the empire with increasing regularity after A.D. 100. The next major Roman naval engagement after Actium was a battle between Romans in A.D. 323 when two rival emperors, Constantine and Licinius, met in sea battle with Constantine's 200 *liburniae* emerging victorious over Licinius's 350 *triremes*. It was a reminder of the lesson learned at Actium; smaller ships, used effectively, could beat a larger fleet of more substantial ships.

Enemies sacked a weakened Rome in the early 5th century. The power and authority of the Roman Empire transferred east to Constantine's new imperial city, Constantinople, on the shores of the Bosporus at Byzantium, today's Istanbul. From there, the Byzantines controlled the flow of trade from east to west, while also trying to maintain control of the Mediterranean. But as Roman troops were withdrawn back into the heart of the empire, and as citizens on the edges of the empire were absorbed into the local cultures, or were slaughtered by barbarian raids, Roman control of the far fringes of the empire collapsed. The end of the fleet on the Rhine may be indicated in the Mainz boat wrecks; they were stripped of their fittings and abandoned to the mud by the early 5th century, showing perhaps that the Roman troops were gone, or those who remained had priorities other than patrolling a river frontier.

In Northern Europe, the contraction and final collapse of Roman control allowed the native seafaring peoples to commence raiding one another by sea. At the same time, diverse groups of tribes joined confederations that allowed for a greater concentration of resources and men against Rome's political, economic, and military weakness. Between the 3rd and 7th centuries, Germanic peoples pushed by ship out of the North Sea, into the English Channel, and finally into the Mediterranean itself.

Roman historians record sea battles against the Germanic peoples as early as 12 B.C., and throughout the next few centuries, these same peoples, operating essentially as pirates, kept the pressure up on Rome. The pressure grew overwhelming after A.D. 200 when confederations of Germanic tribes began to coalesce. A Roman funerary monument from Rome itself, dating to this time, explains that the deceased had participated in an action against a Germanic fleet.

Two hundred years later, Germanic fleets had increased their activities to the point that the "barbarian" push against Rome was as much by sea as it was by wild tribes marching down from the interior of Europe into Italy or pouring across Hadrian's Wall into Britannia. The success of these ship-borne raids is particularly evidenced by the 3rd-century construction of coastal watchtowers and fortifications by the Romans in Germania, Gaul, and Britain as defensive measures against attack by sea. There are also a number of "hoards," or groups of coin and jewelry buried in the ground in order to protect them that date from this period.

The success of these Frankish and Saxon raiders, both in the range of their depredations and the ability to carry sufficient men and arms to strike effectively and return home shows that they had sophisticated vessels built specifically for war. By the fifth century, and for the next 200 years, these boats were capable not only of raiding but of conquest and migration as the Saxons poured out of Europe and into Britain. Archaeological study of ancient boat finds in Northern Europe shows a well-developed shipbuilding tradition progressing quickly from dugout logs to planked boats of considerable size.

Some archaeologists and historians have suggested that the merging of building traditions found in the Mainz boats probably worked both ways. Thanks to exchange with the Romans, the Franks, and other Germanic peoples, as well as the Picts, Scots and Irish built boats that incorporated Roman styles and techniques. Other archaeologists argue for a separate tradition coming out of the forests and coastal communities of Scandinavia. An important piece of evidence in this argument is two boats and an amazing array of boat parts, roughly dating to the same time as the Mainz boats.

THE NYDAM SHIPS

The Nydam ships, excavated from a Danish bog known as Nydam Mose from 1859 through 1863, illustrate the type of ship used by the Germanic peoples to raid both Roman and "barbarian" settlements in Europe. Dating to the 4th century A.D., the ships at Nydam were deliberately sunk as a sacrificial offering to the gods along with a large number of weapons, including axes, swords, bows, arrows, spear and knife shafts, and shields. They were probably spoils from a defeated enemy, deposited in the bog as offerings of thanks for victory. The bog, once a freshwater lake, and now a rapidly drying peat field, has yielded the remains of three ancient boats and a tantalizing trace of a fourth. The boats were ritually destroyed, or "killed," before they were deposited in the bog. The ancient people who lived at Nydam Mose cut one boat up and cut into the hulls of the others with axes to sink them.

The most amazing of the finds, and the most famous, is a large oak warship known as the "Nydam Ship." It is about 25 meters long and narrow, with a 3.5-meter beam. Its builders made it out of five large planks that overlap one another in a style of building known as "clinker-built." The planks were fastened together with iron rivets clenched inside the hull. Frames or ribs cut from curved branches and lashed to cleats carved into the planking strengthened the hull, making it a strong, flexible craft. Rowlocks for 30 oars were lashed to the gunwale, and a large steering oar was lashed or otherwise fastened to the starboard end of the ship. There was no mast or sail.

Some scholars suggest the lack of a sail is not because the boat's builders did not know about sailing technology. As early as the 1st century B.C., during Julius Caesar's conquest of Gaul, his naval forces fought a large number of sailing warships of the Celtic peoples known at the Veneti, at the

■ The Nydam boat, now displayed in the Nydam Hall in the Archaeological Museum in Schloss Gottorf, Schleswig (Holger Ellgaard/Wikipedia Commons)

western end of the English Channel off the coast of Brittany. Rome's defeat of the Veneti, and the next four centuries of a Roman presence in Northern Europe doubtless suppressed the use of sail and led to the development of stealthier warships like the Nydam ship. The addition of a mast and sail would make the boat more visible. Historian Owain T. P. Roberts has suggested that Northern European warships "remained as small, many-oared pulling boats until the constraints of a patrolling foreign navy were removed."

A number of archaeologists view the Nydam ship as a Scandinavian shipbuilding tradition that would ultimately lead to the more famous "Viking ships." But, as historian John Haywood suggests, the Nydam ship is more than a precursor to the Viking ship. It should be viewed as a fully developed ship in its own right and indicative of a specific type of warfare. Without a sail, and with a low profile, the Nydam oak warship was a good ship for a stealthy raid on one's neighbors. Instead of success, the owners of the Nydam ships doubtless died, and their vessels and weapons ended up in a bog both as spoils of war and an unwitting legacy to future generations. Today, the preserved remains of the ship, surrounded by its incredible trove of sacrificed weapons and valuables, are among many impressive exhibits in the National Museum of Denmark in Copenhagen. Every time I go to Copenhagen, I stop there and pay homage to the Nydam Mose ships and finds.

THE BYZANTINE NAVY

The collapse of the Western Roman Empire by the late 5th century gradually allowed the rise of small kingdoms, fragmented and often isolated, that warred on one another in Northern Europe, Britain, Spain, and Italy. In the east, however, Byzantium reigned supreme, controlling trade between Europe and the Far East.

The Byzantine navy protected the sea approaches to Constantinople as well as Byzantium's overseas colonies. The warship of the Byzantine navy was the *dromon* (racer), a two-banked oar-driven warship that also carried sail.

Most probably a descendant of the *liburniae*, these warships represented a return to simpler form that continued to emphasize speed and maneuverability. In their push for simplicity, the naval masters of Byzantium eventually lost either the secret or the desire to build the more complex *triremes* or *quinquiremes* of antiquity. But the Byzantine navy performed well in action.

Decisive military actions, supported by the navy, helped the Byzantine emperor Justinian regain control of the western Mediterranean in the 6th century. In 533, the "barbarian" Vandals who had sailed across the Mediterranean to seize North Africa after the collapse of Rome were defeated and their capital, Carthage, fell to Justinian's commander, Belisarius. This victory was followed by the conquest of Sicily in 535, and the reconquest of Italy by 562.

Byzantium's control of the Mediterranean would not last long. Within a century, Arabs united under the Islamic banner conquered vast areas around the Mediterranean. Arab Muslims took Egypt, Persia, and Northern Africa—including the Byzantine naval bases at Tyre in 638 and Alexandria in 641. Armed Arab *dhows*, along with captured Byzantine ships, swept into the Mediterranean, pushing across the Straits of Gibraltar to seize the Iberian Peninsula. Arab ships pushed into the Indian Ocean, encountering no resistance from small, isolated kingdoms.

Alarmed, the Byzantine navy responded with a program of new construction, developing three versions of the *dromon*: the *ousakio, pamphylos,* and the *dromon* proper. The older Roman technique of ram and board remained the principal tactic, with the two-banked *dromon*, with 25 oars at a bank, and 100 oars overall, crewed by 200 men, 50 of them marines. The *pamphylos* carried a crew of 120 to 160, while the *ousakio* carried 100 men, 50 to row on a single level, and 50 on an upper deck to fight. Aiding the rowers were sails, not the older square sails of antiquity, but the far easier handled, more maneuverable lateen, or fore-and-aft rig favored by the empire's Islamic foes. Other than these few facts, we know very little about Byzantine warships. The accounts of contemporary historians and a few poor illustrations are all that exist. Archaeologists have not yet found or studied the wreck of any type of *dromon*.

Ultimately, Islamic power gained the upper hand over Byzantium. A naval battle off Cyprus in 655 saw the defeat of the Byzantine fleet. A five-year naval siege of Constantinople followed. It ended only when the Byzantine navy employed a new weapon for the first time. "Greek fire," an intensely hot, burning liquid that could not easily be extinguished, was shot from projectile tubes mounted on the bows of *dromon*. Developed around 650 century A.D., "Greek fire" was a naval technological advantage that helped keep Byzantium's capital from falling.

But the Muslims gained the upper hand elsewhere, taking Carthage in 698, followed by Sicily, and then Crete in 827. Byzantium maintained a strong navy, repulsing another siege of Constantinople in 718, and retaking Crete in 961. New powers were also emerging to hold off the Islamic advance in the Mediterranean by then, sometimes allied with Byzantium, sometimes not. The Franks, led by Carolus Magnus (Charlemagne) defeated a Spanish Muslim force in the Balearic Islands, and galleys from the powerful island state of Venice were able to control the Adriatic, warring against both Muslim and Byzantine rivals.

THE BYZANTINE *GALEAI* OF YENIKAPI

Starting in 2004 and continuing through 2010, Turkish and American archaeologists excavated a collection of 37 Byzantine ships that had lain buried beneath the streets of Istanbul. The ships lay in what had been the 4th-century harbor of Theodosius, one of the major commercial harbors of Constantinople until the 7th century. Progressively silting until finally abandoned around the 11th century, the harbor was subsequently filled over and forgotten until construction of a major railway station unearthed the harbor, ships, and other structures and finds going back thousands of years. The excavation site, known as Yenikapi (New Gate) essentially encompassed nine millennia of Istanbul's archaeology and history. The excavation stripped away 8,500 years of accumulated structures, soil, and silt from more than 58,064 square meters in what will likely be forever known as one of the great archaeological excavations of the 21st century.

Among the well-preserved ships excavated were six Byzantine warships that dated from the 9th to 10th centuries. Known as *galeai*, or galleys, these rowed craft are the first Byzantine warships discovered and excavated by archaeologists. Teams from Istanbul University excavated and are studying four of the galleys, while the US- and Turkey-based Institute of Nautical Archaeology (INA) excavated two others. The *galeai* were smaller than the classic Byzantine warships, or *dromon*, and were used as scouts, dispatch ships, and in combat. INA archaeologists Cemal Pulak, Rebecca Ingram, and Michael Jones found that, as described in ancient sources, the *galeai* were open-decked, long (close to 30 meters), sleek (four meters at their widest), and light craft propelled by a single bank of oarsmen.

The *galeai* seem to have sunk along with merchant ships during a violent storm in the ancient harbor about a thousand years ago. Torn open, split, and battered into the mud, they were not salvaged. Silt continued to settle on to the wrecks, burying them completely. Their burial in thick mud, shut

■ Cemal Pulak and Sheila Matthews of the Institute of Nautical Archaeology discuss the excavation of one of the *galeai* at the Yenakpi site in Istanbul. (Author Photo)

off from light and air, meant that when they were excavated, the archaeological teams discovered details that had been suspected but never documented other than in ancient images. Trying to understand how these fast, light, and strong warships were put together and worked from a picture is like trying to decipher how a car works from an advertising photo. The *galeai* at Yenikapi were so nicely preserved that benches where the rowers sat, side by side, were preserved, along with the oar ports.

It is in these details that crew "come to life" on these wrecks. The ergonomics of moving an ancient rowed warship with human power alone was revealed for the first time thanks to these wrecks. The placement of the oar ports, the spacing of the benches, and wear marks preserved in the wood show how the crew sat, close together, pulling on their oars at the minimum practical distance. Their oars, close to the water, passed through leather sleeves that served as watertight gaskets to keep their boat from taking water.

I visited the site during the excavation of the most intact of the *galeai*, and it was remarkable, standing on an elevated framework that allowed the team to excavate without lying on the fragile timbers, to see the details of the construction as well as human traces like what seemed to be scuff marks on the bottom where men's heels had dug in as muscled arms pulled at oars in unison. Also impressive was the realization, as Cemal Pulak, Rebecca Ingram, and Michael Jones explained, to see how sophisticated and expensive these craft were. Each had been exceptionally designed and built with high-quality wood. It was a reminder, whenever we excavate the lost warships and other sites from the past, that what we are digging up is more than a thing. It is something designed and built and used by people, and what they leave behind tells us a great deal about them.

THE VIKINGS

As Byzantine and Islamic forces struggled against each other in the Mediterranean, a new naval force arose on the North Sea. The Scandinavians—the future ancestors of the Danes, Swedes, and Norwegians—developed open-decked, versatile warships and used them to war against neighbors and to mount extensive raids. The Scandinavians, in particular, as they went off "Viking" (which is not the name of a people but the Old Norse word for the voyages), pushed as far south as the Mediterranean. The Viking age saw the development of North Sea and Baltic ships made from planks split with axes from tall northern forests. From smaller 24-oared, single-masted galleys, the "Viking ship" evolved into large, 60-oared *drekkar*, or dragon ships. Whether fighting hand-to-hand, ship-to-ship, or raiding coastal settlements, the Viking ships with their dragon-headed figureheads became well-known, far-ranging, and feared warships.

Viking naval warfare was more of a hit-and-miss affair, with raids against coastal settlements the more common fight than a battle between ships on the water. When battles happened, the defending ships often tied up alongside one another to form a larger fighting platform, while the attacking ships closed, until bow to bow, best warriors forward, with sword and ax they fought for control of the decks. As archaeologists A. W. Brogger and Haakon Shetelig explain, Viking sea battles "were simply contests between floating fortresses moved to the scene of action," or more precisely, "a fenced arena for hand-to-hand fighting, a boxing ring." Viking ships were particularly valuable and potent expressions of power and status, so the objective in battle was to seize a ship, not sink it. Fights between ships focused, as they did for the Romans, in killing the other crew and gaining control of the enemy vessel, which, as historian Paddy Griffith notes, "could be used equally well by friends and enemies alike."

There was no single type of "Viking ship," or even a generic Viking warship. A diverse assortment of vessels—some cargo carriers, other warships, with a range of rowing craft and barges—was built and used by the seafaring Scandinavians. While the Nydam ship is the only archaeologically documented pre-Viking warship, there are numerous sites throughout Scandinavia, Northern Europe, and Scotland that provide a detailed sense of "Viking" shipbuilding and warships. Of all these sites and ships, a few stand out as exemplary. They include two "Royal" ships elaborately buried as part of a funeral rite, and two wrecks—one at Roskilde, the other at Hedeby—and both in Denmark.

THE VIKING WARSHIP

The Oseberg ship, excavated in 1904 near Oseberg, Norway, is a 9th century, 22-meter-long ship. This, the earliest Viking ship yet found, is an interesting comparison to the Gokstad ship, discovered under a Norwegian burial mound in 1880. Like the Oseberg ship, the Gokstad ship was well preserved by the wet soil. Built around 895, it is a ship with a graceful curving hull made of clinker-fastened strakes. Propelled by oars or a single mast and sail, the ship has a stout oak keel cut from a single timber. The keel, and the strength of the overlapping, clinker-fastened planks, made the Gokstad and Oseberg ships flexible and light, but fast on the water and light enough to beach. They also had a shallow draft. The Gokstad ship, for example, drew about 1 meter of water. Like the ancient Greeks, the Vikings built and used their ships more for amphibious warfare than battles at sea. The Oseberg and Gokstad finds were not run-of-the-mill warships, even though archaeologists discovered the remains of 32 painted wooden shields mounted on the sides of the Gokstad ship. It was a *karve* or *karfi*, a royal Norse ship used interchangeably for trade, travel, or war.

Five Viking ships from around A.D. 1000, excavated from the harbor mud at Skuldelev, Denmark, in 1962, provided archaeologists with a

■ The bow of the Gokstad Ship, which dates to around A.D. 880 to 900, in the Viking Ship Museum, Oslo (Jim G./Wikipedia Commons)

detailed look at various types of Viking ships, including two round-hulled *knarr* or merchant ships, and two warships. None of the ships were lost in battle or storm but were purposely scuttled to blockade the harbor, probably to defend it against attacking ships. The smaller warship, about 18 meters in length, with a 2.5-meter beam, shows how the quest for speed defined warship form for the Vikings as it did for the ancients—the warship is seven times longer than it is wide, while the *knarr* is only four times longer than its width, focusing on carrying capacity, not speed. Thwarts or seats for 24 oarsmen, 12 on a side, and oarlocks cut through the top plank, or gunwale strake, join the intricately built hull in a demonstration of exceptional Scandinavian woodcraft. Everything is carefully fitted, down to the step for a single mast, which mounted the square sail, retained by Northern European mariners even as Mediterranean sailors were shifting to the lateen sail.

■ The Skuldelev 1 boat from the excavations at Roskilde, conserved and displayed with metal framework approximating the missing sections, in the Viking Ship Museum, Roskilde. One of six vessels recovered during the initial excavations, it is an ocean-going cargo ship scuttled to block the entrance to Roskilde as a defensive measure. (Boatbuilder/Wikipedia Commons)

The second warship, a larger vessel, was recovered in pieces and with much of its hull missing; only 25 percent of the ship was pulled from the mud. But like the first warship, also recovered in waterlogged fragments and slowly, carefully preserved and reassembled, the second warship revealed much. Archaeologist Ole Crumlin-Pederson estimates that between 20 to 26 pairs of oars, or 40 to 52 rowers, propelled the ship, which was a late–Viking period warship built at a time when larger ships known as *drageskib* or dragon ships were needed for voyages of conquest.

The two warships were the type used by the Danes and the Normans to conquer England. The smaller warship is a type found on the Bayeux Tapestry, which illustrates the Norman invasion across the English Channel in 1066. An "ideal amphibian in sheltered waters," said Crumlin-Pederson, the ship was reconstructed for experimental trials and "rode like a swan upon the water." It also performed well, as shown in the Bayeux Tapestry, ferrying troops and their horses. The modern copy of the larger Skuldelev ship, in a 1967 experiment, loaded four horses, cruised, and then landed the horses with "an ease, which confirmed most convincingly the qualities of this type of ship as a landing craft."

■ Viking-style vessels transporting horses for the Norman invasion of England, AD 1066, from the Bayeux Tapestry (Wikipedia Commons)

The second ship, larger and able to carry more cavalry and horses, was another type used in 1066. With its size, it probably is the type of ship used by the Vikings to reach Constantinople in 1043 with a fleet of 400 ships. Fleets with combined warrior-sailors and cavalry packed into them made fearsome amphibious forces whose impact could be felt strategically as well as tactically. And yet the second warship was not a giant for its age. According to Norse chronicles, vessels larger than the Skuldelev ships were built: the Olaf Sagas, one such account, talks of ships with 32 benches for oarsmen and 200 warriors, and in another account, a 60-bench ship.

Large ships could be built with the clinker method in lengths greater than 37 meters. This allowed the Vikings to build tall, large, yet light and maneuverable ships that carried a crew that could outnumber a foe through their numerical advantage and with higher sides that allowed warriors to rain their blows on an enemy who sat lower in the water. The advantage of fighting in a larger warship was not only the size, and decks that towered

■ One of the hallmarks of the Viking Ship Museum at Roskilde is the reconstructions of the ships discovered during the archaeological excavation. This is a copy of Skuldelev 2, a ship described by the museum as a "war machine" designed to carry 65 to 70 men. Analysis of the original ship found it had been built in the vicinity of what is now Dublin, Ireland, around the year A.D. 1042. (Christian Bickel/Wikipedia Commons)

over an opponent, but also in carrying a larger crew who could physically outnumber their foes. The lessons inherent in the Viking ships were not lost on the English, who, under Norman rule, continued to use Scandinavian shipbuilding techniques well into medieval times. Crumlin-Pederson points out that shipbuilding terms derived from Old Norse words for ship parts were used in English warship contracts for "galleys" dated 1300.

THE HEDEBY WRECKS

Another group of Viking wrecks was excavated from Hedeby harbor in southern Denmark in 1979. Hedeby Wreck 1, a partially burned fragment, was removed from thick mud by archaeologists working inside a cofferdam after the water was pumped out. Crumlin-Pederson, reconstructing the ship's fragile planks both physically and then on paper, brought to life an exquisitely modeled, long, sleek warship "of high status that ended its days in the harbour...after having been set ablaze."

The Hedeby warship was "unusually long, slender and low in comparison with other known finds of Viking warships." It is also lightly built but cleverly reinforced and supported with braces and knees to give it strength; Crumlin-Pederson admiringly called it a "luxury version." This ship of war shows the hand of a master shipbuilder. Crumlin-Pederson contrasted the Hedeby warship with Skuldelev Wreck 5, one of the two warships excavated from the mud at that Danish harbor. Crumlin-Pederson identified the Hedeby find as a royal longship designed "for high-speed sailing and rowing in relatively protected waters," as opposed to the more utilitarian Skuldelev ship, "which shows signs of having been built and repaired as a burdensome duty with the employment of recycled materials."

The Hedeby warship was built around 985 and sank between 990 and 1010. Like the Skuldelev ships, it was a casualty of war. The Hedeby ship was burned, apparently ignited with piles of flammable materials such as brushwood or hay. The extent and pattern of the burning on the surviving timbers show that the ship's loss was not an accident, but a deliberate act. The ship at some stage tipped or listed to starboard, burning the planks well below the original waterline and finally causing the ship to sink. Crumlin-Pederson, looking not just at the ship but also at other finds in the harbor, noted that the wreck lay against pilings. An elaborate system of piling-supported watchtowers and palisades enclosed Hedeby harbor, rising out of the water to fortify the seaward approaches to the town. Crumlin-Pederson believed that the Hedeby warship may have been adapted to another military use as a fireship, and then set adrift to burn a watchtower or a section of the palisade during a harbor attack.

VIKING SHIPS AND THE VIKINGS

Ships built in the clinker-style of the Vikings, with square sails, remained the standard vessel type throughout Northern Europe until the Renaissance. Not surprisingly, warships of larger sizes, but directly descended from the "dragon ships," remained the key to naval power until larger-scale wars and new weapons combined with Mediterranean influences to change them. Still remembered centuries later, the Viking ship entered popular imagination and, with the "Vikings," remain pop culture icons in the 21st century. Archaeology has provided a richer understanding of Viking culture, and a more nuanced view of these people beyond their martial nature. It has also, in some cases, offered forensic evidence of their lives and in one dramatic find, of death in combat.

In 1991, Scottish archaeologists performed a quick emergency rescue dig at the edge of the sea at Scar, a farm on Sanday, a northern Orkney island. High tides and surf eroding the sandy shore were exposing human bones and rusty iron rivets. They proved to be from a Viking boat burial dating to around A.D. 900. Three skeletons—an elderly woman, a young child, and a male warrior—rested inside the boat. By the time the grave was excavated, the sea had already claimed half of the boat and some of the bones and artifacts inside of it. Not much of the boat's timber had survived a thousand years of burial. Most of the wood was gone, but the positions of the rivets that once held its planks together and impressions in the sand allowed archaeologists to reconstruct this "ghost boat" on paper to reveal a sleek seven-meter-long craft. A rich variety of grave goods buried with the boat's occupants included the man's iron sword and a bundle of iron-tipped arrows.

While the "ghost" of the boat survived as outlines in the sand, giving us a glimpse at the past thanks to careful archaeological work, the bones of the dead also revealed much. Forensic analysis of human remains is a subject well known both to readers of archaeological reports and murder mysteries. Even with the flesh gone, bones can reveal much about how a person looked, how they lived, and occasionally how they died. Archaeologists are unsure how the middle-aged warrior died, but his bones indicate that he had been to sea and rowed heavily as a young man.

Forensic anthropologist Daphne Home Lorimer, who examined the bones, deduced this from changes to some of the bones because bone "is a plastic medium and responds to the pull and stress of active muscles." The bones of the lower body, particularly the hips, showed strong evidence of hyperextension, and the knees showed changes occasionally caused by constant squatting but also "constant checking of the inward rotation of the knee." What caused these changes to the bones? Lorimer points out that similar changes are seen in the skeletons of drowned sailors from the 1545 wreck *Mary Rose* and come from young bones adapting to the heavy stresses caused by a ship moving on the sea. In the case of the Scar burial, his bones were not changed from standing on deck, but from bending and rowing in low seats. Archaeologists are not sure if the man was a warrior, because his grave goods included both trading implements and weapons. The evidence of the bones and the presence of the weapons might suggest that as a young man he had participated in Viking war at sea, rowing long distances to raid or fight, before settling down to a more peaceful middle age as a trader.

Another site offered graphic evidence of a maritime raid's violent end. In 2008, construction workers digging a ditch to lay an electric line on a bike path in the village of Salme on the Estonian island of Saaremaa discovered human bones less than a foot below the surface. There were also a handful of artifacts that Marge Konsa of the University of Tartu recognized as being from the Viking era. Konsa and team began to carefully excavate around the construction trench, which had cut through more than a burial—it was a

Viking ship. Much of the ship had rotted away, but the excavation revealed scattered iron rivets that had once held together the boat, and then, close to where the bottom of the boat had been, lines of regularly spaced rivets that allowed Konsa's team to outline what had been a 12-meter-long ship.

What lay inside the ship were the remains of seven men who had met a violent end. They had been hacked, stabbed, and then buried with their weapons and personal goods, likely sitting upright in their boat as they had sailed it in life. The items buried with them suggested that they were high-status individuals, with one man, buried in the center, perhaps the highest ranking. Nestled inside his jaw was the king figure from a Viking game. Its placement suggested it had been placed inside his mouth when he was buried. The weapons scattered among the men were richly decorated with gold and jewels. Other symbols of high status included two decapitated hunting hawks, and a dog that had been cut in half.

The boat lay at the edge of what had been the shoreline 1300 years ago, and Konsa and her team, as they excavated, determined the boat and its dead had been buried sometime around A.D. 650. The circumstances of their death were unclear. Had they been ambushed and killed on a coastal voyage, or were they a ritual burial? More questions, and possible answers, came two years later when a second ship was found, just 30 meters away, by a team led by archaeologist Jüri Peets of the University of Tallinn. Like the first ship, it had also rotted away, but was largely undisturbed, its rivets outlining what had been a 17-meter-long craft. It also contained dead men. Thirty-three bodies, stacked like cordwood, four deep, lay inside. Their weapons were buried with them—swords, axes, and shields lay piled, all of them broken and deformed.

What happened at Salme has remained the subject of ongoing study since the excavation ended in 2012. One possibility is that this was a group of diplomats, or a ruler traveling to conduct negotiations or trade who were ambushed and slain in battle on the beach where they landed. Another is that they were raiders, also killed in battle. They were not locals. Forensic analysis by anthropologist Raili Allmae showed that they had been born and lived in Sweden, not Estonia. The forensic work also showed how they had died extremely violent deaths, with stab wounds, the top of one head cut off, an ax blow to a face, and an arm chopped into three pieces. Some of their comrades seem to have survived, because all 40 had been buried with respect, the high-ranking men in position in their ship, the warriors who had fallen with them laid together and covered with their shields before the ship was buried by quickly scooping sand over it.

The Salme ships and their dead warriors date some 100 years before the start of the era of Viking raids by sea and are the only Viking ships found in this eastern part of the Baltic. Boat burials like the Oseberg or Gokstad ship had one person inside. Nautical archaeologist Jan Bill notes that old accounts talk of warriors who died in battle being buried in their ships—not pushed out to sea on a blazing vessel. The Salme burials are the first archaeological evidence of this, but they also have suggested to archaeologists that a reappraisal of when the age of "Viking" raids from the sea began is now needed. More immediately clear, as Andrew Curry points out, "the remains of these bold, unlucky adventurers are enough to sketch out a powerful scene of a voyage gone badly wrong, and a warlord slain while leading his men into battle on a far-off shore."

3

The Age of Gunpowder

The enemy inflicted such damage upon the galleons *San Mateo* and *San Felipe* that the latter had five guns on the starboard side and a big gun on the poop put out of action....In view of this, and seeing that his upper deck was destroyed, both his pumps broken, his rigging in shreds, and his ship almost a wreck, Don Francisco de Toledo ordered the grappling hooks to be brought out, and shouted to the enemy to come to close quarters.

—Pedro Coco Calderon, 1588

n Northern Europe, the Viking style of warfare, with oarsmen rowing and sailing in fast raids or with many ships in a fleet swooping in onto a beach, faded away after A.D. 1000. The emergence of royal power in England, Scandinavia, France, Hungary, and Poland suppressed raiding and sporadic attacks in favor of trade alliances forged either by negotiation or war. To maximize their trade, the Northern European powers built larger ships, propelled by sail rather than oars. These new, larger ships, called "cogs," required much more timber than the earlier, smaller Scandinavian cargo carriers. A strong regional ruler, be they king or emperor, who held under their control a considerable number of ports and resources was able to build a substantial navy in times of necessity. The high cost of building these new ships led to the use of the cog as both a merchant trader in times of peace and a platform for fighting in times of war.

With this shift in strategy came the reintroduction of royal ships and navies. The change in naval strategy was already underway in the late Viking period, as 9th-, 10th-, and 11th-century Scandinavian campaigns were organized by the emerging kingdoms rather than by tribal leaders. These campaigns employed large fleets numbering into the hundreds of ships. These powerful naval forces represented that important shift from the "Viking" voyages in which several ships might join in a piratical raid to a more concentrated invasion force or seaborne extension of power. Such forces inspired others to counter them. England's first "navy" was an organized royal fleet assembled by the Anglo-Saxon kings of England, notably Alfred of Wessex, to repulse the Vikings.

While navies arose in Northern Europe and England, the kingdoms of the Mediterranean continued a centuries-old tradition of standing navies. The typical Mediterranean warship of A.D. 1000 was still the oared fighting ship. The two-banked *dromon* of the Byzantine Empire and the oared galleys of the various Islamic powers battled back and forth across the Mediterranean, supported and countered from time to time by the oared galleys of the powerful Italian city-states that were emerging from the shadow of Byzantine domination.

The rise of new kingdoms like the Italian city-states altered the balance of power in the region while Byzantium's power waned. Venice, Genoa, Pisa, Spanish Aragon, France, and the Kingdom of the Two Sicilies vied for power in the Mediterranean between 1253 and 1381. Venice finally won the upper hand. The key to Venetian success was a large navy, with impressive fleets of two-banked, three-masted "great galleys." Unlike the descendants of the Vikings, these Mediterranean powers returned to the multi-level oar-powered warship. In the south, rowing and ramming, the time-honored tradition of naval warfare in the Mediterranean for nearly 3,000 years, remained the principal tactic. By 1380, following a decisive defeat of Genoa's navy, Venice controlled the western Mediterranean with its own fleet of 80 great galleys.

However, the rise of a new power threatened Venice and the rest of Christian Europe. Whereas the scattered Islamic caliphates had been unable to break the power of Byzantium or conquer the new kingdoms rising on the Mediterranean's northern shores, a new consolidated power was pushing out of the east. The Ottoman Turks took to the sea to establish their power in the region. They built a fleet at Gallipoli and met Venice in a sea battle in 1416. Venice's navy defeated the Ottomans. Undeterred, the Ottoman ruler, Mehmet the Conqueror, built a new fleet and with it and his army besieged and took Constantinople in 1453. The Ottoman navy moved on to conquer the Aegean and the Black Seas. Venice was able to hold off the Ottoman advance into the rest of its territory, but, weakened, lost three naval battles to the Ottomans off Greece in 1499. The age of Venice was passing. However, new naval powers such as England, France, Portugal, and Spain were on the rise in the West. Some of these powers, particularly the recently united Iberian powers and the "Holy Roman Empire" of Germanic and Balkan states, would stand against the Ottomans in the early 16th century.

HULKS, COGS, AND CRUSADERS

A different type of warship was employed by the new European powers. The Northern and Western Europeans built hulks and cogs. These clinker-built ships grew out of both the Scandinavian ships and Germanic-designed, flat-bottomed coastal trading vessels of the Hanseatic League. Much of what we know about these ships comes from literary references, and images such as the official city and port seals from Northern Europe of the 13th and 14th centuries that depict both the curving hulk (sometimes described as being curved like a banana) and the stocky cog modified for war. While no "war cogs" have been discovered by archaeologists, one essentially complete merchant cog was found and excavated near Bremen, Germany, and other cog wrecks and parts of cogs have emerged from other underwater sites and river mud to reveal how these round, clinker-built ships were constructed.

With their large, stable hulls, they were not the longships of war developed by several cultures over the past millennia. They were stout platforms with flat bottoms that not only kept them stable but also made them capable of carrying great weight. In times of war massive timber structures could be erected on them, making seagoing fortresses. These structures, sometimes only at the stern, other times at bow and stern, were known as stern castles and forecastles. Occasionally, a castle was added to the top of the mast. Experience gained in the Crusades showed how these larger ships, with greater height, allowed men to carry the day by towering over the row galleys, which rested lower in the water. They also prevailed in fierce sea battles by overpowering other ships with sheer numbers, or by delivering death from a great height with archers, heavy stones, or Greek fire.

These ships fought by approaching with the wind, then turning and heading for the midships area at right angles to try and ram the enemy amidships. The men in the castles would sweep the enemy's decks with arrows and missiles before coming alongside. Men in the mast tops hurled heavy stones or pointed iron javelins known as gads (both javelin and gad derive from the Celtic language) down onto the decks of the enemy vessels. Only then did the troops from each ship attempt to board the other's ship and fight. The defending ship would maneuver to place its stern to the enemy, so that the heavily fortified castle was the focus of the attackers.

This type of sea battle influenced the conduct of war at sea in the north. It also influenced the ships, as the larger ships allowed builders to add more masts and introduce the lateen rig, gunpowder, Greek fire and other fire weapons, and finally guns. But from 1000 to about 1400, warships closed in range, archers and crossbowmen rained death from the skies, and then ships grappled as men swarmed the other ship's deck to fight it out with sword, javelin, battle-ax, or pike.

The earliest castles on ships were temporary structures added to the vessels as needed. This worked while rulers and naval powers equipped their merchant fleets for war on an as-needed basis. But as the need for standing fleets grew, the castles were built into the ship to become a permanent part of the structure. The seal of the Baltic seaport town of Stralsund, dated 1329, shows the sides of the hull extended above the main, or weather-deck level to create an enclosed space with a watertight, "castle" deck running the width of the hull at the stern. Over the next few decades, shipbuilders integrated the superstructures into the main body of the ship. This was an important step in the evolution of the fighting ship, particularly galleons with their high, armed stern castles. But these new ships were not descended from cogs. The Northern Europeans replaced their flat-bottomed cogs with hulks. Based on the archaeological study of several wrecks, written evidence, and graphic depictions from the time, we know that the hulk's rounded bottom made it stronger and better equipped to ride the waves, while its blunt bow and stern created more room for carrying cargo, armament, or fighting men.

THE BREMEN COG

In October 1962, workers dredging the banks of the River Weser, near Bremen, uncovered the remains of a wooden ship. This fortuitous German discovery yielded the best-preserved example of a cog yet found. The Bremen Cog, excavated in 1965, chemically treated, and carefully reconstructed at the Deutsches Schiffahrtsmuseum, provides a detailed, three-dimensional look at a cog—the typical Northern European cargo carrier and warship of medieval times. Analysis of the timbers showed the cog was built around 1378.

Until the discovery of the Bremen Cog, details of how cogs were built and how they looked were unknown. The Bremen Cog has a flat bottom, a sharp turn at the bilges, and rounded sides made up of overlapped, edge-sided planking. The bow and stern rise from the keel at sharp angles, with a rudder, only recently introduced to Europe, fixed to the sternpost. A single mast carried a square sail. The stern castle at the aft end of the ship, trapezoidal in shape, overhung the sides of the deck. Study of the Bremen Cog allowed archaeologists to identify other wrecks, not as well-preserved as cogs, adding to the body of knowledge about these long-lost types of ships.

The Deutsches Schiffahrtsmuseum has built a sailing replica of the Bremen Cog. The replica gives us a much better, hands-on appreciation of the ship and its qualities. The angled sides, towering out over the water, gave men on the deck an advantage over attackers in smaller ships or boats who had to climb up the sides while defenders on the deck fired down into them. The large size of the cog made it capable of carrying a large cargo or a number of fighting men. The cog was a worthy successor to the Viking ship and the next major step in the evolution of what would become the gun-carrying wooden warship of the 16th century.

MEDIEVAL ASIAN WARFARE ON THE WATER

While Mediterranean kingdoms and empires rose and fell, ancient cultures at the other end of the world were also taking to the sea. One of those cultures, the Chinese, created a naval force unrivaled by any other in the world of its time. The medieval rulers of the Southern Sung, Yuan, and Ming dynasties built tremendous fleets of thousands of vessels. By the Ming dynasty, they controlled the sea lanes from Korea and Japan to the north, Vietnam and Thailand to the south, and ranged as far west as the Indian Ocean and the shores of Africa. Then, amazingly, the Chinese retreated from the high seas in a period of anti-expansionist, anti-foreign sentiment, leaving the waters of the world open to the growing power of the Mediterranean and European states.

Had China not withdrawn from its control of the seas, early modern and modern history might well be different. By the time the Europeans were first venturing into longer voyages on the open seas, Chinese shipbuilding stood at the apex of thousands of years of development. Chinese merchant craft and warships of the 15th century surpassed anything built in Europe, and Chinese innovations and inventions, when introduced to the Western world, radically changed the form and design of European ships and the art of war on land and sea. While the Chinese themselves were influenced by innovations from the West, such as Greek fire, which arrived in China by the 9th century, China's contributions to the West far outweighed those the West introduced to China.

Chinese innovations—gunpowder in particular—first radically changed warfare in Asia, and then warfare in the West. The introduction of gunpowder, and the development of cannon, dramatically altered the form and design of European warships, as did other Chinese nautical innovations, such as watertight bulkheads and the rudder. The Chinese compass improved the efficiency of European navigation. China's contributions to shipping and naval warfare ultimately led Europe to abandon the millennia-old tradition of row galleys, ramming, and close-in combat. They also gave Europeans the means to reach the Far East and ultimately dominate the seas. Amazingly, while archaeologists have extensively studied the dramatic changes in European warships and war afloat introduced from the Far East, very little work has been done in Asia. Not one Chinese warship wreck has been located or excavated. What we do know about the millennia-old Chinese naval tradition comes from scattered accounts, a few scraps of evidence from archaeological sites on land, and guesswork.

The earliest Chinese warships were limited to inland waters and fought on China's lakes and rivers. They included massive "tower" ships that warriors used to pour fire, molten metal, and stones onto their enemies. Described in the 8th century A.D. in one Chinese account as giving the appearance of a "city wall," they were considered impregnable "floating fortresses." There were also smaller warships, including small, fast, patrol boats. The limitations of an inland navy gave way to an embrace of the sea after the 9th century. Copying the designs of Arab seafarers who had come to trade via the maritime Silk Road, Chinese ships were among the world's most sophisticated, seaworthy craft by the 10th and 11th centuries. By the 12th century, China's Sung dynasty saw a blossoming of overseas trade and the creation of China's first permanent navy.

THE SUNG NAVY, 1100–1279

The Sung were China's first maritime power. They built up inland water transportation links with new canals, locks, and a haul-way for moving cargo-laden craft up the Yangtze against the current. Chinese shipping, although with large and multi-storied ships for trade and war, was a largely inland, river-based fleet. Foreign ships from the Indian Ocean carried on most of China's ocean-going maritime trade. But this began to change after the 8th century. About this time China experienced a boom in shipbuilding, in which Chinese shipbuilders learned from innovations brought into China by Arab, Singhalese, and Persian traders. With these new influences, the Chinese built improved craft that reflected a merging of those traditions with Chinese designs. The result was a significant merchant fleet that grew larger in both the number and size of ships from the 8th to the 12th century.

When they came to power, the Sung used this new fleet to directly trade with Indochina, Malaya, Korea, and Japan. Foreign invaders from overland, the Ruzhen Jin, had taken the interior of China, cutting off access to inland trade. Sung strategist Chang I, writing in 1131, argued that "China must now regard the Sea and River as her Great Wall and substitute warships for watchtowers." In response, the Sung court expanded the navy through an energetic campaign of warship construction, and the creation of China's first permanent navy. Within a few decades, the fleet stood at more than 700 ships. That navy held off a Ruzhen Jin invasion in 1160 not only with a superior force, but with new weapons, including gunpowder-filled bombs thrown by catapults, and Greek fire, the secret of which they had acquired from the Byzantine Empire. Another chemical weapon used by the Sung were bombs filled with lime and sulfur that burst on the water near the Ruzhen ships and filled the air with choking clouds of fumes.

The Sung navy continued to grow. By 1232, the navy stood at 20 squadrons and 52,000 men. Joseph Needham, in his landmark assessment of China's science and technology, sums up the Sung contribution to China's naval history. "The navy of the Southern Sung held off the Chin Tartars and then the Mongols for nearly two centuries, gaining complete control of the East China Sea. Its successor, the navy of the Yuan, was to control the South China Sea also—and that of the Ming the Indian Ocean itself."

Archaeologist Jun Kimura, who has studied Asian shipwrecks and shipbuilding, points not only to the technology of the ships themselves but to an important factor—the Sung state centralized control of shipbuilding, developed industrial capacity, and saw the strength of a naval policy in which the protection of trade was paramount.

MONGOL NAVAL POWER

Despite the power of their navy, the Sung ultimately fell to the Mongols. Genghis Khan's conquests stopped short of China, and his successor was unable to take the Sung. However, Genghis's grandson, Kublai, sensing weakness in a complacent Sung empire, and internal dissension that had spread even to military and naval commanders and troops, began a war of conquest in earnest in 1268. It took Kublai 11 years to succeed. In part, his victory was due to the horse-borne warrior Mongols adopting naval power. Through ships and sailors who defected, as well as building his own fleet on the rivers, and then on the sea, Kublai won key battles that gradually cut off the remaining Sung heartland.

The largest naval battle of the war was a five-year-long siege of the Han River city of Xiangyang. With a force said to number 5,000 boats and about 100,000 men, the Mongols slowly strangled the city and then overwhelmed its forces in 1273. Three years later in 1276, the Sung surrendered, but a diehard faction with what remained of the navy took to the sea and fought a desperate ongoing battle for the next three years, fleeing from port city to port city as the Mongols, now the rulers of China under Kublai, who had crowned himself emperor, pursued them. Guangzhou, the last major port city, fell in 1279.

The last of the Sung navy, a force of 700 ships, clashed with the new Yuan (as Kublai named his dynasty) fleet off Yaishan Island, a two-day sail from Guangzhou. The Yuan crushed the Sung forces after blockading them to exhaust supplies and men, and then moving in for the final kill in a morning surprise attack in one direction, followed by another, afternoon attack in another direction by a separate Yuan force. When it was over, the Sung fleet was gone, and 100,000 had died. Only one surviving firsthand account survives, in which one Wen Tianxiang wrote of seas "upon which human corpses are scattered like fibers of hemp. Foul smelling waves pound my heart to bits."

Kublai Khan's Yuan dynasty of China represented a dramatic change not only in the size but the form of the Mongolian Empire. The largest in world history, the Mongolian Empire had spread out of the Eurasian steppes under the leadership of Kublai Khan's grandfather, Temujin, or Genghis

Khan, into both Europe and the Middle East. By 1242, Mongol invaders stood at the gates of Europe after occupying much of Russia and sweeping into Hungary. Fierce resistance and their own disorder led the Mongols to retreat from both Europe and the Middle East. In 1260, Egyptian troops halted the Mongol advance and retook Mesopotamia. Following these setbacks, the Mongols turned their attentions east, taking Korea, northern China, and then, finally, the Sung empire in southern China.

Kublai's new empire, centered in China, controlled the largest country on earth. Future expansion beyond China was possible, but only by going overseas to other areas in the Far East. To do so, Kublai relied on the large naval force that he had both captured and built to defeat the Sung, and continued the Sung policy of expansive trade abroad. But Kublai also sought to enlarge trade by using the navy as a tool for Mongol expansion, conquering distant lands otherwise isolated from the Mongols by sea. Japan was the first target.

Even before the defeat of the Sung, Kublai had sent envoys to the Japanese court to demand subservience to the Mongols. It was more than an arrogant imperial demand by the khan. The port city of Hakata (modern Fukuoka) was the primary port for maritime trade between Japan and the Sung. By cutting off the flow of that trade, Kublai could economically damage his enemies and perhaps speed up his conquest of China. The Japanese military dictatorship, the *bakufu*, ignored these demands. Kublai responded by ordering his vassals in the Korean state of Koryŏ to build a large fleet of 900 ships and prepare to invade Japan. The relatively narrow straits of Tsushima, spanning some 110 miles between Korea and Japan's Kyushu coast, long a highway of trade, would now be the highway of war.

The fleet departed Koryŏ on October 3, 1274, after embarking 23,000 Mongol, Chinese, and Korean soldiers and 7,000 sailors. They attacked the island garrison of Tsushima, in the middle of the strait, two days later, overwhelming the 80 troops stationed there. The island garrison of Iki, closer to the Japanese coast, fell next. On October 14, the Mongol fleet attacked the coastal port of Hirado, and then moved north to land at various points along Hakata Bay. The Japanese, thanks to spies in Koryŏ, knew of the

Mongol advance. Groups of samurai and their retainers rushed to Hakata Bay. In all, modern Japanese historians estimate that some 6,000 defenders stood ready to fight the substantial Mongol army.

The battle was unequal in both numbers and tactics. Mongol weapons were more advanced than those of the samurai. Their bows had greater range, firing poisoned arrows. The Mongols also had the benefit of explosive shells hurled by catapults. The Mongols advanced en masse and fought as a unit, while the samurai, true to their code, ventured out to fight individual duels. In a week of fighting, the Japanese slowly gave way. By October 20, the Japanese had retreated from the beach, falling back to an ancient abandoned fortress at Mizuki. The tide of battle then shifted in favor of the Japanese.

Reinforcements were pouring in from the surrounding countryside in response to the entreaties of the *bakufu*. An arrow shot into the eye of the Mongol commander left him alive but half blind and in excruciating pain. The sailors aboard the ships, wary of shifting winds that threatened the fleet in its crowded anchorage along the rocky shores of Hakata Bay, warned that the time to leave was now. The primary objective of cutting off trade, at least for a while, had been achieved when the freshly landed Mongols burned Hakata to the ground. It was indeed time to go. The invading troops withdrew to their ships and departed. As they did, shifting winds blew some of the warships to the beach. Swarmed by samurai, the warriors and ships' crews were overwhelmed and killed.

Alarmed at their near defeat, the *bakufu* ordered defenses built at Hakata Bay and troops massed there to meet another invasion. Laborers erected a 40-kilometer-long, two-meter-high stone wall, set back from the beach. The samurai organized their vassals into a compulsory defense force, the *ikoku keigo banyaku*. The *bakufu* requisitioned small fishing and trading vessels to build a coastal force. Angered that some of the samurai who met the Mongols in battle had not more eagerly engaged them in battle, the *bakufu* replaced many of the feudal lords of the region around Hakata Bay with samurai allied to the ruling shogun's family. The *bakufu* also made preparations to retaliate with an attack on Koryŏ and ordered a naval force built, but those plans came to naught.

Meanwhile, Kublai had not forgotten Japan. A Mongol envoy arrived in April 1275. After four months, the *bakufu* summoned the envoy and his entourage to their headquarters at Kamakura, where they killed them all. Kublai renewed his demands for surrender in June 1279, sending more envoys to Hakata just as the last remnants of the Sung dynasty were destroyed at Yaishan Island. Mongol power still did not impress the *bakufu*. They executed the envoys on the beach, making them kneel on the sand as they sliced off their heads, and again sent a grisly answer back to Kublai. Furious, the khan ordered Koryǒ to build a new fleet and prepare for invasion as his officials assembled another fleet and soldiers in China.

In China, the khan assembled a fleet of what legend says was nearly 3,500 ships—most of them captured Sung warships—and an invasion force of 100,000 Chinese warriors. In Korea, the Koryǒ-built force carried 30,000 Mongol and 10,000 Korean warriors and 17,000 sailors. A note here: modern scholars are not convinced that the numbers for the ships and warriors are real, and they may represent an exaggeration perhaps as high as by a factor of 10. Notwithstanding, this was still a large invasion force.

Kublai ordered the two fleets, the Koryǒ "Eastern Route Division" and the Chinese *Chiang-nan* Division, to coordinate their attack after a rendezvous at Iki. The Eastern Route Division sailed first on May 3, 1281, retaking Iki on June 10. Within a week, not waiting for the arrival of the *Chiang-nan* Division, the impatient commanders of the Eastern Route Division sailed from Iki and landed at Hakata Bay. The new fortifications thwarted the landing, and the troops pulled back to occupy Shiga Island in the middle of the bay. The Japanese used their small defense craft to cut into the Mongol fleet. Armed samurai sprang onto the enemy ships and killed the crew and soldiers. The Eastern Route Division, badly mauled, retreated to Iki Island, with the Japanese pursuing them.

The *Chiang-nan* Division, delayed in China, finally sailed in June and rendezvoused with the Eastern Route Division at Hirado in an attempt to bypass the defenses at Hakata Bay. The combined fleet struck the garrison on the small island of Takashima in Imari Bay, 30 miles south of Hakata, and then poured ashore. The Japanese met the Mongols on the beach. A two-week battle ensued through the less-defended, but hilly and rugged countryside. The crews of the Mongol ships chained their vessels together and constructed a planked walkway to build a massive floating fortress in preparation for the inevitable waterborne assault by the small defense craft of the Japanese.

The Japanese force, including fire ships, struck at the Mongol fleet but were unable to do much against the massive fleet in Imari Bay. The principal fight was ashore, where losses on both sides mounted as the invasion dragged on. The stalemate was finally broken when the Mongol fleet was mauled by a sudden storm on the evening of July 30. The legends state that as the Japanese emperor, Kamayama, beseeched the goddess of the Ise Shrine for Japan's deliverance, his prayer was answered. "A green dragon had raised its head from the waves . . . sulfurous flames filled the firmament." Driving rain, high winds, and storm-driven waves smashed into the Mongol fleet. Ships sank as the fleet tried to disengage from one another and flee the bay through the narrow harbor entrance. Most did not make it, drowning their entire crews.

The exultant Japanese dragged exhausted survivors out of the water and killed them. Troops now stranded on the beach, demoralized and cut off from escape, were rounded up and executed by the victorious samurai. The shores were littered with debris and bodies. According to Japanese accounts, "a person could walk across from one point of land to another on a mass of wreckage." Despite mulling revenge and perhaps a third invasion, Kublai never again sent troops to Japan.

The Japanese for their part did not build a strong navy or take to the seas to pursue their enemies following the Mongol defeat. Internal struggles caused Japanese leaders to neglect naval power and overseas expansion. Japan's shoguns left their shores to what they now viewed as a heaven-sent weapon that had proved Japan was under divine protection. The divine emperor's ancestors, the deities of Japan, had sent a divine or god (*kami*) wind (*kazi*) to protect Japan. The powerful myth of the *kamikaze* would live, with terrible consequences for Japan in the 20th century, for almost 700 years.

THE LOST FLEET OF KUBLAI KHAN

Much of what a visitor sees at Fukuoka from the *Genko* (Mongol War) are relatively modern memorials, most of them erected in the early 20th century by a resurgent, militaristic imperial government. A massive bronze sculpture of Kameyama overlooks a park. Nearby stands another statue of nationalist monk Nichiren, a contemporary of the war who had preached of Japan's special nature and the need to keep itself safe from foreign influences. The base of Nichiren's monument is decorated with graphic bronze panels depicting the Mongol invasion and atrocities, including wailing women, stripped, hands slit open by swords, bound to sides of the Mongol ships as human shields. There is no mistaking the message about the nature of the enemy. Other panels show the valiant fights of the samurai, and then the divine intervention of the god wind.

As for archaeological evidence, there is a monument said to be a mass grave of the executed Mongols of the first invasion. A stone anchor from a ship at a nearby temple is said to have come from one of the wrecked ships. There is no way to know, as it is a typical stone anchor of the era. Sections of the stone wall built after the first invasion, excavated by Japanese archaeologists in the 1920s, stand restored in a few scattered city parks.

In a quest to learn whether the *Genko* was a myth or a real war, Torao Mozai, a professor of engineering at Tokyo University, commenced a search for any traces of it in 1980. Mozai was a former Imperial Japanese Navy officer and a survivor of World War II. While most of his shipmates had been killed, Mozai lived because he had contracted tuberculosis and missed his ship's final, fatal wartime voyage. Consumed perhaps by grief and regret, and curiosity, Mozai learned to dive at age 65 and began searching Hakata and Imari Bays for traces of the lost fleet of Kublai Khan.

He found nothing in Hakata Bay, just stone anchors that could have come from any number of ships that had lost them through the centuries that Hakata was Japan's major trading port and oceanic link to the Asian mainland. Hearing that fishermen had been pulling other artifacts from the sea in Imari Bay, especially off Takashima Island, Mozai shifted his work there. Mozai used a sonoprobe, a device that geologists use to discover rocks buried in ocean sediment through sound waves, to scan the seabed. He found what he interpreted as shipwrecks in waters up to 19 meters deep, but buried in thick mud. He also found a fascinating array of artifacts that his divers pulled up.

They included spearheads and swords, stone balls for catapults, ceramic pots for provisions, iron ingots, and stone mortars and mills he interpreted as being used both for preparing food and gunpowder. The greatest find, however, came from farmer Kuniichi Mukae, who had pulled a bronze seal used for stamping documents from the water while digging along the beach for clams in 1974. When he showed it to Mozai, the professor took it to a nearby university for translation, as it had a strange writing on its face. The writing was *Phagspa*, a Tibetan-based script used by the Mongols. It was dated 1277, and was the personal seal of a military officer, reading *gon geun dzung bayin*, "Commander of a thousand." It was, essentially, a smoking gun. Mozai went public with the finds in a *National Geographic* magazine article in 1981, and the story made international headlines. The timing was impeccable, as it was the 700th anniversary of the second invasion and the "kamikaze."

■ The bronze seal from Takashima (Wikipedia Commons)

The events of 1981 led to the creation of a small museum on Takashima to house Mozai's finds, Mukae's seal, and other items donated by fishermen who had snagged them through the years in their nets. In time, it also inspired Japanese archaeologist Kenzo Hayashida to form a multi-year project with volunteer divers, with occasional government funding, to survey the near-shore areas of Takashima and conduct archaeological excavations. They found wooden anchors with stone stocks with broken cables stretched toward shore, suggesting that a storm had hit, and a vast array of artifacts that definitely came from the khan's lost fleet. In a multi-year excavation inside Takashima's Kozaki Harbor, Hayashida and his team stripped away several meters of gelatinous mud to expose the seabed of 1281 and the broken remains of ships, scattered weapons, storage jars, bricks from hearths, lacquerware, personal effects of the crews and warriors, and the remains of supplies and provisions, including animal bones.

In 2002, I was introduced to Kenzo Hayashida by Torao Mozai, and visited Kozaki Harbor and watched the work underwater as part of a documentary we were filming for National Geographic. The site was an amazing array of scattered timbers, rusted iron, and broken pottery, all of it looking, as archaeologist Randall Sasaki would later quip, like it had all come from a blender. Among the finds I watched the team work on was the broken skeleton of a soldier, face down in the mud, with scattered bits of laminated leather armor mixed between his bones. An iron helmet lay close by, as did a sword and iron crossbow bolts. Close enough to probably also be his was a ceramic bowl with Chinese characters that spelled out the name Wang and the rank of commander of a hundred.

Analysis of his bones showed that he was from the Guangzhou region. He was a vassal, fighting for his new, Mongol emperor. Not every man on the khan's fleet was a Mongol. In fact, analysis of the artifacts at Kozaki suggests to the Japanese archaeologists that perhaps only 10 percent of the fighting force was Mongol, with most of the others Chinese or Koreans from Koryŏ. The excavations also yielded hollow ceramic balls that the Japanese referred to as *tetsuhau*. They are shells that with a lit fuse were hurled from trebuchets and catapults at the enemy. In this case, they were likely used for shore bombardment, or landed, in a siege. One of the *tetsuhau*, when X-rayed,

■ An iron helmet from Takashima in the Museum (Wikipedia Commons)

had bits of iron scrap inside it, suggesting it was used to spray shrapnel when it went off. The world's oldest explosive ordnance and the earliest-known naval "shells," the *tetsuhau* are another archaeological example of advanced technologies of the past. They are also reminders of the damage technologies of war can wreak.

Archaeologist Randall Sasaki analyzed the hundreds of fragments of the ships that lay scattered around Kozaki Harbor. In all, he studied 502 timbers that ranged from large sections of bulkheads that once subdivided the hulls, planks, and fragments. Only five timbers were still fastened together. The site, close to shore, had been violently affected, Hayashida told me, but was it one big storm or seven centuries of storms? The answer, after the excavations ended, was a cycle of regular disturbance, but with some items, such as the likely remains of Wang, left in place. Sasaki's work documented well-built ships, likely from the Yangtze River area of China. Some were large ships, estimated to measure more than 30 meters in length. Sophisticated craft, these ships had watertight bulkheads, rudders, and catapults that threw exploding bombs. In summary, they were far more sophisticated than contemporary European ships on the other side of the world.

■ Takazaki Suenaga wounded by a *tetsuhau* bomb, from the *Moko Shurai Ektoba* (Wikipedia Commons)

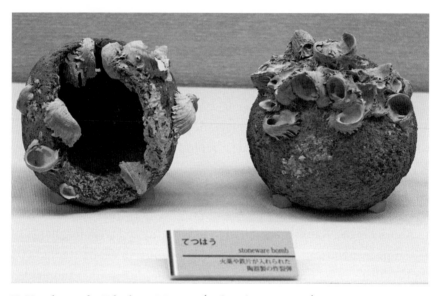

■ Tetsuhau in the Takashima Museum (Wikipedia Commons)

The armor and weapons from Takashima suggest a heavily armed, organized force. These were not simply Mongol horsemen, as I noted earlier. This was a Chinese and Korean army, with some Mongols. They had gunpowder, they had semi-automatic, hand-cranked crossbows that fired short iron darts, and they had plenty of supplies. So why did the khan's invasion force fail? Was it just the bad luck of being caught in a seasonal typhoon, or a storm sent by the gods?

The evidence from Takashima, compared with a brilliant analysis by historian Thomas Conlan of the surviving written sources, including an extensively illustrated account from one of the Japanese warriors, tells a different story. Sasaki found evidence in the fragmented timbers of some ships being hastily or poorly built. He also found closely spaced nail holes indicating repairs to older ships once tightly held together with mortises and tenons like fine pieces of furniture that were then quickly fixed by hammering in a bunch of nails.

A lacquerware plaque from the excavation retained its writing and explained that whatever it had been fastened to—a ship, or a large piece of equipment—had been repaired and then inspected. If this was from a ship, notes Sasaki, then it shows that older vessels were assembled for the invasion, repaired—perhaps not too nicely—and sent off to battle. Hayashida told me of clay storage jars they had excavated that were poorly fired and misshapen, a sign of hasty preparations and not too much care. If the fleet was being prepared by recently conquered people, would they put their all into the job? Or is this the result of haste to answer the demands of an angry, impatient khan?

There are also historical accounts that speak to internal rivalries between the khan's generals and their forces. We know that the Koryŏ Eastern Route Division did not follow Kublai's instructions to coordinate the attack on the islands in the straits of Tsushima and at Hakata. It suggests rivalries between the Koreans and the Chinese. That would translate down the line among the officers and probably even to the troops. A diverse army and navy made up of vassals was not a unified fighting force. But they faced one.

Conlan describes how the Japanese mounted a fierce defense, harrying and cutting into the invasion fleet as it lay at anchor, sending in fire rafts to burn ships. Hayashida's excavation recovered pieces of burned logs and branches, but it is impossible to say if it was used to cook on board the ships or was part of a deadly load from a fire ship sent in by the Japanese.

What emerges from a merger of documents and physical evidence is a clear sign that the fierce response of the samurai, fighting on the beaches and swarming onto enemy ships from smaller vessels, stalled the invasion. Then came a seasonal typhoon. There was, Tom Conlan notes, little need for divine intervention. Imagine then, upon returning to China and lying prostrate before Kublai Khan, how his generals would characterize their loss. Backing up Japanese claims of divine interference makes some sense.

INDOCHINESE AND INDONESIAN WARS AND INVASIONS

With his campaign to conquer Japan in shambles, and the prestige of the Mongols undermined by the destruction of two invasion fleets, Kublai Khan turned his attention to Indochina and Indonesia. The Indochinese kingdoms of the region did not possess large naval forces like those of the Yuan dynasty, but they were no strangers to war afloat. Using both the rivers and the coast for fishing and as water highways, the earliest cultures developed long war canoes, single-banked row galleys, to wage war, which consisted largely of piratical raids.

Bronze drums of the Dong-son culture of Vietnam, dating from after 500 B.C., show long narrow warships with armed warriors. No examples of the actual craft have yet been located, so whether these were dugouts or planked boats is unknown. The discovery of eight sewn-plank boats at Butuan in the southern Philippines suggests that they may have been the latter. Made of shaped planks that were carved to fit together, edge on edge with dowels, they were also sewn together to make a watertight, flexible craft capable of extended voyages of trade or war. The Butuan boats date from A.D. 320 to about 1250. The continuity of the type and the method of construction over a 1,000-year span may indicate that the Butuan boats preserve an even earlier period's boat building. Artifacts found with the boats show a well-developed maritime trade with China, Vietnam, and Thailand, so perhaps the type of boat was endemic to those areas as well as the Philippines.

The exercise of naval power by the peoples of the region, from Vietnam to Malaysia, centered on using their boats to raid one another or passing ships—usually Arab or Chinese traders. Beginning around the 2nd century B.C., one of the principal powers of Vietnam, the Champa kingdom, based much of their coastal economy on piracy, going so far as to build a fleet of armed boats for raids on northern, non–Cham Vietnamese kingdoms and

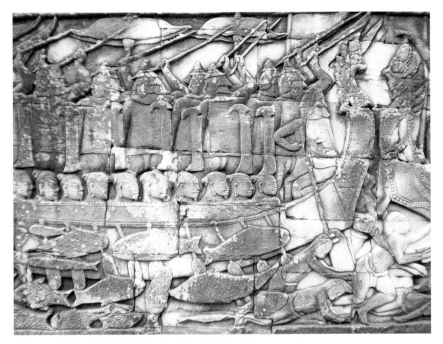

■ This section of the Bayon Temple at Angkor, Cambodia, depicts a naval battle between Cham and Khmer soldiers. The Cham war canoe is bow to bow with the Khmer war canoe. (Wikipedia Commons)

riverine incursions up the Mekong against the neighboring Khmer of Cambodia. The Champa boats, equipped with wood and ivory rams to sink any enemy they encountered, raided the Khmer. This inspired retaliatory assaults by both the Khmer and the northern Đại Việt people. These foes allied, built their own fleet, and swept into Cham waters and conquered the Champa in 1471.

The Đại Việt achievement succeeded where the Chinese had failed, though not for lack of experience or ships. Beginning with the Han dynasty in the 1st century A.D., the Chinese invaded Vietnam to extend their rule and stop pirate attacks. But the distances over the sea made conquest difficult and control, if won, impossible to maintain. That lesson was hammered home during Kublai's abortive conquest. Demands for Vietnamese subjugation met with resistance, and in 1281 the Mongols invaded Champa with 100 ships and a force of 5,000 men, later reinforced with another 15,000 men. A six-month war of guerrilla attrition ensued as the Mongols pursued their foes into the jungle.

To end the war, the khan sent an army overland to march south across Annam, the territory of the Đại Việt, and link up with the southern force. The Đại Việt objected, and as soon as the Mongols had advanced as far south as Hanoi, snared them in a trap. Guerrilla warfare, ambushes, and battles along the Hong River stopped the link-up between the southern army that had landed in Champa and the overland invasion force from China. The Vietnamese annihilated the southern Mongol army and forced the withdrawal of the northern force. A second invasion, in 1287–1288, was likewise defeated, this time through a brilliant ambush and destruction of the Mongol fleet along the banks of the Bạch Đằng River in 1288 on the delta below what is now Hanoi.

Kublai then turned on the rulers of Java, whose power and trade was growing in direct challenge to the Yuan dynasty. A fleet of 1,000 ships and 20,000 men invaded Java in 1293, but the canny rulers of Java diverted the Mongol-Yuan army into killing their enemies, intervening in a Javanese civil war. When it ended, the victorious Javanese ruler turned on the weary Mongols. The army, far from their ships, had to fight their way back to their fleet. In the running battle, 3,000 of the Mongol-Yuan troops were killed. The survivors sailed for home, with Mongol prestige again diminished. The overextension of the Yuan dynasty into foreign waters is proof that the vaunted Mongol military machine, despite its adoption of the Sung-style navy to conquer China, never realized the full potential of naval power. The successors of the Mongols, the Ming, did however realize the potential and developed the world's most powerful navy in the 15th century, only to abandon it after a short time.

THE NAVAL BATTLEFIELD OF BẠCH ĐẰNG

Driving east from Hanoi, if traffic is light, it takes a few hours to reach the coast and the port city of Haiphong at the mouth of the Song Hong, or Red River. The route you drive by car was once a highway for war, as carrier-based planes roared overhead and followed the river to drop their payloads on the capital. Haiphong is a place made famous by the Vietnam War. US forces bombed Haiphong from 1965 to 1968, and then again in 1972 when President Richard Nixon ordered the resumption of bombing and the mining of Haiphong Harbor. The river was also the route that the Mongol fleet took in 1287 to seize the Dai Viet capital of Thăng Long (now Hanoi).

When the Mongols invaded, they faced no opposition. The Đại Việt had left them with abandoned towns and no crops. The occupying Mongols then dug in and began to build a base for their troops and fleet. That was stymied as the Đại Việt harried them with hit-and-run ambushes and attacks. Without provisions and facing starvation, the Mongols asked the khan to send relief. It never arrived. To reach Thăng Long, supplies had to come up the river from the port of Van Don, which sat on the northern shores of Halong Bay. Unknown to the Mongols, the Đại Việt were waiting with their own naval forces in the bay, and they ambushed and burned the relief ships. Their situation now dire, the Mongols had no choice but to retreat. Eighteen thousand troops and 400 ships poured out of Thăng Long and headed for the coast. To do so, they had to run a gauntlet of islands, shallows, and rocks as they threaded the delta. At the critical junction of the Song Bạch Đằng and the Song Chanh, the Đại Việt forces struck just as the tide was falling.

Under the command of warrior prince Trần Hưng Đạo, the Đại Việt launched rafts filled with blazing tinder, setting ships afire. As the Mongols and Chinese abandoned ships stuck in the shallows or impaled on suddenly exposed, sharpened logs set into the riverbed as massive stakes, the Đại Việt attacked with arrows and hand-to-hand combat. It was a complete disaster for the forces of Kublai Khan. Twice now, in the space of several years, he had lost hundreds of ships and thousands of men. For the Đại Việt and their descendants, the Vietnamese, the battle of Bạch Đằng took on mythic significance. Statues of Trần Hưng Đạo are found in most major cities, and his portrait adorns the country's currency, the đồng.

The area around the battlefield on the Bạch Đằng was not settled until the 15th century. Some of that settlement may have started around monuments and memorials to the 1288 battle and Trần Hưng Đạo, who has assumed a somewhat religious significance. Since the wars with France and the United States, and subsequent clashes with China, the warrior prince who defeated the foreign invaders is also a popular figure with the political leaders of Vietnam. Among the temples and shrines erected to Trần Hưng Đạo are reminders of how the distant past is used as a link to the more recent. One of those is a shrine placed where Trần Hưng Đạo, alone, was visited at the water's edge, in the shade of a tree, by a spirit who guided him to the use of the sharpened stakes made from this type of tree to snare his enemies.

The shrine includes a now decades-old tree planted by General Võ Nguyên Giáp, North Vietnam's victorious military commander in the wars with France and the United States. The first time I stood in that courtyard, next to the river, and looked at the tree, I was reminded of how commemoration at battlefields can offer victors an ideal platform. That tree at the shrine underscores the message that Giáp had learned from his country's history and how he adopted the strategies of the Đại Việt and Trần Hưng Đạo. The tree, the shrines, and the various modern monuments to Trần Hưng Đạo on the shores of the Bạch Đằng for me spoke not only to the symbolic importance of the battle. They also spoke to how, like Takashima, there is an almost religious feel to what happened, albeit at Bạch Đằng, divine interference came from spirits that helped the general with his tactics. Unlike the mythic story of the *Genko* in Japan, Bạch Đằng's narrative largely focuses on the human factor in the victory.

Like the Japanese at Hakata and Takashima, the Vietnamese have saved relics and sought archaeological evidence of the battle. Among the more common relics—found in provincial and town museums, and prominently in Hanoi's *Viện Bảo tàng Lịch sử Việt Nam*, the National Museum of Vietnamese History—are a number of the stakes. This French colonial-era building served as an archaeological institute until Vietnamese independence, and its former use is reflected in the majority of the exhibits, which are archaeological. Among them are truncated stakes rising from low-lying, painted pedestals. They are placed in front of a massive mural painted by Le Nang Hien that shows ships ablaze and sinking, as men struggle in the water to reach the shore as troops on foot and horseback swarm

■ Archaeologically recovered stakes from the Bạch Đằng battlefield, with a mural of the battle, in the National History Museum in Hanoi (Bùi Thụy Đào Nguyên/ Wikipedia Commons)

and kill them. It is a powerful display, but looking beyond the emotional impact of it, we had questions. How many of these stakes could be archaeologically traced to the battle of 1288? Were there more still in place in the mud and water of the site?

Black-and-white photographs in the museum document that Vietnamese archaeologists excavated the stakes on display in 1958 and left others exposed at Yen Giang, a commune near the town of Quang Yen.

An Australian-Japanese-Vietnamese partnership since 2009 has conducted a detailed study at that site with additional excavation. This groundbreaking, or perhaps more aptly mud-breaking, work is the first medieval Asian naval battlefield studied by archaeologists. What has emerged is the realization that the "battlefield" is much larger than previously realized as shown by the spread of the various areas where "stake yards" have been found. One popular concept, that the Đại Việt created a vast, mile-long barricade of stakes to close the main channels of the rivers, is now known to be incorrect.

Working from old navigational charts dating to before the Vietnamese began to settle on and plant the river's banks in the 20th century, altering the landscape, the team has plotted the positions of the various temples and shrines on a geographical information system (GIS). They then added the locations of the various excavations of stakes from 1958 to 2010 and the finds reported to them by local farmers. Viewed from above, and examined in layers that peel away modern roads, paddies, and houses, the GIS shows the 19th-century river and reveals a complex landscape. Extrapolating changes to the river in the 700 years prior to the first charts, the stake beds are positioned in now-vanished channels. Stakes are not found where natural features would block the passage of ships, including rocks, shoals, or swamps.

The key to the Đại Việt naval victory of 1288 was knowing the terrain and using it as a tactical advantage. There were only a few places ships could navigate, and the Đại Việt blocked those channels with the stakes. Like the Japanese, Trần Hưng Đạo then relied on his troops. Emerging from hiding to distract the Mongol fleet as it headed down the river, he delayed them until the tide had fallen, exposing the stakes. The fire rafts brought panic and destruction, leaving the Đại Việt to mop up their erstwhile conquerors as they struggled to reach shore.

THE INTRODUCTION OF GUNPOWDER AND THE GUN IN EUROPE

The Chinese invention of gunpowder around A.D. 300 led to its use as a weapon of war primarily as an explosive, as we've seen archaeologically at Takashima. The Chinese invented *t'u huo ch'iang* or "eruptors" around the same time, the 13th century. In 1956, Chinese archaeologists in Jinan excavated a long, narrow, nearly flat-bottomed boat from what had once been the ancient Ji River, which had disappeared in 1852 when the larger Yellow River had shifted. Well preserved because it had been sealed in mud, the wreck had two artifacts with dates written on them. Among those finds was a bronze "hand cannon" that has the date 1377 cast into it.

While an earlier example, the Heilongjiang hand cannon, excavated by Chinese archaeologists in 1970, is dated to 1287–1288, the Jinan hand cannon is the earliest example of a gun from a ship, although by the time this weapon was cast and placed aboard what archaeologists believe was a Ming dynasty river patrol boat, guns and cannon had made their way to sea not only in China but in Europe. Gunpowder and hand and larger cannon probably made their way into the Islamic world and Europe via the Silk Road or with the Mongols as they spread their empire into those regions during the Yuan dynasty, and perhaps earlier.

CHINESE SEA POWER

The introduction of the cannon came just as the Chinese reached the apex of their naval power in the 14th and 15th centuries. During these centuries, the Chinese built the world's most incredible ships and a navy unrivaled elsewhere on the globe. It all grew out of the eagerness of the Mongol rulers of the Yuan dynasty to continue to expand China's overseas trade.

Annam, Champa, and Java, despite their successful defeat of the Mongol fleets and armies, wanted to continue to tap into China's lucrative trade market. Therefore, the rulers of these kingdoms accepted nominal Mongol sovereignty and sent "tribute" in order to continue their trade relationship with China. The reverses of the Mongol navy notwithstanding, China's merchant fleet continued to expand and trade far and wide, taking control of the spice trade and ranging into the Indian Ocean. But while overseas trade to Southeast Asia grew, China's coastal trade declined. The Japanese, eager to avenge the Mongol invasions of 1274 and 1281, ravaged the coast with pirate raids. The Mongols responded by pulling much of China's internal trade off the coastal routes and back into the interior and building fleets of patrol boats to police the canals and rivers.

The build-up of the internal waterways and an inland navy were signs of growing weakness in the Yuan dynasty. The Mongol rulers of China and their dynasty were overturned, beginning in 1351, by rebellions that spread through the country. The struggle only ended when one rebel leader, Chu

Yuang-Chan, defeated both his rival rebel leaders and the remaining Mongol forces to found the Ming dynasty nearly two decades later. Chu came to power gradually, amassing both territory and control of the Yuan navy on the lower Yangtze. By 1359, the war for control of China centered on the Yangtze and a struggle between the states of Han and Ming. Ming controlled the lower Yangtze, but the middle part of the river remained under Han control. The matter was decided in climactic battle, on Lake Po-yang, on the Middle Yangtze, in 1363. The Han ruler, Ch'en-liang, built a fleet of large, three-decked warships, armored with iron plates, armed with heavy cannon, and manned by crews as large as 2,000 to 3,000 men. Chu met the fleet with a mixed force. Some of the Ming ships were large, but most were smaller vessels and no match for the giant Han warships.

Chu's ships were pushed back across the lake by the Han fleet, and several of the Ming vessels ran aground in the shallows, including Chu's flagship. In desperation, the Ming ruler fell back on the ancient tactic of fire ships. As the Han fleet massed to renew their attack, Chu sent a number of fishing boats, manned by a few volunteers and packed with reed and gunpowder, into their midst. The Han fleet, caught by the ruse, began to burn as cannon and powder magazines exploded. According to contemporary accounts, "several hundred" ships were destroyed and 60,000 Han troops and sailors died. But a number of the Han ships remained afloat and ready to fight. Chu and the Ming fleet finally won by harassing the Han fleet as it split up to avoid more fire ships and tried to retreat back up the Yangtze. The smaller Ming ships cut off the huge Han warships and whittled them down, one by one, in a battle marked by cannon blasts, flames, grappling, and boarding. When it ended, Ch'en was dead, the survivors on the last Han ships surrendered, and Chu was master of much of the Yangtze.

Using the victory at Lake Po-Yang as a springboard, Chu pushed into northern China, seizing the remaining states and pushing out the Mongols. Incorporating the remaining Han ships into his fleet, Chu swept into the South China Sea and conquered the coastal ports. Ming completed its seizure of control in China from 1363 to 1382. Amazingly, the country emerged from these wars both prosperous and powerful. The new Ming rulers did not forsake naval power, and under Chu's 30-year reign, as well as his successors, the emperors Hui-Ti and Yung-lo, a large navy was built to control not only the interior and the coast but also distant seas. By the 1420s, China's navy was the largest in the world, with 400 large war junks stationed at Nanking, 1,350 warships, river and canal patrol boats stationed elsewhere, 3,000 merchant vessels that could be converted into fighting ships if needed, 400 huge grain transports, and 250 "treasure ships," overseas warships that brought back riches from far-flung missions of trade and diplomacy.

Under the command of Admiral Zheng Ho, a fleet of these huge junks—some over 60 meters long—armed with cannon, rockets, and guns, carried Chinese naval power and trade throughout Southeast Asia and into the Indian Ocean, pushing back pirates and reopening trade with India, Arab East Africa, and the Ottoman Empire between 1405 and 1433. These large warships may have even been larger, but in the absence of archaeological remains, archaeologists and historians argue over the size of Zheng Ho's ships, with some suggesting 400-foot-long ships. There is no archaeological proof, but by way of comparison, Chinese warships of the 1400s outweighed, out-gunned, and out-classed anything afloat in a European navy.

European powers, just then adapting cannon to warships and starting the progression toward large warships of their own, never came into contact with the full flower of Chinese naval might. After 1433, a new emperor, fearing the perils of foreign contact, withdrew the overseas and coastal navy and scrapped it as China withdrew into its borders and again confined most of its trade and traffic to rivers and canals. Chinese merchant junks on the high seas and coast were left to the mercy of Indonesian, Vietnamese, and Japanese pirates. And the seas were left open to the arriving Europeans, primarily the Portuguese, Spanish, and Dutch, who by the early 16th century were regularly arriving. They seized control of the overseas trade in spices, silks, and other commodities with ships that could not have withstood the might of the Ming navy at the height of Chinese naval power decades earlier. One of the greatest archaeological prizes that remains to be discovered in the ocean is the wreck of one or more of Zheng Ho's "treasure ships." Had they remained on the seas, the history of the world might have been very different.

THE OTTOMAN EMPIRE

Like the Mongols, the Ottoman Turks were fierce warriors who created a vast empire. Sweeping out of Northwestern Anatolia into Europe in the 14th century, they challenged and then defeated the Byzantine Empire. With the fall of Constantinople in 1453, the Byzantine Empire, which had persisted a thousand years after the fall of Rome, came to an end. By that time, the empire, shrunk to a small area, had lost much of its territory through internal weakness, civil war, and hundreds of years of war with Islamic Arabs. The Turks took the Balkans, the Peloponnesus, and then, after the fall of Constantinople, the Middle East and North Africa.

A key part of Ottoman victory and expansion was its navy, which was born of necessity with the need to spread from the Turkish Aegean coast into the nearby islands. Thwarting the Byzantine Navy was also key, and the Turks won their first battle at sea with Byzantine forces off Chios in 1090. Ottoman sea power played a role in the gradual strangulation of Constantinople in the 14th and 15th centuries, cutting off the Dardanelles and the Bosporus, which they then fortified, while also pushing into the Aegean and Black Seas, especially after the fall of the Byzantine Empire. From there, in conflict with Venice, they spread into the Mediterranean, with naval forces playing a role in raids and sea battles off Italy, pushing into the Adriatic, while also expanding into the Red Sea. With fleets of galleys, the primary warship of the Mediterranean for both Islamic and Christian powers, the Ottomans defeated the naval forces of Venice, the Knights of St. John, and then the Holy League of Spain, Venice, Genoa, and the Papal States in the same waters as Actium off Preveza, Greece.

The Battle of Preveza in September 1538 brought an Ottoman fleet of 122 vessels up against a superior force of more than 300 ships of the Holy League. The Ottoman commander, Kheir-ed-din Barbarossa, fought an aggressive battle, using his oared galleys to effect on a largely windless sea that kept close to half of the Holy League fleet becalmed. Barbarossa had destroyed 13 enemy ships, captured another 36, and lost none of his, although hundreds of his men lay dead or wounded. The Holy League's admiral, Andrea Doria, fled the scene, leaving Barbarossa the victor. A second

Christian-Ottoman clash, next to the island of Djerba off the Tunisian coast in May 1560 again brought an inferior Ottoman force of 61 vessels against a combined force, the Christian Alliance, and its 200 ships. Within a few hours, the Ottoman navy again prevailed, sinking or capturing more than half the enemy's ships and killing thousands.

Described as the apex of Ottoman sea power, Djerba did not lead to further Ottoman expansion by sea. What followed was a running campaign of Christian and Muslim corsairs attacking each other's shipping in the Mediterranean, raiding islands, and taking slaves. Indeed, the corsairs of the Mediterranean, while condemned as pirates, were legally sanctioned semi-naval forces. They carried out what essentially was a holy war on the water. The centuries-long conflict left the modern era with the lasting notoriety of Muslim corsairs like Barbarossa and Dragut Reis, whose successors in the 17th to 19th centuries were known as the "Barbary pirates" and a counterforce of Christian corsairs from the Knights of St. John, as well as other Europeans. The strongest image of these times, ships, and actions is that of the galley slave, chained to a bench, whipped, and worked to death.

The Ottoman Empire's plans were not to simply wage a war of attrition at sea. They included the complete conquest of the Mediterranean starting with Malta, base of the Knights of St. John, whose fleet of galleys was a potent force. From there, Sicily could serve as a base to strike Europe. However, the twice-stung European powers regrouped and clashed with the Ottoman navy following the failed Ottoman naval invasion and four-month siege of Malta in 1565. The October 1571 Battle of Lepanto, again off Greece in the Ionian Sea, saw yet another Holy League fleet of 212 ships, led by Don Juan de Asturias, defeat a 251-ship Ottoman fleet led by Ali Pasha. In a close-fought battle, the Christians lost 17 ships and about 10,000 men, while the Ottomans lost some 200 vessels through capture, fire, or sinking, and some 40,000 men.

Lepanto is seen by some naval historians as the climactic battle at sea in which coming close and boarding the enemy took place. It is also a battle where new, larger rowed ships, galleasses, brought more firepower into play, and the effective positioning of some of these ships in the front lines helped disrupt the Ottoman fleet at the start of the battle. Like the Christians after

Djerba, the Ottoman navy rebuilt, and ongoing conflict followed in the Mediterranean for the next few centuries, but Europe was never again seriously threatened with Ottoman invasion.

Archaeological survey has failed to locate evidence of lost ships at the site of the Battle of Lepanto despite two efforts, one in 1971 and the other in 2002. As is the case with the near-by, earlier Battle of Actium, the waters off Preveza have also not yielded any remains from the battle of 1538. However, archaeologists have discovered three Ottoman or Ottoman-era wrecks off the Turkish coast. They lie in the Straits of Rhodes, an active theater of maritime trade and naval conflict. In 2005–2006, the RPM Nautical Foundation conducted a deep-water survey of the straits in collaboration with the Turkish Ministry of Culture and Tourism. The survey disclosed 14 shipwrecks, three of which were, as archaeologist Jeffrey Royal noted, ships "likely prepared for combat."

All three wrecks dated from between A.D. 1450 to 1600. Each of them speaks to the dynamic, often perilous nature of the straits and the Eastern Mediterranean at that time. One of the wrecks was a large, sturdy ship about 35 meters long. A mound of artifacts lying inside the wreck suggested to Royal that it was likely an English merchant ship engaged in trade with the Ottoman Empire and lost sometime during the reign of Elizabeth I between the years 1560 and 1590. Those were dangerous times, and the ship was armed with cast iron cannon, four to each side. Originally mounted on the main deck, these were an effective defense. Mixed into the wreckage were at least four iron crossbows, which Royal believes were on hand for the crew to use. The second wreck, also a merchant vessel of unknown origin, was also armed with cannon. These were small, approximately five-foot-long, banded iron guns that Royal identified as swivel-guns, which were small, effective antipersonnel weapons. Mounted on the ship's bow and stern and along the gunwales, if loaded with shot or scrap iron, they would have been a deterrent for anyone trying to board and take the ship. In the case of both of these vessels, however, they likely sank in storms.

The third wreck, a mound of wreckage some 26 meters long, and centered on a narrow pile of stone ballast approximately nine meters long and three meters wide, three iron guns with separate-cast breech blocks common to cannon of the period. One was a larger gun that appears to have been a centerline gun mounted at the bow; the others were small swivel guns. The site had few other artifacts besides the four anchors. All of this pointed to the likely identity of the wreck, "a small galley of the *fusta* or *galiota* type" used by both the Ottoman navy and the Knights of St. John, and pirates. We don't know who operated this small warship, but its discovery is important. If it is a *fusta*, a small, rowed galley, only one other has been studied by archaeologists. It was scuttled in Lake Garda in 1509 and, thanks to fresh water, revealed much about its construction. The Straits of Rhodes warship wreck, also probably lost in a storm, lies only several hundred meters away from the second merchant wreck. Not only a rare archaeological example of the most common type of Mediterranean warship from a period that spans the great battles of Preveza and Lepanto, lying close to the merchant ship, it joins the other wreck, notes Jeff Royal, in representing the reality of a strait dangerous not only due to weather, but to the turbulent political realities of two empires and faiths waging a constant war against each other's shipping "toward the end of the age of the galley."

THE RISE OF THE GUN IN EUROPE

Historians, working from literary sources and illustrations, date the wide-scale introduction of guns on European ships to after 1400. While ship crews used guns to fight before 1400, the practice was not widespread. Archaeologist Ian Friel, looking at the evidence, finds that longbows and crossbows were the most effective shipboard weapons for killing the other crew, with "guns coming a very poor third, at least before the late fifteenth century." This is certainly what we see with the Straits of Rhodes wrecks.

Archaeologists have discovered and studied a number of other European wrecks from the same period (1400 and 1650) in Mediterranean and European waters. These wrecks, and the guns and equipment aboard them, have provided a detailed look at lost warships, life, combat, and death aboard them. One of the largest changes as medieval naval tactics gave way to Renaissance innovations and technology was the use of cannon aboard ships.

The archaeology of warships from this period shows an increase in the size of ships to accommodate more cannon, changes in the form and construction of the ships to better distribute the weight of the guns, and what disasters could happen when these changes dangerously compromised a ship's stability.

The earliest guns on ships were small, swivel-mounted cannon mounted on the rails, out in the open, like those on two of the Straits of Rhodes wrecks. Firing small balls, or scrap iron known as langrage, these weapons were used to kill men, not ships. A shotgun-like blast of langrage was a cheap and effective way to cut down a group of fighters on another ship's deck. The larger guns, made of iron staves (much like a barrel) and held together by metal bands, were mounted on the main, or weather deck, or in the castles. The earliest guns at sea rested on wooden platforms, not wheeled carriages. Unwieldy and hard to maneuver, these cannon were not powerful enough to breach another ship's hull.

Three warship wrecks from between 1416 and 1545 demonstrate how the first purpose-built warships were adapted to the gun. The first wreck is a "great ship," presumably *Grace Dieu*, a massive ship built for King Henry V of England as part of a naval build-up in response to French raids on the English coast. *Grace Dieu* is a departure from the tradition of the war cog and the rowed galley of the Mediterranean. It is a direct ancestor of the wooden ship of the line, the standard warship of the world's naval powers until the 19th century.

The wreck of *Grace Dieu* rests in the thick mud on the banks of the River Hamble in England. Antiquarians rediscovered the wreck in the 19th century, and for over 100 years people have probed, prodded, and even blasted the thick timbers to learn the identity of the ship. It was not until 1933 that researchers were able to identify the wreck as *Grace Dieu*. Since then, archaeologists working during spring low tides and underwater have partially excavated the wreck and learned more. Historical records show that *Grace Dieu* was a large ship, built to tower over cogs and hulks with a huge forecastle that allowed the ship's archers and other fighting men to overlook and overpower their opponents. *Grace Dieu* also carried four cannon. Built in 1417, the ship never saw action. A brief 1420 voyage ended in mutiny, and the ship was laid up in the River Hamble. It remained there until a fire burned it to the waterline in 1439. Today, only the very bottom of the hull survives to about a meter above the keel.

Archaeologists studying the wreck mapped the long, broad hull and discovered that *Grace Dieu* was the largest European warship when built. *Grace Dieu*'s builders constructed the ship by the Scandinavian method of clinker construction of overlapping planks. But this centuries-old method was reaching the limits of its utility with *Grace Dieu*. In order to build the ship so large, the builders used three layers of planks, effectively giving the ship a triple skin. Closely spaced frames attached to them by thick wooden treenails reinforced the planks of the hull.

The warships of this period—large, clinker-built craft—were the ultimate expression of Viking and Anglo-Saxon shipbuilding technology, built plank-by-plank, "skin-first" and then reinforced with a skeleton of frames or ribs. The introduction of the gun at this stage had no effect on their construction. But by 1500, major changes were afoot. While earlier guns were mounted on the superstructure or on open weather decks, by 1501 a new innovation, guns below the deck, introduced a major change. In order to cut gun ports through a hull, a new type of ship construction was needed, one that did not rely on the planks of the hull for strength, but used instead an internal skeleton or frame.

Archaeologists identified the remains of a ship discovered during excavation of the Thames riverbank at Woolwich in 1912 as probably being the warship *Sovereign*, built for King Henry VII in 1488. The surviving bottom of the hull is carvel (or flush) planked, but the frames show that they were originally notched to fit a clinker-built hull. The huge *Sovereign* carried 141 guns, according to a 1495 inventory, but these were probably small, light guns carried above deck. A push for naval supremacy, particularly by Henry VIII, led to larger, more powerful guns and a need for larger, stronger ships to carry them. The new ships needed to carry these guns close to the waterline and below the deck in order not to capsize. Henry VIII rebuilt *Sovereign* in 1509 to better accommodate his new guns by having his shipwrights strip off the old clinker planks, shave down the frames, and attach a new carvel hull.

Another benefit of this "frame-first" construction was that the hull, without clinker-style planks overlapping one another for strength, now provided a simple, reinforced surface that could be pierced for gun ports and other portholes. The earliest warship wreck with gun ports is a Genoese ship. *Lomellina* foundered off Villefranche-Sur-Mer, France, on September 15, 1516. The ship was under repair when it sank; archaeologists discovered sawdust and chips of wood between the frames and a worker's plane lying nearby. Resting on its port side, the ship had heeled over as it sank. *Lomellina*, according to archaeologist Max Guerout, who led the excavation, was a cross between the Mediterranean row galley and the Northern European "round ships."

This sleeker, well-armed type in time became the basis of the new fighting ship, the galleon. *Lomellina* was a hybrid in more than its hull. The wreck site included 15 guns, some of which may have been for combat ashore since the wreck site included huge wheels for gun carriages. Other guns were intended for the ship, as both their carriages and the gun ports show. But guns alone were still not seen as the key to naval victory. Among the finds from the wreck of *Lomellina* were crossbow parts, and four different types of hand grenades. Like the Straits of Rhodes wrecks, *Lomellina* shows that guns were still just part of the equation as fighting ships came into conflict.

THE WRECK OF *MARY ROSE*

The earliest warship wreck to yield a tremendous amount of information to archaeologists and historians is the well-preserved *Mary Rose*. The ship, with a crew of 600 to 700 men, sank suddenly on the morning of July 19, 1545, off Portsmouth, England. Maneuvering into battle with an invading French fleet, *Mary Rose* was top heavy and heeled over as the crew set sail and ran out the guns. Water poured into open gun ports, which lay dangerously close to the sea. The ship capsized onto its starboard side, quickly filled, and sank as men fought to get out and away. As guns, ballast, equipment, and men crashed through broken compartments and into a broken

▪ *Mary Rose* from the Anthony Roll, a contemporary depiction of Henry VIII's navy (Wikimedia Commons)

jumble inside the ship, *Mary Rose* settled onto the bottom. Less than 40 of the crew escaped to nearby boats.

The wreck gradually sank into the mud and the exposed port side was swept away as it weakened and collapsed. But the remainder of the hull was buried in mud that sealed the ship as a time capsule. Archaeologists slowly excavated the wreck from 1971 to 1982 and recovered more than 19,000 artifacts. The excavation revealed that *Mary Rose* lay on the starboard side, with more than half of the ship, four deck levels in all, intact with guns, equipment, and personal belongings jumbled in the hold, decks, and cabins exactly where they had fallen when the ship capsized and sank. Archaeologists raised the intact hull in 1982 and studied it in a massive shelter that constantly sprayed it with preservatives and cold water for decades until it could be safely dried and opened to the public. I visited it twice, marveling at the size and the survival of this Tudor naval time capsule.

The remains of the ship, from its keel up to the stern castle, allowed archaeologists to make a detailed reconstruction of *Mary Rose*. The ship was a carrack, a huge and modern (for its day) purpose-built warship. *Mary Rose*'s

■ A rosary recovered from the wreck of *Mary Rose*, 1982 (The Mary Rose Trust, Wikipedia Commons)

■ A wooden tankard recovered from the wreck of *Mary Rose*. Among the most powerful artifacts excavated were personal items. (The Mary Rose Trust, Wikipedia Commons)

builders equipped it to fight as much with guns as other weapons like bows and arrows. Among the weapons found inside the ship were swords, daggers, pikes, bills, and incendiary darts used to set an enemy ship on fire. But the most common weapons discovered in the wreck were bows and arrows. Accounts of medieval battles talk about the power of the English longbow and how lines of archers would fill the skies with deadly volleys of arrows.

■ A boxwood comb and its container, recovered from *Mary Rose*, also spoke to personal hygiene on crowded warships. (The Mary Rose Trust, Wikipedia Commons)

Some bows were capable of piercing armor. Even more amazing is that until the discovery of *Mary Rose*, not one medieval bow or arrow had survived.

Thanks to the wreck of *Mary Rose*, we have detailed knowledge of the weapons and the men who used them in battle on both land and sea. Excavators found 137 complete and three broken English longbows, 2,497 complete arrows, and 1,471 broken arrow tips. Some of the bows and arrows were still stowed inside boxes, and groups of the arrows were bundled together, 24 to each bundle. A leather disk, with 24 holes, kept the bundles together but prevented the arrows from crushing one another's feathering. Archaeologist Margaret Rule, who led the excavation, compared them to an ammunition clip. "When the archer removed the arrows from the spacer and tucked them into his belt the spacer could be recharged from the nearby box of arrows. In practice the spacer served in the same way as a .303 rifle clip of ammunition, and groups of ready-to-use charged spacers may have been assembled at battle stations on the upper deck and the fighting tops."

A number of skeletons also lay buried inside the sunken ship. One of the men's bones lay on the deck with the remains of his leather jerkin, or undershirt. A leather belt or thong with a spacer full of arrows loosely circled his spine, showing he was an archer. Another body, with only the bones left, was also discovered to be an archer. His bones showed that the man had worked with the bow for many years. Two of the vertebrae in his spine showed changes from twisting repeatedly to the left. His lower left arm bone, the ulna, was thicker than his other arm bones, and the end of that bone, where it joined the rest of his arm, was flattened at the joint by repeated pressure. These changes probably resulted from a lifetime of holding his bow in his left hand, twisting sideways to the left, pulling back the shaft with his right hand, holding tight against the pressure of the drawn bow, and then letting the arrow fly—an action he would have repeated again and again in battle.

Other skeletons lay tangled beneath a mass of rope that covered the open deck when *Mary Rose* sailed into battle and sank. The rope, woven

■ A set of Bollock daggers recovered from the wreck of *Mary Rose* (The Mary Rose Trust, Wikipedia Commons)

into a diamond-shaped mesh, formed anti-boarding netting to keep the enemy off the decks when *Mary Rose* closed and grappled with another ship. But the netting also trapped the crew when *Mary Rose* sank. The netting was strung atop a planked wall of panels that armored the deck. Called "blindage," these planks were movable. The crew could pull them out to provide a protected port for an archer or gunner to fire at a nearby ship's crew. The blindage, the netting, and the numerous hand weapons all point to a continued reliance on fighting at close quarters. While *Mary Rose* and contemporary warships represented the ascendancy of the gun, it was a time when the guns were meant for the other ship's crew, not its hull.

Mary Rose had a long gun deck and gun ports, and a number of iron and bronze cannon, some of them still mounted to their wooden gun carriages, lay inside the wreck. The types and ages of the guns are mixed. Some of them were practically antiques. Archaeologist Margaret Rule argues that the mix of guns represents a hasty arming in a time of national emergency. Anthropologist Richard Gould points out that gun manufacture and guns themselves were rapidly changing at this time. The mix of types could reflect tactical indecision as to which types worked best. Three "hailshots" are primitive—rail-mounted shotguns fired cubes of cast-iron shot into groups of enemy soldiers or marines. The hailshot is a weapon that predates the cannon and was used both in Asia and Europe beginning in the 14th century. The presence of the hailshots may not indicate a desperate attempt to obtain any weapons at hand. It may have been a deliberate decision to include antipersonnel weapons in the time-honored tradition of killing the enemy crew and not just damaging their ship.

Mary Rose carried many deadly antipersonnel weapons, even for use with the large "modern" guns. Archaeologists working on the wreck discovered wooden cases, some of them made with staves like small barrels, others hollowed-out cylinders split into two halves. These artifacts are canister shot, much like giant shotgun shells. Each was packed with different materials—including sharp pieces of flint—that would scatter when the gunners fired the shot at an enemy ship. The canister, bursting open, would send a deadly rain of the flint through an enemy's ranks with results like shattering a thick glass window at high velocity.

The weapons aboard *Mary Rose* clearly indicate that the officers envisioned a typical sea fight, with the ship as a floating castle pitting men against men. But they also took advantage of adaptations to the ship to fit newer, heavy guns more suited to damaging enemy ships than picking off their crews. The invention of the gun port and the development of the gun deck, shown so strongly in the wreck of *Mary Rose*, was the essential step in turning the warship into a destroyer of other ships, and not just a platform on which men fought at sea.

The hull of *Mary Rose* gives archaeologists a rare opportunity to physically see how these early gun ports and decks were fitted into a carrack hull. One amazing feature is that the ship's hull has notched frames, or ribs, that were originally cut for clinker planking. But this type of planking does not allow shipwrights to cut many holes for gun ports. The strength of a clinker-built hull is found in the joining of the overlapped planks. At the same time Henry VIII's shipwrights were building *Mary Rose*, in 1509–1511, they were also converting *Sovereign* from a clinker- to a carvel-planked hull. Why spend time and effort to remodel one ship while at the same time building another with the older, out-of-style method? It may be that the ship was a more conservatively built throwback. Although records of the time list it with many guns, *Mary Rose* probably carried them on the open weather deck and in the superstructure.

Henry VIII had *Mary Rose* rebuilt in 1536. This may be the time the ship was re-planked with a carvel hull, and the continuous gun deck and ports were added. The strategic position of England had changed with Henry's divorce of his wife, Catherine of Aragon, and his excommunication by the pope. The Catholic powers of Europe, particularly France and Spain, were foes worth considering, and these international tensions may have led Henry to rebuild ships like *Mary Rose*. The gun deck is supported and braced with internal frames and riders. The evidence of these timbers—some are poorly fitted—suggested to Margaret Rule that they were quickly added in response to a deteriorating political and military situation. Analysis of the wreck discovered that dry rot inside the ship's older timbers was neglected in the rebuild. The reconstruction of *Mary Rose* to enable it to take heavier guns appears to have been a quickly made decision driven by emergency. Leaps forward in military technology, particularly risky ones, are usually the result of exigency and the need to take action despite the risks.

One of the greatest risks, of course, was that a hull strong enough to take more guns was not necessarily safer. *Mary Rose* sailed into battle on July 19, 1545, carrying some 91 cannon. The higher the guns were placed on a ship with high fore and stern castles, the more unstable and easier to capsize that made *Mary Rose*. The surviving superstructure shows evidence of lighter planking inside to make it less top-heavy, and the gun decks and ports are placed lower in the hull to help balance the ship. Unfortunately, this effort to diminish the risk of capsizing the ship did not work, and within moments of moving into position for battle, *Mary Rose* heeled over and sank.

Another factor in the loss is suggested by the forensic analysis of the bones of *Mary Rose*'s dead. Out of 415 men on board who died that day, archaeologists recovered the bones of 179 men. The forensic scientists who studied the skeletons determined, from the substance of the bones themselves, that "a significant proportion of the crew did not originate in Britain," and instead came from "warmer, more southerly regions." In all, they suggest that somewhere up to 60 percent of the crew may have been nonnatives. That means they may not have spoken English, or that it was a second language. Just before *Mary Rose* capsized, and the ship was heeling, Sir George Carew, the ship's commander, shouted to a nearby ship that he had "the sort of knaves whom he could not rule." The forensic scientists argue that poor communication, thanks to the need for able-bodied sailors and not necessarily English-speakers for the English king's massive warship may have contributed to the loss of *Mary Rose*.

THE RISE OF THE SAILING WARSHIP

While *Mary Rose* and other carracks of the 16th century represent the rise of the large, heavily armed warship, two types of fighting ships, the caravel and the galleon, quickly replaced them. These ships were responsible for spreading European control over a broad area of the globe, particularly the empires of both Spain and Portugal. The caravel was developed on the Iberian Peninsula, probably from coastal fishing boats that increasingly ventured offshore. Starting around 1440, Portugal used caravels as the principal ships of exploration and commercial expansion. Pushing down the coast of Africa, around the Cape of Good Hope and into the Indian Ocean, and thence into Asian waters, the Portuguese used their caravels and larger galleons to win tremendous trade advantages. They did so literally at the end of a gun, seizing control of principal trade routes, defeating Ottoman, Indian, and Southeast Asian naval forces that tried to oppose them.

Spain, Portugal's neighbor and rival, also used the caravel and galleons to push west across the Atlantic and into the Americas. The caravel in American waters was the first naval assertion of Spanish power in the New World. Amazingly, given the significance of their role in expanding the Iberian kingdoms of Spain and Portugal into global empires, we know very little about these ships. We know far more about Viking ships or Roman merchant ships than we do about caravels. Archaeology has provided much detail on those older ship types thanks to the excavation of many wrecks. The fragmentary remains of three probable caravel wrecks in the Caribbean, a few documents, artistic representations, and informed speculation are all we currently have to go on for caravels.

One of the wreck sites, at Molasses Reef in the Turks and Caicos Islands, dates to the early 16th century. Very little of the wooden hull had survived in the shallow, six-meter-deep water of the site. But a number of iron guns and composite lead and iron shot provided a detailed look at ship's armament. The guns included breech-loading *bombardetas* and a number of breech chambers. The fact that more of the chambers were found than guns suggested to archaeologist Joe Simmons that they were kept loaded with powder in a "ready" state for battle so that a rapid rate of fire could be maintained. Smaller, swivel-mounted guns known as *versos*, along with the *bombardetas*, indicate that the guns of the Molasses Reef wreck were intended to kill men, not seriously damage ships. The other weapons excavated from the wreck, including crossbows, swords, shoulder arms, and grenades are consistent with this.

Similar guns and more extensive hull remains from another site, at Highborn Cay in the Bahamas, give us some clues about these small, but sturdily built ships. The caravel hull was used for both warships and armed merchantmen and served as powerful tools for 16th-century imperial expansion. Ironically, the caravels sailing into the Indian Ocean, arriving within decades of China's withdrawal from the seas, could have been met by larger, better-armed Ming warships under Zheng Ho's command and easily defeated. Instead, as both Portugal and Spain expanded their reach and strengthened their grip on the world's oceans, they built larger, better-armed ships—galleons—to meet any foes. Galleons supplanted caravels and fought in a series of actions that not only pitted Spain and Portugal against each other but also witnessed the rise of new naval powers in the Netherlands and England.

As these new, sail-powered warships came into ascendancy, the heyday of oar-powered warships was passing. The switch to larger hulls, capable of carrying many guns, gradually made the row galleys that dominated the Mediterranean obsolete. Lepanto was the last major battle under oars in the Mediterranean. Within two decades of Lepanto, another series of naval engagements demonstrated that the age of the gun at sea was at hand. These were the clashes between English sea dogs and the armada or navy of Spain in 1588.

MARS THE MAGNIFICENT

In 2011, Ocean Discovery, a team of highly experienced divers and archaeologists led by Richard and Ingemar Lundgren, made one of the most significant shipwreck discoveries in the history of underwater exploration of the Baltic after several years of research and surveys. They found the long-sought-after massive Swedish warship *Mars the Magnificent*, built as part of a military expansion by King Erik XIV's push to increase Swedish influence in the Baltic. *Mars* was a huge warship for its time, but as archaeologist Patrick Höglund notes, *Mars*'s complement of guns was diverse and if the crew fired all cannon at once, they would have thrown about 619 pounds of shot at an enemy. By way of comparison, the Swedish warship *Vasa*, built and lost 60 years later, could have hurled 1,212 pounds, or twice as much as *Mars*'s broadside.

The 16th century was a time of nearly unremitting war between Sweden and its neighboring states in the Baltic, and key battles at sea were the hallmark of most of these conflicts. During Sweden's seven-year-long war with Denmark, the Hanseatic League city of Lübeck, and Poland, *Mars* was part of a fleet of 37 Swedish warships that fought a two-day battle at the end of May 1564 with a Danish-Lübeck fleet of 25 ships off the island of Öland. The Danish-Lübeck ships endured a pounding from the superior firepower of the Swedish ships, and so their admirals ordered the fleet to close with the Swedes and try to take the largest ones, including *Mars*, by boarding them and fighting it out in hand-to-hand combat. After a fierce fight, with cannon balls smashing through *Mars*, the ship caught fire. As the enemy swarmed the decks, *Mars* exploded and sank, killing over 1,000 men.

The discovery of *Mars* 447 years later disclosed a broken ship that, despite the explosion and nearly half a millennium underwater, is still remarkably preserved by the cold, dark, brackish waters of the Baltic. Richard Lundgren, writing about the first dive to the wreck, 70 meters down, described the wreck's "looming presence" as they dropped to find half of *Mars* lying on its side with open cannon ports. Moving off the wreck, they found a jumble of bronze cannon, shattered timbers from the other half of the ship, and a variety of artifacts that speak to life and war on board. The study of the ship itself fills in a gap in our knowledge of the details of warships built in the period between the wrecks of *Mary Rose* (1545) and *Vasa* (1628).

Archaeological work on *Mars* is ongoing, with my colleagues Niklas Eriksson and Johan Rönnby describing the initial discoveries in a March 2017 report in the *International Journal of Nautical Archaeology*. What is clear from their reports is that despite the destructive end of *Mars*, the site is a time capsule cracked open on the seabed, with two-thirds of the ship present and identifiable, including the stern and the admiral's cabin, a number of personal artifacts, and reminders of the violent end of *Mars* as evidenced by human bones mingled with the wreckage.

THE SPANISH ARMADA

The running sea battle between England and the Spanish Armada (July 31 to August 8, 1588) between Spanish and English ships has been described by historian Geoffrey Parker and archaeologist Colin Martin as "the longest and fiercest artillery action, which had ever taken place at sea." In the end, England prevailed, and the armada retreated into a series of storms that lashed and wrecked many of its ships. Queen Elizabeth celebrated their destruction with a medal that proclaimed "God Breathed." Like Japan's deliverance from Kublai Khan, the defeat of the Spanish Armada was a combination of poor and rushed planning, internal discord, and a staunch English defense. The storms that ended the fleet, like the typhoon that lashed the khan's fleet at Takashima, left a rich archaeological record on the sea floor. Over the last several decades, archaeologists studying the wrecks of ships from the Spanish Armada have added much to our understanding of the ships, the weapons, and naval combat of the time, as well as aiding a new understanding of the reasons why the armada failed to successfully engage the English fleet and invade England's shores.

Philip II of Spain's intended invasion of England was the result of decades of tension between the Catholic Church and Protestant England in the aftermath of Henry VIII's divorce from Catherine of Aragon and his subsequent renunciation of Catholicism. Spain's control of the overseas trade, Philip's conquest of Portugal, and Spanish involvement in plots to replace Henry's daughter Elizabeth with a Catholic monarch angered the English court. England's support for the rebellious Netherlands in their fight against Spanish rule, and the increasingly outrageous attacks on Spanish ships and New World ports by English freebooters enraged Philip. An undeclared war between the two nations, one a mighty, global empire, the other a beleaguered island kingdom, culminated in Philip's orders for a large fleet to seize control of England's shores. A Spanish army, aided by European mercenaries, would then cross an English Channel swept free of English ships, march on London, and depose Elizabeth.

Initial Spanish plans called for a fleet of 500 ships and 30,000 troops. When the "invincible armada" finally sailed, only 130 ships drawn from various parts of Philip's empire and 20,000 troops were available. The Spanish fleet included Mediterranean row galleys; hybrid galleasses that carried guns, sails and oars; galleons from the New World treasure fleets; and huge merchantmen from Portugal, Italy, Dalmatia, and Northern Europe that the Spaniards had converted into fighting ships. Some of the fleet were transports, loaded with artillery, siege trains, fortifications, and weapons for the invading troops.

The Spanish Armada entered the English Channel on July 31, 1588. The English fleet, 170 ships strong, included 70 merchantmen converted to warships. Over the next several days, the two fleets closed and fought a series of actions that demonstrated a new approach to war at sea. The English ships sailed in a line, keeping just within firing range of the armada, and unleashed a barrage. Spanish naval tactics, unchanged from the last several decades, called for their ships to grapple with the enemy, use their guns to sweep the other's decks, and then board and take the enemy with overwhelming force. The well-armed, well-trained troops on the Spanish ships never got a chance in the armada's encounters with the English. In a few hours, the furious rate of English fire peppered the galleon *San Juan* with over 300 rounds. The Spanish response was not as intense; one Spanish officer estimated they had fired 750 rounds against 2,000 English shots.

The battles continued over the next week as the armada, massed together into a large formation, lumbered up the Channel. The English picked off a few stragglers that separated from the armada's massed bulk. Their success was not in destroying the armada as a fighting force but instead in preventing it from landing. When the armada reached Calais for provisions and to rendezvous with the invasion force on August 6, it was still intact and formidable. The pursuing English disrupted the anchored armada with a bold attack with blazing fire ships. Panic instead of flames swept the Spanish fleet, and many ships cut their anchors free and fled to sea, where the English rejoined the battle. Again, the English gunners outshot their opponents. The galleon *San Mateo*, surrounded by English ships that kept their distance and peppered it, was described as "a thing of pity to see, riddled with shot like a sieve."

When the smoke cleared, the armada, thwarted in its plans to land on England's shores, but still substantially intact, began a slow return home, circumnavigating the British Isles. Of the 130-ship fleet that sailed against England, only 60 returned home. Very few were lost in battle. The majority foundered on the shores of England, Scotland, and Ireland, or on the open seas, lashed by storms that mauled the retreating armada. The ships, weakened by battle damage, and many of them missing anchors left behind at Calais during the English fire ship attack, stood little chance against the fury of the sea and storms the English believed were heaven sent. The *Santa Maria de la Rosa*, which wrecked on the Irish coast on September 20, 1588, had sailed past another armada ship, *San Juan*, whose officers watched as it sailed by, noting "all her sails were in shreds" except the foresail. "She cast her single anchor, for she was not carrying more" and hung on against the racing tide. After a few hours, the tide ebbed, dragging *Santa Maria de la Rosa* and *San Juan*. The horrified crew of *San Juan* watched helplessly as the other ship began to sink. "We could see that she was going down, trying to hoist the foresail. Then she sank with all on board, not a person being saved."

WRECKS OF THE ARMADA

Divers, treasure hunters, and archaeologists have discovered a number of armada wrecks on the shores and waters of Scotland and Ireland, and careful archaeological work has revealed the identity as well as tremendous detail about four of these ships. One wreck, *San Juan de Sicilia*, was systematically plundered for treasure. Evidence was scattered and removed, destroying its archaeological value. However, the dean of armada shipwreck research, Colin Martin, working with the evidence from four excavated wrecks—the transport *La Trinidad Valencera*, the armed merchantman *Santa Maria de la Rosa*, the galleass *Girona*, and the armed merchantman *El Gran Grifón*, rewrote the history of the armada. Since then, new work on *La Trinidad Valencera* has documented more of the site and revealed new artifacts that have been exposed in the wreck's dynamic environment. More recently, archaeologists discovered and have worked on the wrecks of three transports lost off Ireland, *La Lavia, La Juliana* and *Santa Maria de Visión*. The wrecks, lying off County Sligo's Streedagh, had initially been discovered in the 1980s by private divers, but were for the most part buried. The wrecks were exposed in 2015 when the seabed was found to have been stripped by two years of heavy storms.

In the past, historians have suggested that the armada's failure was the result of their huge ships being outmaneuvered by smaller, more agile English ships; from firing all of their heavy shot early in the battle; or having too many short-range guns. Martin, working with historian Geoffrey Parker and others, and combining the evidence from the wrecks with meticulous research in English, Spanish, and other archives, has determined that none of these suggestions are correct. The problem lay in Spain's failure to adapt to the technological revolution sweeping Europe. The explanation is not just in the English tactic of line-on attack and bombardment without boarding. It lies in the disparate rate of fire between the two fleets.

The Spanish ships, with 2,500 pieces of artillery, were a match for the English. And the armada sailed into action with their guns loaded, ready for action. A cannon recovered from the wreck of *El Gran Grifón* demonstrates the Spanish practice of always keeping a gun loaded, so that a volley of shots would precede a ramming and boarding. The excavation of the armada wrecks also yielded a tremendous amount of information about the individual armament of the soldiers who sailed aboard, including the earliest surviving examples of fire pots and pole-mounted *bombas* that spewed flames and projectiles—the same types of weapons used by the Chinese a continent away in their sea battles.

But the Spanish fleet was not ready to repeatedly load and fire. The principal problem, Martin found, was one of standardization. The "Spanish" guns and shot, nominally standard, were actually different. These guns, coming from various parts of the empire and Europe, manufactured by different foundries, unlike those of the English, meant the shot simply did not match. In the heat of a battle, the men of the armada had to search among their shot, measuring each cannon ball to see if it would fit into their guns. In the wreck of *La Trinidad Valencera*, archaeologists discovered a wooden "gunner's rule," used to calibrate shot. This vital tool was "useless," Martin notes, because "the graduations are so inaccurate and inconsistent" on one side, while on the other "a fundamental arithmetical misconception has rendered these graduations entirely spurious." Martin also discovered that some of the guns, such as one raised from the wreck of *El Gran Grifón*, were hastily cast to meet the needs of the armada. The bore of the gun was cast off-center, making it worthless.

Archaeological excavation of *La Trinidad Valencera* also recovered huge gun carriages. These six-meter-long wooden carriages mounted two wheels at the front and swept back to rest on the deck. These carriages sat on a gun deck about 12 meters wide. They were unwieldy and difficult to manhandle. After firing, each gun was pulled back, swabbed, and reloaded by its muzzle. In a telling display of experimental archaeology, Martin supervised a test in which a crew loaded, fired, cleaned, and reloaded a gun on this type of carriage. Then the crew did the same with an English gun on its shorter, four-wheeled carriage. Examples from the wreck of *Mary Rose* show that the English were mounting their guns on these small, stout, more maneuverable carriages in the 16th century. Not surprisingly, the modern gunners completed their job with the four-wheeled carriage in half the time.

Two decades ago, I spent a day in rapt conversation with Martin as he shared his thoughts on a variety of shipwreck studies, notably the armada wrecks. After decades of analysis, study, and simply thinking about it all, Martin had a great deal to say. What had caused the Spanish ships to be so ill-served by a lack of standardized guns and shot and plagued by essential instruments with fundamental math errors? The probable answer was Spain's rejection of much of its Islamic and Jewish population following the Alhambra Decree, or the Edict of Expulsion in March 1492, which required all practicing Jews to leave Spain, and the ongoing effects of the Inquisition in rooting out heretics among the *conversos*, former Muslims and Jews who had converted to Catholicism but whose faith was doubted.

In the space of the next decades, two distinct groups who in Moorish Spain had composed a large percentage of the peninsula's intellectuals and scientists fled Spain. Do the issues seen with the armada guns and instruments correlate? Consider what happened when Nazi Germany enacted its anti-Jewish laws before the war, leading to an exodus of those who could flee, among them Albert Einstein, and those from other countries who fled after Nazi takeovers. Many who left would have been invaluable to the Axis war effort, but Hitler's policies and actions led to a "brain drain" powerfully demonstrated by the number of refugee scientists who worked on the Manhattan Project and developed the atomic bomb. Martin felt, and I agree, that an earlier brain drain had helped defeat the Spanish Armada. The work on these wrecks is a reminder, once again, that what we learn about is ourselves, as people, when we study the past through that which we leave behind.

4

The Age of Sail

Whosoever commands the sea commands trade, whosoever commands the trade
of the world commands the riches of the world, and consequently the world itself.
—Sir Walter Raleigh

The hallmark of this age was the expansion of Europe's wars to a
global stage. After centuries of conflict within the confines of the
Mediterranean, large-scale naval warfare expanded into northern seas by
the 16th century, then spread with the development of overseas empires
throughout the world. The sea fights of Portugal, Spain, the Netherlands,
France, and England sent ships and fleets into combat far from home, leaving sunken warships in African, Indian, Asian, and American waters. At the
same time Russia, Sweden, and Denmark fought for control of the Baltic.

The 17th century witnessed the growth of European trade and warfare in
the Far East. It was a time when the result of China's decision to destroy its
navy was clearly demonstrated. China's rulers had abandoned the naval
legacy of the Mongol dynasty by the early 16th century, leaving the coast
weakly guarded by a small, ineffective force that was no match for regular

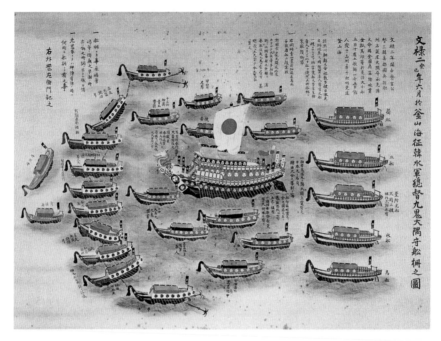

■ Japanese *atakebune*, warships used in the invasion of Korea in from 1592 through 1598. (Wikipedia Commons)

raids by Chinese and Japanese pirates. In this naval vacuum, the Japanese moved to become the dominant power in the region. In 1592, a Japanese fleet of hundreds of ships launched an invasion of Korea, intending to press on and take China.

Under the leadership of Admiral Yi Sunsin, Korea pushed back the Japanese advance on both land and sea. One of Yi Sunsin's keys to victory was Korea's newly developed "turtle ships." These oar-powered ships were equipped with rams and guns. A turtle-backed, armored casemate protected the decks and gave the ships their name. Japan tried again in 1597, defeating the Koreans twice. But in 1598, a reinforced Chinese navy aided Yi Sunsin, who defeated and destroyed a 400-ship Japanese force at Chinhae Bay. Japan withdrew from its quest to expand overseas, and both the Korean and Chinese naval forces atrophied, leaving no Asian power capable of stopping the influx of foreign traders and warships into the region. The Pacific and Asia became another stage for the struggle between European powers.

船龜營水左羅全

■ The Korean *Geobukseon*, or "turtle ship," from the wars with the Japanese during the Japanese invasion of Korea from 1592 through 1598. These are considered the world's first armored ships. (Wikipedia Commons)

The rise of the gun in the late 16th century and widespread adoption of weapons designed to smash and sink other ships led the various sea powers to build larger ships capable of mounting increasing numbers of cannon. The typical heavy warship of the early 17th century, the galleon, gradually developed into two types of ships in the 18th century—the "ship of the line" and the frigate. It was not just an age of hulking, towering ships bristling with cannon. Smaller warships, carrying smaller numbers of guns, joined the wrecks of the large ships to provide a rich archaeological record of the age of the "wooden walls."

Archaeologists studying warship wrecks from this period have also examined an extensive collection of artifacts. These finds not only document fighting at sea and the use of weapons. They also provide a detailed look at life aboard. The man-of-war from 1550 to 1850 housed increasingly complex societies aboard ships that carried crews the size of small towns and villages. Archaeology reveals much about how these men worked, ate, slept, sought recreation, and fought.

THE WRECK OF *VASA*

One of the world's great archaeological treasures is the completely intact Swedish galleon *Vasa*. Built for King Gustaf II Adolf of Sweden, the great galleon was part of a naval expansion designed to prevent the Habsburg Empire from extending its control into the Baltic. Gustaf II Adolf wanted to expand Sweden's own power over the Baltic, and with the aid of Dutch shipwrights, built up a navy to control the region. One of those ships was *Vasa*. The threat of a Habsburg fleet from Spain entering the Baltic pushed forward the completion and launch of the new ship, a giant by the standards of its day.

On August 10, 1628, *Vasa* cleared the naval dockyard in Stockholm and crossed the harbor on its maiden voyage. As a crowd of some 10,000 watched from the shore, *Vasa* fired two salutes with its guns and set sail. Strong gusts of wind made the huge ship career sharply, and as the officers shouted orders for the men to take their stations and loosen the sails, the ship heeled again. Water poured in through open gun ports and flooded the lower decks. The ship continued its roll, the water pouring over the rail as the ship went under on the port side. Sails still set, flags flying, *Vasa* sank. Out of a crew of 133, little more than half survived.

According to Swedish records, an English salvor managed to get the wreck off its side and upright within days of the sinking. Attempts to raise the wreck were not successful, but between 1663 and 1665, divers working from a diving bell suspended over the wreck managed to pull up many of the ship's guns. After a brief salvage project in 1683 that raised one cannon, the wreck of *Vasa* was abandoned and forgotten for more than 300 years.

In 1956, persistent efforts by researcher Anders Franzen were rewarded when he rediscovered the wreck resting in 32 meters of water in Stockholm harbor. Hardhat divers sent down to find the ship in the murky water reported walking up to a solid wall of wood. The dark waters of the Baltic are

■ *Vasa* after it was raised. (Vasammuseet)

not as salty as other oceans, and the marine organisms that eat submerged wood elsewhere in the world are absent. Other than the damage from early salvage attempts, centuries of anchors hitting the submerged hulk, and the rusting away of iron fastenings, *Vasa* was completely preserved. The discovery prompted the Swedish government to devote both the time and money to raise the intact ship from the depths.

Between 1958 and 1961, divers cleared the wreck and prepared it for raising. Working with high-pressure hoses, they cut into the clay beneath the hull in order to pass slings underneath her. These were then used to slowly move *Vasa* into shallower water. Finally, the hull was raised out of the ocean in April 1961 and moved into a special dry dock for treatment and restoration. Continually spraying the hull with preservatives until 1977, the Swedes rebuilt missing portions of the decks and stern castle and reattached sections of the ship and its ornate, carved decorations that divers had recovered from the original wreck site. The reconstructed ship, masts once again stepped and with its lower rigging in place, now rests inside a new, specially built museum that opened to the public in 1990.

Vasa was both large and exceptionally well decorated for its time. It was a special *royalskeppet* or royal ship. It also embodies the new role of the warship as a symbol of both regal power and national pride, as well as the changes in ship design that fully adopted the gun as the principal weapon of war at sea. Galleons like *Vasa* were the next step in warship development after huge carracks like *Mary Rose*. Sleeker, without a heavy forecastle, and with a more compact stern castle, galleons were built with cannon in mind as their principal armament and were the first purpose-built all-gun warships. The guns were carried below the main deck on a gun deck that ran the length of much of the hull.

By the time of *Vasa*, the galleon was a ship in transition. Galleons were growing larger to accommodate more guns below the decks. *Vasa* has two gun decks mounting an impressive number of cannon. It held 64 guns in all, 48 of which were large 24-pounders. Firing a solid iron ball weighing 24 pounds, these guns were potential ship killers. To counter the threat of the enemy's guns doing just that to *Vasa*, it was built with thick timber sides and heavy framing to help the hull absorb the hits. An impressive amount of timber and money went into *Vasa*'s 69-meter length, 11.7-meter width, and 1,210 tons.

■ The cleared gun deck. (Vasamuseet)

Vasa was designed to carry 145 crew and 300 soldiers. While the guns were the primary armament, fighting men on the ship discouraged boarders who might still try to close and attempt to take the ship in hand-to-hand fighting. *Vasa*'s masts, when recovered, included a fighting top, a large platform from which men armed with muskets could shoot at the enemy's decks or at boarders on their own deck. *Vasa*'s ammunition for the cannon also included bar-shot and pike-shot. These balls and spikes, mounted on sliding bars, spread to whip through the air and cut through rigging to drop masts or plow through the unprotected flesh of the enemy's crew.

One of the most striking conclusions reached by the archaeologists and other scientists who removed more than 14,000 artifacts from the wreck was the disparity between the ship's majestic, imposing appearance and life aboard the ship as experienced by its crew. *Vasa* is covered with hundreds of carvings, in their time brightly painted and gilded, with symbols depicting

■ Archaeologists work inside *Vasa* after it was raised, clearing the mud. (Vasamuseet)

the power of the Swedish crown, images of life and death, religious icons, and mockery of their enemies. Carvings show two Polish noblemen, enemies of Sweden, humbled and crouched under the king's toilet, which is a bench perched on a railing outside of his cabin. My immediate thought when I was shown this on my archaeologist's tour of the ship was that Gustavus Vasa was no stranger to bathroom humor. The figurehead, a huge, snarling lion, and the roaring lion's heads on the gun port lids were all part of a deliberate attempt at floating propaganda to awe and impress and put down the enemy, for all who saw *Vasa*.

Lars-Ake Kvarning, the director of the *Vasa* Museum, noted how the archaeological finds, when cleaned and analyzed, turned "a rare mixture of apparently worthless bits of wood" into "imaginative carvings," while other finds showed what life aboard was like "behind this showpiece façade." Life, Kvarning pointed out, was discovered by the finds inside the ship to be "plain and hard." The sailors and soldiers did not have uniforms and had to wear whatever they themselves brought aboard. Archaeologists, unpacking well-preserved sea chests belonging to the sailors, found no "extra clothing for cold nights on deck and no wet-weather clothing." The men, who sailed with their families, lived on the decks. Hammocks for sleeping were unknown. The food, eaten on wooden plates with wooden spoons, was boiled salted beef and pork, as well as salt herring. Fishing gear found inside the hull indicates that the crew caught fresh fish to augment their diet.

The excavation revealed the remains of 25 people in or around the wreck. Their bones showed the traces of hard work and previous injuries, including healed fractures of arms and legs that had been broken by "severe blows." Teeth were ground down by poorly milled flour, and "some wretches bore clear testimonies of virulent pus-formation in their jaws" from poor dental hygiene. Many of the bodies showed the results of poor bone formation from malnutrition. The conscription laws of Sweden at that time were explicit that healthy men between the ages of 18 and 40, free of disease and injury, were to be provided by towns and villages for warship crews. But as Kvarning pointed out, the bodies from *Vasa*, not surprisingly, show that "peasants and citizens did not voluntarily let their best men go. Nor was life

The steerage compartment in *Vasa*. This is where one of the bodies, perhaps the ship's helmsman, was found. (Peter Isotalo/Wikimedia Commons)

Excavation of *Vasa* revealed a number of skeletons, including this individual next to a gun carriage. (Vasamuseet)

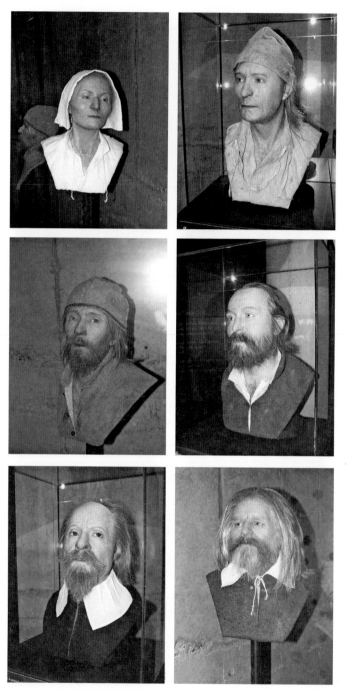

The reconstructed likenesses of some of *Vasa*'s dead, as displayed in the Vasamuseet. This is a powerful and emotional part of the museum. (Wolfgang Sauber/ Wikimedia Commons)

on warships of the day anything men voluntarily allowed themselves to be conscripted to."

Finally, the wreck of *Vasa* points out that the transition to many-gunned warships came at a price. Like *Mary Rose, Vasa* was top-heavy and prone to capsize. Surviving Swedish archives describe a lengthy investigation that came to no definite conclusion as to why *Vasa* sank. There were accusations of poor design and of the crew's failure to lash down the gun carriages, so that when the ship rolled, the heavy weight of the guns helped pull *Vasa* over. What seems clear from looking at the ship today is that it was built top-heavy, without enough room for ballast in the hold. The gun carriages, often still on their four wheels, were discovered lashed in place. *Vasa* sank because it was built in a time of national emergency, built larger than other ships, and quickly rushed into service with a critical design flaw that sent it to the bottom before it even cleared the harbor.

KRONAN

The incredible preservation of wooden wrecks in the Baltic, first seen with the wreck of *Vasa*, was demonstrated again by the 1980 discovery of the wreck of *Kronan. Kronan*, built at Stockholm between 1665 and 1672, was a huge, three-decked 60-meter-long, 2,140-ton warship. Armed with 126 guns, *Kronan* was a heavily armed and lavishly decorated symbol and instrument of Swedish naval power.

Sweden's quest for domination of the Baltic, beginning in the late 16th century and lasting into the early 18th century, led to a series of conflicts in that enclosed sea. By 1660, though, Sweden's power in the Baltic was at its peak, with a Baltic empire that controlled most of the coast and the sea itself. But Sweden's empire was contested by other European nations, notably Russia and Denmark. In 1675, Denmark and her ally, the Netherlands, declared war on Sweden. *Kronan*, the flagship of a Swedish fleet sent against a Danish-Dutch fleet, engaged the enemy off the southwest coast of Sweden on June 1, 1676.

While turning to fight, *Kronan* capsized in a squall. One survivor reported, "The ship simply fell on her side with her sails and masts on the

■ One of the ornate carvings from the wreck of *Kronan*. (Wikimedia Commons)

surface of the water. And she sank almost at once and nothing was visible but her starboard side. Then the ship exploded amidships, in her main magazine I should think. And people who had gathered on her starboard side flew into the air" as they clung to the overturned hull. Only 42 members of some 500 crewmembers survived.

Archaeological excavation of *Kronan*, which lies in 26 meters of water, under the direction of Lars Einarsson of the Kalmar County Museum, has documented the preserved remains of about two-thirds of the port side of the ship and recovered more than 23,000 artifacts. The wreck site has been described by the archaeologists as "a fantastic sight that is at the same time frightening," as they swim over large, scattered timbers, bronze cannon, ornate decorations and wooden sculptures from the ship, pewter plates, clay pipes, and skeletons. Like *Vasa*, the wreck of *Kronan* is an incredible archaeological legacy from the heyday of Swedish naval power, offering

▓ Recreation of the gun deck of *Kronan*, with cannon recovered from the wreck, displayed in the Kalmar Lansmuseet. (Boatbuilder/Wikimedia Commons)

insights into the ship, its guns and other armament, and the personal effects of the crew. Given the overwhelming tragedy of the sinking, this is also a chance to learn a great deal from the skeletons of the hundreds of drowned crew about their ages, health, and old, healed injuries that left traces in their bones.

LIFE ON BOARD BALTIC WARSHIPS

A recurrent theme in shipwreck archaeology is the shift away from the study of individual wrecks to assessing groups or collections of ships, and all elements in underwater landscapes including battlefields. A recent study by archaeologist Edgar Wróblewski looks at life at sea and in war for Danish-Norwegian sailors during the Great Northern War of 1700–1721. It is excellent work. The thesis draws from archival and archaeological evidence, with finds from the wrecks of the frigates *Mynden, Lossen, Schleswig,* and *Fredericus,* and the ships of the line *Dannebrog* and *Hedvig Sophia.* The study brings the human element into focus, and not through an illustration of violent death or the discovery of their remains. He examined finds of sailors' chests, and from them as well as isolated finds, he discusses clothing and shoes, tools, eating utensils, the evidence of how they spent their time on and off duty with handcrafts, sewing, games, reading and writing materials, smoking, fishing, and sleeping, and questions about hygiene.

FROM GALLEON TO SHIP OF THE LINE

The battle for domination of the seas was more than a succession of wars. The naval arms race of the 17th and 18th centuries was characterized by competition not only to build large numbers of ships but also to build bigger, heavier ships to carry more guns. These large ships were also a reflection of prestige for the monarchies that commissioned them. The crowns of Europe used these large ships as symbols of their greatness and as a means of instilling nationalistic pride. The development of the "great ships," as the English called them, also changed the way battles were fought.

The only way to place larger numbers of guns (and heavier guns, too) on a ship was to build gun decks to mount them, side by side. Two-decked ships like *Vasa* and three-decked ships of the same period, like the famous English warship *Sovereign of the Seas*, had only one effective way to fight. They sailed alongside the enemy and fired all the guns on whatever beam, or side, faced the other ship. These "broadsides" ultimately led to ships fighting in rows or lines, sailing alongside each other to discharge as much shot as possible into each other. The naval powers built their ships heavy not just to carry as many heavy guns as they could but also to absorb as much punishment from the enemy's guns and keep afloat. The huge wooden fortresses, the "ships of the line," became the standard warship of the 18th century.

But it would be a mistake to focus just on the "great ships" of the period. In the 18th century the European naval powers also reintroduced the concept of specialization. Throughout the period between 1650 and 1850, they developed a range and variety of warships that for the first time in over 2,000 years launched diverse fleets capable of carrying a fight to rivers, lakes, coastal shallows, and the high seas. Smaller, more maneuverable (and also cheaper to build) frigates with two decks and mounting less than 60 guns were built by many nations, including emerging naval powers like the United States, whose famous frigate *Constitution* of 1794 remains afloat more than two centuries after launch thanks to several rebuildings.

Several wrecks from the late 17th and early 18th centuries provide a detailed look at warships in this time of naval expansion. They indicate that these large fleets reintroduced the concept of standardization. The problems of standardization of guns and shot, one of the elements that helped defeat the Spanish Armada, were resolved in the 17th century, and wrecks of warships, beginning in this period, include guns captured from an enemy adopted for use on a rival's ships. The hulls of the ships, too, show the beginnings of standardization in construction, the development of "classes" of ships as more than one vessel was built to a single plan, and the transition of ideas and techniques as the naval innovations of one power were copied by another as a result of capturing each other's ships—just as Rome had done with Carthage two thousand years earlier.

THE DUART WRECK

A chance discovery by a diver in the waters off Duart Point, near Mull, Scotland, has provided archaeologists with a detailed look at a small warship lost in 1653. Under the leadership of archaeologist Colin Martin, excavation of the wreck is slowly yielding its secrets and identity. The Duart Wreck is probably *Swan*, a small warship built in 1641. If *Vasa* was a 17th-century battleship, then *Swan* was a destroyer. Light and fast, *Swan* represented a class of warship built to defend the English Channel. In the early 17th century, North African, Turkish, French, and Dutch pirates and privateers regularly raided English shipping and settlements in the Channel with small, fast pinnaces that out-maneuvered the English navy's galleons. A contemporary observer describes a galleon as a giant, "strong and invincible at a close and grappling, but for all that so weak and impotent in his legs that any active and nimble dwarf, keeping out of reach, may affront and scorn him."

The "nimble dwarfs" of the pirates inspired the English to copy them. During the reign of King Charles I, the navy launched English-built pinnaces. These ships were not as successful as the pirates' ships, largely because English shipwrights insisted on bulking up the pinnaces to make their hulls stronger than the lightly built enemy ships. But while the pirates' ships were light and hence did not have a long life, they were faster than the English pinnaces. In 1637, an Irish noble, Thomas Wentworth, bought a Dutch pinnace for the protection of the Irish coast. In 1641, King Charles I ordered a copy of Wentworth's "extraordinarily good sailer." The new ship, *Swan*, entered service in July of that year, patrolling Irish waters and Scotland's west coast.

Swan was soon swept up in England's Civil War and in 1645 was "captured" by parliamentary forces when its unpaid crew, at anchor off Dublin, were approached by a parliamentary ship whose captain offered to pay their wages. By 1649, when Parliament proclaimed the English Commonwealth under Oliver Cromwell, *Swan* had spent much of its eight-year career with the crew fighting their own countrymen. The pinnace's end came during another campaign in home waters, this time in the Sound of Mull on Scotland's west coast.

Following the execution of Charles I in 1649, Cromwell moved to crush royalist sympathizers in Ireland and Scotland. The dead king's heir, Charles II, landed in Scotland in 1650 to fight for his crown, but in September 1651 he was defeated by Cromwell's forces. Charles escaped to the continent, but his supporters fought on. A 1653 rebellion in Scotland, supported by the Macleans of Duart, inspired Cromwell to send a naval force and troops to subjugate the region and capture the Macleans' castle at Duart Point. The Commonwealth's six-ship, 1,000-man force landed at Duart Point to find that the Macleans had retreated. The success of the expedition came to an abrupt end on September 22, when a fierce storm swept through the sound, sinking some of the ships and leaving the others dismasted and crippled. "Wee lost a small Man of Warre called the *Swan*," a correspondent wrote Cromwell. Two other ships were also lost, all of them "in sight of our Men att land, where they saw their friends drowning, and heard them crying for helpe, but could not save them."

The wreck of *Swan* was not seen again for more than 300 years. In 1979, naval diving instructor John Dadd discovered the wreck, but kept his find quiet for 12 years. In 1991, Dadd finally reported his discovery to authorities, who visited it and agreed with him that it was a significant find. Other divers, from the Dumfries and Galloway Branch of the Scottish Sub-Aqua Club, also discovered the wreck in 1992. The Archaeological Diving Unit (ADU), acting on both discoveries, found that the wreck was being exposed by erosion of bottom sediments. Iron cannon, wood—including carved decorations—and human bones were in danger of being swept away by the sea in a high-energy environment of surf and current. Colin Martin began excavating the wreck in 1993 to preserve it from the ravages of the sea.

Swan lies jumbled and collapsed into itself, with the retreating sediments exposing exceptionally well-preserved organic materials such as fabric, rope, leather, bone, and wood. In the remains of the cabin of Edward Tarleton, *Swan*'s captain, archaeologists retrieved paneling, "an elaborate door, more suited to an elegant drawing-room than to the interior of a small warship," the ship's binnacle, one compass, and the disarticulated remains of a human skeleton—or skeletons. Two of the discoveries, as Martin explains, hint at the richness of the site. Two masses of rusted concretion, when X-rayed, revealed an "almost intact pocket watch, its brass shell miraculously preserved within an outer shell of corrosion," and a steel rapier with an ornate handle. When conservators cleaned the rapier, corrosion had claimed the steel, but the concretion had preserved the shape, outline, and details of the blade, guard, and tang. The conservators were able to extract and save the hilt, an elaborate creation of tightly wound silver and gold wire.

While excavation did not expose major portions of the ship's hull, a series of beautifully carved decorations did "come to light." They include a helmeted warrior's head; a winged cherub; a scroll; and a portion of a heraldic badge with three ostrich feathers, a coronet, and the words *Ich Dien*. The carvings are amazing on two counts, according to Martin. They are the remnants of the ornate stern decorations of *Swan* and date to her construction as a royal ship. The badge is that of the heir apparent of England—a hated item that Cromwell's men would have, or should have, removed from the ship once it came into Commonwealth hands. The decorations might have been covered over, or removed and stored aboard *Swan*, since Martin found no trace of their attachment to the hull. No matter where they were hidden, the fact that the carvings remained aboard *Swan* eight years after its capture by the Commonwealth is a reminder that ships, like men, can and often do change sides. Perhaps *Swan's* crew kept the carvings in case the Commonwealth's fortunes changed, and the monarchy returned to power.

The ornate and heavy carvings and the lavish paneling and door from the captain's cabin seem inappropriate for the ship, notes Martin. For a ship designed to be fast and out-maneuver the swift pirates of the Channel, they were "an unproductive addition" to both weight and expense. "Every surplus pound, or piece of structure which imparted excessive rigidity, was a liability" for a ship that needed to be flexible and light. Their presence on *Swan* suggests that to the ship's builders, or perhaps to the king himself "for whom royal dignity and symbolic embellishment always took precedence over practicalities" *Swan's* effectiveness lay more in its visual impact than in her performance.

DARTMOUTH

The archaeological study of a small English warship, an early frigate of the late 17th century, offers a detailed look at the origins of standardization. It is also a reminder that more warships were lost to age and accident than combat. *Dartmouth* was a fifth-rate ship of the line. It was so designated because in the progression of a naval fighting force, the more guns a ship carried, the higher its rate. A first-rate carried 100 guns while a fifth-rate like *Dartmouth* carried 32 guns. Built at Portsmouth in 1655, *Dartmouth* carried up to 135 men. The 32 guns were a mixture of nine-, six- and three-pounder iron cannon. Colin Martin describes *Dartmouth* as "an early member of a small, lightweight class of warship . . . which were designed for patrol and reconnaissance work."

After a long career at sea, which included participating in several actions and lengthy patrols in the Caribbean and Mediterranean, *Dartmouth* was not retired. Rather, the Royal Navy "refitted" the ship with extensive repairs in 1678. On October 9, 1690, *Dartmouth*, now an aged, decrepit ship, wrecked on the coast of Scotland in a gale when the worn-out anchor cable parted. Driven onto the rocks, *Dartmouth* sank with most of its crew. Only six men survived the wreck.

Divers rediscovered the wreck in 1973, and two seasons of excavation recovered the scattered remains. These included the intact hull structure as well as guns and many other artifacts. Martin, analyzing the hull remains, found evidence of standardization in the placement of the frames or ribs of the hull. The shipwrights who built *Dartmouth* placed each frame exactly one foot apart. One surviving lodging knee, used to support the main deck, showed that it fit exactly within a five-foot module, and that the deck was laid out and built in a modular fashion, much like a modern home. The need for nations to build large fleets of many similar ships led to the standardization not only of types of ships, but of ship construction. Martin's analysis also showed that the keel, or backbone, of the ship, was built of three large pieces of timber, each carefully fitted together with a complex joint. Each section of the keel was just about as long as a mature English elm could grow.

Archaeological study of the surviving hull of *Dartmouth* also showed that the ship had been pushed beyond her limited life, even with a major rebuilding. The keel had been cut out and replaced, and the thick frames or floors of the hull were clamped down with a thick timber. But outer hull planks showed that some of the wooden treenails used to fasten the planks to the frames had been placed nearly atop older treenails, probably to tighten up loose fastenings. And the hull was, at the time of the wreck, worm-eaten and leaking, with the rigging worn, confirming Captain Edward Pottinger's complaint to the Admiralty, just a few weeks before the ship was lost, of these defects. Pottinger's list of the ship's defects included the anchor cable "so extremely worn as not to be trusted." Indeed not, as the loss of the ship and the remains of *Dartmouth* show a navy grappling with the need for growth into a large force both by building standard ships but also pushing them and the men who crewed them beyond their limits. The lesson here isn't one about a decrepit ship, but about lives needlessly lost.

STIRLING CASTLE AND *NORTHUMBERLAND*

The wrecks of two other English ships of the period, the third-rates *Stirling Castle* and *Northumberland*, provide two more examples of a standardized warship. Built at Deptford in 1679, *Stirling Castle* was a 70-gun ship. *Northumberland*, built at the same time, was the product of Baylie's Shipyard in Bristol. Like *Dartmouth*, *Stirling Castle* and *Northumberland* represent a building-up of the Royal Navy and the introduction of a fleet of similarly designed and built "rates" of various sizes and armament.

After naval service in the English Channel against the French, *Stirling Castle* was bound for the Mediterranean in November 1703 when caught by what became known as "The Great Storm of 1703." When the wind and waves subsided, 12 ships and over 1,500 men were gone. Daniel Defoe, author of *Robinson Crusoe*, watching from another ship, described the end of *Stirling Castle* as the storm drove it past:

> It was a sight of terrible particulars, to see a ship...in that dismal case; she had cut away all her masts, the men were all in the confusions of death and despair; she had neither anchor, nor cable, nor boat to help her; the sea breaking over her in a terrible manner, that sometimes she seem'd all under water; and they knew, as well as we that saw her...they could expect nothing but destruction. The cries of the men, and the firing of their guns, one by one, every half minute for help, terrified us in such a manner, that I think we were half dead with the horror of it.

Stirling Castle sank at the Goodwin Sands, off the southeast corner of England. In 1979, the Underwater Research Group of the Thanet Archaeological Unit investigated reports that the shifting sands had exposed a large wooden wreck. Their divers found a large warship, listing to starboard, half buried in the sand but substantially intact. Scattered artifacts on the decks and the seabed allowed the archaeologists to determine that the ship was *Stirling Castle*. Limited visibility and shifting sands hampered the ability of the divers to work on the wreck, but a number of recovered artifacts provide a detailed look at life aboard. A bronze six-pounder gun recovered from *Stirling Castle* is a Dutch gun cast in 1629 and probably captured during the Anglo-Dutch Wars. Like the ship itself, the gun is evidence of standardization and shows how a captured piece of ordnance (and entire warships) could easily be adopted by an enemy.

The expense of work and conservation kept the number of artifacts raised from *Stirling Castle* to about 200. The intact hull itself, holding the bones of many of the drowned crew, still rests in the Goodwin Sands. The sand reburied the wreck in 1980. It reappeared in 1998, and archaeological surveys that year and in 1999–2000 disclosed more information about the ship, as well as the fact that it was starting to fall apart. In that latter year, the archaeological team recovered a cannon and its wooden carriage, which was an archaeological rarity, and a 2002 excavation found evidence that suggested that the ship may have been fitted with a steering wheel, an apparatus just being introduced to ships at the time of the ship's loss.

Northumberland, also lost in the Great Storm of 1703, went down with all hands. Rediscovered in 1980 by the same team that found *Stirling Castle*, the Underwater Research Group of the Isle of Thanet Archaeological Group. Their recoveries of the ship's bell, dated 1701, and pewter plates marked "J.G.," and thought to be the personal possessions of Captain James Greenway, as well as a large copper kettle, helped prove the wreck was HMS *Northumberland*. The team went on to find all of the warships lost in the "Great Storm," by 1981. Work on *Northumberland* took place in 1993. Since 1998, volunteers from the Seadive Organisation, led by Robert Peacock, have documented the sites, as have the Archaeological Diving Unit and Wessex Archaeology, a private firm contracted by English Heritage. They have completed detailed surveys of the various sites but with much attention focused on *Stirling Castle*, which has progressively become more exposed over time and is in danger of collapse and loss of artifacts and information.

This is not to make the work sound easy. The sand is constantly shifting, and as Robert Peacock explains, portions of the ships and amazing finds surface and then disappear in a season—or a day. Scattered remains and intact portions of hulls, and a wide range of artifacts that speak to how these time capsules of 1703 are cracking open and spilling their contents make the Goodwin Sands an intriguing, exceptional place to work both in terms of challenges and archaeological results.

LOSSEN

Norwegian archaeologists discovered the wreck of the frigate *Lossen* in 1963 near Hvaler at the entrance to Oslo Fjord. Built in 1684, *Lossen* entered service in 1686. In 1717, the 24-gun frigate was protecting convoys running from Norway to Denmark during the "Great Nordic War" with Sweden. That conflict was but one of many Sweden engaged in. Sweden was the dominant power in the Baltic and fought several wars with its Scandinavian neighbors as well as against Northern European states for centuries. With few interruptions, the Baltic was in a state of war from the 15th through the early 19th centuries. The war was then in its 17th year. *Lossen*, caught in a storm on December 23, ran north for the protection of Oslo Fjord, only to be driven onto the rocks at the entrance. Of the 109 aboard, only 54 men survived.

The wreck, lying in about nine meters of water, was buried in soft mud that preserved the lower hull of the frigate. Inside the hull were thousands of well-preserved artifacts that included all 24 cannon—18 six-pounders and six three-pounders—as well as shot, grapeshot, and barbell-headed bar shot. The galley equipment, including a large copper cooking pot recycled from an older, just retired Norwegian warship, joined cutlery and eating utensils to give a sense of how the crew ate. Barrels of salted pork and sheep, as well as fish, were cooked in the pots and served on round wooden trays. Small barrels of butter and liquor, as well as numerous wine and other liquor bottles, showed that alcohol was no stranger to the ships, either for the officers or the men.

While clothing had disintegrated, the excavation produced 925 buttons, most of them different, which suggested to the archaeologists that the crew of *Lossen* did not wear uniforms, but like the crew of *Vasa*, nearly a century earlier, wore their own clothes. But while the crew of *Vasa* slept on the deck or wherever they could find a spot, *Lossen*'s crew slept on hammocks.

Brooms and brushes showed that the Norwegian navy was concerned about hygiene aboard ship, as did combs with double rows of closely set teeth used to comb out lice. Among the more interesting finds was evidence of how the crew spent their time when not working the ship or fighting.

Like countless generations of sailors, they smoked pipes, took snuff, and carved wood. Twenty-four half-finished wooden spoons, carved wooden boxes, and a small, "elaborately carved child's rattle" were discovered in *Lossen*, all evidence of the very human activities of a crew seeking relaxation, or an extra way to make money in the midst of the rough-and-tumble world of a warship in the midst of a long war.

COPYING THE ENEMY'S SHIPS: THE WRECK OF *INVINCIBLE*

The wreck of an 18th-century French ship of the line, captured by the English and incorporated into the Royal Navy, speaks not only of standardization—and one navy using the captured arms and ships of another—but also of how navies of the time, notably the English, copied one another's ships. *L'Invincible*, built at Rochefort and launched in 1744, was part of France's naval build-up. It also embodied a new design perfected by the French for large, seaworthy, 74-gun ships. *L'Invincible* proved its mettle in battle with the English in 1745, when alone it fought off three English warships—its 74 guns against 134 English cannon. But on May 14, 1747, *L'Invincible* met its match when confronted by a fleet of 14 English ships at the First Battle of Cape Finisterre off the Spanish coast. Captured and towed back to Portsmouth, *L'Invincible* excited the interest of English naval officers, including Admiral Lord Anson, its captor, who proclaimed the French 74 "a prodigious fine ship, and vastly large."

While the Admiralty did not immediately pursue Anson's plans to copy *L'Invincible*, and two ships laid down to copy the French warship were canceled due to lack of funds (and the end of the war with France), in time the ship was copied. In 1757, the Royal Navy laid down two new "74's" on *L'Invincible*'s lines, and thus began a long line of English 74's—the "backbone" of the Royal Navy—that lasted for nearly a century. The original, incorporated into the Royal Navy as HMS *Invincible* in early 1748, remained in service for 10 years. At the end of that career, *Invincible* was used against France in the Seven Years' War to raid and seize French possessions in North America. After one season in Canadian waters, the ship was ready to sail with a large squadron when it ran aground on a sandbank off Portsmouth on February 19, 1758. Despite the efforts of the crew, *Invincible* was holed by its own anchor and sank. After some salvage, the Royal Navy abandoned the ship to the sea.

The wreck of *Invincible* remained undisturbed until fisherman Arthur Mack snagged it with his nets in 1979. Excavation began in 1980 and continued in 1991 as a volunteer effort undertaken with great difficulty—inadequate funds and political troubles plagued the project—but sustained by the personal energy of Arthur Mack, the wreck's discoverer and champion, and archaeologist John Bingeman. *Invincible's* wreck is a veritable time capsule of ship and ordnance stores as remarkably well preserved as those excavated two centuries earlier from the nearby wreck of *Mary Rose*. The artifacts include the most diverse collection of mid-18th-century rigging blocks, lines, bosun's tools and stores, navigational instruments, and the mess kits of the crew. The mess kits included square wooden platters from which the crew ate. Plates like these were the origin of the term "a square meal."

While the guns themselves were salvaged after *Invincible's* loss, a number of fragile, expendable items listed in records or known only from illustrations were remarkably well preserved by the mud of the Solent. They include 50 intact powder barrels and tampions used to plug the ends of cannon to keep moisture out. The tampions, spooled together in groups of six, suggested to Bingham that they were constantly replaced, and that the ship's guns were kept loaded with the tampion in place. The first shot of the gun would have cleared the tampion, which would be replaced after battle.

Wooden cartridge cases loaded with charges of gunpowder for the guns were excavated. The light poplar of the cases had "the consistency of *papier-mache* when raised" but they were carefully conserved because they are the only known examples of these eminently expendable charges. Another exciting discovery was a 14-foot roll of slow match (the fuse used to fire guns) that was covered with red wool. A feedhole allowed the gunners to pull out a length of the match.

The excavation also yielded structural information about *Invincible* that provides a good sense of the ship's construction. One of the features of interest to the English was the use of iron fittings such as braces and knees to help support the heavy weight of the gun decks. This feature was adopted for use in many warships in the late 18th century, helping "stretch the limits" of wood to build stronger vessels, and also to satisfy the requirements of the Royal Navy as it built up into the world's largest naval force, overwhelming the ability of England's forests to provide the necessary timber.

Excavation of *Invincible*'s lower gun deck revealed many of the iron knees and an interesting feature—a nut at the lower extremity that apparently was used to tighten the knee, which could—and would—work loose in heavy seas or from the vibration of gunfire. This suggests that the French shipwrights were taking advantage of the new material—iron—in a way not possible with the thick, heavily pinned wooden knees of the past. *Invincible* was not only a harbinger of change for the Royal Navy as the progenitor of a new class of 64s; it anticipated the changes wrought by the increasing use of iron.

THE RISE OF RUSSIAN SEA POWER

The 18th-century struggle for naval supremacy occupied regional as well as global concerns. The end of the 17th and the first decades of the 18th century were a time of war as the Dutch, French, and English sparred. But they were also a time in which the restive Baltic states of Sweden, Denmark, Poland, and Russia fought for control of the northern seas. Russia, beginning with Tsar Peter the Great, established a navy, learning by copying foreign warships and hiring experienced constructors and officers to assist the Russian Navy. Peter's ambitions in both the Black Sea and the Baltic, and Russia's desire to thwart the designs of the other Baltic states and the Ottoman Turks, brought decades of war to both seas. By 1721, Russia was the dominant sea power in the Baltic, but it maintained an uneasy stalemate with the Ottomans. Another Russian-Ottoman war in the 1730s ended with an Ottoman victory, aided by Britain, which sought to maintain a balance of power in Europe by discouraging a more powerful, dominant Russia.

The European wars of the mid-18th century shifted the balance of power, particularly as Britain, France, and their allies slugged it out in the Seven Years' War of 1755–1763. The Russian ruler, Tsarina Catherine the Great, pulled Russia out of the war after she ascended the throne in 1762. The respite allowed Britain's continental ally, Prussia, fighting Russia and Sweden, to be more of a counter to France and helped end the war. Britain rewarded Russia by supporting Catherine's ambitions in the Black Sea and Mediterranean.

Catherine built up a larger navy, pulled some of her heaviest warships out of the Baltic for duty in the Mediterranean, and hired British naval officers to command some of her ships as she determined to end Ottoman naval power in the region. The Russo-Turkish War of 1768–1774 commenced in earnest in 1770, when the new Russian Mediterranean fleet arrived from the Baltic. The Russian fleet, only 12 ships in strength, met the Ottomans off the Aegean island of Chios, close to the Turkish mainland at Cesme, on July 5, 1770. The Turkish fleet—21 ships of the line and a number of row galleys—were pushed back into Cesme's harbor when the Russians launched a fierce attack. A follow-up attack at dawn on July 7 ended in Russian victory as their ships destroyed the Ottoman fleet. The war continued for the next four years, with Russian victories on land and sea, a blockade of the Dardanelles, the creation of a Russian Black Seas fleet, and Russia's occupation of the Crimean peninsula in 1774 just as the war ended. Russia ended the war as a major new naval power, both in the Baltic and the Mediterranean.

EVSTAFII AND SLAVA ROSSII

Two Russian warship wrecks from this period recall the war and Russia's rapid rise to naval power. The first, the pink (naval transport) *Evstafii*, wrecked off the Shetland Islands on September 17, 1780. Built at Archangelsk in 1773, *Evstafii* was a 38-gun ship. Sailing south from Archangelsk to Kronstadt, Russia's Baltic naval fortress, *Evstafii* struck the rock Griff Skerry in a gale and sank with 189 officers, crew, and passengers. Only five of the crew survived the wreck. Wreck hunter Robert Stenuit discovered the wreck of *Evstafii* in 1972. Stenuit's divers did not find or recover any portions of the ship's hull or rigging. But a number of metal artifacts, including guns; shot; pieces of muskets and pistols; sword hilts; belt buckles; hardware; and 220 Russian and Dutch gold, silver, and copper coins were found. One of the more interesting finds was a corroded silver medal, struck to commemorate the Russian victory at Cesme.

The other Russian naval wreck of the period is the 66-gun warship *Slava Rossii*, also lost in 1780. Part of a Russian naval visit to the Mediterranean to underscore a new treaty of armed neutrality, *Slava Rossii* sailed from Kronstadt with five other ships, visiting Copenhagen, Texel, Dover, and Lisbon before heading into the Mediterranean to reach Livorno, Italy. Bad weather caused Captain Ivan Abrasimovich Baskakov to lose his position. Separated from the rest of the flotilla, *Slava Rossii* struck the rocks off Levant Island, a French possession off the Provencal coast and sank in 40 meters of water with a loss of 11 lives. A fisherman, Louis Viale, snagged the wreck with his nets in 1957. Pioneering French archaeologist Philippe Tailliez raised 10 cannon from the site that year, but scientific excavation of *Slava Rossii* did not start until 1980.

Under the direction of archaeologist Max Guerout, divers surveyed and excavated the wreck in a project that continued for another two decades. Additional guns, including three bronze cohorns (8-pdr. mortars) for use by the ship's infantry ashore, shot (including hollow shells, grapeshot, chain shot, and round shot), equipment, small arms and apparel, and equipment for both the crew and the Russian naval infantry were taken from *Slava Rossii*. A portion of the hull survived and helps demonstrate a continuity of form and construction for Russia's 66-gun warships. The first Russian "sixty-six" was built in 1731 by Scotsman Joseph Nay, hired and brought to Russia by Peter the Great several years earlier. The Russians not only learned to draw from the experience of other nations but also to adhere to what was viewed as a successful design for many years. *Slava Rossii* when launched in 1774 was one of the last of a line of 51 66-gun ships built for the Russian Imperial Navy between 1731 and 1779.

Guerout noted that the excavation also recovered shipboard equipment and fittings that "if not always spectacular, certainly gave insights into the way the very young Russian navy absorbed the knowledge brought in from abroad… [T]here are no significant differences … between the wreck of *Slava Rossii* and other naval wrecks of the period," except one. The French archaeological team discovered 63 copper alloy religious icons in the wreck. This amazing collection of "travelling icons" made of more durable copper rather than painted wood were "physical expression to the religious feelings which are known to have pervaded the Holy Russian Empire," while also providing a closer look at the popular feelings of *Slava Rossii*'s own officers and crew. Like so many other artifacts from lost warships, the icons are also a powerful reminder of how humanity faces the realities and risks of war.

THE HEYDAY OF THE WOODEN WALLS

Throughout the 18th and 19th centuries, the world's most powerful navy belonged to the world's most powerful nation: Great Britain. The united kingdoms of England and Scotland (joined by an Act of Union in 1707) expanded into a global empire. Although Britain's control of the seas was never absolute and was constantly challenged by other nations, the Royal Navy remained the world's dominant navy, expanding British trade into North America, the Caribbean, Pacific, Indian Ocean, and the Far East. It was also a period of overseas scientific study and exploration, using the resources of the Royal Navy to map the Pacific, the southern continent of Australia, and the Arctic and Antarctic regions. The major challenges of this incredible expansion overseas were the colonial wars for the Americas and the drawn-out conflict with France and its allies from 1783 through 1814. The wars of the period were global, as Britain fought in American waters, the Mediterranean, Caribbean, and the Baltic.

Other naval powers fought extended wars during these years, including renewed conflict between Russia, Sweden, and Ottoman Turkey. Catherine the Great's navy fought a two-year war between 1788 and 1790 for greater control of the Baltic and Black Seas. But the principal struggle was between Britain and France that began in 1792. A series of engagements, skirmishes, and battles involved hundreds of ships and resulted in horrendous loss of life. But the wooden walls had grown so big and formidable that very few ships were sunk as a result of action. Heavy-caliber guns smashed through the thick hulls, blasting splinters and pulverizing wood through the enclosed gun decks to leave a gory wake of destruction. Grapeshot and chain shot swept across open decks and into the masts, slashing rigging, sails, yards, and occasionally cutting through the masts and dropping them into the water. In a heavy battle, huge ships of the line would lie crippled, unable to maneuver or to fight, thousands of the crews dead or dying. But unless a ship's magazines were hit, setting off a fire and explosion, these massive wooden fortresses, with their thick hulls, did not sink.

The 18th century was an age of new tactics as well as a return to older forms of fighting. Like war on land, where troops lined up, facing each other to kneel, stand, and fire as they marched toward the enemy's line, ships also fought in lines. Opposing lines of ships sailed alongside each other, firing broadsides of shot into each other. But these fights were often a mutual slaughter and an effective standoff. Ships cut off from the main line could be captured, and in an age where the ships and guns of the combatants were essentially interchangeable, tactics to close, grapple, and board a crippled enemy, and take its decks in hand-to-hand fighting were encouraged. These circumstances inspired some commanders, like Britain's Horatio Nelson, to abandon the strict discipline of the line-on attack and try bold "melee" attacks—sailing into an enemy's line to break it up allowing ships closing in for individual, one-on-one duels—in short, reliance on personal initiative and daring.

The toll of war at sea in this age was better measured by the number of mangled bodies and amputated limbs dropped over the sides of the ships after a battle than by sunken vessels. But a number of ships did go down, sunk in accidents or by storms. Divers, fishermen, and archaeologists have discovered several warships from this period, and these submerged time capsules join a small group of surviving ships still afloat—notably Nelson's *Victory*—to provide insights into the world of the ships of the line in the climactic age of wooden warships.

HMS *SWIFT*

A small British warship wreck at the bottom of the world speaks to the far reach of the Royal Navy in the 18th century. A small, 14-gun sloop-of-war, *Swift* was a typical warship on the ocean frontier as Britain's navy explored, charted, and carried the flag to the distant parts of the globe. *Swift* was lost in the Deseado Estuary in Patagonia on March 13, 1770, while surveying the southernmost coast of the Americas. Based in the recently occupied base of Port Egmont, in the Falkland Islands/Islas Malvinas, *Swift* hit a rock and sank, taking three of the crew with it. They were the cook and two marines. The body of the cook washed ashore, but the other two men were never found. The survivors lived in desperate circumstances until a group of volunteers rowed the ship's open cutter to Port Egmont in an epic, difficult journey across 643 kilometers of the South Atlantic to bring help, which came a month later.

The story of the wreck fascinated a local group of high school students from the modern town of Puerto Deseado, and in 1982 they discovered the wreck and ensured it would be studied and protected. Under the direction of Dolores Elkin, a team from the Argentinean National Institute of Anthropology began excavations in 1998 that continued over the next several years. It was an epic, pioneering project in South American maritime archaeology. While artifacts were recovered, studied, preserved, and displayed in a local museum, the wreck itself, well-preserved by the cold water, mud, and a lack of wood-eating organisms, remains in place as a heritage site. Publications tell the story, in Spanish and English, of HMS *Swift*.

During the excavation of the captain's cabin, Elkin's team found a shoe with a human bone inside. After contacting the British Embassy, which granted permission, the team proceeded to excavate the nearly complete skeleton of a young man, approximately 25 years of age, who stood five feet, six inches tall, and had been right handed. The scant remains of a uniform confirmed that at last one of the sloop's two marines had been found, but as to whether he was 21-year-old Robert Rusker or 23-year-old John Ballard was never determined despite forensic work. He now lies in the Cemeterio de Chacarita in Buenos Aires beneath a marker that notes he is an unknown marine from *Swift*.

HMS *PANDORA*

The frigate *Pandora* is best known as the ship sent into the Pacific by the British Admiralty to apprehend the mutineers from HM Armed Transport *Bounty* in 1790. It is also the focus of one of the most detailed, lengthy archaeological examinations of a late 18th-century warship wreck ever conducted. Built at Deptford, England, in 1778 by shipbuilders Adams & Barnard, the 24-gun frigate *Pandora* served in the Royal Navy's Channel Fleet for the first eight months of its career. In May 1780, *Pandora* began a three-year stint of convoy duty, escorting ships to Britain's Canadian possessions. Laid up in 1783, *Pandora* re-entered active service in 1790. The Admiralty originally intended to return *Pandora* to the Channel Fleet, but news of mutiny aboard *Bounty* in the distant Pacific led to a change of orders. On November 7, 1790, *Pandora* sailed for Tahiti, arriving there on March 23, 1791.

After apprehending 14 of *Bounty*'s crew, Captain Edward Edwards searched for *Bounty* until August. On the evening of August 28, while trying to sail *Pandora* through the shoals and islands that mark Australia's Great Barrier Reef, Edwards and his crew lost the ship when she ran aground on a submerged reef. Badly damaged, *Pandora* sank on the morning of August 29 after several hours of desperate work to save the ship. It sank in about 30 meters of water with 31 of the crew and four prisoners from *Bounty*'s crew.

Rediscovered in 1977, *Pandora*'s wreck was the focus of a detailed archaeological survey led by archaeologist Graeme Henderson in 1979. Archaeologists from the Queensland Museum, assisted by colleagues from other museums and government agencies, began excavating *Pandora* in

1983. After more than a decade of meticulous excavation, the archaeologists, under the direction of Peter Gesner, exposed about one-sixth of the wreck. Their work suggests that *Pandora*'s lower deck and platform deck (from the waterline to the keel) may be intact. *Pandora* lies heeled over on its starboard side, with the bow more deeply buried than the stern. The exposed stern and port side have disintegrated, allowing archaeologists to excavate inside the wreck.

While the hull is the major artifact, tens of thousands of smaller artifacts lie inside the ship, many of them in groups or clusters that correspond to cabins or storage areas. While larger artifacts such as a 6-pounder gun, and an ornate portable fireplace, probably from the captain's cabin or the great cabin on the upper deck, were recovered, hundreds of others offer a tantalizing look at the contents of a wreck that is a late 18th-century time capsule much like *Mary Rose* or *Vasa* are for their period of history. Medical equipment and an ornate, well-preserved gold and silver pocket watch suggest that one area of excavation encountered the remains of the ship's surgery or the surgeon's cabin; the watch may have belonged to ship's surgeon George Hamilton.

Navigational instruments, personal effects, and what may be souvenirs—Polynesian artifacts and seashells—have been recovered from inside *Pandora*. Peter Gesner noted that the excavations exposed "large clusters of personal effects which have been deposited against partitions and onto the lower deck," many of them "separated by preserved portions of cabin partitions" that allow the archaeologists to "ascribe artifacts to individuals." To do so allows us a unique opportunity to take an intensely personal tour through a British warship of the end of the 18th century, as well as examine the stored provisions and equipment in the hold, including an "extra set of fittings and stores" to refit and resupply *Bounty*.

DE BRAAK

The remains of a small, 16-gun Royal Navy "brig-sloop" provide a detailed look not only at another lost warship but also at what can go tragically wrong with important underwater archaeological sites. HMS *De Braak* capsized off Cape Henlopen, Delaware, on May 28, 1798, taking with her the captain, James Drew, 34 of the crew, and 12 prisoners from a Spanish ship, *San Francisco Xavier*. *De Braak*, assigned to convoy escort by the Royal Navy, was helping protect shipping between Britain and the United States in a period between the animosity of the Revolution and the War of 1812. Separated from its convoy by a storm, *De Braak* finally reached American shores with her Spanish prize after seven weeks' absence. *San Francisco Xavier*, laden with copper, cocoa, and other goods, had the misfortune of flying the flag of an ally of France (and a traditional enemy of Britain) when the lost *De Braak* encountered it at sea.

With its prize, *De Braak* reached Cape Henlopen and was trying to enter the harbor when a strong gust of wind or a squall pushed it onto its side, sending guns crashing across the decks, tossing men, and sinking *De Braak* within minutes. Only 33 of the crew survived the wreck. Rumors that *De Braak* was carrying treasure, magnified through the years, inspired many to hunt for the wreck in the 19th and 20th centuries. Treasure hunters finally succeeded in locating *De Braak* in 1984 and gained legal control of the wreck as "salvors in possession." The salvage of *De Braak* turned into one of the greatest archaeological disasters in American history. Historian and archaeologist Donald G. Shomette writes of "human remains...illegally disposed of" when divers encountered some of *De Braak*'s dead, and "artifacts requiring expensive conservation...cast overboard."

The "De Braakle," as some with wry humor termed this debacle, culminated in a highly publicized lift of the unexcavated hull by a crane in August 1986. The hull twisted and broke, spilling artifacts into the sea. The damaged remains of *De Braak*, placed on a barge, were towed away and excavation of the seabed with a clamshell bucket began. The excavated "spoil" was then loaded on a barge and then "processed on an industrial gravel separator." Artifacts plucked from the separator were sifted again in an increasingly desperate search for treasure that simply did not exist. I went out to inspect the work as a young federal archaeologist, and three decades later still vividly recall the shock of seeing a backhoe scrape the dredged-up contents of the wreck onto the conveyer belt of the gravel separator as artifacts stuck up out of the reeking mud.

Shomette notes, "Although 26,000 artifacts were recovered, fewer than 650 were coins." The assessed monetary value of what had been wrenched from the wreck was less than $300,000—and it had cost the salvagers $3 million to get it. The hull and artifacts ultimately ended up in the hands of the State of Delaware. The story of what happened to De Braak helped spur the passage of the United States's Abandoned Shipwreck Act of 1987, ending the application of the laws that had given title to wrecks like De Braak to treasure hunters.

Despite the incredible damage to the wreck and the loss of much information, archaeologists who stepped in to preserve the artifacts and recover as much information as possible for the State of Delaware have reaped incredible results. Work by archaeologist David Beard on the ship's hull remains suggests that De Braak, ostensibly a Dutch warship, may have been a British ship, perhaps a privateer, captured by the French around 1781, sold to the Dutch, and then seized by the British in 1793 when the shifting alliances of Napoleonic Wars linked Holland with revolutionary France. Beard documented how De Braak's construction closely matched British practice, not Dutch, and discovered copper fastenings incised with the name of an English manufacturer. Beard's work not only highlights the changing fortunes of war—much like Colin Martin's work on Swan—but it also again demonstrates how standardization of warships and their equipment could see a vessel like De Braak change flags at least twice, if not three times, to serve different navies.

Analysis of De Braak's rigging, particularly its blocks and tackle—by Shomette and archaeologist Fred Hopkins Jr.—provides a close look at why the ship capsized. Contemporary accounts suggest the brig-sloop was "overmasted," or that the rigging was too heavy for the ship, making it unstable. Shomette and Hopkins discovered that De Braak's blocks were about twice as heavy as a "typical Royal Navy vessel of her size and rig" and that about 25 percent of the Royal Navy's brig-sloops of the period had been lost not to enemy action but to accidents. The brig-sloops, altered from a one-masted design to two masts, and heavily rigged to press for as much speed as possible by pushing a ship with as many sails as possible, were probably a flawed experiment. The search for speed, a re-rig that shifted the ship's center of gravity (making it top heavy), and an unfortunate squall combined to send *De Braak* and nearly 100 other brig-sloops to the bottom.

Archaeologist Charles Fithian carefully documented the ordnance and arms from *De Braak*, particularly the ship's guns. Known as "carronades," these short, stocky, meter-long guns were manufactured by the Carron gun works in Scotland. Their size and lighter weight than a traditional "long gun" allowed the carronade to be fitted on smaller warships, as well as on the upper decks of larger warships. Mounted on a sliding carriage, not wheels, the carronade hugged the deck, could be rotated and swung around on a front pintle to come to bear on an enemy, and packed a powerful punch. The intense naval combat of the Napoleonic Wars widely introduced carronades into naval service, giving smaller ships a deadly firepower.

Fithian's analysis of *De Braak*'s guns not only showed that it was armed with "the very latest technology in naval ordnance," but that the ship only carried two types of shot. Round, 24-pound ball shot, delivered close-up, gave the carronade its nickname of the "smasher" as it tore through enemy hulls. Tin canisters of smaller iron balls "canister shot" had an equally deadly effect on an enemy crew when fired like a shotgun at a crowded deck. The carronade was an ideal murdering weapon for the Napoleonic Wars' return to up-close and personal fights at sea. Fithian also documented innovations developed to speed up the bloody work—fixed ammunition for *De Braak*'s two 6-pounder "bow chasers"—in which the charge to fire the gun is attached to the projectile. Fixed ammunition meant faster loading than the older method of loading the charge, wadding, and the projectile before firing. The 6-pounder charges aboard *De Braak* are the earliest archaeological evidence of fixed ammunition at sea. Fithian also documented 14 brass gunlocks—a flintlock firing mechanism for guns that was just then replacing the slower and older match fuse. The gunlock allowed a warship to fight with a "more dependable and rapid rate of fire," and *De Braak*'s are the earliest examples "encountered to date on a Royal Navy shipwreck site."

The dedicated work of the archaeologists and conservators has made a tremendous difference, saving not only artifacts but also significant information from a devastated archaeological site. Had they directed the work, and had the excavation proceeded like that of *Pandora, Swan,* or *Mary Rose,* the *De Braak* site would have doubtless joined the other ships as one of the world's great archaeological success stories. But in many ways, thanks to Shomette and his colleagues, the final work on *De Braak*'s surviving collection is still an archaeological success. They have shown how this wreck is a physical reminder of the demands of an intense series of wars at sea, and how an emerging industrial and technological revolution was changing both warships and the way they fought.

NUESTRA SEÑORA DE LAS MERCEDES

In April 2007, international headlines trumpeted the discovery and recovery of more than a half million silver and gold coins from a deep-water site off Portugal by Tampa-based commercial salvage company Odyssey Marine Exploration. According to Odyssey's news release, the site, code-named "Black Swan," appeared to be where someone had dumped a vast treasure overboard, but without evidence of a shipwreck. The Kingdom of Spain believed otherwise. The coins shown on the news were Spanish, and previously Odyssey had unsuccessfully sought permission to recover lost Spanish treasure. Spain's cultural ministry had demurred. What followed was a five-year legal battle in the US Middle District of Florida Court that ended with a judgment that what Odyssey had found was the Royal Spanish naval frigate of war *Nuestra Señora de las Mercedes*, a warship that exploded and sank in battle against a British naval fleet on October 5, 1804. It was carrying money belonging to both the king and private merchants, under the protection of a naval force, the royal funds part of a payment to Napoleon as part of an agreement that kept Spain out of Bonaparte's wars.

The 38-gun *Mercedes* was 16 years old, and a veteran of an earlier engagement with Britain, the Battle of the Cape of St. Vincent in February 1797 and another action in 1800, all part of Spain's role as an ally of France in their war with the British. The Treaty of Amiens of 1802 brought a brief hiatus in the Napoleonic Wars, but when they resumed in 1803, Spain stayed out of active conflict after France made payments to them. Great Britain considered the payments a "direct subsidy of war," and so when, in

September 1804 the British government received intelligence that the Spanish warships *Medea, Mercedes, Clara,* and *Fama,* under the overall command of José de Bustamente y Guerra, were on their way from South America with specie and copper and tin ingots (to make bronze), they dispatched a Royal Navy squadron to intercept the Spanish ships and take the money.

On October 3, the British Navy frigates *Indefatigable, Lively, Medusa,* and *Amphion* took station south of Portugal to intercept the Spanish squadron before it reached Cádiz. Two days later, they spotted the Spanish squadron to the southwest. As the two squadrons met, the Spanish kept on course as the British lined up and fired a warning shot to lay to and prepare to be boarded. After receiving an "unsatisfactory answer," the British opened fire and the Spanish responded. Ten minutes later, a shot penetrated into the hull of *Mercedes,* which exploded so violently that one of its cannon flew into the rigging of nearby HMS *Amphion.* Hundreds of crew, and the wives and children of a number of Spanish officers who were returning home to Spain, were killed instantly. Only 40 men clinging to a fragment of the frigate's bow survived.

The stunned Spanish officers in the other ships surrendered to the British. Considered prisoners, and their ships prizes of war, they were taken to British ports. Spain declared war on Great Britain, and in turn, Britain declared war on Spain. The bloody legacy of the war that followed included the defeat, a year later, of the Spanish and French fleet at Trafalgar, and the long nightmare of the Peninsular Wars, during which France turned on Spain, occupying it in 1808. That led to a protracted guerilla war between Spanish patriots and the French, and British intervention until its end in 1814. The war so weakened Spain that much of its overseas empire in the Americas was lost by the early 1820s, leaving only Cuba and Puerto Rico as colonies in that hemisphere.

What Odyssey discovered in 2007 was the broken, scattered remains of *Nuestra Señora de las Mercedes* lying on a plain of sand and mud in 1,037 meters of water. I reviewed a great deal of data that the courts ordered Odyssey to provide by royal marines during the course of the five-year legal battle over whether there was a wreck there, and if so to whom it belonged.

The basic legal principle of sovereign, or government, ownership applies to warships, embassies, and consulates, and so to the king's money on board. As for the private funds, they too were found to belong to Spain, because the Spanish Crown had reimbursed every private merchant and family whose money had been guarded by royal marines and carried in a time of potential conflict in the warship.

Odyssey never provided a map, only a photomosaic of the seabed, and so with lawyer James Goold, counsel for Spain, I worked to identify fragments of the ship, cannon, and scattered artifacts using videotapes of the remotely operated vehicle dives on the site and screen-captured images that we had to try and match to the mosaic. It took time, but what emerged was a wreck site that in many ways resembled an airplane crash site. That impression was underscored by a Spanish expedition to the site in 2015 by the National Museum of Underwater Archaeology. The blast that destroyed *Mercedes* sent large chunks of the hull to the bottom, some of them with cannon and their carriages entangled. Damage from the explosion included deformed metal reinforcing members and a dented cannon.

Anchors, ceramics, an officer's sea chest with his pewter plates and a gold snuff box, fittings from the decks, cannon, copper and tin ingots, and hundreds of chests of silver coin lay strewn in an ovoid zone formed from the epicenter of the blast. It was graphic, and when you realized that some 250 lives were lost in that instant, a reminder of the costs of war—in this case the innocent families of the officers who were coming home, in troubled times, but until that moment *Mercedes* exploded, a time when they were still at peace with Britain.

THE WRECKS OF TRAFALGAR

The most significant naval battle of the Napoleonic Wars, the Battle of Trafalgar on October 21, 1805, was a classic face-off between warring ships of the line near the southwest coast of Spain. Under the command of Admiral Horatio Nelson, a British fleet of 27 ships engaged a Franco-Spanish fleet of 33 ships commanded by Admiral Pierre-Charles Villeneuve.

Nelson's philosophy that "no captain can do very wrong if he places his ship alongside that of the enemy" unfolded as two columns of British ships, one led by Nelson in his flagship, the 100-gun HMS *Victory*, the other by Admiral Cuthbert Collingwood in HMS *Royal Sovereign*, engaged the enemy and punched through the enemy's line of ships, hammering each other, often at point-blank range.

Shot dismasted ships, punched huge holes through the thick oak sides, spraying men with splinters that blinded them, gouged flesh, and tore off limbs; and carronades—short, stubby guns—mowed down men on decks with shotgun-like blasts. French and Spanish losses were horrific, with more than 2,200 dead, and more than 1,000 men injured, some of them badly maimed. The British lost 458 men, including Nelson, shot down by a sharpshooter as *Victory* fought a close battle with the French ship of the line *Redoubtable*. The French lost the 74-gun ship *Achille*, which exploded after catching fire during the battle, and the British captured 22 ships and some 7,000 men. A coming storm threatened the decisive victory's full measure of spoils, as well as badly damaged ships on both sides. Ultimately, several of the ships were burned by their British captors, while other damaged French and Spanish ships wrecked on the Spanish coast near Cádiz.

Trafalgar left Britain in control of the seas, but the Napoleonic Wars continued for another decade. Nelson, enshrined in British memory as the empire's greatest naval hero, is commemorated in many places, most famously at London's Trafalgar Square, where many of us who study the history of the sea make pilgrimage, as well as the preserved *Victory* at Portsmouth. Originally built in 1758, and rebuilt and repaired many times since, *Victory* rests in No. 2 Dock, where it is open to visitors. The ongoing struggle to preserve the ship has lasted for a century and a half, with extensive rebuilding, treatments to keep deathwatch beetles from eating the ship's timbers, an ongoing £16 million restoration, and the creation of the HMS Victory Preservation Trust.

Spanish archaeologists searching for the remains of the shipwrecks from the Battle of Trafalgar have focused their efforts on the Andaluz coast near Cádiz. Their work located the wrecks of the French ships *Fougueux* and *Bucentaure*, Villeneueve's flagship, which wrecked in the storm on October 23.

The dismasted, battered 74-gun *Fougueux* came ashore October 22, breaking up three days later off Camposoto Beach. Only 25 men, a mix of the British prize crew and French prisoners, survived the wreck. The Spanish archaeological excavation of *Fougueux* conducted by the Centro del Arquelogía Subacuática (IAPH), has documented a site both scattered but also concentrated around the remains of the midships portion of the bottom of the hull, with a range of artifacts that speak to life on board, including broken wine bottles, ceramic jars, navigational instruments, including half of a minute-glass sand-clock, iron cookware, and two very pertinent reminders of the consequences of naval warfare of the time. One is a bronze screw mechanism used to fix a tourniquet, allowing a ship's surgeon to cut off a badly injured arm or leg. The other was a broken serving dish with the English inscription:

From Rocks & Sands,
And Every Ill,
May God Preserve the Sailor Still

My colleagues with the RPM Nautical Foundation, with support from the National Geographic Society, and working with the Centro del Arquelogía Subacuática, conducted a survey in 2004 to find some of the Trafalgar ships that lie in deeper water, including the 120-gun Spanish ship of the line *Santísima Trinidad*, one of the largest and most powerful ships at Trafalgar. Captured at great cost to both sides, *Santísima Trinidad* sank in deep water on October 24. The sonar survey they conducted found mud-shrouded outlines of what is likely *Santísima Trinidad* and the Spanish ship *Argonauta*, which sank nearby. Conditions were not ideal for photographic documentation of the wrecks due to the soft mud. *Santísima Trinidad* is buried in the black silty sediment that comes from the Guadalquivar and Rio Negro in the rainy winter, so any disturbance of the bottom causes immediate and total loss of visibility.

While that was frustrating, the evidence of Trafalgar on the seabed will continue to emerge. Meanwhile, as a reminder that archaeology takes many forms, and particularly continues in the laboratory, one of the most compelling artifacts preserved from the battle is the torn and tattered fore topsail of HMS *Victory*, which is in the collection of the National Museum of the Royal Navy next to *Victory* in Portsmouth. The second-largest sail on the ship, it was hit some 90 times by French and Spanish shot that day, with holes, rips, and tears that offer a forensic and graphic sense of the battle that the repaired and restored *Victory* itself does not. Studied, cleaned, and preserved by Mary Rose Archaeological Services, the 336-square-meter sail is displayed at the museum with a specially designed presentation that uses sound, film, and lighting that allow the sail to essentially "tell its story." Like all artifacts, the story of the sail is not only the story of the battle, but a reminder of the men who stitched that mass of canvas into a sail. It speaks for those who worked aloft, above the decks, both unfurling and furling the heavy weight of the sail from its yard. It speaks to those who, like it, were pierced with shot, splinters, and bullets on October 21, 1805, a fateful day remembered as the apex of the age of the wooden walls at sea.

5

Colonial Conflicts in the Americas

We have met the enemy and they are ours.

—Oliver Hazard Perry, US Navy, September 10, 1813

The struggles between various European powers for empire played out across the world, with the New World and American waters as a constantly contested theater of war. This began with contact and conflict with the indigenous peoples and extended into wars of conquest. At the same time, the European powers with a stake in the New World, as well as those who desired a stake, also came into conflict with the Americas and its waters as their battlefields. Following Columbus's voyages into the Caribbean, Spain's first major incursion into the heart of the Mexica-Aztec Empire came with the expedition of Hernán Cortés in 1519. Landing on the Gulf of Mexico coast in April, Cortés established the settlement of Villa Rica de Vera Cruz and began his alliances with the Totonac, recently conquered and unhappy Aztec vassals.

Cortés came to Mexico with a fleet of about 11 ships (the exact number is debated), and in July 1519, in a famous act that set the path of his expedition forward, ordered his fleet scuttled. That point of no return is commonly and falsely believed to be an order to burn the ships, but they were stripped and scuttled in deeper water offshore of Villa Rica de Vera Cruz. In 1520, Cortés returned to Villa Rica when news came that an expedition led by Pánfilo de Narváez had come to oppose him. Cortés overcame Narváez, convinced Narváez's men to join his forces, and then scuttled Narvaez's fleet.

Today, the site of Villa Rica de Vera Cruz is a fishing village outside of modern Veracruz. I visited it with my friend George Belcher while working on the 19th-century wreck of the US brig *Somers* in 1986. A scatter of ruins, and a tree that the locals tell you Cortés tied his ships to, is not that impressive a site unless you let your imagination roam. It is easy to picture what took place here in the spring of 1519 when those ships, laden with arms and men, inaugurated the colonial wars for America. Archaeology on land began in 1951, and in the late 1980s and early 1990s, Mexico's Instituto Nacíonal de Antropología e Historia (INAH) conducted excavations at the town site.

In 2018, a National Geographic Expedition Council–sponsored expedition led by Roberto Junco of INAH, Christopher Horrell of Texas State University's Meadows Center, and Frederick "Fritz" Hanselmann of the University of Miami commenced a survey to search for the scuttled ships of 1519 and 1520. If found, the earliest wrecks from the wars for the Americas may yield more direct archaeological evidence of the first naval invasion of Mexico. The initial victory that came with the fall of Tenochtitlan in 1521 was the precursor of six decades of *conquista* in Mexico. That effort was supported by ongoing naval and maritime supply. While there is no direct archaeological information for that effort, as yet, there is high hope that the 2018 expedition's results will yield evidence of the lost ships of the Aztec conquest.

We have one clue from deep-sea images from a survey of the sea route from Cuba to Mexico that shows two small Spanish ships of the period that appear to have been loaded and lost during the early stages of the conquest. There are no cannon or firearms, but scattered crossbows speak to understanding the need for resupply of Spanish technology as well as horses and men.

LA TRINITÉ

Spain had explored, conducted slaving raids, and made multiple attempts at colonization in La Florida (which included modern Georgia and South Carolina) within a few years of Columbus's voyages through the mid-16th century. The failed expeditions of Pánfilo de Narváez in 1527, Hernando de Soto in 1539, and Tristán de Luna y Arrellano in 1559 left Florida open to the colonial ambitions of France. French incursions into La Florida included settlements and fortifications at what is now Parris Island, South Carolina, and Jacksonville, Florida, in 1562 and 1564, setting the stage for a Spanish counter thrust in 1565. It came as a French fleet under the command of Jean Ribault sailed to reinforce France's colony in Florida with seven ships, supplies, and up to 1,000 soldiers, sailors, and colonists. A Spanish fleet of five ships, with 200 sailors, 500 soldiers, and 100 other Spaniards under the command of Pedro de Menéndez de Avilés arrived soon after the French on September 4, 1565.

Menéndez's fleet appeared as Ribault's transport ships offloaded supplies at their river outpost, Fort Caroline. A brief encounter and an exchange of cannon fire ended with Ribault's warships heading out to sea, where they would regroup to tackle the Spanish ships. Menéndez's ships sank one of the French supply ships, but the ultimate outcome of the encounter was in doubt. That ended two days later when a powerful storm drove the French fleet ashore on the coast, with three of the ships sinking near Ponce Inlet on the coast, and the flagship, *La Trinité*, sinking off Cape Canaveral on September 12, 1565. On September 18, Menéndez assaulted Fort Caroline and took it, slaughtering most of its garrison with the exception of women and children and some of the men who escaped.

With news of French survivors from Ribault's wrecked fleet now ashore, Menéndez organized his troops and marched to meet them at the end of the month. Finding the French split into two groups, exhausted, bedraggled, and in no position or mood to fight, he accepted their surrender. Despite their pleas for mercy, he slaughtered most of them, including Ribault. The storm that destroyed Ribault's fleet ended France's efforts to gain Florida, and Menéndez founded settlements at both Fort Caroline and on the coast at the site of what is now the city of St. Augustine in 1565.

The wrecks of Ribault's fleet have been the objects of interest and desire for archaeologists, historians, and treasure hunters for some time. In 1970–1971, relic hunters discovered French artifacts along what would become Cape Canaveral National Seashore, and National Park Service excavations at four of these sites from 1990 to 1995 confirmed the suspicions of the relic hunters that they were survivor campsites from the wreck of *La Trinité*. With support from NOAA's Office of Ocean Exploration, the nonprofit Lighthouse Archaeological Maritime Program (LAMP), headed by Chuck Meide, surveyed off shore of Cape Canaveral in partnership with the State of Florida and the National Park Service in July–August 2014. A variety of buried targets were located.

In August 2016, treasure hunters announced that they had found "three 16th century Spanish shipwrecks" during a state-permitted survey off Cape Canaveral that they believed to be linked to the Ribault fleet, with one striking artifact, a marble column with the Royal Coat of Arms of France, as well as ornate bronze cannon. The treasure hunters released images of the artifacts and filed suit in court to gain possession of the wreck site, which inspired a response from the State of Florida and France. The treasure hunters had acted in violation of the terms of their state permit because like LAMP's survey, they were granted permission to survey but not dig. More to the point, their find was not from Spanish ships, but from the wreck of French *La Trinité*. What followed was a lengthy legal dispute over exactly what is down there, who owns it, and who has the right to follow up on the discovery. At the end of June 2018, the court ruled, as had been the case with *Nuestra Señora de las Mercedes*, that the site was one wreck, and that it was *La Trinité*. With that, plans for a comprehensive survey and excavation in an international partnership were formed, and the project was poised to begin as this book was completed.

LA BELLE

The excavation of a French warship lost off the Texas coast 120 years after Ribault's disastrous end is a shining example of what archaeological projects can do to bring back lost and forgotten history, provide powerful details of past events and people, and inspire partnerships that continue well past the time the digging is complete. In the century following the end of France's ambitions in Florida, a new French colony on the northern Atlantic seaboard took root in what is now Canada, establishing Quebec in 1608 and exploring the Great Lakes in the decades that followed. Spanish colonies, other than Florida, spread up from the Valley of Mexico north into Baja California and into the southwestern portion of North America, centering on the province of Santa Fe de Nuevo México, established in 1598. British colonies had spread up along the east coast.

At that stage, French ambitions were focused on the rich fur trade of the Americas, and exploration and expansion from modern Canada into the Great Lakes, rich in possibilities, ultimately led to exploration of the Mississippi River. The 1673 expedition of Louis Jolliet and Jacques Marquette followed the great river through the heart of North America to the Gulf of Mexico. In 1682, Rene-Robert Cavelier, Sieur de La Salle, eager to expand both France's and his own personal fur trading empire, explored the Great Lakes in 1679–1680. In 1682, he turned his attention to the Mississippi. In his canoe-based explorations of 1682–1683, he built forts and, naming the region *La Louisane*, claimed it for France. La Salle reached the river's mouth on April 9, 1682.

With that, La Salle pursued what would be his final quest, which was to establish a French colony at the mouth of the Mississippi. That colony would cement a fur trade highway from the Great Lakes to the Gulf of Mexico, split Spanish control of the Gulf, isolating La Florida, and keep English ambitions pinned to the eastern seaboard. With royal approval and sponsorship, including the gift of four ships, supplies, and 300 colonists as well as 100 soldiers, La Salle's expedition sailed from France in July 1684. Landing in what is now Matagorda Bay in Texas in early 1685, La Salle set up a fort and commenced land exploration in a series of efforts to find the Mississippi as they had missed their intended landing site by some 400 miles. It ended badly with disease, fights with the indigenous peoples they encountered, and La Salle's death at the hands of some of his men in 1687.

Only three ships had reached Texas, one having been lost to Spanish privateers, and on entering the bay, the crew of the supply ship *L'Aimable* stranded and wrecked their ship. La Salle's largest warship, the 36-gun man-of-war *Le Joly*, remained long enough to see La Salle's flagship, the barque longue *La Belle*, anchor and its crew rescue what they could before departing. *La Belle* alone remained, with much of its supplies and arms for the soldiers on board, as well as its crew. During one of La Salle's searches, the crew stranded and lost *La Belle* in the bay. In 1686, following the capture of a stranded French colonist, the Spanish government learned of La Salle's attempt, sailed to the bay, and discovered the broken wreck of *La Belle* in shallow water, as well as a campsite ashore.

Historical research and interest in rediscovering *L'Aimable* and *La Belle* led to surveys, the magnetic mapping of Matagorda Bay, and, in 1995, a State of Texas–sponsored expedition that discovered *La Belle* in shallow water, buried in soft mud. The "smoking gun" from the discovery was a bronze cannon spotted by archaeologist Chuck Meide that was both French and with markings that showed it could not have been cast past 1683. What followed was a massive effort, funded by the Texas Historical Commission and led by archaeologist Jim Bruseth. The million-dollar, one-year project

■ This 800-pound. bronze cannon with its French insignia was the first artifact found that identified the wreck of *La Belle*. (Texas Historical Commission)

■ Excavating *La Belle*. (Texas Historical Commission)

■ Personal artifacts excavated from the wreck of *La Belle* (Texas Historical Commission)

completely excavated *La Belle* in 1996–1997. The dig took place inside a specially built cofferdam that surrounded the wreck.

With the water removed, and *La Belle* exposed in its shallow grave, the excavation proceeded to recover exceptionally well-preserved artifacts that included ship's equipment, supplies, tools, arms, and trade items intended for the local people La Salle encountered. Out in the open, the work on the wreck was visible to more than the team, but also the public, and the dig was closely followed as this aspect of Texas's and US history, largely forgotten by most, was literally resurrected from the bottom of Matagorda Bay. Among the discoveries was the skeleton of one of La Salle's men, lying atop a coil of anchor cable at the bow, so well-preserved by the mud and a lack of oxygen that his brain remained in place inside his skull. The *La Belle* sailor's name remains unknown, but his reconstructed facial features are now well known to two generations of Texas schoolchildren and the public.

Analysis and preservation of the artifacts, as well as the raised and recovered hull of *La Belle* at the Conservation Research Laboratory at Texas A&M University in College Station took many years to reverse the effects of the long burial in mud and sea water. In 2014, the hull was moved into the Bullock Museum in Austin, where it and the artifacts went on prominent display in the exhibit "*La Belle*: The Ship That Changed History." The exhibition is not the only legacy; there are scholarly and popular books, an award-winning educational program, a film, and web-based access to the collection that share this wreck's story with the public. In 2018, the wreck of this small French warship and its contents, now integrated into a new

■ The conserved hull of *La Belle* displayed at the Bullock State History Museum in Austin. (Larry D. Moore/Wikimedia Commons)

exhibition, "Becoming Texas," help tell a 14,000-year-old story through documents, human stories, and the power of artifacts.

THE CARIBBEAN

The American colonies of the various European powers were closely tied to the Caribbean and in particular its sugar-based plantation economy, all part of the triangular trade fueled by slavery, sugar, rum, and manufactured goods. The evolving global economy was taking precedence over colonial expansion in the name of King and Country, or the simple plunder of commodities such as gold and silver. While Spain held sway over much of South America, all of Central America, and portions of North America, Portugal held Brazil, and the French, Dutch, Danes, and the English challenged Spain and Portugal's 16th-century domination of the New World through the establishment of their own colonies. These included settlements in the Caribbean, where Spain held the Spanish West Indies, notably Cuba and what is now the Dominican Republic, while the other European powers constantly warred to gain more of the islands, including those beyond the Spanish Antilles. While wars in Europe helped shape the destiny of the Caribbean colonies, so did war in the Caribbean itself.

The sea was the basis of economic exchange, and as elsewhere in the world, the oceanic paths of commerce also served as highways of war. The wars for "America" evolved from colonial counterpunches for territory to the taking of assets for economic gain. This played out at sea with the weaker powers of the time, such as England, relying on privateering and raids against Spanish ports and shipping, with the career of Francis Drake exemplifying the daring and range of an English "sea dog" of the 16th century. As a teenager, sailing with his second cousin, John Hawkins, he attacked Portuguese ships off West Africa, raided the Mexican port of Veracruz, raided Panamá and seized the "silver train" transporting bullion and coin across the isthmus, and embarked on a global voyage from 1577 through 1580 in which he rounded South America and pushed into the Pacific to raid and sink Spanish ships.

SATISFACTION

Another English freebooter whose exploits define the age and the nature of war at sea in the Caribbean is Henry Morgan. Based in Jamaica, which Spain lost to England in 1655, Morgan's greatest exploit was his raid on Panamá in 1671. Massing a fleet of 38 ships, with his flagship a captured French 14-gun ship renamed *Satisfaction*, Morgan headed for Panamá in late 1670 with an advance force of 470 men in three ships sent to capture the Castillo de San Lorenzo at the mouth of the Chagres River on Panamá's Caribbean coast. When Morgan and the rest of the fleet arrived off the river's mouth on January 12, 1671, the advance force had taken the fort, and so Morgan headed in.

Satisfaction struck a shallow reef off the fort, followed by three or four other ships. Smashed and scattered, they warned the rest of the fleet off. Morgan and most of his crews escaped, with a loss of some 11 people. Regrouping on land, Morgan and a land force proceeded up the river and crossed the mountains into Panamá City—which they took, plundered, and left partially destroyed. The "Sack of Panamá" made Morgan both a legend and a rich man.

The wreck of *Satisfaction*, known to lie somewhere on or just off Lajas Reef, beneath the Castillo de San Lorenzo, has been the subject of private and organized searches by both history-minded divers and treasure hunters in Panamá since the 1950s. Various accounts speak of finds on the reef and of a wake of devastation. In 2008, I headed to Panamá with fellow archaeologists Frederick "Fritz" Hanselmann and Dominique Rissolo, with the support of the Waitt Foundation, and under permit from the Instituto Nacíonal de Cultura (INAC), to conduct a comprehensive survey of the maritime archaeological landscape of the mouth of the Chagres. As part of that, working in shallow water, we found a scatter of eight iron cannon lying inshore of the reef and a largely buried, small iron anchor. The guns were recovered by Hanselmann the following year and taken to the conservation laboratory at Panamá Viejo, the archaeological park centered in the heart of the city Morgan had once destroyed.

There, a team of conservators stabilized the corroded iron, removed the encrustation of centuries, and revealed the true shapes and character of the guns.

■ A tangle of cannon lie off Lajas Reef, likely from the wreck of Morgan's *Satisfaction*. (Author Photo) M0010016

They are right for the time and are a mixture of French and English guns. The laboratory work revealed, with the first gun treated, that it was still loaded, and that a fabric sash was wrapped around the breech hole where the gun would be fired. Are they Morgan's guns from *Satisfaction*? It appears they are, and as such, are the first direct archaeological evidence of Henry Morgan's amphibious assault on Panamá.

THE ROCKLEY BAY PROJECT

In time, voyages of privateering and outright piracy gave way to colonial wars between men-of-war and naval squadrons and fleets in the 17th and 18th centuries. To date, archaeologists have for the most part studied individual wrecks, but under the direction of archaeologist Kroum Batchvarov from the University of Connecticut, an ongoing project in Rockley Bay in Tobago is examining the larger battlescape and losses of a key naval engagement between French and Dutch naval forces in March 1677. The battle came during the French-Dutch War of 1673–1678. During that European war, both sides used their navies to attack each other's colonies abroad.

The battle of March 3 came after a two-week assault on Tobago by a French naval and land force at Rockley Bay, where the Dutch fleet lay at anchor. The French squadron of 15 men-of-war tried to force the bay and destroy the Dutch, but ultimately retreated after the loss of four ships. The cost to the Dutch was high, with eight men-of-war lost along with three transport ships in which the island's women, children, and slaves had been evacuated. France ultimately prevailed, taking Tobago, and ended Dutch colonial, economic, and military ambitions in the Caribbean.

In the 1990s, a survey of an area where modern port expansion had hit discovered the buried remains of shipwrecks. Archaeologists from the *Mary Rose* Trust and the Nautical Archaeology Society excavated and documented one of the wrecks in 2000 in the face of ongoing erosion and probable destruction as cruise ship propeller blast washed over the sift mud that buried them. That was followed by Kroum's project in 2013–2014 with co-leads Doug Inglis and Jason Paterniti. They found more than a dozen targets, investigating three of them as well as previously located sites. One of them is the wreck of a warship marked by 18-pdr. cannon.

While the latest team found that most of the wrecks encountered date to a century or so after the battle, and are associated with the island's subsequent colonial history, the 18-pdr. wreck may be the 1653-built 56-six gun Dutch man-of-war *Huis te Kruiningen*, a veteran of earlier battles lost on March 3 in the battle of Rockley Bay. The government of Tobago announced the discovery in November 2014. The discovery is significant, as an obscure and yet historically significant naval battle for control in the Caribbean, as an engagement of importance in the development of Tobago, and because the likely *Huis te Kruiningen* wreck is a rare source of detailed information on the construction and fitting of a Dutch man-of-war of the age, something poorly documented in the historical record. That's amazing when we consider that these huge floating wooden fortresses were as technologically advanced and as important as an intercontinental ballistic missile is in our times.

BRITAIN VS. FRANCE

Conflicts in Europe also extended to North America, where by the 18th century the principal colonial powers contending with one another were Britain, France, and Spain. Russia extended its colonial ambitions to the New World in the North Pacific in the mid-18th century, but the tsar's possessions were a concern only for a weak Spain, which belatedly extended its own colonies up the Pacific Coast in the late 18th century in response to Russia. The principal contest in the Americas centered on conflict between Britain and France. The battleground was the northeastern end of the continent, both on the coast of New England, Nova Scotia, and Newfoundland, as well as the reaches of the St. Lawrence and the waterways that ran between Quebec and New England such as Lake Champlain.

Four major conflicts raged between France and Britain in the eight decades between 1690 and 1760. The first, known as King William's War (1690–1697), was followed in 1702 by Queen Anne's War (known in Europe as the War of the Spanish Succession). The next, King George's War (the War of the Austrian Succession in Europe), erupted in 1744 and ended in 1748. The final conflict, the French and Indian War (known in Europe as the Seven Years' War) began in North America in 1756 and spread to Europe. It ended in North America in 1760 with the British conquest of New France, although hostilities did not formally conclude until 1763 and the signing of the Treaty of Paris.

THE LOST WRECK OF *ELIZABETH AND MARY*

England's struggle with France left a rich underwater archaeological legacy in Canada and the northeastern United States. The earliest wreck associated with one of America's colonial wars is the ship at L'Anse aux Bouleaux on the north shore of the Gulf of St. Lawrence. A local diver, Marc Tremblay, discovered the wreck in December 1994 as he was pulling in the mooring lines for his boat. The wreck, lying just in front of Tremblay's cottage, was in less than two meters of water and had probably been exposed by winter storms that stripped away sand to reveal timbers and artifacts in a small area. Tremblay reported his discovery to Parks Canada and worked with archaeologist Marc-Andre Bernier. Over the next three years, the team completely excavated the wreck and identified it as the merchant bark *Elizabeth and Mary*, lost in 1690 while retreating from a failed siege of Quebec.

In 1689, as war raged in Europe between France and England, British colonists in New England were alarmed to learn of French plans to invade from Canada and seize New York. The French plans called for a naval push down Champlain and the Hudson River. The plan was formulated, notes archaeologist and historian Kevin J. Crisman, by government officials in Paris "who had no appreciation of the difficulties of logistics and warfare in the wilderness." Instead of following the plan, the governor of New France instigated a guerrilla war, with attacks by French troops and their Indian allies against isolated outposts, farms, and towns on the frontier. The war that followed was known as "King William's War" in America. The British colonists raised troops and prepared to strike back with two invasions, one by way of Lake Champlain, the other by sea and down the St. Lawrence to strike at Quebec, the heart of New France.

The Champlain invasion stalled for lack of boats to travel up the lake, but the St. Lawrence expedition, commanded by Sir William Phips of Massachusetts, sailed from Boston in August 1689 with 34 ships and 2,200 militiamen. Phips's fleet, many of them merchant ships pressed into wartime service, anchored off Quebec City on October 16 and demanded the French surrender. The French governor-general, the Count of Frontenac, replied he would answer Phips *"par le bouche de mes canons"* (from the mouths of my cannon). Phips bombarded the city and landed troops, but Quebec held fast, and in early November Phips retreated with the winter. Four of his ships did not make it home, wrecking along the way. While the fates and general locations of the lost ships were generally known, *Elizabeth and Mary* was lost without a trace with a company of militiamen from Dorchester, Massachusetts. Marc Tremblay's discovery solved a 300-year-old mystery.

While not a warship, *Elizabeth and Mary* was in use as a ship of war and the impressment of this merchant ship for naval use reflects just how much

Phips's campaign against New France was on a distant frontier, with a fleet of only six warships and more than two dozen hastily impressed merchant ships filled with citizen-soldier volunteers. The majority of artifacts excavated from the wreck are the arms of the militiamen. They include muskets, pistols, bandoliers for powder and shot, cartridge boxes, the remains of a cartridge pouch with 12 incredibly preserved paper and powder cartridges, shot, belt axes, and swords. Many of these items were personally owned, with some of them decorated with the initials of their owners. A small lead plaque on one musket, for example, marked "CT," identified it as the gun of Cornelius Tileston of the Dorchester Company.

Other artifacts recovered from the wreck also speak evocatively of the militiamen—the remains of their clothing and shoes, personal items like combs and clay pipes, as well as fish and mammal bones from the provisions that they ate. One of the most poignant personal artifacts was a small pewter porringer. The handle's decoration included three letters—"M, S and I." The initials are those of Increase and Sarah Mosley of Dorchester, and the porringer is a personal link to Increase, who carried it with him as he sailed with Phips's expedition. Increase Mosley died with his fellow militiamen when *Elizabeth and Mary* wrecked. Sarah waited patiently for news of him for 13 years, remarrying finally in 1703 when it was clear Increase would not be coming home. The wreck of *Elizabeth and Mary* is more than a look at the human face of war. It is also a reminder of how the sea swallows men and ships. Glory and conquest notwithstanding, the tiny porringer plucked from the sands of L'Anse aux Bouleaux speaks powerfully of the ultimate costs of war at sea.

SAPPHIRE

The second-oldest warship wreck in Canada is the 364-ton, fifth-rate English frigate *Sapphire*. Built in 1675, the 32-gun ship was scuttled to prevent her capture on September 11, 1696, after a squadron of nine French ships cornered her at Bay Bulls, Newfoundland. Captain Thomas Cleasby used his ship's guns to protect the settlement of Bay Bulls from the French, but outgunned and not wishing to hand his ship over to the enemy, set fire to *Sapphire* and rowed ashore. According to local tradition, a French boarding party had just gained the decks when *Sapphire* exploded and sank.

Local divers discovered the wreck in 20 meters of water in 1960, and through the years, a number of artifacts were removed from the site, including three cannon that were sold by commercial divers in 1972. The plundering of the wreck inspired other divers to form the Newfoundland Marine Archaeology Society to help preserve the site. Starting in 1973, the society surveyed the wreck, excavated a portion in 1974, and were successful in having the wreck designated a Provincial Historic Site in 1975. The society documented at least 10 cannon, wooden hull remains, and some 300 smaller artifacts, many of which were raised. *Sapphire*, like *Dartmouth* and *Anne*, provides an opportunity to study English warships of the late 17th century, just at the advent of British naval power.

BATEAUX BELOW AND THE *LAND TORTOISE*

The French and Indian War left a number of wrecks in US and Canadian waters. Many of them are located in Lake Champlain and Lake George, which lie near each other on the New York–Vermont-Quebec border. Lake Champlain in particular was one of North America's most strategic waterways, its 107-mile length and nearby waters, like the Hudson River, connecting New France with New England. Running from New York and Vermont into Quebec, the north-south axis of the lake made it a natural water highway for trade or invasion. During the French and Indian War, both sides used Champlain's waters to ferry thousands of troops. Battles to control Lake Champlain's land-locked waters resulted in a rush to build ships to control it. Once the war was over, many of the ships and boats not lost in combat were laid up in the backwaters of the lake, as well as nearby Lake George, only to slip beneath the surface and be rediscovered by archaeologists centuries later.

Fortification of Lake Champlain's shores to control the waterway proved ineffective in times of war, as troops in large numbers overwhelmed defenses to take the forts. France and Britain both used lake-built ships and boats to ferry troops and supplies and attack each other on Champlain's waters. The French schooner *Le Vigilente*, launched in 1742, was the first warship to patrol Lake Champlain, but others would soon follow.

Both sides used bateaux, which are sturdy, flat-bottomed craft averaging 10 meters in length, to conduct the first campaigns on the lake. Easy to build, bateaux carried troops and arms as easily as the heavy cargoes they transported down rivers and across the lakes during peacetime. Carpenters built hundreds of them during the French and Indian War. To safely store the boats in winter, the British sank a number of bateaux at the southern end of Lake George, where they would be safe beneath the water and ice until the next spring and the resumption of the war. A group of dozens of bateaux were never recovered—perhaps because they were sunk too deep. British military records report that hundreds of bateaux were intentionally sunk in 1758 to preserve them in the cold lake waters. Local divers rediscovered the bateaux in the 1960s, and portions of several were raised. Work on the bateaux continues to this day by a dedicated volunteer group of avocational archaeologists known as Bateaux Below, Inc. Led by Joseph Zarzynski, the Bateaux Below divers have mapped dozens of bateaux on the lakebed as well as the construction details of these once-common but until recently undocumented craft.

A far more amazing and significant discovery made by Bateaux Below, however, came in 1990 when the divers encountered a multisided wooden wreck in nearly 32 meters of water near the sunken clusters of bateaux. The oldest intact warship wreck in North America, it is also the only known example of a *radeau*, which is a floating, self-propelled gun platform. Shipwright Samuel Cobb of Maine built two *radeau* on Lake George in 1758 to assist a planned British assault on Fort Ticonderoga. Launched in October, the *radeau* were apparently scuttled for the winter along with the bateaux fleet. If dozens of bateaux were sunk too deep, so too was one of the *radeau*, a vessel named *Land Tortoise*. Never mentioned again by the British, it was this stocky gun ship that the divers encountered in 1990.

Other than a sketch in a journal kept by a Connecticut militia colonel and a brief note of *Land Tortoise*'s dimensions, no documentation of this unique colonial warship has surfaced. But the intact, well-preserved wreck, still solid after two and a half centuries in Lake George's cold, fresh water, has yielded its secrets. Seven-sided with a pointed bow and more blunted stern, *Land Tortoise* is essentially a flat-bottomed barge with sloping sides forming a floating casemate for seven cannon. The dimensions of the actual craft, recorded underwater, are a close match to the historical description at 15.85 by 5.9 meters.

Large, curved, wooden frames and stanchions support the wooden walls, and while the construction is crude, it is solidly held together with hand-forged iron nails and wooden treenails. But if the crudeness of the construction indicates haste, the layout of the *radeau* reflects the skill of the shipwright and the military engineers who helped design it. The gun ports are asymmetrical with three on the starboard and four on the port side. This staggered the cannon and allowed the crew to work their guns without interfering with one another. This also kept the guns from hitting one another while they recoiled when fired. There are also two view ports on the upper slope of the bow, on each side, allowing an observer to steer the ship without exposing himself to enemy fire.

While the divers discovered the steps for two masts in the lower hull, sailing *Land Tortoise* would be impractical. The Bateaux Below crew documented the holes for 26 oars, or sweeps. Protected by the sides from gunfire, the crew of the *radeau* could slowly maneuver their clumsy craft into position. The *Land Tortoise* provides a rare look at a unique colonial warship. Its discovery and documentation by Bateaux Below is another example of the significant contributions volunteers make to maritime archaeology.

BOSCAWEN

Another group of avocational archaeologists ultimately transformed their hobby into their profession, forming the Champlain Maritime Society and founding the Lake Champlain Maritime Museum. They are now the leading practitioners of archaeology in Lake Champlain, surveying shipwrecks, excavating some, and sharing the artifacts and information they scientifically recover from the lake with the public through the exhibitions, programs, and publications of the museum.

In 1983, the Champlain Maritime Society, the Fort Ticonderoga Association, and the Vermont Division for Historic Preservation sponsored an underwater survey that discovered the remains of three abandoned warships off the shores of Fort Ticonderoga. One of the wrecks proved to be the 16-gun British sloop *Boscawen.* Under the supervision of archaeologists Art Cohn and Kevin Crisman, the two-year excavation of *Boscawen* between 1984 and 1985 revealed a small hull that they called an "incredibly crowded" ship with all of its 180-man crew aboard. Built quickly to meet the needs of a military crisis, much like *Land Tortoise*, *Boscawen*'s excavated hull showed that it was framed and planked simultaneously, with a few "guide frames" fastened in place to allow the shipwrights to attach the planking before the rest of the frames were added.

Other evidence of hasty construction included lower deck beams made from white pine logs. Rather than remove the bark and make the logs into square timbers, the shipbuilders fitted them in place and adzed the top to make a flat surface to attach the deck timbers. *Boscawen* was also launched with wood chips, sawdust, and construction debris choking the spaces between the frames. Ordinarily kept clear in ships, these spaces fill with water as a ship is worked, but the unimpeded flow of the water allows the pumps to get at it and keep the bilges dry. *Boscawen*'s clogged spaces meant the ship always sailed with "a foot or more of stagnant water in its bilges."

The sodden mess of the bilges, filled with what Crisman describes as "untidy heaps of wooden sticks and fragments, broken glass, scrap metal, food remains, charcoal, ballast stones and straw" was a nasty place and an archaeological treasure trove. Lost tools, equipment, ordnance stores, gaming pieces for the crew's recreation, buttons, and numerous parts of muskets and small arms, lost in the bilges, revealed much about life and fighting aboard *Boscawen*. Even the discarded food in bilges showed that the sailors "supplemented their monotonous army diet with local wild foods" including deer, wild fowl, wild plums, grapes, and nuts. But the compelling message of the wreck of *Boscawen* was that this hastily built warship was not intended to last and was not well maintained after its brief but important service in seizing the lake from the French. Within a year of victory, the stripped-down hulk was left to rot and sink, only to be rediscovered two centuries later. The discarded *Boscawen* is now the earliest known warship wreck excavated in America.

THE WRECKS OF LOUISBOURG

France formally established New France in 1608 with the founding of the settlement of Quebec on the St. Lawrence River. The St. Lawrence was an ideal water highway for seagoing trade to connect Europe with the rich fur-bearing regions of Canada, particularly the Great Lakes. The river's run to the sea, through the Gulf of St. Lawrence, passed the large offshore islands of Newfoundland, Cape Breton, and Nova Scotia before encountering the open Atlantic. It was on these approaches to Quebec that France also established colonies, notably Acadia (now Nova Scotia). And it was on these shores that Britain and France clashed during their wars. Phips sacked Port Royal, Acadia, easily reached by New England ships, in 1690 before his ill-fated expedition to Quebec. It fell again, this time permanently, to the British in 1710. With their command of the sea the British maintained some level of control over Acadia even though another naval expedition to Quebec, this one in 1711, also ended in failure. With the end of Queen Anne's War in 1713, Britain retained Acadia and Newfoundland under the terms of the Treaty of Utrecht.

To counter the British presence at the gateway to the St. Lawrence, the French established a colony, Louisbourg, at the eastern tip of Cape Breton Island. In 1720, the French began work on a massive fortification at Louisbourg, making it a prime target for British and colonial forces. The outbreak of King George's War in 1744 and a provocative French raid on the Nova Scotian fishing village of Canso led to a British invasion in mid-1745 that captured Louisbourg. French reinforcements and supplies were blocked at sea by the superior Royal Navy, which also thwarted two French expeditions that sought to retake the fortress in 1746 and 1747. France finally regained Louisbourg in 1748 under the terms of the Treaty of Aix-la Chapelle, which ended the war.

Britain established a colony, fortress, and dockyard at Halifax, Nova Scotia, in 1749 to meet the continued threat of Louisbourg. In 1755, when war with France resumed, the fortress remained untouched for three years, as French troops defeated various thrusts by land and water. It was not until 1758 that the power of the Royal Navy again began to cut off supplies and troops to New France. A huge force of ships and men descended on Louisbourg in July 1758, and with overwhelming force destroyed or captured a fleet of 12 French ships anchored there before besieging the fortress. The French sank six ships at the harbor entrance to keep the British out, but the Royal Navy stood off and rained mortar shells into the anchorage, setting three of the trapped ships on fire. On the evening of July 25, British sailors and marines in small boats swept past the sunken hulks and captured two ships, burning one, *Le Prudent*, when it went aground, but keeping possession of the other ship, *Bienfaisant*. Only one French ship managed to escape the conflagration and capture. The destruction of the French fleet and the fall of Louisbourg, notes archaeologist Kevin Crisman, "effectively ended French sea power in North America."

A British officer described the scene as the Royal Navy took possession of Louisbourg:

> Indeed when our ships came into the Harbour, there was hardly any part of it, which had not the appearance of Distress and Desolation, and presented our View frequent Pieces of Wrecks, and Remnants of Destruction—Five or Six Ships sunk in one Place with their Mast-Heads peeping out of the Water—the Stranded Hull of *Le Prudent* on the muddy shoal of the other Side, burned down to the Water's Edge, with a great deal of her Iron and Guns staring us in the Face…the whole a dismal Scene of total Destruction.

The fall of Louisbourg was followed, in 1759, by the British capture of Quebec and victories on the Great Lakes and Lake Champlain. Final victory was not yet in hand, and would not come for another year.

In 1960, the bicentennial year of the end of the French and Indian War, the Canadian government began an intensive program of archaeology and architectural reconstruction to resurrect Louisbourg, which the victorious British had razed to the ground. As part of the program, archaeologists from Acadia University surveyed the waters of Louisbourg Harbor and eight 18th-century wrecks. Since then, archaeologists from Parks Canada have surveyed four of the wrecks and mapped two of them in detail. They include the burned-out hulk of *Le Prudent* in just five meters of water. The floor timbers of the hull of the 74-gun warship are exposed on the bottom, as is a large mass of round shot once stored around the ship's mainmast and now solidly concreted together. Fragments of iron cannon, shattered by the heat of the fire that destroyed the ship, are scattered around the wreck along with shot.

Another wreck surveyed by the Parks Canada team is the 64-gun *Celebre*, burned and sunk on July 21, 1758, during the bombardment of the harbor. Lying in seven meters of water, this wreck has a well-preserved bottom, with several construction features like its pump wells and mast steps also preserved. Like the wreck site of its contemporary, *Invincible*, the wreck of *Celebre* also features the French shipbuilding innovation of iron reinforcement. The site is also marked by large numbers of artifacts, including 33 iron guns and the broken remains of four other cannon. Two other wrecks, *Entreprenant* and *Capricieux*, were also studied. Largely buried by sand in an exposed position in just four meters of water, they join the other two lost French warships as physical reminders of the final British naval assault on Louisbourg.

MACHAULT

The end of New France came in 1760. Following the fall of Louisbourg and Quebec, only Montreal and a portion of the St. Lawrence remained in French hands. With supplies running low, a desperate expedition sailed from Bordeaux with arms and supplies in six ships. Only three ships, the flagship *Machault*, *Bienfaisant*, and *Marquis de Malauze* reached the Gulf of St. Lawrence. Unable to reach Montreal because a British fleet was ahead of them on the St. Lawrence River, the French anchored in the Bay of Chaleur at the mouth of the Restigouche River, south of the St. Lawrence's mouth. Learning of their arrival, the British sent a five-ship flotilla to capture the French ships. Two weeks of maneuvering and fighting finally ended when the crews of *Machault* and *Bienfaisant* burned their ships. Afloat and abandoned, *Marquis de Malauze* met the same fate when a British crew boarded and set her on fire.

Parks Canada archaeologists searched for the three wrecks between 1967 and 1969, and located them all before selecting *Machault* for excavation. The Parks Canada archaeologists, under the direction of Walter Zacharchuk, began work on the wreck in 1969. When the project ended in 1974, thousands of artifacts and portions of the hull had come to the surface, revealing much about the ship and its contents. The artifacts included three iron 12-livre cannon, a small antipersonnel swivel gun for use on the deck or in the "fighting top" of a mast, varieties of shot, hand grenades, iron mortar shells (not part of this ship's armament, these were doubtless intended for other ships or for service ashore), and some of the ship's arms for in-close fighting on the decks. They include two pistols with "Le Machault" engraved on their wooden stocks, muskets, iron boarding axes, and cutlasses.

Many personal items, shipboard fittings and rigging, and trade goods were found, including Chinese export porcelain, an amazing discovery for a ship supposedly on a hard-pressed relief mission. The Parks Canada archaeologists believe that some enterprising soul aboard *Machault* was gambling on a highly profitable sale of the goods to a blockaded Montreal merchant and had quietly stowed them away. One other find of interest was two British 12-pdr. cannonballs, prominently marked with the broad arrow of the Royal Navy.

The archaeologists think that these balls may have been fired into *Machault* as it grappled with the British ships, lodging in the hull and going down with the ship as she sank. The failure of *Machault* and the French relief effort at the Battle of the Restigouche was one of several final, fatal blows to New France. On September 8, 1760, the governor-general surrendered Montreal and the rest of the colony he still had control of to the British, ending three centuries of French rule in Canada.

THE AMERICAN REVOLUTIONARY WAR

The American Revolutionary War of 1775–1781 is largely known to most Americans as a war defined by struggles on land at Lexington and Concord, Valley Forge, Saratoga, Camden, and Cowpens, to name a few. It was also a war in which Britain came to fight by sea, shipping in troops and arms, and used its fleet to blockade and seize American colonial ports. Britain's colonial rivals, notably France, Spain, and Holland, all took part, overtly and covertly, to aid the American cause. France formally recognized the government of the United States and waged war on Britain; Spain provided covert support and supplies, then joined the French in a siege of the British fortress of Gibraltar, and finally marched into Louisiana and West Florida to take strategic ports, including New Orleans.

There were naval and land battles in the Caribbean as part of the proxy war. The greatest naval victory of the conflict was the interception, defeat, and capture of a British convoy of ships bound to the West Indies in September 1778 by a Franco-Spanish fleet that took 52 British merchant ships loaded with tens of thousands of muskets, supplies for troops, and 294 cannon. Meanwhile, Dutch merchants in the islands sent supplies and arms in their ships to American ports. Without international, naval, and maritime support from Britain's rivals, the American colonies might not have won their independence.

It was the war that created the US Navy and Marine Corps and launched a dedicated fleet of American privateers who attacked British maritime commerce. The Continental Navy, formed to also wage a war against commerce, and not necessarily battle the ships of the superior Royal Navy, nonetheless fought valiantly, albeit losing the frigates built for the American cause. With French support, and ships, American captains, and crews sortied from French ports to attack British shipping, the most famous being John Paul Jones, who made naval history with the former French merchantman *Duc de Duras*, renamed *Bonhomme Richard* in his daring attacks on ships with a joint American-French squadron in 1779.

In the climactic battle of that sortie, off Flamborough Head, on September 23, 1779, Jones's ships were engaged by the British HMS *Serapis* and the armed HM *Countess of Scarborough*. Jones alone engaged *Serapis* with *Bonhomme Richard* in an epic sea fight. At the height of battle, the badly damaged *Bonhomme Richard*, close to *Serapis* and with many of the crew dead and wounded and a number of the guns out of action, was hailed by *Serapis's* captain, who asked if Jones surrendered. "Sir," replied Jones, "I have not yet begun to fight!" Ultimately, the captain of *Serapis* was the one to surrender. While *Serapis* outgunned *Bonhomme Richard*, and was more maneuverable, Jones grappled *Serapis* and tied his wounded vessel to the British ship, negating *Serapis's* advantage. Jones transferred his flag to the captured British ship.

A number of searches for *Bonhomme Richard* have been mounted by colleagues and friends off the English coast, but to date, despite exhaustive and careful research, meticulous survey, and numerous dives on probable targets on a seabed marked by centuries of wrecks, the site remains elusive. It will be found. As for *Serapis*, Jones handed it over to the French, and while in their service as a privateer, it was lost in an accidental fire off Madagascar in July 1781. Rediscovered in November 1999, it has been periodically studied ever since.

THE AMERICAN REVOLUTION ON LAKE CHAMPLAIN

The ultimate British triumph in North America in 1760 was followed within decades by the American Revolution, in which France achieved a measure of revenge by using its navy to support the rebellious English colonies in their successful quest for independence. French warships returned to American waters to fight the Royal Navy. At the same time, the new nation of the United States took to the sea to fight for its independence and for the right to trade on the high seas.

When Britain's American colonies rose up in revolt in 1775, the power of the Royal Navy was seemingly absolute. Britannia ruled the waves, and control of the seas and a blockade of the American coast ensured the isolation of the rebellious colonists and the confinement of the war to skirmishes and battles on the land. France aided the colonial cause, and battles on the sea in favor of American independence were therefore between the French and the British. As a weak, new power, the United States could not hope to build a fleet capable of joining the conflict as an equal. But the United States did take its war to sea, outfitting armed merchant ships as privateers to prey on British merchant shipping. It also hastily built fleets of small warships for fights on the inland waters, particularly Lake Champlain, once again a strategic waterway.

American forces seized the lake in 1775 and used it as a highway to raid British-held Canada. The promise of British retaliation led American forces, under the command of General Benedict Arnold, to prepare for a naval assault by hastily building a fleet of vessels to keep Champlain in American hands. Arnold's fleet included a new design: a flat-bottomed gunboat. In the summer of 1776, shipwrights assembled eight gondolas and other craft. While under the command of the Continental Army of the United States, the Lake Champlain squadron of 15 vessels was the first American navy.

The two naval forces met in battle on Lake Champlain for the first time on October 11, 1776. Arnold's small squadron went into battle with soldiers joining the ship's crews because there were not enough sailors. The British, with a larger force of 29 vessels, sank two of Arnold's fleet—the schooner *Royal Savage* and the gunboat *Philadelphia*. Arnold was able to withdraw from the action, but on October 13 the British caught up with him and destroyed most of Arnold's remaining ships. Only four of the American ships escaped. By November 2, 1776, though, the British fleet withdrew to the northern end of the lake for the winter, giving the Americans time to build up their forces. The delay caused by the Lake Champlain campaign kept the British from linking their troops in Canada with troops in New England. In October 1777, the Continental Army defeated unreinforced British troops at Saratoga, New York. The American victory was a deciding factor in France's decision to support the United States's bid for independence, and for France's navy to take to the seas in support of the Americans.

In 1935, diver and salvage engineer Colonel Lorenzo F. Hagglund of New York rediscovered the wreck of Arnold's gunboat *Philadelphia* in 17 meters

■ *Philadelphia* being raised. (Naval History and Heritage Command)

of water off Valcour Island. The cold, fresh waters of Lake Champlain had preserved the completely intact ship. Hagglund simply patched a hole in the bow where a British 24-pdr. had punched through, pumped out the water, and raised *Philadelphia*. The colonel toured Lake Champlain with the wreck on a barge, charging tourists to visit the oldest American warship. After his death, Hagglund's heirs donated *Philadelphia* to the Smithsonian Institution in 1961.

Archaeologists and historians have carefully studied *Philadelphia* and drawn detailed plans. Originally built without plans by shipwrights who followed Arnold's basic instructions, the gunboats were based on flat-bottomed cargo-carrying boats from New England known as "gondolas." The construction of *Philadelphia* used heavier, stronger timbers to support the weight of a 24-pdr. cannon at the bow and eight ¾-pdr. swivel guns mounted on the gunwales. The wreck demonstrates the resourcefulness as well as some of the desperation of the American cause. Cannon were in

■ *Philadelphia* on display in the Smithsonian Institution's National Museum of American History. (Laura A. Macaluso, PhD/Wikimedia Commons)

short supply, and so the 24-pdr. at the bow was discovered to be a Swedish-manufactured gun about 100 years older than the ship. Paint was in short supply, so *Philadelphia*'s builders coated the gunboat with tar instead.

A single mast carried two square sails, but to manuever the gunboat in action, the crew used 14 sweeps, or oars. In battle, the gunboats had to come in close to the enemy, and hand-to-hand fighting, not heavy gun action, defined the American tactics. The swivel guns were anti-personnel weapons, and when Hagglund raised the wreck, he found army muskets—with bayonets, balls, and buckshot—ready for use by the soldier crew. Sitting on deck, the crew were "protected" only by bundles of saplings and twigs known as fascines. The fascines and wooden hull were little protection, and before *Philadelphia* could close to fight, a British 24-pdr. cannonball sank it. Hagglund discovered the fatal cannonball still lodged in the broken timbers of *Philadelphia*'s bow.

In 1997, archaeologists from the Lake Champlain Maritime Museum, as part of a comprehensive underwater survey of the lake, discovered the remains of another gunboat, *Spitfire*, in 122 meters of water. The gunboat lies upright and intact in the mud bottom. The bow gun remains in place, mounted on its carriage, and the mast rises toward the surface, almost as if *Spitfire* sat down not long ago, as opposed to the nearly two and a half centuries since it sank. In the summer of 2017, the Lake Champlain Maritime Museum announced plans to raise the funds to recover *Spitfire* and preserve it after a careful archaeological investigation. All told, from beginning to end, the project will last some two decades. Nearly identical to *Philadelphia*, *Spitfire* is another incredible legacy from the beginnings of America's navy, and a desperate fight to control a strategic waterway. The sunken ships also recall a tactical defeat for the Americans that bought time for a more strategic victory on a distant battlefield.

DEFENCE

Another sunken warship recalls a more disastrous defeat, when the United States lost 30 ships during the Penobscot Expedition on the coast of Maine. The destruction of that fleet was one of the greatest naval disasters in US history. The Penobscot Expedition's 37 to 41 ships sailed from Boston in 1779 with some 2,000 troops to drive out a British force that had come out of Halifax to occupy the Maine coast and control the Penobscot River. The force that sailed from Boston was the largest American naval expedition of the Revolution. It faced a smaller British force, protected only by three warships. But six large British warships, easily outgunning the smaller American transports and gunboats, were on their way.

The Penobscot Expedition landed and dug in; had the troops pressed their advantage they could have won, but instead they waited for the British reinforcements to arrive and retreated in the face of the enemy's superior strength. Blockaded in Penobscot Bay by the British ships, the American fleet could not retreat down the coast. Running up the Penobscot River, the fleet was pursued by the British. Trapped, the American commanders decided to scuttle their ships to keep them out of British hands. Most of the ships, on fire, sank before the British could capture them. The small brig *Defence*, one of the last left afloat and uncaptured, was chased into Stockton Harbor. The crew set *Defence* on fire and rowed to shore. As the British closed in, *Defence* blew up and sank.

Since 1779, periodic dredging of the Penobscot has yielded cannon and fragments of the lost fleet. In 1972, a detailed survey of the area by students and faculty from the Maine Maritime Academy revealed the remains of *Defence* in eight meters of water. Excavation of the wreck began in 1975 under the auspices of the Institute of Nautical Archaeology, the Maine Maritime Academy, and the Maine State Museum. Five years of excavation seasons, under the direction of archaeologist David Switzer, revealed a well-preserved wreck and artifacts beneath the mud of the Penobscot.

The crew of *Defence* set the fire to scuttle the ship at the stern, where the ship's powder magazine was located. Before the flames swept through the ship, the magazine exploded, sinking *Defence*. The blast damage was enough to tear out the sternpost and several frames, as well as crack the keelson, but *Defence*, thankfully for future archaeologists, had not been blown apart. The results, when the ship's interior was carefully excavated, were a detailed look at the ship's fittings, furnishings, and equipment, most of them lying in close proximity to where they had been used aboard. The finds included the gear and tools of the bosun, ship's carpenter, the gunner, and the sailors in the crew. The highly regimented life of the "wooden walls" of the large ships of the line was duplicated, in a smaller scale, as shown by the recovery of the crew's mess kits near the galley.

To organize and feed a large number of people quickly, warships separated the men into "messes" of eight men. Like the larger ships of the time, *Defence* was also organized into messes. The discovery of 16 carved wooden tags at first mystified the archaeologists until they realized these tags were "markers" placed with cuts of salted meat. Sailors ate salted pork or beef packed in barrels—a number were discovered, bones still inside them, as work progressed on *Defence*. One member of each mess would approach the pork or beef barrel as the cook doled out a portion, receive the "whack" for his mess mates, and mark it with the wooden tag engraved with their mess number. The mess then retrieved their boiled meat, with the tag, at mealtime. Spoons, mess kits, pewter plates, and ceramic mugs—some of them marked with the initials of the crew—were also excavated. The initials on the items marked them as personal property, not ship's issue. The days of a navy issuing mess gear or bedding was still far off, and a sailor was responsible for his own "kit," whether on a man-of-war or a merchantman.

The Revolutionary War "time capsule" also included shoes, belt buckles, and clothes. None of the crew wore naval uniforms, a practice that had not yet come into use, but a small button, marked "USA," came from a soldier's uniform. The button may be a clue that soldiers were used to fill out the crews of the Penobscot fleet, or that a sailor was wearing a discarded or otherwise acquired army uniform item. The button may have also been a souvenir kept by one of the sailors. A range of ordnance, including grape- and canister shot, round shot, and the gunner's equipment was recovered, but the ship's 16 6-pdr. cannon were not. Probing the mud outside the hull revealed that some of the guns were buried there after falling off the wreck, but the archaeologists did not excavate outside the hull for fear of collapsing *Defence*'s hull once the mud cradling it was removed.

But the excavation of *Defence* did completely clear the interior of the hull. The relatively small, 33-meter-long *Defence* was crowded with equipment, guns, and a 100-man crew that ate and slept in a tight amidships section. And yet this crowded, small warship was able to work effectively, leading historian John Sands to reflect that she was in all "a remarkably complex machine." *Defence* was also not a slow, crudely built ship. The remains of the hull showed that *Defence* was built quickly, with a few shortcuts, like a roughly shaped crutch hacked from the trunk of a large oak and placed at the bow with two lopped-off branches still attached to the trunk to reinforce the ship's stem.

The shortcuts could not disguise the sharp lines of the hull, with a *v*-shaped form and a sharp bow. Too small and outgunned by larger British ships, *Defence* was a precursor to the later "clipper"-formed merchant and warships built in the United States in the 19th century. Built to outrun a larger, heavier ship, *Defence* was better suited to attack the unprotected merchant ships of an enemy. Trapped with no place to run, and up against a superior force, all *Defence*'s crew could do was send their ship to the bottom, denying its fast hull and arms to the British.

YORKTOWN

The last major land battle of the Revolutionary War took place in September–October 1781 at Yorktown, Virginia, not far from where English colonists set foot ashore to establish the first permanent English settlement in the Americas at Jamestown in 1607. The British Army, under the command of General Charles Cornwallis, was bivouacked in Virginia and building a naval base where the British fleet, then in New York, could winter in a once-free port. Situated on the York, a branch of the James River, Yorktown sat on bluffs overlooking the river, with a commanding position that could be fortified. Cornwallis and his troops, already based in Virginia, had waged the British Army's southern campaign throughout 1780 and into the fall of 1781. Under the banks of the river, a fleet of more than 60 supply and transport ships and armed men-of-war—including the 44-gun HMS *Charon*, the 28-gun HMS *Guadeloupe*, and the 24-gun HMS *Fowey*—assembled, while Cornwallis's troops built a fortified enclosure of trenches and earthwork redoubts to protect from an attack by land.

The Americans with their French allies decided to besiege Cornwallis's forces both by land and sea, with a French fleet under the command of the Comte de Grasse heading to the Capes of Virginia to both blockade Cornwallis's position and prevent either escape or support by sea. The siege by land, bombardment, and the storming of defensive redoubts, as well as the end of any hope of reinforcement led Cornwallis to surrender his force of several thousand on October 19, 1781. Cornwallis's defeat brought the British to the negotiating table, and with the Treaty of Paris of 1783, formally ended the war and recognized American independence. Those basic facts should be known to every student of American history. What is less known is the naval side of the final campaign and the naval archaeology of Yorktown.

George Washington knew the importance of naval support, stating that "no land force can act decisively unless it is accompanied by maritime superiority." The French West Indies Fleet, under the command of the Comte de Grasse, gave the Americans and French land forces at Yorktown that superiority. De Grasse's fleet of 37 ships bypassed British naval forces in the West Indies and delivered funds, supplies, and French troops after arriving and mooring inside Chesapeake Bay. As news reached the British, a squadron of 19 British warships moved south to meet the French, and nearly caught them unaware. The two fleets met at sea off the Capes of Virginia, just outside the bay, and fought a heavy action that left six British ships damaged to only two of the French. After more French ships arrived, the British commander decided to withdraw, leaving Chesapeake Bay to the French, and Cornwallis and his troops isolated.

Back at Yorktown, meanwhile, Cornwallis had ordered 10 of the supply and transport ships scuttled in a line, bow to stern, with pilings driven around them to block the French fleet. While that protected Cornwallis's forces at Yorktown from an attack from the river, American and French troops on land were able to bring their guns to bear on the fleet anchored below, and hit and sank a number of the British ships, which, as one account notes, "were enwrapped in a torrent of fire." Ultimately, some 50 British ships ended up on the bottom of the river by the end of the siege and battle.

Following the centennial of the battle in 1881, interest in commemoration—and in time, preservation—of the battlefield led to the inclusion of Yorktown in a Colonial National Monument, later designated a National Historical Park, in 1930. The park includes Jamestown, Yorktown, and other historic sites in the area, linked by a 37-kilometer-long scenic parkway. As part of the establishment of the park, the National Park Service embarked on what is now a several-decades-old park archaeology program on the battlefield. One aspect of that was a 1934–1935 project in the York River, in partnership with the Mariners' Museum, to locate the sunken Cornwallis fleet. Several sites were located, and hardhat divers recovered hundreds of artifacts, but it was not archaeology.

Among the wrecks encountered and salvaged from was HMS *Charon*. The 44-gun frigate was relatively new—it was only four years old—when American and French bombardment set it on fire. Burning to the waterline, it sank with great loss of life. While it cannot be said, at least with certainty, how many of the artifacts are from *Charon*, the National Park Service displays a number of naval artifacts in a partial replica of Charon at the Yorktown visitor center. In the 1970s, the approaching American Revolution Bicentennial renewed interest in locating, preserving, and studying the sunken fleet. That led to volunteers and graduate students from Texas A&M University's Nautical Archaeology Program and its affiliated Institute of Nautical Archaeology (INA) conducting surveys and test excavations in the river starting in 1976. In 1980, the Texas A&M and INA team relocated *Charon*, exposing the lower hull and matching it to the frigate's surviving plans.

By 1980, surveys of the river had located nine 1781 wrecks in the river, including the probable site of HMS *Fowey*. That in turn led to a multi-year project to completely excavate the most intact wreck, known by its official state archaeological registration number, 44YO88. One of the largest, most complex, and important American shipwreck excavations of the 20th century, the Yorktown Project, led by archaeologist John D. Broadwater, worked inside a specially constructed cofferdam that surrounded it and allowed the archaeologists to work on the wreck without having to fight the current. The cofferdam, constructed of steel sheet piles driven around the well-preserved hull, shielded divers from current and stinging jellyfish, and a water filtration system cleared the otherwise muddy river water to allow archaeologists to actually see what they were excavating.

I was able to dive on the wreck in 1985. As you dropped into the cofferdam, the water, stained to the color of lightly steeped tea, was clear enough so that with your lights on, you could look from above and at a distance at the exposed wooden sides that curved up from the keel to form the tub-like hull. While that was fascinating, the wreck proved to be a veritable physical "treatise" on 18th-century naval architecture, it was what was inside the wreck, sealed in the mud like the contents of a time capsule, that captivated the team excavating 44YO88.

As John Broadwater notes, the wreck contained the tumbled furniture inside the captain's cabin that swirled about and broke as the water poured in during the scuttling of the wreck, the personal possessions of the crew, and an incomplete gun carriage. The quick sinking and burial in mud also preserved the evidence of the ship's use at Yorktown. In addition to being a supply and transport ship, while anchored off Yorktown, it had served as a floating workshop for the British Army. Among the finds were barrels being rebuilt and patched, shoes being repaired, and, next to a pile of wood chips, an adze. "It seems very likely," says Broadwater, the crew "spent the time before sinking their ship fabricating fortification elements and repairing military equipment." A hole cut below the waterline, also well preserved, showed how they had scuttled the ship.

Broadwater was ultimately able to identify 44YO88 as the 1772-built British merchant brig *Betsy*, a coal transport ship used at Yorktown as a "victualler," carrying food supplies, but also a transport, bringing 100 men of the 43rd Regiment of Foot to Yorktown in July 1781. Among the finds from the excavation were five 43rd Regiment uniform buttons. Budget cuts and waning political interest ended the Yorktown Project, but Broadwater has maintained scholarly interest, as well as ongoing research, recently surveying an erosion-exposed site in the river with fellow archaeologist Gordon P. Watts that is another 1781 wreck. John is both a pioneer and an innovative thinker who stays with the times. He was one of the first maritime archaeologists in the United States to propose looking at warship sites as part of battlefields, making a brilliant point not only with the Yorktown fleet but also within the larger context of the Battle of the Virginia Capes.

THE WAR OF 1812

The wrecks of *Defence* and *Philadelphia* are the only two American warships of the Revolutionary War studied by archaeologists. They stand in sharp contrast to the numerous British warship wrecks of the period found elsewhere in the world, like *Pandora*. A small, inferior force, the American navy was an auxiliary of the Continental Army, and at best American privateers on the high seas could hope only to raid British merchant shipping while the major sea battles were fought on behalf of the United States by a vengeful French navy.

At the conclusion of the Revolutionary War, the few surviving ships of the United States's navy, mainly gunboats and schooners, were sold and their sailors sent home. But American ships were appearing on every sea, trading with other countries. The United States was a weak nation without a navy to protect it, and American ships were seized and American sailors forced to become members of the crews of British warships, or slaves of Barbary "pirates" in the Mediterranean. Almost begrudgingly, Congress voted to build a new navy in 1794. Unable to afford the costs of the 100-gun ships of the line, they opted for a number of smaller 44-gun frigates, including the famous "Old Ironsides," USS *Constitution*. These ships were to play a major role in the establishment of fledgling American sea power over the next few decades, first in a struggle with revolutionary France known as the "Quasi-War," and then again with Britain in the War of 1812.

To many, the most famous naval battles of the War of 1812 were those engagements on the open sea, particularly the exploits of "Old Ironsides." But most battles afloat during the two-year conflict were fought close to shore, particularly on the lakes. Like the French and Indian War, and the Revolutionary War, Lake Champlain and the Great Lakes were a strategic theater of war that have left a number of warship wrecks on their lakebeds. Some of the most significant underwater archaeology in North America has taken place on the lakes. But other work, particularly on the reaches of Chesapeake Bay, provides a detailed look at the amazingly unprepared navy, a victim of political whims, which nonetheless struggled against the odds against a superior navy and managed to play a role in the United States' retention of its independence.

The War of 1812 commenced in June 1812, and in the next few months, the frigates of the US Navy met and defeated British warships in single-ship actions—some of them, like the defeat of HMS *Guerriere* and HMS *Java* by USS *Constitution*, were important symbolic victories that had little strategic value. The first significant naval contest came in 1813, on the waters of Lake Erie. Lieutenant Oliver Hazard Perry took command of a nonexistent squadron in early 1813, but in short order, the hard work of a group of workers under the direction of New York shipwrights Adam and Noah Brown had hastily assembled and built a fleet of warships, including the 20-gun brigs *Lawrence* and *Niagara*.

The British and American fleets met in battle at the southern end of the lake on September 10, 1813. The fleets, more or less equally matched, fought a fierce battle with heavy casualties. Perry was forced to leave the badly damaged *Lawrence* for *Niagara*, breaking the British line with her and finally winning the battle. The entire British squadron was taken, and Perry sent a famous dispatch to his superiors, "We have met the enemy and they are ours." Lake Erie was now under American control, but adjacent Lake Ontario remained contested as both sides built ships and skirmished without any climactic battle. But the actions did result in the sinking of two ships that today are the best-preserved wrecks of the War of 1812.

HAMILTON *AND* SCOURGE

The inland naval battles of the War of 1812 were marked by an arms race in which both sides tried to put as much firepower as possible on the water. This included building warships as well as refitting merchant vessels for war. Not all of these converted "warships" were particularly effective, as the loss of two topsail schooners on Lake Ontario in 1813 demonstrates. At the outbreak of war, the British naval presence on the lake was larger than that of the United States. The 16-gun brig USS *Oneida* was the only American warship, countered by Britain's 22-gun ship *Royal George* and as many as five smaller warships. After a thwarted British attack on the US base at Sackets Harbor, New York, the American commander, Captain Isaac Chauncey, assembled a larger fleet of merchant schooners, and in November 1812 launched a 20-gun ship, *Madison*. By 1813, Chauncey had added two more warships, the 24-gun *General Pike* and the 16-gun schooner *Sylph*, as well as a fast dispatch schooner. The British met the challenge by building two 24-gun ships.

Archaeologist Kevin Crisman, the pre-eminent authority on the shipwrecks of the War of 1812, points out that the two sides exchanged long-range cannon fire and skirmished without much result, both of them "reluctant to risk a full-scale battle unless victory was absolutely assured." Chauncey was worried about the performance of his squadron, for although he had twice as many ships as his British counterpart, "the unequal sailing qualities" of the custom-built warships stood in sharp contrast to the armed schooners. It was a "very clumsy squadron under sail." It was also a risk for some of the ships to sail at all. The schooners *Hamilton* and *Scourge*, one an American-built vessel, the other a seized British trader, had been armed by Chauncey to build up his forces in 1812. *Hamilton* was 22 meters long, with a beam of 6.7 meters, while *Scourge* was smaller at 18 meters by six meters. Each of the two-masted topsail schooners was fitted with cannon, *Hamilton* with 10 and *Scourge* with eight guns. The additional weight of the guns made each ship dangerously unstable.

Ned Myers, a crewmember aboard *Scourge*, reported, "This craft was unfit for her duty, but time pressed, and no better offered. The bulwarks had been raised on her, and she mounted eight sixes [guns], in regular broadside." As well, Myers complained, the "accommodations were bad enough, and she was so tender that we could do little or nothing with her in a blow. It was often prognosticated that she would prove our coffin." Myers's prediction came true on the evening of August 8, 1813. The two squadrons had skirmished without effect on the seventh, and each stood off for the evening. A storm came up suddenly and the top-heavy schooners capsized, sinking within minutes. Ned Myers later wrote that as the ship rolled, he sprang to save himself:

The flashes of lightning were incessant, and nearly blinded me. Our decks seemed on fire, and yet I could see nothing. I heard no hail, no order, no call; but the schooner was filled with the shrieks and cries of the men to leeward, who were lying jammed under the guns, shot-boxes, shot and other heavy things that had gone down as the vessel fell over. The starboard second gun, from forward, had capsized, and come down directly over the hatch, and I caught a glimpse of a man struggling to get past it.

Myers made it into the water, while other men, trapped on or in the sinking *Scourge*, struggled to get free. Myers watched an officer try to wriggle out of one of the stern windows, and then the ship and the man were gone. Myers saved himself by finding the ship's boat adrift, and went on to rescue several of his shipmates. But both the top-heavy *Hamilton* and *Scourge* had gone down with most of their crews.

The intact, exceptionally well-preserved wrecks were found, close together, in 97 meters of water in 1973. A survey led by a St. Catherine's, Ontario, dentist, Dr. Daniel Nelson, and sponsored by the Royal Ontario Museum, located targets that year believed to be the ship's, and in 1975, a sonar survey revealed the ghost-like image of the intact *Hamilton* on the lake bed. Since then, surveys of the wrecks by Jacques Cousteau in 1980, the National Geographic Society with archaeologists Kenneth Cassavoy and Kevin Crisman in 1982, and a 1990 detailed mapping of both ships by a team led by Dr. Robert Ballard and Dr. Anna Marguerite McCann captured incredible photographs and produced detailed site maps of *Hamilton* and *Scourge* as they lie in the darkness. In 2008, another detailed survey undertaken by the Canadian Navy and the ASI Group (Ltd.) of *Hamilton*, and working under the supervision of archaeologist Jonathan Moore of Parks Canada, conducted a detailed sonar and video survey with remotely operated vehicles (ROVs) to determine the ongoing condition of the two wrecks.

The significance of *Hamilton* and *Scourge* lies entirely in their level of preservation. The 12-pdr. carronades and single long 24- or 32-pdr. on *Hamilton* and the 6- and 4-pdr. guns on *Scourge* remain on their carriages, on the decks. Lying nearby are powder ladles, rammers, and other equipment, with cutlasses and boarding pikes. The open hatches, the masts rising toward the distant surface, the unbroken glass in the stern windows, and *Hamilton's* ship's boat, still at the stern where it was suspended from davits, make the wrecks unique time capsules. It is as if the crew was standing ready to fight, although the upended guns and scattered equipment are clear evidence of each ship's roll into her grave. Archaeologists have spotted the remains of at least five of the crew, with one skeleton lying alongside *Scourge's* port side, bones tangled in rigging that dragged him down with the ship. The bodies are harsh evidence of the necessities of war compelling the US Navy to put out to fight an enemy—and the elements—with ill-suited ships.

THE CHESAPEAKE FLOTILLA

Hamilton and *Scourge* were unsuitable warships, and yet they were better equipped than the US Navy's largest group of fighting vessels: hundreds of gunboats. The result of an ill-advised naval policy of the Jefferson administration, the small, shallow-draft gunboats were constructed in large numbers to patrol and defend the coastal waterways of the United States. Jefferson, in response to increasing tensions with Britain and France, had placed an embargo on all foreign trade and virtually isolated the United States by sea. The government reasoned that without an overseas merchant trade, a large seagoing navy was not required—only sufficient numbers of gunboats to keep watch at the coast for smugglers and hostile visitors.

At the outbreak of the War of 1812, the US Navy was no match for the Royal Navy as a result of the government's emphasis on gunboats. The victories of USS *Constitution* and its sister ships were important morale boosters, but did nothing to stop the Royal Navy from blockading the American coast and landing an invading army. The "Jeffersonian Gunboats" have come down through history as an ineffective force ill-suited to the defense needs of the United States. Swept aside by the superior forces of the Royal Navy, the gunboats were unable to prevent the British from attacking coastal settlements, towns, and ports—and ultimately, from sailing up the Potomac to capture and burn the capital at Washington, DC.

The Royal Navy blockaded the entrances to Chesapeake Bay and the numerous ports and settlements in the "Tidewater" on the shores of Delaware, Maryland, and Virginia in early 1813. The British actively raided the region with impunity, inspiring a Revolutionary War veteran and hero, Joshua Barney, to petition the navy to place him in command of a defensive force of gunboats and hastily built armed barges. By the spring of 1814, Barney's "flotilla" was not yet ready, but increasing British pressure led him to attack the principal Royal Navy stronghold at Tangier Island on Chesapeake Bay. Joining forces with a gunboat squadron from Norfolk, Virginia, Barney's armed barges, along with his flagship, the sloop *Scorpion*, a row galley, and a number of merchantmen, attacked the British on May 31, 1814.

The British outgunned Barney's flotilla, and after a brisk fight, as rein-forcements arrived to crush the Americans, Barney withdrew his ships from the bay and into the Patuxent River. They would never leave. The Royal Navy blockaded the river, pushing Barney's flotilla further up into a shallow tributary, St. Leonard's Creek. Six separate British attacks, in barges and schooners, tried to destroy Barney's forces, but failed. Finally, the cornered Barney struck back in a daring raid. Coming out of the creek and into the river in the darkness of June 26, 1814, just before sunrise, Barney's ships badly damaged two British frigates before retreating again. In the retreat, two gunboats and several merchantmen were scuttled to avoid capture.

The end for Barney's flotilla finally came in August 1814 as the British pushed up the Patuxent to capture Washington, DC. Pulling back up the river as the British advanced, Barney was trapped by shallow water by the third week of August. Unable to continue upriver, and not wanting his fleet to fall into British hands, Barney ordered the barges, gunboats, schooners, and the sloop set on fire and scuttled in the river on August 22. Sixteen vessels slipped beneath the muddy waters of the Patuxent. Barney's men joined the land forces opposing the British advance. Two days later, on August 24, they were defeated at the Battle of Bladensburg, leaving Washington open. As the government fled, the triumphant forces of Admiral Sir George Cockburn put Washington to the torch. The burning of the capital did not bring surrender or the end of the war, as other important cities remained uncaptured, among them Baltimore, which held out even after a fierce bombardment of its defender, Fort McHenry, with mortar shells and rockets.

In 1978, archaeologist and historian Donald Grady Shomette, with the assistance of the Calvert Marine Museum of Solomons, Maryland, and with federal funding, began a survey of the Patuxent to locate Barney's flotilla. Years of dredging and wreck removal by the US Army Corps of Engineers to clear the river as a navigable waterway had left few traces, but in 1980, Shomette's persistence paid off with the discovery and test excavation of a wreck in the mud of the upper Patuxent. Shomette believed the wreck to be Barney's flagship, *Scorpion*. His excavation of a portion of the wreck revealed charred and scattered timbers at the bow—traces of the scuttling fire and blast that sank many of Barney's flotilla. As the digging continued, it became clear that this was indeed *Scorpion*.

Like the wreck of *Defence*, the blast damage was confined to a small area, with a thick plank bulkhead keeping the blast and fire out of the hold. As divers slowly vacuumed up the thick mud from inside a cofferdam and groped in the dark water, they discovered the surgical tools and medicines lost by the ship's doctor, Thomas Hamilton. Some of the bottles still had salves and ointment inside. Other finds included a cup with the name of the ship's cook, Ceaser Wentworth, clothing and shoes, carpenter's tools, weapons, a box of munitions, and the oars and benches the crew sat on while rowing the ship into action.

Between 2010 and 2013, a new team of archaeologists returned to the site to excavate more of *Scorpion* in time for the bicentennial of the War of 1812. Drawn from the ranks of the US Navy's Underwater Archaeology Branch, the State of Maryland's maritime archaeology program of the Maryland Historical Trust, and the Maryland State Highway Administration, they exposed more of the battered *Scorpion* and recovered more artifacts. Led by my colleagues Susan Langley, Robert Neyland, and Julie Schablitsky, the project cleared the mud into the ship's cabin, and recovered ship's stores and medical equipment. The wreck of *Scorpion* was reburied after the project. Substantially intact, it is again sealed by mud, a rare survival of the naval war of 1812 and of a brave but woefully inadequate defense against a superior naval force.

Shomette also located two buried wrecks in the mud of St. Leonard's Creek in 1996 that he believed were gunboats Number 137 and 138. Limited excavation of the wrecks began in 1997 and continued through 1999 with a diverse group of participants including Maryland state archaeologists and volunteers from the Maritime Archaeological and Historical Society, all under the direction of Shomette and archaeologist Lawrence Babits of East Carolina University. The excavation of the small vessels revealed that these small craft were nearly identical, heavily built to carry the weight of cannon, but unwieldy and slow. The excavation revealed that an extra mast was placed inside one of the gunboats, perhaps in an effort to help it speed up with the help of more sail.

There are other wrecks from the Chesapeake flotilla left to discover. They and those already discovered and excavated are more than a reminder of a desperate action to stop the British naval advance. They are tangible evidence of a misguided US naval policy that allowed the British to carry the war past the American coast and into the towns and settlements, and finally to the capital of the United States.

EAGLE

While the naval war went poorly for the United States on the mid-Atlantic coast, the US Navy was able to seize naval control of the Great Lakes and Lake Champlain. Oliver Hazard Perry's victory at the Battle of Lake Erie on September 10, 1813, is perhaps the most famous American naval engagement on inland waters, but the more significant battle in terms of ending the war was the Battle of Lake Champlain a year later on September 11, 1814.

The outbreak of the War of 1812 found Lake Champlain practically undefended, although the US Navy did maintain a negligible presence on the lake with two half-sunk, laid up gunboats. The navy sent Lieutenant Thomas Macdonough to Lake Champlain to build up a naval force in October 1812, and for the next few months Macdonough purchased and armed six merchant schooners that gave him control of the lake—for a while. In 1813, two of Macdonough's ships, *Growler* and *Eagle*, sailed into a British trap after entering the Richelieu River in pursuit of three gunboats. Well inside Canadian waters, the two vessels were surrounded by troops on the banks and started to retreat. Harassed by the gunboats, the two American ships ran low on ammunition and finally surrendered. The British repaired the damaged *Growler* and *Eagle*, and with their gunboats and a small flotilla of bateaux, descended onto Lake Champlain to wreak havoc, burning buildings and military equipment at Plattsburgh, New York, at the end of July as well as capturing several American merchant vessels.

Macdonough added two more armed merchant sloops and two gunboats to his squadron and managed to keep the British at bay for the rest of

1813. But during the winter of 1813–1814, Macdonough learned that the British were busy building a squadron of their own at Isle aux Noix, on the Richelieu River. To counter the British threat Macdonough needed to add more vessels to his own squadron. Macdonough had shipwrights built six 25-meter-long, 4.5-meter-wide row galleys with carronades at each end—and, in response to news that the British were building a warship, Macdonough also ordered a 24-gun sloop of war. Under the supervision of master shipwright Noah Brown, workers built and launched Macdonough's new vessels within an amazing 60-day period.

They also purchased an unfinished steamboat, still on the stocks in its shipyard, and completed it as the armed schooner *Ticonderoga*. This naval force was able to keep the British at their end of the lake, but by the early summer, Macdonough learned that his enemies were rushing to complete even more vessels to gain naval supremacy. The anxious lieutenant pushed his superiors for funds to build one more vessel, and with approval from President James Madison in hand, Macdonough signed a contract for the additional vessel with Noah and Adam Brown in early July. Adam Brown rushed men and supplies to Vergennes, Vermont and built the new vessel in 19 days, launching the 39-meter-long brig *Eagle* on August 11.

Eagle joined Macdonough's squadron with just enough time for two weeks of maneuvers and training, with the crew, also hastily assembled, including soldiers, convicts from an army chain gang, and army musicians. On September 11, 1814, the long-awaited British invasion swept down the lake and along its shores as ships and troops moved south. Macdonough, thanks to *Eagle*'s quick launch, was able to match the British, gun for gun. Meeting at Plattsburgh Bay, scene of the earlier successful British raid, the two fleets clashed in a bloody two-and-a-half-hour action. Macdonough and his ships won the battle, losing 52 men in the action while the British lost at least 54. Shot and splinters horribly wounded many more. All of the British warships were captured, and the troops who had followed the ships in their advance into the United States hastily retreated back into Canada.

The victory at Plattsburgh ended British plans to invade the United States from the north and left all the lakes bordering Canada with superior American naval forces. The situation was a deciding factor in Britain's agreement to end hostilities and sign the Treaty of Ghent on December 24, 1814. Under the terms of the peace, the lakes were demilitarized, and Macdonough's painstakingly assembled squadron was laid up at Whitehall, New York. The navy sold some of the converted merchant vessels and sank the six row galleys in the fresh cold water to preserve them. The remaining ships, many of them rotting and half-sunk, were finally sold in 1825 to salvagers who stripped the hulks.

Archaeologists Kevin Crisman and Art Cohn surveyed the Whitehall area in 1982, locating the remains of *Eagle*, the row galley *Allen*, the captured Royal Navy brig *Linnet* and the armed schooner *Ticonderoga*. Between 1983 and 1984, archaeological teams from the Lake Champlain Maritime Museum, working under Crisman and Cohn, excavated and studied *Eagle*. While stripped and with half of the hull surviving, *Eagle* yielded much information about its hasty construction. Built of several different types of wood, some of them amazingly soft and ill-suited, such as white pine and spruce for the frames, *Eagle* also had no reinforcing wooden or iron knees to support the decks. The deck beams were clamped between two thick timbers—a shelf of sorts—that would have allowed the beams to pull free and the decks to fail in rough seas. As Crisman has pointed out, Macdonough did not need a durable ship; he needed a platform for more guns as fast as it could hit the water. Time was of the essence, and the wreck of *Eagle* clearly shows that this imperfect warship was nonetheless completed just in time, thanks to its shortcuts, to balance the scales of naval power and win the battle.

LAS GUERRAS DE INDEPENDENCIA

The Napoleonic Wars in Europe, in particular the occupation and weakening of both the Spanish and Portuguese royal houses, had a profound effect on the American colonies of the two powers. The greatest impact was on Spain, which had dominated nearly all of South and Central America and a fair portion of North America for four centuries. The collapse of Spain's American empire was essentially, as historian Jaime Rodríguez has noted, a transatlantic Spanish civil war that took place from 1810 to 1821. The first half of that time was marked by sporadic attempts that failed, but after 1815, Spain's grip on its colonies faltered and then ended.

In some cases the loss of Spain's colonial possessions came through rebellion and war. In other cases, they were lost through peaceful means. Diplomatic negotiations between the United States and Spain added Florida to the United States in 1821 following the signing of the Adams-Onís Treaty in 1819. In 1821 came the independence of Mexico, then the Mexican Empire, and the independence of Central America, which became a united republic. Much of South America was also free. Chile had gained independence in 1818. The republic of Gran Colombia, which beginning in 1819 controlled northern South America and Panamá, won decisive battles in 1821–1822, and while smaller campaigns continued through the 1820s, by the end of that decade, Spain was left with only Cuba and Puerto Rico as its colonial holdings in the New World.

In addition to the land battles that largely defined the conflict, naval activities played a role. In the aftermath of Trafalgar, Britain had emerged as the world's greatest naval power. Historian Rafe Blaufarb notes that it was in Britain's interest to hold the Spanish world together rather than create openings that its traditional enemy, France, could exploit, and so it used the Royal Navy to enforce a "muscular Pax Britannica throughout the Atlantic world." While the British did not intervene in the Spanish conflicts, their presence prevented others, including the United States, from taking a more active role through intervention.

Britain did intervene in Brazil. The Portuguese prince regent, Dom João VI, had fled to Brazil in early 1808 following Napoleon's 1807 invasion of the Iberian Peninsula. The Portuguese government-in-exile was under the protection of Britain, which had sent an army to Portugal in August 1808. One of the means by which the crown prince thanked his protectors was to open Brazil, formerly closed to foreign trade, to the world's commerce with an imperial decree signed after arriving in Brazil. That move, long sought by British merchants seeking to build a global economy, greatly aided British trade. Over the next several years, Brazil increasingly developed, thanks to trade and the presence of the royal court and the transfer of power, from a colony into what historians have noted was a co-kingdom if not a rival of the occupied mother country, Portugal.

Following Napoleon's defeat in 1814, Dom João VI returned to Portugal, and in 1818, was crowned king. It was not an absolute rule, as royal power was limited by a sovereign assembly, the *Cortes Gerais*. What followed over the next few years, as Portugal, through the *Cortes*, strove to re-establish dominion, were moves by Brazilians for independence, leading to rebellion when the now–prince regent, Dom Pedro, who had remained in Brazil, and had defied the *Cortes*, was crowned Emperor Dom Pedro I of Brazil. What followed were a series of conflicts within Brazil, as loyal Portuguese military units fought against the new government through early 1824. Eager to maintain its trade and relationship with both governments, but with Brazil now the third-largest customer of British goods, Britain moved to enforce a peace and mediated the Treaty of Rio de Janeiro, signed in August 1825.

In the former Spanish colonies, the Spanish Royal Navy destroyed a small Argentine naval force in March 1811 at the Battle of the Río de la Plata. It was three years before Argentine patriots formed a new rebel naval force. That small navy, commanded by an expatriate Irishman, William "Guillermo" Brown, defeated the Spanish in two engagements, blockaded Montevideo, and took that Spanish naval base. That opened regional waters, and ultimately the Pacific, to naval ships and government-commissioned privateers sent out to attack Spanish merchant shipping. With assistance from newly independent Haiti, Latin American rebels fought a series of successful actions in the Caribbean, which was also the setting for privateers raiding Spanish shipping.

In the Pacific, Chilean and Peruvian independence also involved naval forces, with Chile building a navy through the acquisition of modern warships from Britain and the United States to form the *Armada de Chile*. Those forces, commanded by Lord Cochrane, a British veteran of the Royal Navy, played a key role in securing independence for both Chile and Peru in cooperation with land forces led by Jose de San Martín. After capturing all of Spain's warships off their coasts and key ports like Peru's El Callao, they were forced to fight again when resurgent Spanish naval forces retook Callao. The final major battle of the war was the Battle of Callao in October

1825. What followed were continued sorties by South American privateers against Spanish shipping for the next few years. Thus ended, as historian David Head notes, the "last major conflict in the Atlantic world for a generation."

THE MONTERREY SHIPWRECK: A WRECK FROM THE END OF EMPIRE?

Lying 273 kilometers off Galveston in more than 1,219 meters of water in the Gulf of Mexico, the copper-clad lower hull of a shipwreck may be one of the privateers that warred on behalf of Latin America's republics during their decades-long war with Spain. Initially discovered during a survey for offshore development for Shell, the wreck has been studied since 2012 with ROV missions in 2012, 2013, and 2014. When discovered in 2012, the wreck included more than its partially worm-eaten hull. There were two piles of muskets, scattered plates and dinnerware, a glass decanter, many bottles, navigational instruments that included the remains of the ship's compass, telescopes and an octant, and five cannon.

It was clear from the artifacts and the form of the hull and its fittings that it was an armed ship from the first quarter of the 19th century. Archaeologists have studied two other Gulf wrecks from that period, one known as the

■ The stern of the possible privateer wreck, *Monterrey A*, as revealed by robotic cameras in 2012. (NOAA Office of Ocean Exploration and Research)

■ This octant from the Monterrey A wreck, shown after recovery, is a clue that the vessel was lost with all hands. It was too valuable to leave behind. (Amy Borgens)

■ Scattered ceramics and glassware from the captain's cabin of the *Monterrey A* wreck, 2012. (NOAA Office of Ocean Exploration and Research)

Mardi Gras wreck, another deep-water site discovered in 2001 56 kilometers off the mouth of the Mississippi and studied and partially excavated by a team of government and private industry archaeologists in 2005–2006. The Mardi Gras wreck is an early 19th-century armed vessel that was either a privateer or a merchant ship armed for its own defense in a volatile gulf of its time. In addition to one cannon, the Mardi Gras wreck carried an assortment of pistols, muskets, and swords in an arms chest, which was a catch-all locker on deck for weapons on board armed ships. The wreck may be that of the American privateer *Rapid*. *Rapid*, stationed off the mouth of the Mississippi during the War of 1812, sank after capsizing while tacking to avoid a British warship in December 1813.

The other early 19th-century gulf wreck lies inside Pass Cavallo, which heads into Texas's Matagorda Bay. Clive Cussler's National Underwater Maritime Agency (NUMA) discovered it while searching for LaSalle's *L'Aimable* in 1998. The Texas Historical Commission investigated the site and excavated more than 200 artifacts. Analyzing the finds, which included lead shot, cannon shot, musket fragments, saber fragments, and bayonets that date the wreck to the early 19th century, they believe it is an armed vessel, perhaps a privateer. One possible candidate, the New Orleans schooner *Hannah Elizabeth*, is known to have wrecked in Pass Cavallo in 1835 while running guns to support the Texian revolution against Mexico.

The partial excavation of the Monterrey shipwreck found a small bag of silver coins that were likely the ship's purser's funds for supplies and food for the ship. The two piles of muskets yielded examples of British, Spanish, and French guns, and documented but did not recover a pile of sabers.

■ Archaeologists Amy Borgens and James Delgado recover bottles archaeologically excavated by the remotely operated vehicle *Hercules* after it was brought on board E/V *Nautilus*, 2013. (Ocean Exploration Trust/ Meadows Center)

The cannon include a long, likely 18-pdr. gun that had been mounted mid-ships on a centered-rotating gun carriage, and four sturdy carronades. The hull remains show that it was a fast, sleek two-masted "clipper" schooner, brig, or brigantine, and that it may have been built on Chesapeake Bay or Baltimore.

The War of 1812 and these ships' use as privateers made "Baltimore clipper" schooners and brigs famous. After the war, a number of these fast ships were purchased by navies, smugglers, and slavers (one example is the famous *Amistad*). More than 100 also entered service as privateers for revolutionary and emerging Latin American states, raising Spanish commerce while still owned by American interests but serving under new Spanish names and with American masters and crews, some of them with new names. Their actions were against US law, but that did not dissuade them to strike a blow for Latin American freedom while lining their pockets with prize money.

What is clear is that regardless of whose flag it flew, the Monterrey shipwreck comes from a time when the last wars for the Americas were coming to an end, and the Gulf of Mexico was a vast naval background where ships like *Monterrey A* waged a war on Spanish shipping that helped end an empire and give rise to new republics. The three Gulf wrecks—Mardi Gras, Pass Cavallo, and Monterrey—all reflect the waning years of Spain's American empire. The gulf was a dangerous place, filled with privateers, pirates, and foreign men-of-war, and its waters were no longer friendly for Spanish ships and commerce.

6

Iron and Steam

Inequality of numbers may be compensated by invulnerability. Not only does economy, but naval success, dictate the wisdom and expediency of fighting with iron against wood.

—Stephen Mallory, Confederate Secretary of the Navy, April 20, 1861

The Industrial Revolution that began in the 18th century brought tremendous change in the 19th century. Metal-hulled ships supplanted wooden ships and new, more powerful weapons emerged from factories. Steam power and those weapons gave rise to new ways to fight. Change was rapid and dramatic. The United States launched the first steam-powered warship in 1815. Britain followed, but it was decades before the new technology was fully trusted and adopted. The pioneers were fully rigged for sail as "steam frigates," a type quickly adopted by Britain, France, and the United States by midcentury. These wooden hulled warships arrived on the scene just as shell-firing guns did, occasioning a return to the ancient technique of armoring. France introduced the first ironclad in 1859, but it was not until 1861 that two ironclads engaged in combat. When they did, they changed the face of naval warfare. Over the next few decades, many naval powers built armored warships with turrets and shell guns, each successive generation growing larger in terms of the caliber of the guns, the thickness of the armor, the power of the engines, and the size of the ship itself.

The 19th century began with traditional battles between wooden ships of the line at Trafalgar and the naval actions of the War of 1812. The last battles between wooden ships in the Mediterranean came with the war for Greek independence at the Battle of Lissa in 1839. Harbingers of change were apparent as well in Russia's battles with Ottoman Turkey in 1856, when a Russian fleet, armed with shell-firing guns, completely destroyed a Turkish squadron. The use of the new technologies, particularly against weaker powers, was readily apparent in the 1840s, as Britain used steam and shell guns to push aside Chinese resistance during the Opium Wars, and the United States began to flex its muscles in the expansionist war with Mexico in 1846–1848.

Then came the American Civil War of 1861–1865, where both sides of the conflict demonstrated the efficiency of steam, ironclads, turrets, mines, and submarines. That war accelerated the shift from wooden navies to iron and steel ships, heavier guns, and the end of sail. It also led to an industrialized naval competition that accompanied growing international tensions as "Great Powers" vied for overseas territories and control of the sea, a principle propounded by American naval theorist Alfred Thayer Mahan.

Archaeologists have documented the wrecks of a number of 19th-century warships, finding evidence as they do of stubborn adherence to old, "tried and true" technologies and strategies in the face of new developments, as well as of navies embracing the wrong new technologies and innovations, including some evolutionary dead-ends. A striking example of blind adherence to an older technology is demonstrated in an American warship wreck, built well after the introduction of steam, but focused instead on the quest for speed under sail in heavily armed, smaller wooden warships.

THE BRIG *SOMERS*

The 10-gun brig *Somers* is one of the most notorious ships in the history of the US Navy. *Somers* was the product of a US Navy still adhering to wooden warships and only just starting to experiment with steam when it was launched in 1842. The American experiments with knife-like hulls with sharp bows and large areas of sail, beginning in the later 18th century (as seen in the wreck of *Defence*), had continued in the 19th century with fast privateers in the War of 1812, known as "Baltimore clippers" since many came from shipyards in that southern port. The development of the "clipper" spread, after the war, to merchant shipping, reaching its heyday in the 1840s and early 1850s. The navy also flirted with clipper hulls. Sleek and faster than any other ships, clippers, when armed, were effective commerce raiders, a role well suited to the US Navy, then still inferior in terms of the numbers and sizes of its ships as compared to Britain.

Somers was built primarily as a training ship, a fast, well-armed floating school for young naval officers. Launched from the New York Navy Yard on April 16, 1842, *Somers* was very much a clipper with a knife-like bow and stern only gradually swelling along its 33-meter length to reach a maximum width of 7.6 meters amidships. *Somers* still packed a punch with 10 32-pdr. carronades and two long 32-pdr. guns on the deck. The two masts were heavily sparred, carrying a large amount of sail. The result, when the canvas was fully spread, was 12 to 14 knot speeds, which, when compared to a lumbering ship of the line's several knots, was remarkable.

Somers's career as a training ship took a tragic turn on its second voyage. Sailing from New York on September 13, 1842, the brig carried 120 crew, many of them boys aged 13 to 19. Among them was 19-year-old Philip Spencer, scapegrace son of the secretary of war. Spencer's short naval career had been distinguished by drunkenness, brawls, and insubordination, and Captain Alexander Slidell McKenzie and his officers did not relish the thought of having the prominent, troubled teen aboard their ship. Spencer lived up to his reputation during *Somers*'s voyage to Africa, clashing with the captain, and finally committing the unpardonable act of privately confiding a plan to seize the ship, murder McKenzie and the officers, and take *Somers* on a piratical cruise.

When McKenzie learned of Spencer's discussion with another crewmember, he promptly arrested the boy and chained him to one of the carronades. Spencer's pleas that he was joking notwithstanding, McKenzie and his officers began to seek other members of the "conspiracy," arresting the bosun's mate, Samuel Cromwell, and seaman Elisha Small. Fearing that mutiny was spreading, McKenzie hastily assembled a court martial. The court quickly found the three guilty, and sentenced them to death. Spencer, Cromwell, and Small were hastily executed from the main yardarm on December 1, 1842.

When *Somers* reached New York, news of the executions was at first praised, but under scrutiny occasioned by the complaints of the elder Spencer, the hangings were condemned. A highly publicized court martial acquitted McKenzie of murder and other charges, but the controversy over the "*Somers* Affair" dogged him for the rest of his life. The US Navy decided to abandon the concept of a training ship, instead creating the shore-based US Naval Academy in 1845 as a direct result of the *Somers* executions. The most famous outcome of the affair was the interest of Herman Melville, whose cousin, Guert Gansevoort, served as *Somers*'s first officer. Melville mentioned the "mutiny" in his 1850 book *White Jacket*, citing "the well-known case of a United States Navy brig...a memorable example, which at any time may be repeated. Three men, in a time of peace, were then hung at the yardarm, merely because in the captain's judgement, it became necessary to hang them. To this day the question of their complete guilt is socially discussed." Melville also used the events aboard *Somers* in his last work, *Billy Budd*.

Sailors considered *Somers* an unlucky, cursed ship. Reassigned to regular duties, the brig was part of the navy's Home Squadron when the war with Mexico broke out in 1846. Sent into the Gulf of Mexico to help blockade the principal Mexican port of Veracruz, *Somers* was chasing a suspected blockade runner on December 8, 1846, when a sudden squall came up and capsized it. The top-heavy brig, with too much canvas, required heavy ballast in the shallow 3.35-meter-deep hold. Low on provisions, "flying light" with only six tons of ballast when the gale hit, *Somers* went over in an instant and sank in 10 minutes with 32 of the crew. The navy never salvaged the wreck, but its tragic history and notoriety lived on, not only in the oral traditions of the US Navy as its only recorded "mutiny" but also in the public mind thanks to *Billy Budd*.

■ George Belcher discovering a ceramic jug on the wreck of the US brig *Somers*. Inscribed "Alexandria, D.C.," it was an early clue that he had discovered the wreck of *Somers*. (Author Photo)

San Francisco underwater explorer George Belcher and his brother Joel discovered the wreck of *Somers* in 32 meters of water off Veracruz in 1986. Reporting the discovery to Mexican and US officials, the Belchers worked with both governments to study the wreck and ensure its preservation. Surveys of the exposed portions of the wreck in 1987 and 1990 revealed much about the ship, its fittings, and armament, and provided more clues about its loss. I was part of the 1987 survey and led the 1990 project. Diving on *Somers* in the darkness off Veracruz was a unique opportunity to explore a notorious ship. *Somers* lies on its starboard side, just as it was when the squall knocked it down in 1846. The side of the hull is intact and buried in the sand, but the copper-sheathed keel, some of the port side's frames, and the keel and rudder rise out of the bottom to delineate the extreme sharpness of the clipper hull.

The long, extremely narrow *Somers* was an exceptionally crowded ship, with little room below decks and a flush, open deck. As you swim over the wreck, it is easy to see how a crew of unruly boys and men could become restless and contentious in such crowded quarters. It was also easy to see, with little physical separation from the crew, and without the psychological advantage of an elevated quarterdeck or physical barriers, how the officers could become anxious, if not paranoid, in the face of trouble.

Whether Spencer was only joking about seizing *Somers* or not, McKenzie and his officers' decision to hang the boy becomes more understandable as a fearful reaction of a small group of men feeling outnumbered and surrounded on a ship with no place to run but over the side should violence erupt.

Somers's carronades lie on the wreck, many in their original positions. The starboard side guns lie buried, muzzle down in the sand, just as they once lined the deck. The semicircular tracks and rollers of the gun carriages lying near them are a reminder of the maneuverability of these small but deadly smashers. A gun crew could swivel a gun to bring it to bear on an enemy on these rolling, sliding carriages. The crowded hull still holds the ship's pumps, the cast-iron galley stove, rows of stored anchor chain, and jars and bottles of provisions. But some of the more interesting items lie far from the hull. Resting in the sand, far beyond sight of the mounded wreck, are the fittings for the masts and rigging, the farthest more than 30 meters from the hull.

Somers's masts were long and heavily sparred, carrying a great deal of sail. This weight along with the guns on the deck, made the ship top-heavy. The narrow, knife-like hull was a very unstable platform for all of that weight, and required heavy ballast to safely sail *Somers*. The need for a fast, heavily armed (for its size) ship led the navy to compromise with little margin for safety, and when *Somers* was put into a position where it was light, without enough ballast, and the wind came up, the brig easily capsized and sank. This event illustrates that at the end of the age of the wooden sailing warship, centuries after *Mary Rose* and *Vasa* capsized and sank, navies still took risks with unstable warships—which resulted in their occasionally or oftentimes becoming lost. More warships in the age of fighting sail foundered in storms or capsized than were ever lost in combat.

USS *CUMBERLAND*

The sloop-of-war USS *Cumberland* is best remembered as a symbol of the end of an era. A member of the last generation of steam frigates built to fight under sail, *Cumberland* was the first victim of a steam-powered, ironclad ship of war. The navy launched *Cumberland* in 1842 from the Boston navy Yard. The frigate served for 20 years in American, Mediterranean, and African waters. The navy "razeed" or cut down the frigate to a sloop of war, mounting fewer guns in 1856. In 1861, with the outbreak of civil war in the United States, *Cumberland* was one of several US warships at Portsmouth, Virginia's Gosport Navy Yard. The Navy Yard and its ships were caught behind enemy lines when Virginia seceded from the Union and demanded the surrender of all federal property, arms, and warships within its territory. The commanding officer of the Yard decided to destroy what he could of the Yard's facilities, ordnance, and those vessels that could not flee. *Cumberland* was one of the ships to clear the burning Navy Yard on April 20, but other ships were not as lucky, including the steam-powered frigate USS *Merrimack*, scuttled at the dock and set afire.

The two ships would meet again soon. On March 8, 1862, *Cumberland* and several other warships stood off Newport News, Virginia, blockading the James River. *Cumberland*, with a single 70-pdr. rifled gun, two 10-inch Dahlgren pivot guns, and 22 nine-inch Dahlgren guns, was a formidable opponent for any Confederate vessel that might challenge the blockade. But the Confederacy had adopted the latest technological innovations in naval warfare. Raising the sunken *Merrimack*, Confederate engineers cut the hull down, removed the masts, repaired the steam machinery, and placed a battery of guns inside a sloping armored casemate. Commissioned as CSS *Virginia*, it was not the world's first ironclad, as both France and Britain had already built their own, but *Virginia* would be the first to be tested in battle.

Steaming into view of the blockading ships on the morning of March 8, *Virginia* headed for the wooden frigate USS *Congress*. Raking *Congress* with gunfire, *Virginia* continued on unscathed as cannon fire bounced off its armor. *Cumberland* was next. The captain was not aboard, and executive officer, Lieutenant George Morris, was in command. As Franklin Buchanan, *Virginia*'s captain, called out for *Cumberland* to surrender, Morris yelled, "Never! I'll sink alongside!" *Virginia* lined up to sink *Cumberland* with a six-foot armored ram projecting from its bow. Buchanan later wrote that he "steered directly for the *Cumberland*, striking her almost at right angles, under the forerigging on the starboard side . . . backing clear of her, we went ahead again, heading up river, helm hard-a-starboard, and turned slowly . . . the *Cumberland* continued to fight though our ram had opened her side wide enough to drive in a horse and cart."

Guns still firing, *Cumberland* sank by the bow within minutes, taking about 120 of the crew down with it. Confederate Brigadier General R. E. Colton, watching from shore, "could hardly believe my senses when I saw the masts of the *Cumberland* begin to sway wildly. After one or two lurches her hull disappeared beneath the water, guns firing to the last moment." The age of the wooden walls had effectively ended decades earlier, but *Virginia's* on-slaught and *Cumberland's* sinking were a definitive illustration of the end of the age of wooden warships.

Archaeologists working with author and explorer Clive Cussler rediscovered the wreck off Newport News in 1980. Intact decking, an anchor, the exposed remains of the bilge pumps, scattered artifacts including the ship's bell, cannon fuses used to fire the guns, a gunlock cover inscribed "USNY, 1856," and calipers used to measure the gauge of shot were visible to the divers who first visited the wreck. They also found evidence of considerable damage to the ship. This was not surprising, given the heavy blow from *Virginia's* ram and the speed with which the heavily timbered *Cumberland* sank.

But after the discovery, archaeologists and the navy virtually ignored *Cumberland*, designating it as historic but not pursuing further study or excavation. The wreck remains on the bottom of the James to this day, unfortunately heavily looted by souvenir-selling relic hunters who plundered the site. After learning about the despoliation of USS *Cumberland* from the Confederate Naval Historical Society, the FBI arrested the looters and the US Navy and the State of Virginia accepted responsibility for actively working to study and preserve what was left. An archaeological survey of *Cumberland* in 1993 revealed extensive damage to the wreck. The relic hunters had used oyster dredges to rip into the hull in their search for artifacts that were then sold off to the highest bidder.

The second destruction of USS *Cumberland* is a striking example of what can happen to significant shipwrecks when insufficient resources to pursue an important find or official indifference leave the door open for looters. As a result, much of the archaeological value of USS *Cumberland*, including an opportunity to study the damage to the hull caused by *Virginia*'s ram, had been lost. In the aftermath of the damage, navy archaeologists and curators have studied the artifacts recovered from the looters, with many of them now displayed in the Hampton Roads Naval Museum in Norfolk. Navy archaeologists from the Underwater Archaeology Branch have documented the hull's exposed remains with three-dimensional sonar to map the wreck, and in the process, have learned that more of *Cumberland* is buried, perhaps sealing more artifacts and the stories they can tell within the wreck.

USS *MONITOR*

Another participant in the momentous naval actions on the James River in March 1862 was an unusual vessel that demonstrated, along with CSS *Virginia*, that the day of the wooden warship was done. News of the Confederacy's work on the raised hulk of USS *Merrimack* led Union officials to seek proposals for their own ironclad. On September 15, 1861, Swedish-American inventor John Ericsson presented the plans for a small steam-powered ironclad with a single rotating turret on its deck. The "Ironclad Board" skeptically accepted Ericsson's proposal, and the race was on to see which ironclad—CSS *Virginia* or Ericsson's *Monitor*—would be finished first. Ericsson launched *Monitor* on January 30, 1862, while *Virginia* slid off the ways on February 17. Both ironclads then steamed for the mouth of the James and the blockading fleet, *Monitor* under tow from New York while *Virginia* steamed under its own power.

Virginia won the race, hitting the blockading fleet hard on March 8 when it engaged and sank USS *Cumberland*. But the next morning, as *Virginia* readied for its next attack, the small *Monitor*, described as a "cheesebox on a raft," stood between the Confederate ironclad and the Union fleet. For the next four hours, the two warships hammered away at each other, firing at one another without effect, at times point blank. The battle ended in a stalemate that changed naval warfare forever. *Monitor* mounted only two 11-inch

Dahlgren smoothbore guns in its rotating, armored turret. But as the *London Times* editorialized after the battle, the arrival of *Monitor* shifted the balance of naval power. The Royal Navy was effectively reduced in number from 149 "first-class warships" to only two "armoured vessels." "There is not a ship in the English Navy, apart from these two, that it would not be madness to trust to an engagement with the little *Monitor*."

The success of *Monitor* was a profound revelation. And yet the actual vessel, while copied by the United States and other powers, was not a lasting success. With its shallow draft and low freeboard (the seas always washed over the ironclad's deck), *Monitor* was not a seaworthy vessel. The short life of *Monitor* is proof of that. After several months on station at Hampton Roads, the entrance to the James River and the site of its famous battle with *Virginia*, with a brief layover in Washington, DC for repairs and public tours, *Monitor* departed for Beaufort, North Carolina, towed by USS *Rhode Island* out into the open ocean. It did not last long. Heavy seas washing over the deck began to fill the ship just a day out, and by the late evening of December 30, 1862, *Monitor* had lost the tow and was wallowing in the waves off Cape Hatteras, the pumps unable to keep back the water. Boats from *Rhode Island* took off most of *Monitor*'s crew, and around 1 A.M. on

THE WRECK OF THE IRON-CLAD "MONITOR."

■ The loss of USS *Monitor*. (Naval History and Heritage Command)

December 31, the ironclad, with a red distress lantern hanging from a flag-staff, slipped beneath the waves with 16 of the crew.

Archaeologists and other scientists located the wreck of *Monitor* in 69 meters of water off the North Carolina coast in 1973. A detailed photo-graphic mapping of the wreck by the US Navy in 1974 showed that the iron-clad had rolled over while sinking. The heavy turret pulled free of the hull, and the overturned hull had landed on top of the turret. Angled down at the bow, the upside-down hull nearly obscured the turret, revealing only a small curved section as it protruded from the starboard quarter. The US gov-ernment designated the wreck and the area surrounding it the nation's first National Marine Sanctuary in 1975. After that, several archaeological expeditions dived to examine *Monitor* and recover artifacts. The first dive to the wreck, in the submersible *Johnson*, in August 1977, was an amazing moment for archaeologist Gordon P. Watts Jr. As the submersible landed on the sandy bottom and moved forward, Watts and his crew discovered a small brass marine lantern lying eight meters away from the wreck. It was probably the same signal light flying from *Monitor*'s masthead atop the turret that "provided rescuers their last contact with the *Monitor* 115 years earlier."

Divers recovered the lantern and a loose iron hull plate in 1977. This was followed in 1979 by a test excavation inside a six-foot-square grid near the starboard side of the bow. "Locking out" of a dive chamber from the sub-mersible *Johnson Sea Link*, archaeologists Watts and John Broadwater used a water dredge to remove sediments and sand from what proved to be the collapsed remains of Captain John Bankshead's cabin. The archaeologists also examined the exposed remains of the wardroom and the engine room, where the intact machinery included the forced-air blowers that had pres-surized that space, creating a forced draft for the boilers. The blowers were an amazing Ericsson innovation, and yet they, like the other machinery, relied on leather belts to run. As *Monitor* took on water, the wet leather belts had slipped off their shafts, stopping the fans and the boilers as well as the ship's pumps. Powerless and unable to stop the incoming water, the ironclad had wallowed on the seas until it flooded.

The National Oceanic and Atmospheric Administration (NOAA) spon-sored a 1983 expedition to recover *Monitor*'s unique four-fluke anchor,

▪ Documenting the remains of the captain's cabin on *Monitor*. (National Oceanic and Atmospheric Administration)

which Ericsson developed to fit inside a hollow anchor well below the deck and inside the bow. A steam-powered windlass inside the ship raised and lowered the anchor without exposing the crew to enemy fire. Later expeditions recovered loose artifacts, more hull plating, and the four-bladed propeller. The expeditions also showed that the wreck was rapidly deteriorating, and so NOAA and the US Navy, with support from Congress, mounted major recovery missions in 2000 and 2002 to raise the ironclad's 30-ton steam engine and 160-ton turret. These were the more revolutionary features of *Monitor*.

While plans existed for the ironclad's hull and machinery, the archaeology of *Monitor* revealed many details that had never been recorded with pen and ink. More important, however, were the many details that emerged from the grime, sand, and rust of a century and a half beneath the sea. Inside the overturned turret, archaeologists found more than the toppled guns and the dents that defined the battle damage from *Monitor*'s 1862 encounter

■ US Navy divers excavating the turret of USS *Monitor*. (National Oceanic and Atmospheric Administration)

with CSS *Virginia*. A variety of artifacts spoke to life and death aboard the ship. These included tools used in the turret and discarded boots left behind as men scrambled for their lives out of the turret when *Monitor* wallowed in the trough of the waves as it sank on that long-ago New Year's Eve.

A drawer of silverware, all of it belonging to the ship's officers, who were responsible for the furnishing of their own wardroom, showed that at the end, someone, perhaps a faithful steward, was attempting to save things of value as *Monitor* foundered. The silverware lay scattered, mixed in with tumbled coal when the ironclad lost its battle to the sea and capsized. The turret came free of the hull and crashed, upside down, onto the seabed 69 meters below the surface of the ocean. Lying on the upended roof of the turret, close to the ladder that they were trying to climb, archaeologists found the skeletons of two of *Monitor*'s sailors. Their bones lay almost perfectly articulated, one man athwart and atop the other.

After the two skeletons were excavated from within the turret, they were shipped to the US Government's laboratory for the identification of the remains of America's recovered war dead in Honolulu. There, forensic scientists learned more about the two men. One was older than the other, both were Caucasian, and likely of European descent, and both men stood approximately five and a half feet tall. The older man's bones revealed that he had led a life of heavy labor, walked with a limp, and smoked a pipe. A simple gold ring on his hand suggested that he had been married. The younger man had recently broken his nose, maybe in a shipboard fight, or maybe by hitting a hard surface on a crowded ship. The two men's bones yielded mitochondrial DNA, but an exact match to hundreds of *Monitor* crew descendants could not be made.

They might have remained in the laboratory for a very long time because of the government's policy to not bury "unknown" service members. In one of my first assignments with the NOAA, I worked closely with David Alberg, the superintendent of USS *Monitor* National Marine Sanctuary, to get those men out of a steel cabinet and buried with full honors. Genealogist Lisa Stansbury tracked down more descendants, but again, no DNA match could be made. Lisa's work, as well as historian John Quarstein's, did provide much more detail about the lost 16 men of USS *Monitor*, their lives, and the impacts their deaths had on their families.

Ultimately, the Louisiana State University's Forensic Anthropology and Computer Enhancement Services (FACES) Laboratory, headed by Dr. Mary Manheim, provided us with recreated likenesses of the two *Monitor* sailors based in the structure of their skulls. We unveiled them at the US Navy Memorial in Washington, DC, in March 2012. The news spread nationally, thanks to coverage by the *Washington Post*'s Mike Ruane, and it gave us a chance to publicly call for the two men, no longer anonymous skeletons, thanks to Mary and her team, someone's son, brother, or husband, to be buried at Arlington. A year later, in March 2013, the two were laid to rest at Arlington National Cemetery beneath a stone with the names of all 16 of *Monitor*'s crew who had been lost with the ironclad.

The turret, now emptied of silt, coal, and artifacts, and no longer a tomb, now rests inside a large fresh-water tank next to the engine in the conservation laboratory of the USS *Monitor* Center at the wreck's permanent

■ The reburial of the two *Monitor* sailors at Arlington. (National Oceanic and Atmospheric Administration)

■ The engine register from the USS *Monitor*. (National Oceanic and Atmospheric Administration and The Mariners' Museum)

dry-land home, the Mariner's Museum, in Newport News, Virginia. The conservation of these massive and complex artifacts will take many years. Meanwhile, they are on display along with already conserved artifacts and contextual displays that allow visitors to experience what it was like to be inside the ship, both as a floating vessel of war and as a wreck. The museum brings to life the crew and a ship that signaled the most dramatic change in the way wars were fought at sea since the introduction of the gun.

CSS *H. L. HUNLEY*

The first battle between two ironclads during the US Civil War was just one significant demonstration of the changing face of war at sea. Another was the first successful use of a submarine to sink a warship. This time, the technological advantage lay with the beleaguered Confederacy. The small submarine *H. L. Hunley* was not the first submersible warship. Proposals for and experiments with submarines date back to the time of the Spanish Armada. The first submarine used in time of war is said to have been a wooden-hulled, one-man craft invented by David Bushnell and taken into combat off Staten Island in September 1776 by Sergeant Ezra Lee to sink HMS *Eagle*, flagship of a British fleet that had escorted an expeditionary force to take New York. Some historians do not believe that this early submarine, which Bushnell named *Turtle*, was ever completed or taken into combat. Whether it did or did not actually does not matter. Patriotic American tales of this ingenious Yankee craft inspired others to follow Bushnell's example.

Among them was fellow American Robert Fulton. Fulton built a small submersible, *Nautilus*, for the revolutionary French government in 1800 as well as floating mines that he called "torpedoes" after the North Atlantic ray *Torpedo nobiliana* because of its ability to use strong electric shocks to stun prey. While Fulton's submarine did not participate in any actions, his "torpedoes" did, although with mixed results. News of Fulton's inventions, inflated by hype, led others to experiment with submarines. British, French, Spanish, and German inventors tried, aided by the Industrial Revolution. German artillery officer Wilhelm Bauer built a working, all-iron submarine in late 1850, following it with another in 1855 for the Imperial Russian Navy. Bauer's ideas and materials were sound, but technology had not yet caught up to safely, repeatedly dive, keep a submarine balanced in the water, and fight. Both of Bauer's submarines sank in operational accidents.

Most naval officers and government officials viewed the various experiments with submarines in the first half of the 19th century with distaste. The submarine, as well as the torpedo, was seen as an evil weapon; one British officer, Vice Admiral Sir George Berkeley, wrote about "the Baseness

& Cowardice of this species of Warfare." It took another conflict, and the desperation of a weaker naval power, to take the risks to both reputation and pocketbook to build the next generation of submarines. The outbreak of the American Civil War and the limited resources of the Confederacy when compared to the larger naval forces of the Federal government (the Union) led Confederate leaders to pursue risky and expensive new technologies like ironclads and submarines. The Confederacy's first submarine, a small iron craft named *Pioneer*, lasted for a few months at New Orleans between its February launch and April scuttling in 1862 after the city fell to the Union. The builders of the submarine retreated to Mobile, Alabama, and built a second boat, *American Diver* (also known as *Pioneer II*) in early 1863, only to lose it when it flooded and sank without the crew aboard while under tow to attack Union ships.

The next attempt by this same coalition of machinists and businessmen who had financed the two submarines was made in Charleston, South Carolina. An important Confederate port, Charleston, was surrounded by a large fleet of Union ships that blockaded the harbor to prevent ships with supplies and munitions from supplying the Confederacy. The cornerstone of Union naval strategy was the use of its overwhelming force to first close off the Confederacy before seizing the rivers and coastal ports, cutting off the flow of guns, ammunition, clothing, medicine, and food to the Confederate Army and the rebellious citizens of the American South. A submarine's stealth and the power of a "torpedo" delivered by it to unsuspecting Union ships could disrupt the blockade.

The new submarine was a long, narrow cylinder made from high-quality boiler iron. A Confederate naval officer described the "very curious machine for destroying vessels" in a letter to his fiancée:

In the first place imagine a high pressure steam boiler, not quite round, say 4 feet in diameter one way and 3-1/2 feet the other—draw each end of the boiler down to a sharp wedge shaped point....On the bottom of the boat is riveted an iron keel weighing 4,000 lbs. which throws the center of gravity on one side and makes her swim steadily that side down. On top and opposite the keel is placed two man hole plates or hatches with heavy glass tops. These plates are water tight when covered over. They are just large enough for a man to go in and out. At one end is fitted a very neat little propeller 3-1/2 feet in diameter worked by men sitting in the boat and turning the shaft by hand cranks...she has a rudder and steering apparatus.

The submarine towed a "torpedo" made of copper, filled with 90 to 100 pounds of black powder that was detonated by a string attached to a primer. In a demonstration for Confederate officers, the submarine's crew approached a target vessel "within about fifty yards of her keeping the man holes just above water. At that distance, the submarine sank down and in a few minutes made her appearance on the other side of the vessel. He pulled the string and smashed her side to atoms."

But the technological wonder had its faults. The submarine sank two times while on maneuvers, killing the crew. The first accident, in August 1863, happened on the surface. The captain, Lieutenant John A. Payne, foolishly approached the sub's berth with both hatches open. It is possible

■ *H. L. Hunley* as depicted during the Civil War by artist Conrad Chapman Wise. (Naval History and Heritage Command)

that the crew had not completely pumped out the ballast tanks used to make the sub dive. With a low freeboard and very little buoyancy, the sub sank when Payne stepped on or bumped the diving plane and the bow dipped, sending water into the sub. Payne and three other men managed to scramble free of the narrow hatches before the sub sank, drowning five other crew members.

The second accident, in October 1863, with another crew, this time commanded by Horace L. Hunley, one of the financial backers for the sub, also ended badly when the sub dived at too sharp an angle because the crew mistakenly flooded the bow ballast tank too quickly, sending the sub slamming into the muddy bed of the Cooper River. Half buried in the river bottom, 15 meters down with the stern rising out of the mud at a 35-degree angle, the sub was trapped, and the crew slowly suffocated. Three weeks later, when the Confederates were finally able to raise the sub, the scene inside when the hatches were opened was "indescribably ghastly; the unfortunate men were distorted into all kinds of horrible attitudes…the blackened faces of all presented the expression of their despair and agony."

Undeterred, another crew readied the craft for a submerged attack on the Union fleet off Charleston Harbor. On February 17, 1864, the submarine, now formally named for its dead backer and captain as CSS *H. L. Hunley*, slowly moved out to sea under the command of Lieutenant George Dixon. Instead of towing a torpedo, *Hunley* carried a charge at the tip of an iron spar attached to the sub's bow. Heading into the night and toward the sloop-of-war USS *Housatonic*, two and a half miles away, Dixon brought his sub and crew right up the starboard side of the Union warship. Lookouts spotted the sub and raised the alarm. As the crew beat to quarters, sentries opened fire, hitting the exposed upper works of the sub with musket fire. Captain Charles Pickering, *Housatonic*'s commander, fired his double-barreled shotgun into the conning tower, which may have been open.

Then, just as *Housatonic* started to back away from the attacking sub, the spar torpedo exploded. *Housatonic* sank in about six minutes. *H. L. Hunley* slowly backed away from the sinking vessel, and then disappeared, not to be seen for over 130 years. The success of the small sub, the first to sink an enemy warship in combat, was as striking an example of the potential of the new technology to change naval warfare as the clash between the ironclads. That and the mysterious disappearance of *H. L. Hunley* inspired numerous searches for the lost submarine that began in 1873 and continued into the next century.

In May 1995, archaeologists Ralph Wilbanks and Wes Hall, working under contract for Clive Cussler's National Underwater and Maritime Agency (NUMA), discovered the wreck of *H. L. Hunley* in nine meters of water, completely buried in sediment. Dixon and his crew had not gotten very far from *Housatonic*: the two wrecks lay about 300 meters apart. Wilbanks and Hall removed enough sediment to expose a diving plane and one of the hatches, verifying that this was in fact the lost submarine. In 1996, archaeologists from the South Carolina Institute of Archaeology and Anthropology (SCIAA) and the Submerged Resources Center from the National Park Service (NPS) returned to the site and did a more extensive test excavation of portions of *H. L. Hunley* as well as detailed study of the wreck and its environment. Under the direction of the two supervising archaeologists on the site, Christopher Amer of SCIAA and Larry Murphy of the NPS, the team exposed both hatches, the top of the sub, the port side diving plane, and a section of the side down to the solid iron bar keel.

The excavation of the submarine provided the first detailed look at a vessel that had never been fully documented during its brief career. Since the Civil War, a number of people, including some of the surviving participants in the *Hunley*'s construction, had provided various estimates about *H. L. Hunley*'s actual size, the placement of the spar torpedo, and the form, or lines of the hull. But no contemporary plans or photographs existed for the submarine. As archaeologists pulled back the mud and sand to reveal the buried hull of *Hunley*, they quickly discovered that most conclusions about the sub's appearance and manufacture had been wrong. What they found was an amazingly sophisticated design and an exceptionally well-constructed vessel. *Hunley*'s hull is hydrodynamic, with a sharp, knife-like bow, shaped to move through the water with minimal resistance. Instead of being fastened with thick rivets projecting from the hull plates that would create drag in the water, the sub is flush-riveted and smooth. This level of craftsmanship surprised the archaeologists, some of whom were expecting this rushed, wartime project to have construction shortcuts, much like those found with earlier warship wrecks like *Defence* or *Eagle*.

H. L. Hunley is 12 meters long. It was small and the inside was cramped for the crew. The hull is only a meter wide, meaning that the crew had to sit, hunched over, as they turned the cranks to drive the propeller. A series of glass deadlights, to let in light, were set into the top of the submarine, but these only worked during the day. Without electrical power, the crew of *Hunley* worked in near darkness, by candlelight in a crowded iron cylinder where they could not stand or stretch out, the air thick and hot. The low freeboard notwithstanding, it becomes easier to understand why they would run on the surface whenever possible with the hatches open.

There was nothing glamorous about serving aboard *Hunley*, particularly after two other crews had either drowned or suffocated inside what some were calling the "peripatetic coffin." It takes a special type of courage to get inside something like that submarine, and with the strength of your own body fight the ocean to reach a warship two and half miles out, and then, at close range, set off an explosive charge that hits your vessel almost as hard as it hits the target.

The 1996 excavation was followed by a complete excavation and recovery of *H. L. Hunley* in 2000, as divers carefully removed sediment from a 36-by-12-meter area to reveal the craft, lying on its starboard side, oriented toward shore. That work, again led by SCIAA, the National Park Service, and the US Navy, culminated in August of that year when a massive floating crane raised the submarine from the sea. Taken to shore by a transport barge, the submarine was lifted into a 75,000 gallon freshwater tank to begin the years-long process of conserving it and excavating its interior.

Eighteen years after its recovery, work still continues on *Hunley*, but the interior has been completely excavated, and the concretion that encrusted and shrouded the hull has been cleared away to reveal the submarine as its inventors and crew knew it. The discoveries made inside the submarine added to an understanding of how the craft was both simple and sophisticated, with a set of differential gears that took the hand-cranked power provided by the crew as they labored, bent over on a wooden bench, and increased it to drive the submarine faster than the men could crank. The 16-foot-long spar itself, when cleaned and studied by conservator Paul Mardikian, revealed that the "torpedo" at its end was also sophisticated. The remnants of the copper casing that held the charge were found firmly attached to the end of the spar. That countered years of speculation that the torpedo was probably a barbed weapon meant to stick into the wooden hull of its target, and then be detonated by a lanyard that pulled a trigger as the submarine backed away, leaving the torpedo behind.

Archaeologists were able to enter the submarine by carefully unbolting hull plates and slowly digging down through the silt and sediment that packed the interior. What they found, according to senior archaeologist Maria Jacobsen, was a "truly unique time capsule" that included the bodies of the eight-man crew and a number of tools and personal effects. Tools included a hammer, an oil can, binoculars, and a lantern—perhaps the one used to signal the shore, or used to light the interior. The bodies of the crew

■ Archaeologists excavate the interior of *H. L. Hunley*. (Wikipedia Commons)

were found at their posts, suggesting that their deaths came without panic, and not long after *Hunley* had moved away from the sinking *Housatonic*. Forensic analysis of the bodies has not found any sign of physical trauma, and the likely cause of death was a build-up of carbon dioxide, with the already exhausted crew slumbering and slowly dying in their sleep as the oxygen inside the submarine ran out, perhaps after setting down on the bottom to wait for the outgoing tide to reverse course.

George E. Dixon, the submarine's commander, lay at the bow, in his combat position. The remains of his clothing clung to his bones, and from them, a variety of artifacts spoke about the man and his love of fine things. His gold pocket watch, with a Masonic Order fob and chain; a silver and antler pocket knife; and a diamond ring tucked into his vest pocket provided this insight. But Maria Jacobsen's discovery of another poignant artifact in his pants pocket told another tale. A post-war tale by a woman named Queenie Bennett, who claimed to be Dixon's wartime sweetheart, told of a gold twenty dollar piece she had given him as a keepsake, and how when

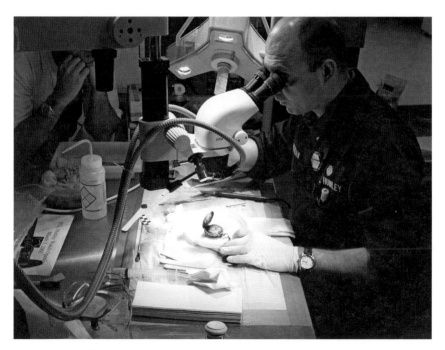

■ Conservator Paul Mardikian conserving the watch of *Hunley*'s commander, George Dixon. (Naval History and Heritage Command)

carried in his pocket, it had saved him when he was struck in the leg at the Battle of Shiloh in April 1862.

As Jacobsen excavated around Dixon's legs, she found a twenty dollar gold piece in his pocket. Dented by the indentation of the bullet, it was inscribed

Shiloh
April 6, 1862
My Life Preserver
G.E.D.

It was one of the most memorable personal moments in the excavation when the coin was rinsed to reveal the inscription.

Other artifacts were simpler but also poignant. A burned matchstick used to light a lantern or candle, a pencil, an empty wallet, shoes, and a pipe still filled with tobacco were found lying scattered about the bodies of the crew. Eight tin canteens were also found, with rope handles and corks, one lying under the bench where the men labored in a hot, stifling iron cylinder to bring *Hunley* to sea and into combat. Another find, preserved both by the silt and then the exceptional work of the conservation team, was the knotted silk bandanna worn around the neck of crewman James Wicks. The remains of the crew themselves told some tales.

Four of the men were European-born, and later genealogical work shows that one was a recently arrived former cobbler-turned-sailor from Denmark. Surviving DNA provided a match for only one of the men to descendants, but working from forensic evidence and where they lay, the *Hunley* team was able to determine who each body likely was. Modern forensic crime reconstruction techniques provided faces for the crew, and in a way added more to our modern connection with these eight brave men who risked and lost their lives to carry out the first successful submarine attack and sinking in history.

The eight men of *Hunley* were buried in Charleston's historic 19th-century Magnolia Cemetery with full honors in April 2004. They joined four men from a previous crew who had also been archaeologically rediscovered and

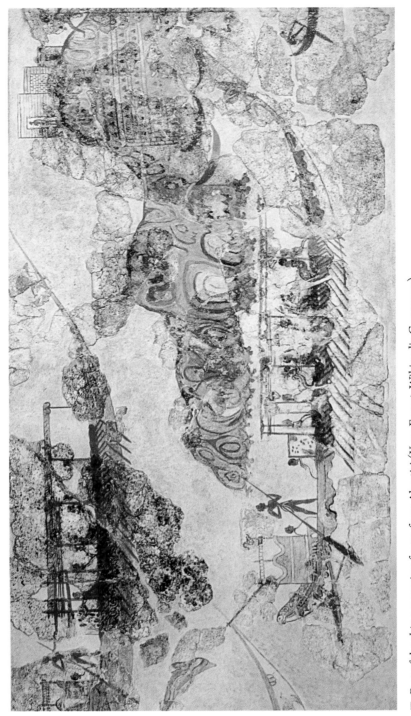

Part of the ship procession fresco from Akrotiri (Yann Forget, Wikipedia Commons)

■ This Byzantine manuscript, the Skilitzes Codex, dates to around A.D. 1000 and depicts the use of Greek fire. It is in the collections of the Biblioteca Nacional in Madrid. (Wikipedia Commons)

■ The Oseberg ship displayed inside the Viking Ship Museum, Oslo (Daderot/ Wikipedia Commons)

Yuan warships as depicted on the Moku Shurai Ekotoba, with samurai Takezaki Suenaga and other Japanese attacking from a small boat (Wikipedia Commons)

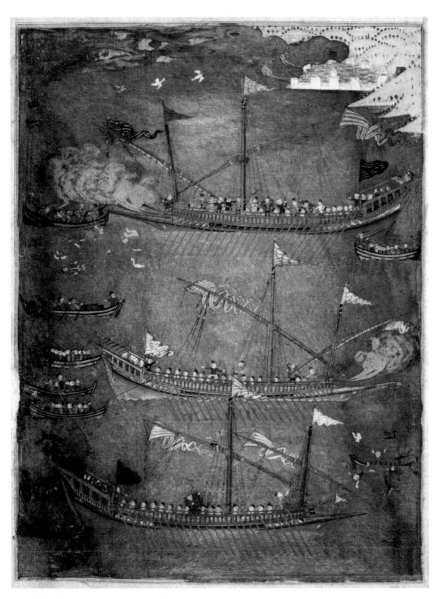

■ This illustrated manuscript shows Ottoman galleys in battle with Black Sea pirates, circa 1636 (British Library, Sloane 3584, f. 78 recto. Wikipedia Commons)

Vasa in the museum, fully restored, view of the port quarter (L-BBE/Wikimedia Commons)

One of the guns at Lajas Reef, likely from the wreck of Morgan's *Satisfaction* (National Geographic Creative/Jonathan Kingston)

The bow of USS *Monitor* (National Oceanic and Atmospheric Administration)

US Navy–issue mustard jar recovered from the wreck of USS *Cairo* (National Park Service)

Color painting of the wreck of USS *Maine* in Havana Harbor (Naval History and Heritage Command)

Dresden's bell as found and the bell on display in the Dresden Museum (Author Photo and Wikipedia Commons)

The wreck of USS *Utah* and the Utah Memorial at Pearl Harbor (National Park Service/Valor in the Pacific National Monument)

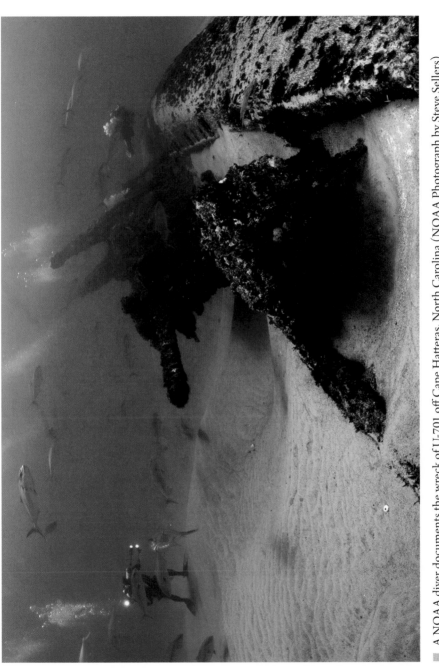

A NOAA diver documents the wreck of U-701 off Cape Hatteras, North Carolina (NOAA Photograph by Steve Sellers)

The conning tower of the Imperial Japanese Navy submarine I-201 (University of Hawaii/Hawaii Undersea Research Laboratory/NOAA)

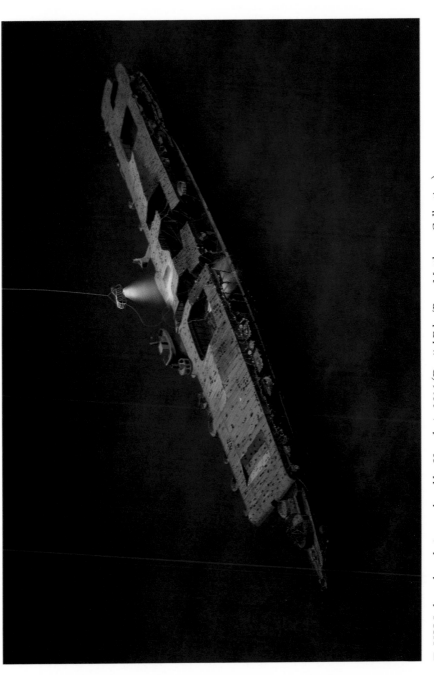

■ USS *Independence* being explored by *Hercules* in 2016 (Danijel Frka/Russ Matthews Collection)

Hellcat fighter in the forward elevator of USS *Independence* (Ocean Exploration Trust/NOAA)

reburied at Magnolia. The first sinking of *Hunley* in August 1863 drowned five men. When raised, their bloated bodies required removal, and so Confederate authorities sent slaves into the crowded craft to dismember the bodies to enable them to clear *Hunley* and clean it for the next crew. The site of their burial in a Confederate cemetery was later built over when the Johnson Hagood football stadium of South Carolina's military college, the Citadel, was built in 1948. The discovery of burials in 1993 and the realization that *Hunley*'s first crew might still lie beneath the stands of the stadium inspired an excavation to find them in the aftermath of the submarine's 1995 discovery.

In the summer of 1999, archaeologists found the four men in two pits, coffins stacked on one another. While the fifth crew member was not found, and matching each body to the crew known to have drowned inside the submarine in 1863 was not possible, Jonathan Leader and his team found graphic evidence that these were *Hunley*'s men—the bodies lay reassembled, with crude hack and chop marks showing where legs and arms had been severed to pull them from the submarine. Just as battlefield archaeology on land can reveal the grisly face of war, so too did the 1999 dig that found the first crew of *H. L. Hunley*.

USS *HOUSATONIC*: *HUNLEY*'S VICTIM

The archaeological examination of *Hunley* also included a look at *Housatonic*. The National Park Service team investigating *Hunley* helped pioneer a broader look at the archaeology of navies with this approach by looking at the naval battlefield that defined *Hunley*'s encounter with *Housatonic* on that February night in 1864. Even though major portions of the wreck were scrapped in 1872, and then again in 1909 to clear the harbor of obstructions, several feet of the lower hull remains buried. The most recent examination suggests that *Hunley*'s spar torpedo detonated close to a powder magazine near *Housatonic*'s stern. The powder—as much as four tons of it—exploded, ripping off much of *Housatonic*'s aft end, below the water, which explains why the Union warship sank so quickly.

USS *CAIRO*

Another American Civil War wreck, USS *Cairo*, is, like *Monitor* and *Hunley*, a reminder of the increasingly technological nature of naval warfare in the 19th century. The ill-fated *Cairo* was one of many steam-powered ironclads built for service on the rivers of the south. *Cairo's* greatest claim to fame is the fact that it was the first warship sunk by an electrically detonated mine—an "infernal device," in the colorful language of her time. Like *H. L. Hunley* and CSS *Virginia*, the mine that sank USS *Cairo* was another cornerstone of the Confederacy's naval strategy to affect a "technical surprise" by adopting innovations like ironclad warships; rifled, shell-firing guns; submarines; and mines.

During the American Civil War, while the Union's naval strategy against the Confederacy was primarily devoted to a blockade of southern ports and harbors, it also included seizing control of the Mississippi River. Controlling the river and dividing and isolating the rebellious southern states would, in the words of one military commander, "strangle" the Confederacy. To wage war on the Mississippi and its tributaries, the Union built specialized ironclads based on the design of western river steamboats. Known as the City-class gunboats, these riverine warships were shallow-draft craft with sloping, armored casemated sides. Inclined, reciprocating steam engines drove a paddlewheel recessed in the hull behind the armor. This armor, made from railroad iron, also protected the crew and the ship's armament.

USS *Cairo*, named for Cairo, Illinois, was built at Mound City, Illinois, in 1862. The vessel was extremely broad, and shallow. It did not enjoy a long career. The gunboat was lost on December 12, 1862, during naval operations in support of General U. S. Grant's siege of Vicksburg, Mississippi, when *Cairo* and a flotilla of other ironclads advanced up the Yazoo River to assault Vicksburg's northern defenses.

The Confederates, using the technological advantage of electrically detonated "torpedoes," had mined the river. As *Cairo* slowly steamed up the muddy waters of the Yazoo to engage a Confederate shore battery, she passed over a minefield. Two sharp explosions rocked the ship, tearing two holes in the hull. As the water poured in "like the roar of Niagara," Captain

Thomas Oliver Selfridge ran the sinking ironclad up against the river's muddy banks. As the crew scrambled to safety, *Cairo* slid off, sinking in 12 minutes. Only the tops of the stacks and the flagstaff rose above the swirling brown water. To thwart Confederate salvage, the crew pulled down these landmarks, leaving *Cairo* to the river. It was never salvaged, slowly sinking deeper into the mud.

Edwin C. Bearss, research historian at Vicksburg National Military Park, and local historian Warren Grabau discovered the wreck of *Cairo* in 1956. Plotting the ironclad's location with naval records and old maps, and working from a rowboat, the two historians found the wreck with a handheld compass that swung wildly because of the huge mass of iron on the hull. Balancing over the side of the boat, they probed with an iron bar and were rewarded with the sound of iron as they roughly plotted the outline of the sloping casemate beneath the mud. In 1959–1960, local divers surveyed the exterior of the wreck, and in September 1960, Bearss and Grabau hired a

■ The pilothouse of *Cairo*, the first part of the wreck to be raised. (Naval History and Heritage Command)

salvage crane to pull the armored pilothouse free of the hull and raise it to the surface. They were also able to grapple an eight-inch naval gun and yank it from the casemate, only to discover that it was still loaded.

Cairo lay buried deep in the silt of the Yazoo, filled with mud, as a perfectly preserved, encapsulated archaeological site filled with the ship's ordnance, equipment, tackle, and the personal items of the crew who had so hastily abandoned the ship on December 12, 1862. Bearss and friends formed a private non-profit group, Operation Cairo, Inc., to bring up the ironclad. Dollars to raise *Cairo* came in, but there was just enough to do the job. No funds would be left to preserve the wreck or its contents. To compound the problems, when the lift finally happened in October 1964, it turned into a disaster. The marine salvors hired to raise the wreck underestimated the ironclad's weight. Using crane barges to pull on wire cables passed under the hull, the salvors broke the intact ship apart, cutting it into three pieces. Only the bow came up relatively intact. The wires crushed the midships portion of *Cairo*, and the stern collapsed and fell back into the river. A large amount of material that fell into the river, such as armor, the wheelhouse, entire sections of the casemates, and smaller artifacts, were never recovered.

The State of Mississippi barged the surviving pieces of the ship down river to a shipyard in Pascagoula, Mississippi, to be cleaned and reassembled. Unfortunately, out of sight, these pieces slowly began to rot and fall apart. The smaller artifacts from inside the wreck, however, fared better. Cleaned, restored, and cataloged by volunteers, the well-preserved artifacts included personal items of the crew such as family photographs; spoons, plates, and cups marked with the initials of the men of each mess; ship's equipment; and ordnance. Many of the artifacts, like these, were evocative reminders of the crew, who despite the difference of a few centuries did not live that differently from the crew of *Vasa* or *Defence*.

The National Park Service restored and reassembled the remains of *Cairo*'s hull between 1977 and 1984. Only 15 percent of the original vessel had survived by then, but NPS architects were able to support the hull fragments, armor, and machinery on a laminated wooden framework that creates a "ghost" of the original ironclad. Displayed outdoors under an open

▦ This stencil, recovered from the wreck of USS *Cairo*, belonged to commanding officer Thomas Oliver Selfridge. (National Park Service)

shelter, *Cairo* and the nearby museum that houses her artifacts tell the story of how quickly one "new" technology—the torpedo—was deployed to counter the threat of another technology, the ironclad, in the rapidly changing world of the 19th century.

MAPLE LEAF

Like USS *Cairo*, another vessel sunk by Confederate "torpedo" proved to be another amazing trove of well-preserved artifacts. However, unlike *Cairo*, it has only been partially excavated. Built in Canada for passenger and freight service on Lake Ontario, the steamer *Maple Leaf* was sold to Boston merchants in 1862. They immediately chartered it to the US Army's Quartermaster Department, which desperately needed ships to transport troops, baggage, and supplies to the theaters of war. On the early morning hours of April 1, 1864, *Maple Leaf* was slowly steaming on the St. Johns

River, 27 kilometers out from Jacksonville, Florida, carrying three regiments—more than 1,000 men—to the Florida port city. Suddenly, a huge explosion ripped a hole in the bow of the wooden-hulled steamer, which began to quickly sink in the 6-meter-deep river. According to Army Captain Henry W. Dale, there was a "tremendous crash, and a heavy report. The saloon filled with a sickening stench, the timbers breaking in the great tumult." Four African American crew members were killed in the blast, but the soldiers and officers were able to safely disembark as *Maple Leaf* settled into the mud with its upper works above the river's surface.

The army was unable to raise *Maple Leaf*, but some items were salvaged. However, the men lost their baggage, equipment, and stores, all of which remained inside the wooden hull, now filled with the St. Johns mud. Nearby Confederates, who had placed the torpedo that sank the steamer, set fire to what remained above water. The remaining portions of the hull that stuck above the riverbed were cleared away in 1889, and the steamer was soon forgotten.

The story of *Maple Leaf* inspired Jacksonville dentist Keith Holland, who with friends used old charts of the river to search for the lost steamer. In June 1984, they succeeded in discovering *Maple Leaf*'s mud-shrouded remains. Negotiations with government officials ensued as Holland wished to excavate the wreck. Because the ship was still owned by the US government, a deal was struck between the government and Holland allowing Holland and his team from his recently formed St. Johns Archaeological Expeditions to begin work in 1989. The recovery effort was guided by East Carolina University archaeologist Frank Cantelas, and for a 10-day period, divers including East Carolina graduate students worked in extremely limited visibility to recover some 3,000 artifacts.

The finds revealed that the steamer is perhaps one of the United States's greatest underwater Civil War archaeological repositories. The range of artifacts included wooden crates still marked with the names of individual soldiers, with their regimental assignments. While the majority of the finds were associated with enlisted men, the belongings of some officers were also recovered. In addition to standard-issue equipment, intensely personal items were found, including a number of family photographs and small sewing and mending kits carried by Civil War soldiers who were known in the ranks as "housewives."

The excavations also recovered standard camp equipment, weapons, sutler's stores—goods and items sold by private merchants who served the private needs of the troops—and goods that the archaeological team believes were looted from southern plantations. High-quality china, porcelain doorknobs, and plate-glass windows found in the *Maple Leaf* excavation were likely looted by the troops from a recent expedition to St. John's Island, South Carolina, where several plantations were occupied by Union troops.

Since the 1989 excavation, the site was listed as a National Historic Landmark—one of only a few shipwrecks accorded that highest of honors in the United States at that time. Inside *Maple Leaf*, another 400 tons of baggage and equipment remain within its well-preserved wooden hull. While for now, without more political interest and funding for the project, excavation has ended, and *Maple Leaf* is perhaps the most fascinating potential Civil War archaeological project that remains to be done in the United States.

CSS *ALABAMA*

While the wrecks of several Civil War naval vessels lie on the ocean floor and riverbeds of the southern United States, a significant wreck that exemplifies both the desperation and the prowess of the Confederate States Navy lies off the coast of France at the bottom of the English Channel. The Confederate States Navy, while confined to the coast and rivers of the southern United States to wage a desperate war against superior Federal forces, sent secret agents to sympathetic Britain to raise funds, purchase arms, and outfit British-built vessels as Confederate warships. Operating under subterfuge to circumvent British neutrality in the conflict, the Confederates built a number of blockade runners and raiders. The most famous was CSS *Alabama*.

Built at John Laird's shipyard in Birkenhead, Englaand, near Liverpool, *Alabama* was a three-masted steam- and sail-powered barkentine. Sailing from Liverpool and entering active service in August 1862, *Alabama* cruised under the command of Raphael Semmes on a 22-month voyage into the Indian Ocean, China Sea, and the Atlantic. In that time, *Alabama* captured and then either sank or ransomed 64 American merchant vessels. The actions of *Alabama* and the other Confederate raiders on the high seas devastated the US shipping industry to the point it never fully recovered after the Civil War.

Alabama engaged the steamer USS *Hatteras* off Galveston, Texas, on January 11, 1863, in a 19-minute battle that sank *Hatteras*. The US Navy dispatched ships to hunt down the Confederate raider. In June 1864, after Semmes slipped into the French port of Cherbourg to land prisoners and drydock his ship, the sloop-of-war USS *Kearsarge* entered the harbor. Rather than try to flee, Semmes decided to fight. The two ships met in the English Channel off Cherbourg on June 19. Circling each other and firing, the two ships fought until *Alabama*, outgunned and not as staunchly built as the Federal warship, sank. Semmes surrendered, but was saved from capture, along with several of his officers and crew, by an English yacht that had stood by and watched the battle.

Years of searching for the wreck finally paid off on October 30, 1984, when a French Navy minesweeper discovered *Alabama* lying in 58 meters of water seven nautical miles off Cherbourg. A joint French-American team led by archaeologists Max Guerout and Gordon P. Watts Jr. then explored the wreck and documented the ship. They mapped many details of the hull, which rests at a 20-degree angle along its starboard side, including the steam machinery. The priorities for archaeological work were studying the ship's technology and living conditions aboard, and finding any evidence of *Alabama*'s 22-month-long career as a raider.

The team recovered more than 100 artifacts. They include the captain's porcelain flush toilet, an ornate fitting not expected in a fighting ship; and souvenirs from some of *Alabama*'s victims, such as a whale's tooth from a burned whaler and a case of soap from Boston seized from a Yankee prize by Semmes for his ship's use. Other artifacts raised from the wreck are one of the ship's Blakely guns, its loading interrupted by the order to abandon ship, leaving a live shell in the barrel, and the remains of *Alabama*'s wheel,

■ Shell and storage box, recovered from the wreck of CSS *Alabama*. (Naval History and Heritage Command)

with its brass bindings still inscribed with *Alabama*'s motto, *Aide toi et Dieu t'aidera*, "God helps those who help themselves."

THE BATTLE OF MOBILE BAY

The shift from studying individual ships of war to better understanding naval battlefields is evident when studying one of the more famous Civil War naval battles in Alabama's Mobile Bay. This gulf port, important to the Confederacy, was blockaded and ostensibly closed to commerce by the Union Navy, but blockade runners still ran the gauntlet into and out of the port, and the powerful guns of seacoast and harbor defense fortifications kept pursuing warships out of the bay. After the fall of New Orleans to the Union in April 1862, Mobile was the only major Confederate port left open in the Gulf of Mexico. By 1864, it was one of only two major Confederate ports left open, the other being Wilmington, North Carolina. To maintain its security, the Confederate Corps of Engineers strengthened defenses and sank vessels loaded with brick amid pilings driven into the channel to block the approaches to the city between 1862 and 1864. In addition to the obstructions, Confederate engineers also placed floating "torpedoes" or mines at the bay's entrance.

In the summer of 1864, a combined Union naval and land force took Mobile Bay and closed the port to Confederate shipping. While troops landed to besiege and take the forts that guarded the harbor entrance, an 18-vessel fleet under the command of David Glasgow Farragut boldly steamed past the forts to fight the Confederate gunboats *Gaines, Selma,* and *Morgan* and the ironclad ram CSS *Tennessee* on August 5, 1864. Farragut had ordered a tight formation, but one of the ironclad monitors, USS *Tecumseh,* strayed into the torpedo minefield. The explosion of a mine quickly flooded and capsized *Tecumseh,* which sank in nine meters of water, taking 96 men with it. The loss of the monitor did not deter the rest of the fleet, and Farragut pressed forward. While doubted by some historians, Farragut reportedly ordered his fleet to "Damn the torpedoes, full speed ahead." Three hours later, the Union fleet was victorious, sinking CSS *Gaines* and pounding CSS *Tennessee* into surrender. Protected by its obstructions, Mobile itself did not fall until the city surrendered in April 1865, but its blockade running days were over.

The wreck of *Tecumseh* was sold by the government for scrapping in 1873, but when the salvager announced he would blast the hulk and raise it in pieces, relatives of the lost crew petitioned Congress to stop him. By Act of Congress, the salvager's money was refunded, and it was stipulated that any future efforts to salvage the wreck had to properly remove and bury *Tecumseh's* dead. It was a century before anyone thought to do so. In 1966, the Smithsonian, as part of a planned national military museum, commissioned a search to find the sunken monitor and investigate what it would take to raise it. In 1967, divers discovered *Tecumseh* off Fort Morgan, lying upside down in the mud, and cut into the hull to recover artifacts that included a large brass engine room gong used to relay orders to the engineering crew. The project never came to fruition due to funding problems, and *Tecumseh* was left in place. A 1993 survey by East Carolina University archaeologist Wilson West found the wreck was still intact, covered with light encrustation. The diver who entered the wreck in 1967 reported that the monitor was intact and only partly filled with silt; for this reason, it is thought that *Tecumseh* is an exceptionally well-preserved time capsule. I led a team that surveyed the wreck site in 2018 and found it completely buried.

Other archaeological surveys in Mobile Bay have expanded our understanding of the larger battlescape, both that of August 1864 and earlier and later events. A variety of surveys mapped a number of magnetic targets, and in 1985, a more comprehensive study and excavations by archaeologists led by Clell Bond and Jack Irion of Espey, Huston and Associates more clearly defined and identified some of the ships scuttled to block the channel as well as some of the obstructions. To protect Mobile, the Confederate-emplaced obstructions ranged from wrecks to pilings and cribs filled with rock and bricks. Much of that, ostensibly cleared post–Civil War, remained as archaeological evidence.

BLOCKADERS AND BLOCKADE RUNNERS

The longest-lasting naval activity of the Civil War was the blockade of the Confederate coastline and its key ports to prevent the flow of goods to and from the rebellious states. Based on the idea of General of the Army Winfield Scott, the "Anaconda plan" intended to economically strangle the Confederacy.

Starting in April 1861, the blockade was at first a paper closure to inhibit shipping, but it became a physical entity over the next several months as the US Navy formed blockading squadrons to close off southern ports. To do that, the navy had to requisition many vessels, including a number of merchant ships that were hastily armed, to patrol the long Confederate coastline. In response, southern businessmen, and, later, the Confederate government, equipped ships as blockade runners—at first wooden-hulled sailing ships, then over time as the trade evolved into low-profile, fast steamships. Hundreds of vessels were engaged in the blockade, and as time passed, both hunters and prey evolved in terms of the ships, tactics, and cargoes carried. More often a game of cat and mouse, blockade running was seen as one of the more romantic aspects of the Civil War at sea. Margaret Mitchell's Rhett Butler, portrayed by Clark Gable in *Gone with the Wind*, was the captain of a blockade-running steamer. Equally daring were the blockaders; by war's end, navy ships and crews had captured over 1,100 blockade runners and had run aground or "destroyed" another 355 vessels.

Archaeologists have studied blockade runner wrecks off the Atlantic and Gulf coasts of the United States, off Bermuda—a hub for blockade runners— and in British waters, as many later runners were built in the officially neutral but southern-sympathetic United Kingdom. Early projects included the recovery of cargoes from several runners, but, increasingly, the archaeology of the blockade has turned into a larger understanding of the evolution of the ships, shifting demands for cargo, and understanding the wrecks of the blockade as part of a larger landscape of war in a 3,549-mile-long battlefield that was in reality a set of intensely focused actions off key ports such as Norfolk, Wilmington, Charleston, Savannah, Mobile, New Orleans, and Galveston.

Much of this work has been led by archaeologist Gordon Watts, who began his research in the 1970s and continues to do so four decades later. In addition to Watts, Mark Wilde Ramsing, Richard Lawrence, and Leslie Bright of North Carolina's Division of Archives and History built on work by Watts and others to define an archaeological district of blockade wrecks off the approaches to the Cape Fear River and the port of Wilmington. The nation's largest number of blockade runner wrecks, 31, lie in North Carolina. Twenty lie off the approaches to Charleston.

There, in South Carolina, work by archaeologist James Spirek has also cataloged what he has termed the archaeology of naval operations in Charleston Harbor from 1861 to 1865. Charleston was the birthplace of the Civil War, both in terms of secession fervor and the opening shots of the war with the cannon barrage against Fort Sumter, a harbor fortification, on April 12, 1861. Spirek has examined the broader battlefield landscape, incorporating wrecks of blockade runners and other craft (including *Housatonic* and *Hunley*), as well as obstructions placed in the harbor to thwart approaches by blockade runners. In a 2008–2011 study, Spirek and colleagues assessed the "stone fleet," 29 former whaling ships laden with stone and sunk in the main channels by Union forces.

They also studied wrecked Confederate steamers used as auxiliary warships, Union warships lost in failed attempts to take the port—including two partially salvaged monitors—and shore side (and in some cases now submerged) harbor gun batteries, as well as sunken blockade runners. Spirek's work with his colleagues truly defined Charleston Harbor as a naval battlefield, a first in Civil War maritime (and naval) archaeology.

Six blockade runners were wrecked off Galveston, where archaeologist J. Barto Arnold has also extensively documented the history and remains of the steamer *Denbigh*, wrecked in 1865. Historians such as Stephen Wise, Andrew Hall, and Kevin Foster have greatly aided our understanding with comprehensive studies of the economics, shipping operations, and naval architecture and engineering.

Modern Greece

The 1960s discovery of the blockade runner *Modern Greece*, a British-registered screw steamer that crashed ashore near the mouth of North Carolina's Cape Fear River, led to a hasty recovery of its cargo by well-intended US Navy divers who turned their 11,000 finds over to the State of North Carolina in 1963. The 753-ton, iron-hulled *Modern Greece* was inbound to Wilmington with a much-needed cargo of military supplies and general cargo when it was intercepted by the USS *Cambridge*. Under fire, the captain of the steamer ran close to shore to get within range of the guns of Confederate-held Fort Fisher to avoid capture. Just a half mile from the fort, *Modern Greece* ran hard aground at 4:15 A.M. on the morning of June 27, 1862. Both Union warships and the guns of Fort Fisher fired shots into the stranded steamer before the blockaders moved off. Troops from Fort Fisher salvaged cannon, small arms, gunpowder, household goods, clothing, and whisky before abandoning the steamer to the tide.

Modern Greece gradually disappeared beneath the sand, some 90 meters offshore. Storms exposed the wreck in April 1962. The centennial of the

Civil War inspired the navy's salvage of the wreck's remaining cargo as well as its anchors and capstan. In 1977, archaeologist Leslie Bright cataloged and documented the *Modern Greece* artifacts, which are the only blockade runner cargo to be extensively studied. The cargo speaks to the times and needs of the Confederacy and its citizens; hardware, house wares, tin, sheet steel and wire are reminders that the South was largely non-industrial. Battlefield necessities included Enfield rifles, bayonets, shells, lead ingots to be melted into bullets, and surgical kits.

Recently, archaeologists from East Carolina University took a second look at the cargo of *Modern Greece*. East Carolina's Chelsea Freeland questioned why not all of the cargo was salvaged in 1862 and found that at that early stage of the war, Wilmington was regularly benefitting from blockade runner cargos that made it in, and there was no shortage of merchandise. What was saved, she found, were readily accessible items needed by the military, and then only luxury items. The selective salvage of *Modern Greece* was in itself an artifact, as within a few years, the effectiveness of the blockade would have compelled the complete stripping of the wreck in more desperate times.

MARY CELESTIA

The excavation of the 207-ton paddle steamer *Mary Celestia* illustrated the role of personal smuggling in highly profitable blockade running. Because of the risks, blockade running merchants sold both basic commodities and luxuries for 200 to 700 percent more than they had in peacetime. More than fancy clothes, ladies' shoes, perfumes, and wines, however, what the government of the Confederate States of America needed were uniforms, boots, medicine, weapons, and ammunition. To counter the tendency of blockade-running companies and captains to load their ships with high-value commodities for better profit, the Confederacy operated government-owned runners and in 1864, the Confederate Congress passed a law banning luxury goods on the steamers to focus the incoming cargoes on what was needed to win the war.

Mary Celestia was one of the hundreds of steamers built to run the blockade. Ordered by William and James Crenshaw, two brothers from Richmond, Virginia, whose business interests in Great Britain and its colonies, including Bermuda, depended on regular maritime trade, *Mary Celestia* was the product of the Liverpool shipyard of William C. Miller & Sons. Launched in February 1864 and completed two months later once its boilers and engines were installed, *Mary Celestia* departed for Bermuda. Arriving in May, the steamer commenced the first of four known and perhaps as many as eight trips to Wilmington, North Carolina, running the blockade with a variety of goods and returning to Bermuda with cotton. Bermuda was an ideal transshipment point for the blockade runners. Its small port of St. George's was crowded with ships arriving from Halifax, Liverpool, London, and Nassau with coal to fuel the runners and commodities offloaded into warehouses awaiting a fast steamer to load and run past the blockaded coast several hundred miles away. The cotton, after landing in Bermuda, also warehoused, would be collected and sent to Great Britain in a large, slow ship without fear of being intercepted by the US Navy, which stayed close to the American coast.

Mary Celestia's career was brief but dramatic. Chased by a US Navy blockader, the runner escaped when the captain threw over 40 bales of cotton to lighten the load and the engineer held the safety valves down to get the boilers running hot enough to push the steamer's engines to 17 knots and outrun the Yankee ship. While a yellow fever epidemic ravaged the crew, and in an act of bravery, the ship's North Carolina pilot—the man who knew the landmarks to safely navigate the hazardous approaches to Wilmington—although himself dying of the fever, stayed at his post as the runner raced past the blockaders. He brought *Mary Celestia* safely into the Cape Fear River, collapsed, and died.

On its final voyage, *Mary Celestia* steamed out of Hamilton, Bermuda, with owner William Crenshaw and Bermuda pilot John Virgin aboard. Loaded with a Confederate government–mandated cargo of canned meat and "general merchandise" (actually munitions and Enfield rifles), *Mary Celestia* steamed along the southern shore of the island to drop off the owner and pilot near the Gibb's Point Lighthouse, where they both lived.

Approaching the shore, the chief mate shouted that there were rocks ahead. The pilot, in control of the ship's movements, shouted back he knew the rocks and reefs as well as he knew his own home. With that, *Mary Celestia* struck the reef. Several minutes later, as all on board scrambled into boats, the steamer sank, taking with it the ship's cook, who ran back below to save something of value he had left behind, only to have a door swing shut and trap him.

Despite more than a century of salvage and gradual structural collapse, portions of the wreck remained intact, notably the steamer's sharp bow, which still lay on its side. When winter storms washed out sand, exposing a crate with intact and still-full bottles of wine, the Bermuda government mounted an international rescue excavation of the bow, which I co-directed in 2011 with Philippe Rouja and Dominique Rissolo. What we found, stored inside the boatswain's locker, where paint, spare gear, and tools were kept, was a secret stash of wine, perfume and cologne, an expensive English hairbrush, and pairs of shoes. This was not cargo, but a private stash probably intended for friends and family behind the blockade. A stash like this might have been what sent the cook back into the sinking ship, only to lose his life.

Chief Engineer Charles F. Middleton, writing his wife back home in Charleston to report he was safe, lamented that while he had grabbed some of his clothes as *Mary Celestia* sank, he "lost a great deal otherwise. I had [unreadable] Barrels Sugar, 1 lb. Best Tea, a case of shoes (59 pair), a whole piece of calico and two dresses of same, but thank God I saved myself." What struck me as an archaeologist is that the items in the bow that we excavated provide more than data. They are a tangible link to the evocative human behaviors of *Mary Celestia*'s crew, an intimate window into a human past often overshadowed by the big names and events of written history. The naval aspects of the Civil War are perhaps one of the best-documented aspects of how archaeology adds to our understanding not only of conflict, but of human roles and consequences in times of war.

7

The Race to Global War

Don't cheer boys; the poor fellows are dying!
> —Captain John Woodward Philip at the Battle of Santiago, 1898

The US Civil War was a naval proving ground, essentially ending a thousand years of wooden warships and illustrating the use of iron-hulled and armored warships. It also demonstrated the effectiveness of the undersea "torpedo," or mine. Throughout the 1860s and 1870s, other navies responded to the lessons of the US Civil War by adding ironclad monitors to their fleets, while others commenced a decades-long quest for effective combat submarines. Over time, the inefficiency of the monitors gave way to the development of the steel-armored cruiser and battleship, culminating when Britain introduced the game-changing HMS *Dreadnought* at the start of the 20th century. By the end of the 19th century, the "Great Powers" were building bigger, faster, longer-ranging, and harder-hitting ships.

This was the era of imperial naval pride and of "gunboat diplomacy," projecting force through the deployment of warships to the far corners of the world. To be a great power then meant having a navy, a lesson taken up by nations like Japan, Germany, Italy, Spain, Chile, Peru, Austria, and Turkey, among others. The United States, weary and sick at the conclusion of a war that remains the largest killer of Americans of all other wars combined that it has fought, pulled back after 1865. The United States maintained a fleet of Civil War veteran ships with little replacement or experimentation in newer, better warships until the 1880s.

This was also a time of overseas expansion by nations using their industries and technologies to build up navies and seize colonies abroad. France occupied Tunisia in Africa as well as Pacific islands, Indochina (Vietnam), Cambodia, and Laos. Italy annexed Eritrea. Britain established a "protectorate" over India, Egypt, Zanzibar, Bahrain, and Palestine; seized the Malay Peninsula; and fought a three-year war to retain South Africa. Belgium conquered the Congo. Germany built up colonies in Africa and the South Pacific. Japan, forcibly "opened" to the world by a squadron of US Navy warships demanding trading rights in July 1853, burst out into the Pacific between the 1870s and 1890s by seizing the Kuril and Bonin Islands, the Ryukyus (including Okinawa), and the Volcano Islands (including Iwo Jima).

The United States, for the most part, stayed out of the fray, opting for a peaceful purchase of Alaska in 1867 and claiming a series of distant Pacific atolls, including one named Midway. They were either convenient way stations used to store coal for steamships, or because they were rich in guano, malodorous bird droppings that enriched crops as fertilizer. A change in American political and military attitudes came with the publication of naval officer Alfred Thayer Mahan's *The Influence of Sea Power upon History* in 1890. It coincided, just three years later, with Frederick Jackson Turner's published thesis that the age of the American frontier had ended. Mahan's argument that control of the seas meant political, military, and economic power resonated in an America racked by economic depression and social disorder. An expanded, powerful US Navy could, particularly in the Pacific, make America a global power to rival Great Britain. Those sentiments hearkened an imperial age in which a strong, modern American navy emerged. The United States expanded overseas, seizing Hawai'i; fighting a war with Spain; and seizing Puerto Rico, Guam, the Philippines, and, for a while Cuba, and then building the Panama Canal through what was essentially an occupied Panamá.

Mahan's book also had a profound effect on foreign naval thinking, particularly with the nascent Imperial Japanese Navy, and with Kaiser Wilhelm of Germany, who eagerly built a powerful Kriegsmarine. The build-up of Japan and Germany in particular was alarming to the Great Powers, especially at the start of the 20th century when Japan twice destroyed two Russian fleets. It was a harbinger of decades of global war that began just nine years after Japan's final decisive naval battle of that war, Tsushima. That war, truly global, saw a brief interregnum, followed by a vaster, bloodier conflict that concluded just 40 years after Tsushima with the near-complete destruction of Japan and Germany. The world's oceans, lakes, and even its rivers are the resting place of a wide range of warship wrecks as well as battlefields from this often-contentious and at times violent age of naval expansion, skirmishes, and wars.

USS *SAGINAW*

When launched in 1859, *Saginaw* was on the brink of being on obsolete warship. Powered by steam, the wooden-hulled sloop-of-war carried 50 crew and only four guns. Constructed at the relatively new US Navy Yard at Mare Island, on San Francisco Bay, *Saginaw* was the first product of that yard. It was also one of a handful of warships in the Pacific representing and projecting American power during and immediately after the Civil War. *Saginaw*'s far-ranging career began in China, where it patrolled to protect US shipping from pirates, and then to Vietnam to search for a missing boat of sailors. This mission led to the destruction of a Vietnamese fort guarding Qui Nhon when it opened fire on *Saginaw*. The French were in the process of conquering Vietnam, and foreign warships were not welcome.

During the Civil War, *Saginaw* stayed close to America's Pacific shores on duties that included searching for Confederate warships and raiders and escorting gold-laden steamships from San Francisco to Panamá. In 1868, the navy sent the ship north following the US purchase of Alaska. There, in another use of naval power to enforce American law, *Saginaw* bombarded Tlingit native villages and forts on the Alaska coast in retribution for the killing of two American fur traders. In early 1870, another mission in the spirit of America's guarded, piecemeal expansion into the Pacific after the Civil War took *Saginaw* to Midway. The low-lying atoll, as its name implies, is halfway between North America and Asia. The first Pacific island formally annexed by the United States in 1867, Midway was seen as an ideal coaling station to fuel warships and the large wooden sidewheel steamers of the Pacific Mail Steamship Company, which that year had commenced regular steamer service between San Francisco, Japan, and China.

Opening a channel through the reef at Midway to allow steamers to enter required not only men and equipment but a warship to guard them and serve as the support ship for the hard-hat divers who were blasting the reef. *Saginaw* had completed that task and was ready to return to Mare Island when news of a shipwrecked crew at nearby Kure Atoll diverted it. On October 29, 1870, as the steamer approached Kure in late-night darkness, *Saginaw* hit the reef and wrecked at 3:15 A.M. After a long, frightful ordeal, with daybreak the crew spotted a narrow opening that led to tiny Green Island. The crew landed supplies and provision as the sea and coral tore their ship apart. They then used their last match to light a fire for cooking and warmth. Ninety-three men were now stranded with faint hope of survival.

Kure Atoll lay off the regular shipping routes, and with food and water in short supply was, as a later navy account stressed, "little more than a sandbank." Five volunteers agreed to sail the captain's gig—a small, 22-foot-long boat—more than 1600 nautical miles to Hawai'i to bring help. After the crew reconfigured the gig into a more seaworthy craft and provisioned it as best they could, the volunteers set out on November 18, three weeks after *Saginaw*'s wreck.

Their 31-day ordeal remains one of the cruelest stories of the sea. The provisions proved largely spoiled, and starvation set in as well as sickness. Wet, cold, wracked by diarrhea, they made it to the island of Kaua'i, where, too weakened to land, they drifted into the surf, flipping the gig on the night of December 18. Only two of the men made it ashore. One died, leaving only one survivor, Coxswain William Halford. Brought to Honolulu, Halford's tale and letters from the wrecked *Saginaw* that the gig's crew had carried in a sealed tin container launched a rescue expedition sent by King

Kamehameha V that reached Kure Atoll 68 days after *Saginaw*'s loss. They found that *Saginaw*'s crew had survived and brought all of them safely off the narrow island where, had no rescue come, they would have all died.

The self-sacrifice of the crew of *Saginaw*'s gig made national headlines and ensured the preservation of the gig as a relic, along with its flag and a sextant made from scrap from broken wrecked instruments. The lost men are commemorated on a memorial plaque in the chapel of the US Naval Academy in Annapolis. William Halford received the Medal of Honor in 1872, dying after a long and distinguished career in 1919, still on active duty after being recalled to service during World War I.

In 1912, *Saginaw* shipmate George H. Read published *The Last Cruise of the Saginaw*, his account of the wreck and the cruise of the gig. A century later, it remains in print as a classic in American naval literature. *Saginaw*'s gig was originally displayed at Mare Island and then sent to Annapolis in 1882. By the 1950s, the gig was displayed in Saginaw, Michigan's Castle Museum, but it recently returned to US Navy custody. *Saginaw*'s gig is more than a

■ The gig of USS *Saginaw*, the setting for epic suffering and heroism (Naval History and Heritage Command)

relic; it is an evocative artifact, with the desperate modifications made at Kure, and bearing the scars of its final night on the reef and beach when the voyage ended and four of the five crew died. When you look at this battered, tiny craft, your eyes are drawn to the names of the five-man crew of the gig— John G. Talbot, William Halford, Peter Francis, John Andrews, and James Muir. The survivors cut these names into the hatch coaming to leave a record should they die before reaching safety and alerting rescuers to the loss of *Saginaw*. The gig is, as archaeologist Hans K. Van Tilburg writes, "the single most evocative" artifact of the last cruise of USS *Saginaw*.

Van Tilburg, an accomplished and highly respected archaeologist who focuses on the Pacific and Asia, led two expeditions to Kure Atoll, now part of Papahānaumokuākea Marine National Monument, a 582,578-square-mile conservation area managed by the National Oceanic and Atmospheric Administration (NOAA). Van Tilburg is the Pacific Regional Maritime Heritage Coordinator. During the first mission, in 2003, the team discovered the broken wreck of *Saginaw* both outside and inside the atoll's lagoon. The 2006 mission discovered artifacts from the ill-fated steamer.

■ *Saginaw*'s engine broke apart during the wreck; NOAA archaeologists found part of it wedged into the reef. (NOAA)

The wooden hull has disintegrated, but the broken steam engines, paddlewheel shafts, the anchors, *Saginaw's* four cannon, parts of the boilers, fasteners from the hull, and other artifacts were found wedged into the crevices of the reef. The major find from 2006 was *Saginaw's* bell, "upside down and half buried…the crown of the bell cracked," as Van Tilburg writes, a "sight both touching and rare." An NOAA team recovered the bell in 2008; after preservation treatment, it is now on display in Hawai'i. The wreck and its artifacts reflect, as Van Tilburg notes, more than the broken remains of a small wooden American gunboat and the first naval ship built at Mare Island Naval Shipyard. They tell the story of America's "first real strides into the Pacific…with the ships and tools of antiquated steam navy."

HMS *VIXEN*

Despite the fame of the two American combatants of the Civil War, CSS *Virginia* and USS *Monitor*, the United States was not the first nation to think about or build ironclads. However, the American experiences with monitors and other ironclads in combat during the Civil War did inspire other powers to embrace the "ironclad revolution." While some naval powers like Russia and Sweden copied John Ericsson's design for monitors, the poor sea-keeping abilities of these essentially coastal craft meant that in many ways they were ill-suited for serious naval use. Architects in Britain, realizing this shortcoming in the monitors, and working from their own experiments with both armored warships and turret-mounted guns, gradually developed seagoing ironclads that in time evolved into the powerful battleships of the early 20th century.

The evolution of the battleship was not a smooth progression, and the wreck of one early British ironclad in Bermuda is a striking example of what one prominent naval historian, David K. Brown, calls the "Age of Uncertainty." HMS *Vixen*, built in 1864 and scuttled to help block a channel in 1896, rests in 10.7 meters of water, her bow rising above the surface at the west end of Bermuda. While built with iron frames and an iron hull as an "armored gunboat," *Vixen* was covered with teak cladding because early iron hulls were easily fouled by marine growth, which slowed them down. The hull below the waterline was also sheathed in copper to keep marine organisms from eating the wood.

The Royal Navy did not consider *Vixen*'s iron hull to be the ship's armor; instead a thick iron box at the heart of the ship protected the machinery. Iron plate used in shipbuilding in the 19th century—as well as early steel—was not as strong as modern metal. Brittle when cold, it had a tendency to shatter. This Achilles heel was serious. During the age of the wooden walls, warships often blasted each other, even at point-blank range, without sinking because the thick wooden hulls had more flexibility and wood is buoyant. But an iron ship, particularly in a new age with the more powerful punch of rifled guns and exploding shells, would sink quickly once buoyancy was lost when the hull was shot through. The answer was armor, but the thick plate needed to protect a ship's machinery, guns, and crew was incredibly heavy. Not only did the weight affect buoyancy, it could also overwhelm early, more inefficient steam engines. *Vixen*, therefore, is an embodiment of compromise with just enough armor to protect the engines and boilers without making it too heavy.

Another compromise is seen in the ship's machinery. Powered by two 160-horsepower direct acting four-cylinder steam engines that drove a set of propellers, *Vixen* and its sister ships were the Royal Navy's first twin-screw warships. But instead of going faster than other ships, as expected, *Vixen* was disappointingly slow. The ship also carried only enough coal to fuel the boilers for twelve days' operation, and so the Royal Navy compromised by equipping *Vixen* with masts and sails. Other than using the engines to maneuver in and out of harbor, or into battle, *Vixen* usually operated under sail. Apparatus at the stern allowed the crew to hoist the propellers out of the water, while a collapsible funnel dropped closer to the deck to allow the ship to work better with the wind. Labor intensive and not efficient, *Vixen* had a short life as a warship on the open seas. By 1868, it was sent to Bermuda to serve as a guard ship for the naval dockyard. With the decks cleared of superstructure and masts, it remained afloat for another 23 years, at which point it was scuttled.

Archaeologists from Brown University and Earthwatch, in cooperation with the Bermuda Maritime Museum, studied the wreck of *Vixen* between

1986 and 1988. Directed by archaeologist Richard A. Gould, the divers mapped the wreck and documented features not fully shown on the vessel's plans, like a projecting, armored ram at the bow. This anachronistic feature seemed to the archaeologists to be a strange emphasis for the Royal Navy when the ship was equipped with modern, breech-loading guns that were not protected by armor. These construction choices "challenged the documentary description of these ships as gunboats," but more to the point is evidence of this period of uncertainty, or, as Gould terms it, "tactical indecision" as the Royal Navy grappled with the benefits of the new technology.

THE IRONCLAD *RUSSALKA*

Another wrecked monitor speaks to more than the European adoption of the monitor-type warship after the *Monitor/Virginia* battle. *Russalka* (Mermaid) was built at St. Petersburg in 1866–1867 for the Imperial Russian Navy. With two turrets, each carrying two heavy-duty cannon, and a four-and-a-half-inch-thick iron belt of armor protecting its sides, *Russalka* was part of a Russian build-up of its navy following Russia's loss of the Crimean War in 1856 and the end of its ability to both fortify and place naval forces in the Black Sea. In response, Russia proceeded to build up its fleet in the Baltic and looked to further naval and military expansion in Asia. A key part of that was to create an ironclad navy.

The first Russian ironclad, built in Britain in 1863, was the floating battery *Pervenetz*. That monitor's design was followed to such an extent that 19th-century naval authority Frederick Jane noted "having taken to the monitor, Russia practically adopted it." Building *Russalka* was part of that adoption. The Russian focus on monitors meant that, as Jane noted, "nothing in the nature of a seagoing vessel was attempted for some time." Russian sea power was relegated to coastal defense, as the monitors were not suited for prolonged or open-water cruises.

The career and the loss of *Russalka* point to this weakness in Russia's post–Crimean War naval expansion. After its launch, *Russalka* had an entirely uneventful career in the Baltic, save one grounding. By 1870, the ship was assigned to artillery training, and for the next 23 years, training, naval exercises, maintenance, upgrades to guns, and changes of command filled *Russalka*'s logbooks. That changed on what would have been just another voyage on September 7, 1893. *Russalka* sailed at 8:30 that morning, escorted by the gunboat *Tutscha*, from the naval base at Reval (now Tallinn), Estonia, bound for Helsinki, a short 43-nautical-mile trip across the Gulf of Finland. It was a rough day, with gale-force winds and heavy seas, and the two ships struggled to make headway. More than halfway across, *Tutscha* lost sight of *Russalka* in a squall, but proceeded to Helsinki. *Russalka* never showed up, and a search along the route found only a lifeboat with a frozen corpse in it. No other sign of the ship or the other 176 men and boys in its crew was ever found.

Where *Russalka* had gone down remained a mystery for 110 years. On the ninth anniversary of the loss in 1902, both the German kaiser and the tsar dedicated a 16-meter-high granite and bronze memorial, topped by a life-sized angel holding aloft a gilded Orthodox cross pointing out to sea. Designed and sculpted by Estonian artist Amandus Adamson, it is decorated with bronze plaques depicting the ship, small-cast guns, anchors, and chain at a busy intersection where Tallinn's Kadriorg Park ends at the waterfront. I have visited Tallinn three times, and each time, I stop and visit the angel of the *Russalka*. My interest is so keen because I am one of a few who has dived to and touched the wreck.

In 2003, archaeologist Vello Mäss of the Estonian National Maritime Museum, and commercial diver Kaido Peremees, set out to find *Russalka*. On July 24, they made a dive on an intriguing sonar target they had found two days earlier, 16 miles out from Helsinki. The wreck lay in 74 meters of water. Dropping through pitch-black water on a line with which they had snagged the wreck, at a depth of only 40 meters, their lights revealed the rudder and the bronze propellers of *Russalka*. The Russian ironclad had sunk bow first, driving into the mud and burying itself nearly upright for about 30 meters of its length. With a National Geographic team, I was able to visit the wreck with Vello and Kaido and dive *Russalka* two years later.

We were the first Westerners to do so, and it was a privilege. Intact, and draped with snagged trawl nets, *Russalka*'s iron hull is rusted, but the bronze of the propellers and a detached Nordenfelt rapid-fire gun caught in the nets gleams as if polished. The aft turret had fallen out, and was nowhere to be seen, but the gaping maw of its barbette marked its place. The wooden decks were intact, and as you drop beneath the nets and look into hatches, you see smashed wooden paneling, doors, and furniture, and gain a clear sense that you are looking into a tomb.

The discovery of the wreck solved the mystery of where *Russalka* lay—within sight of the church spires of Helsinki. They had almost made it to safety. As to why it sank, Vello Mäss points out that *Russalka*, like other monitors, relied on watertight decks, and they were not designed for battling heavy seas because the freeboard was only 76 centimeters. At some stage, through a leaky seam, a sprung hatch, or aged metal seams, the ironclad began to take on water at the bow. At some point, either turning to avoid an oncoming wave, or lost and unable to determine a position, it turned back toward Reval and suddenly plunged to the bottom, propellers still spinning, and drove into the muddy sea bed like a fallen arrow.

Perhaps there was enough time for some of the crew, perhaps on deck, to scramble into boats, which may be why one boat and one dead man from the crew were later found. Next to the hull, another overturned boat rests by *Russalka*'s conning tower. Sticking out of it are what appear to be bones. We did not approach any further. The forensic sense of *how* only partly answers the question of *why*, however. Obsolete, old, and not in the best condition, *Russalka* sailed from Tallinn in the face of a storm with the captain knowing that his ship was not well-suited to the conditions. However, his admirals refused to let him stay in port. *Russalka* needed to get to Helsinki, and so Captain Second Rank Ienish ordered his crew to cast off, and they set out and died in strict obedience to bad orders.

THE WRECK OF *ESMERALDA*

Halfway across the world, another warship wreck in Pacific waters off the coast of Chile is the victim of another battle with a monitor. *Esmeralda* is another exemplar of the standard warship of the world's navies at the brink of the ironclad revolution. Built as a wooden-hulled, steam-powered corvette in England, *Esmeralda* had been ordered in 1855 by the Chilean navy, then a nearly four-decade-old institution that had already fought in Chile's war for independence from Spain and in a three-year-long conflict with its neighboring states of Peru and Bolivia. Chile's political and military leadership believed in maintaining a strong navy, and that remains at the core of modern Chilean politics and pride. *Esmeralda* was part of an expansion of the *Armada de Chile* that had commenced in the mid-1840s in order to maintain its standing as Latin America's strongest naval power. Arriving at Valparaíso in 1856, the new corvette was intended to help counter the ongoing threat of Spain, and, for the Chileans, an even more hated rival, neighboring Peru.

Conflict and *Esmeralda's* first test in battle came during a two-year-long naval war with Spain over control of offshore guano islands. On November 26, 1865, *Esmeralda* captured the Spanish schooner *Virgen de Covadonga* 55 miles north of Valparaíso after an hour-long exchange of gunfire that badly damaged the Spanish ship and left four of its crew dead and another 22 wounded. There were no casualties on *Esmeralda*. The next trial by fire came 14 years later during the *Guerra del Pacifico*, a prolonged, three-year struggle on land and sea between Chile, Peru, and Bolivia.

In the early months of the war, the Chilean navy blocked the Peruvian port of Iquique with *Esmeralda* and its former capture, now squadron mate, *Covadonga*. The Peruvian navy broke the blockade on May 21, 1879, when it sent the Peruvian ironclad *Huáscar* and the armored frigate *Independencia* to Iquique. The Peruvians, in a four-hour-long battle drove off *Covadonga* but lost *Independencia* when it ran aground. *Huáscar*, meanwhile, pounded *Esmeralda* in a bloody exchange of gunfire that holed the corvette's wooden hull repeatedly while *Esmeralda's* shot glanced and bounced off the ironclad's armor. Captain Arturo Prat and the crew of *Esmeralda* fought valiantly, and prolonged the inevitable, but after multiple hits and the explosion of an overtaxed boiler, *Esmeralda* slowed as *Huáscar* closed for the kill and rammed it.

At that moment, Captain Prat and two of his men leaped onto the deck of *Huáscar*, reportedly with a cry for his crew to follow. Peruvian sharpshooters hit Prat twice, killing him and his men. The battle continued as *Huáscar* moved off, ramming again, and then shooting down yet another group of Chileans who leaped onto the deck. A third ramming opened a hole in *Esmeralda*'s side and the ship sank, with the Chilean flag nailed to its mast reportedly the last part to leave the surface. The loss of the ship shocked Chile, but Prat's death roused a patriotic fervor. Arturo Prat and some of his crew are interred beneath a prominent memorial to them in Valparaíso, the *Monumento a Los Heroes de Iquique*, while relics of his as well as artifacts raised from the wreck of *Esmeralda* by Chilean navy divers in the 1960s, 1970s, and 1980s are displayed at the National Maritime Museum. A modern replica of *Esmeralda* is its own museum and *Huáscar* is also a museum ship. Captured by the Chilean navy after another brutal battle in October 1879, it served for decades as a Chilean warship before its retirement and restoration to its 1879 appearance.

Despite the various recoveries, and its long immersion in the sea, *Esmeralda* is substantially intact, as no marine organisms exist on the site to eat the hull. Diving *Esmeralda* is like visiting a ghost ship, with loose artifacts scattered inside the hull, and the death-wound—the large hole opened by *Huáscar*'s bow—visible and stark. In April 2010, a team led by Chilean archaeologist Diego Carabias conducted a full archaeological survey of the wreck in response to a report by navy divers that they had spotted a human skull inside the hull. The skull was indeed there, and the team carefully removed it. A grim reminder of the toll of the battle, the skull is likely from a man who had died at his post when with each close pass of *Huáscar*, the Peruvian gunners had poured shot into *Esmeralda*, killing many of the crew. After forensic study, the Chilean navy interred the skull in the vault of the *Monumento a Los Heroes de Iquique*.

HMS *DOTEREL*

In 2005, I was part of a National Geographic television crew that journeyed to the tip of South America to dive a British gunboat that lies in the Straits of Magellan. The wreck of HMS *Doterel* had laid where it had exploded off

■ *Doterel* memorial in the Royal Navy Chapel in Greenwich (Stephen C. Dickson/ Wikipedia Commons)

Punta Arenas, Chile, on the morning of April 26, 1881, killing 143 of its crew and leaving only 12 survivors. After the sinking, the Royal Navy sent hard-hat divers down to inspect the wreckage to see if they could discern what had happened, such as a boiler explosion. They found the hull of the steel-framed, wooden-hulled *Doterel* half intact forward of the stern, with the engineering spaces undamaged. No trace was found of the ship's bow. After salvaging guns and the propeller from the relatively new, one-year-old ship, the navy divers departed, leaving *Doterel* to the sea.

The tragic peacetime loss of *Doterel* stayed in the contemporary papers of 1881 longer than most accidents because Irish terrorists were suspected of having blown up the ship. Irish separatists, known as "Fenians," had threatened high-profile British targets, and an American-based group's leader, O'Donovan Rossa, outright claimed that his group had placed explosives in *Doterel*. The Royal Navy's committee of inquiry ruled, however, that coal gas emanating from the ship's bunkers had ignited and destroyed the ship. A new probable cause came to light in 1883, when a jar of xerotine siccative, a patent dryer for paint (an essential on always-wet or damp ships), spilled on HMS *Indus*. One of the *Doterel* survivors was now a member of that crew. The odor brought back a memory of smelling it once before on *Doterel* just before a pair of explosions destroyed the ship. Xerotine siccative was by then known to be dangerous, especially when a jar had exploded on board HMS *Triumph* seven months after *Doterel*'s loss. Further investigation found that a jar had cracked inside *Doterel*'s paint locker, at the ship's bow. Two men sent to retrieve and throw it overboard had apparently lit a match to find the xerotine siccative, which exploded. That explosion then set off *Doterel*'s forward magazine's four tons of munitions. The case was considered closed, but questions remained—had this been an act of terrorism or an accident? That's what brought us to Punta Arenas.

The wreck of *Doterel* remains untouched off the city's main waterfront. Working with a local diving and salvage company, our divers, the father-and-son team of Mike and Warren Fletcher, made a hard-hat dive as I talked them through the wreckage from the surface. *Doterel* looked pretty much as it had in an *Illustrated London News* drawing of diving operations in 1881. Warren worked his way forward, and soon moved off the wreckage and onto the sand. He kept going in a straight line, swimming into the gloom, and 46 meters away from the main body of the wreck, he found the tip of the bow.

The explosions had blown the bow free of *Doterel*. As we inspected the bow, the ruptured hull and the twisted steel frames showed that the blast had come from within the bow and had destroyed both the paint locker and forward magazine. Despite the braggadocio of a long-dead terrorist, the destruction of the gunboat had been an accident. As we concluded the dives, we sat on deck and talked about how fortunate it had been that the mysterious destruction of *Doterel* in a foreign port had not led Britain into a war with Chile, or a massive witch hunt for perpetrators who didn't exist. We did so mindful of a recent set of dives we had made in Cuba on the wrecks of a war started when the US cruiser *Maine* had mysteriously blown up in Havana Harbor in 1898.

HMS *VICTORIA*

In addition to *Russalka*, one other pre-dreadnought warship rests on the seabed, bow stuck into the bottom and vertically rising toward the surface. Launched in 1887, HMS *Victoria*, a 103-meter-long, steel-hulled behemoth, was the first battleship in the world powered by the recently developed triple expansion marine steam engine. Previously limited to smaller ships, the 1860s–1870s development of this type of engine proved it suitable for major ships. The installation of a triple expansion engine in *Victoria* was one of the factors that made it the fastest, largest warship afloat when the Royal Navy commissioned it. Heavily armed, *Victoria* was also the most powerful ship in the world's naval forces. It was the epitome, no pun intended, of the Victorian Age.

None of that saved *Victoria* and most of its crew when it sank on June 22, 1893, in a preventable collision with HMS *Camperdown* off Tripoli, Lebanon. While executing a turn with two columns of warships on the orders of Vice Admiral George Tryon, who was on board *Victoria*, *Camperdown* rammed into the starboard side of *Victoria*. Propellers still racing, *Victoria* sank quickly by the bow, stern in the air. Some of the crew, trapped inside or tangled in the rigging, went down with the ship. The vortex of the sinking dragged others down. In all 358 men died. The loss of *Victoria* shocked Victorian Britain, and controversy and recriminations raged in the press. A court martial placed the blame for the accident firmly on Admiral Tryon, who had gone down with the ship, but controversy still remained, including concern over the destitute families of the sailors who had died. A public subscription led by philanthropist and friend of the Royal Navy Dame Agnes Weston raised £50,000 in a matter of a few weeks to aid these families.

The wreck of HMS *Victoria* remained undiscovered until Christian Francis and Mark Ellyatt found it in August 2004. The discovery was the culmination of Francis's 10-year search for *Victoria*. They found the wreck standing vertically from the seabed in 150 meters of water with the stern 75 meters below the surface. The ship's name was still visible on the stern in large 30-centimeter-high letters. The wreck has been visited since by high-qualified technical divers, including Mark Ellyatt. Diving and exploring wrecks without robotic vehicles or submersibles limits the amount of time one can spend there. However, unless a small, remotely operated vehicle (ROV) is available, tech divers have the advantage of being able to explore the interior.

This ship exemplifies how wrecks are time capsules, as videos of the dives reveal guns on carriages, equipment, and personal effects. In 2011, the Lebanese Ministry of Culture declared the wreck of *Victoria* a historic monument of the Lebanese government. In January 2012, Mark Ellyatt reported that he had been able to reach Admiral Tryon's cabin, which he told the *Daily Mail* "is a bit like a shrine, with all kinds of nice things hanging off the walls." Tryon had a collection of memorabilia from Admiral Horatio Nelson, the hero of Trafalgar, including Nelson's sword. Ellyatt hid the sword in the wreck, he reported, to keep it from being plundered.

USS *MAINE*

On the evening of February 15, 1898, the battleship USS *Maine* lay at anchor in Havana Harbor. At 9:40 P.M., a series of explosions split the ship open, sending a pillar of fire into the sky and a shower of debris into the sea. Much of the forward part of *Maine* had disintegrated, taking with it 253 of the 355-man crew. Seven more died of their wounds after being plucked from the harbor's waters. A board of inquiry decided on March 28 that a submarine mine had detonated beneath *Maine* and set off one or two of its forward magazines. Spurred by war-hungry newspapers, a long-simmering anger at Spain, and a desire among some to annex Cuba into a new American overseas empire, the United States went to war with Spain on April 25 to the rallying cry of "Remember the *Maine*! To hell with Spain!"

The war lasted less than four months before it ended in an armistice following the destruction of two Spanish fleets and the defeat of its armies in Cuba and the Philippines. The US Secretary of State John Hay called it a "splendid little war." That judgment is a matter of perspective. In all, just over 4,000 Americans were casualties, half of them lost to disease, with

Spanish casualties at four times that number with approximately 15,000 of them lost to disease. The major naval actions were at Manila Bay, where a fleet commanded by Admiral George Dewey smashed the Spanish fleet on May 1, and the Battle of Santiago on July 3, when the Spanish fleet was either destroyed or run aground. The majority of the fighting on land took place in Cuba, both with landings at Daquiri and Siboney, a bloody fight at Las Guasimas, and then a struggle to take the heights above Santiago, with the actions at El Caney and San Juan Hill gaining fame through the actions of the US troops in the face of fierce resistance from the entrenched Spanish forces. Among those troops were Col. Theodore Roosevelt's "Rough Riders." A naval force also took Puerto Rico, but faced strong resistance there that ended only with the armistice.

The aftermath of the war and the resultant Treaty of Paris, signed in December 1898, essentially ended 500 years of Spain's colonial presence in the Americas with the cession of Puerto Rico and Spain's withdrawal from Cuba, then under a nominal American occupation. Spain also gave the United States the Philippines and Guam. The United States agreed to pay Spain $20 million for its former colonies and thus gained an overseas empire. Cuba remained under American control until 1902, with a second US occupation from September 1906 to February 1909. The Platt Amendment (1901), which ended the initial occupation, forbade any foreign military use of the island and forced the Cubans to accept subsequent United States occupations to protect American economic interests in a subsequent treaty in 1903. Cuba also agreed to lease to the United States its already-occupied 116-square-kilometer naval base and coaling station at Guantánamo Bay.

The wreck of USS *Maine*, for the most part, remained in Cuba. The broken hulk sat in just 10 meters of water in the middle of the harbor off the city's waterfront until 1912. After Cuban demands to clear the wreck from the port, and ongoing pressure from the families of the lost crew to bring their bodies up from the wreck, Congress authorized what in time would total nearly a million dollars to raise *Maine* and sink it offshore. Contractors drove steel pilings to create a cofferdam around the hulk. Steam pumps cleared away the water, and workers then began the laborious task of clearing the ship of broken wreckage, tons of coal, and the remains of the crew as they

U.S.S. MAINE
JUNE 16, 1911
COPYRIGHTED 1911
AMERICAN PHOTO Co.
HABANA-CUBA

▓ Wreck of *Maine* in cofferdam (Naval History and Heritage Command)

were encountered inside the ship. In all, the bones of 36 men were found and sent to the United States, where they were entombed at Arlington National Cemetery, where many of their shipmates had been interred in 1899.

The salvagers built a wooden bulkhead to close off the intact aft section of *Maine*, after it was cleared, and the superstructure cut away, and then re-floated on the ship's own keel. At 1 A.M. on February 11, 1912, after nearly 14 years on the bottom, *Maine* lifted out of the mud as the cofferdam flooded. After the cofferdam was cleared away, a navy tug, USS *Osceola*, towed the hulk out of the harbor on March 16. At a point nearly five kilometers off the harbor entrance, a navy team on board opened floodgates that the salvagers had installed and left *Maine*. Forty-one minutes later, with a large US flag flying from a low pole placed near the stern, *Maine* sank in water reported to be 1,133 meters deep.

The question of what sank *Maine* has continued to the present. The initial 1898 naval investigation claimed an undersea mine planted by parties

▦ *Maine* scuttled (Naval History and Heritage Command)

unknown had exploded and set off the magazines near the bow. A second investigation, conducted in 1911 as the wreck was raised, also concluded that an external explosion had set off the magazines. However, a 1974 reinvestigation led by the navy's "nuclear admiral," Hyman Rickover, agreed that the opinion of the navy's engineer in chief of the navy, George W. Melville (1841–1912), that a spontaneous coal fire had set off the magazines was correct.

Two subsequent, media-driven investigations left us with a verdict essentially unchanged from the Rickover study. In Cuba, investigations notwithstanding, the official verdict, and one I heard from Cuban officials while documenting the naval aspects of the Spanish-American War as part of a National Geographic television documentary, was that the United States sank its own ship to start the war. I did not agree with them then, nor do I now.

In October 2000, a Cuban-Canadian-American science team working off the Cuban research vessel *Ulises* rediscovered the sunken stern of USS *Maine* in 917 meters of water more or less squarely where USS *Osceola* had recorded that the hulk left the surface. Resting upright, the remains of the battleship retained its propellers and had not corroded. Close by, a trail of coal and a boiler suggest that the stern was not completely stripped when it was sunk. Since the rediscovery, no one has returned to examine what is left of *Maine*, but floating over the site of the 1898 explosion, I was told by the Cubans that some of it still lies beneath the mud, and that the site is firmly fixed in the Cuban national consciousness as a result of Fidel Castro's insistence that Cuba "remember the *Maine*," albeit not for the reasons Americans do.

USS *MERRIMAC*

The purpose of my visit to Cuba was to dive and film all of the wrecks associated with the Battle of Santiago as part of an ongoing series *The Sea Hunters*, which I hosted with my friend, author Clive Cussler. The major emphasis of the show, and our principal focus was a US Navy ship lost in a daring night-time action on June 3, 1898, a month before the battle. The ship was the collier USS *Merrimac*, and the actions of its crew that night earned them the Medal of Honor, and made the commanding officer, Lt. Richard P. Hobson, a national hero. The navy bought the four-year-old, British-built steamer at the outbreak of the war to supply coal to the fleet then assembling for the naval and army assault on Spanish forces in Cuba. *Merrimac* made it to Cuba, but it constantly broke down, frustrating its commander and his superiors.

With the outbreak of the war, Spain's Caribbean Squadron, a force of six vessels, had sought refuge in the harbor of Santiago de Cuba at the southeastern end of the island. Cuba's principal port on the Caribbean side, Santiago's harbor was known to 19th-century mariners as a good, commodious port, but with a narrow entrance just about 122 meters wide at its mouth, and a crooked channel past it that required careful navigation. The *Castillo de San Pedro de la Roca*, also known as the *Castillo de Morro*, towered above the entrance, and with its lower levels close to the water, made an effective gauntlet for an enemy to try to pass. The Spanish commander, Admiral Pascual Cervera y Topete, had chosen a safe refuge in the face of an American naval force that outgunned his. The US fleet encircled the entrance to the bay, bottling up the Spanish ships.

At that juncture, Admiral William T. Sampson, commanding the North Atlantic Fleet, decided to take the Spanish ships out of action by sinking

Merrimac in the narrow harbor entrance. Sampson turned to Lt. Hobson, a commissioned naval architect, to execute his plan by swiftly sinking *Merrimac*. Hobson's final plan was for a moonlit dash into the channel, with 10 explosive charges set along the port side of the ship. Dropping an anchor at the bow when the charges fired would stop the ship in its tracks as it began to sink, and as it swung with the outgoing tide, dropping an anchor at the stern would stop *Merrimac* as it settled. The ship would then, according to the plan, sink straight across the channel, so that no ship could get past it.

Hobson also planned on a small crew, eight men in all—one with an ax at each anchor, two in the engineering spaces, one at the wheel, and two men to join the helmsman—in firing the explosive charges. The seven crew—Randolph Clausen, George Charette, Osborn Deignan, Francis Kelly, Daniel Montague, John Murphy, and George Phillips—were all volunteers. Hobson argued that only he could successfully sink *Merrimac*, and so Admiral Sampson replaced *Merrimac*'s captain with Hobson.

THE FAMOUS MERRIMAC CREW.

■ The crew of USS *Merrimac* at Santiago (Naval History and Heritage Command)

On the evening of June 2, *Merrimac* stood off with the rest of the fleet. In the early morning hours of June 3, Hobson made his move. Running full speed ahead for the entrance, and lit by moonlight, *Merrimac* surged toward the fort. At that point, a small Spanish picket boat with a rapid-fire gun opened up, and then the fort's guns responded. Ordering all stop, Hobson then gave the command to fire the charges. Only two went off. Spanish gunfire, meanwhile, repeatedly hit *Merrimac* with a noise that Hobson described as "Niagara magnified." Watching offshore from the battle cruiser USS *New York*, Associated Press reporter "Chappie" Goode wrote: "In a few seconds the mouth of Santiago Harbor was livid with flames that shot viciously from both banks...the dull sound of the carronade and its fiery light were unmistakable evidences of the fierce attack that was being waged on Hobson's gallant crew." Captain Robley "Fighting Bob" Evans, observing from the bridge of the battlecruiser USS *Iowa*, exclaimed: "It looks like Hell with the lid off!"

As shells riddled the ship, Hobson and his crew crouched down on the deck, taking shelter and amazingly suffering only a few gashes and cuts from shrapnel. Instead of sinking as planned, the ship drifted out of the channel and sank in shallow water close to and parallel with the shore. "A great wave of disappointment set over me," Hobson later wrote.

Washed over the side by the inrush of water as *Merrimac* sank, the eight men grabbed an upside-down raft and floated through the night. As the sun rose, a steam launch found them and retrieved them from the water. Admiral Cervera and two of his junior officers had come to inspect the scene and found eight coal-dust– and oil-begrimed men. Hobson swam to the launch, and Admiral Cervera pulled him aboard, followed by *Merrimac*'s crew. "The officers looked astonished at first," said Hobson, "then a current of kindness seemed to pass over them, and they exclaimed; 'Valiente!'" Cleaned, fed, and given dry clothing by their captors on the admiral's flagship, Hobson and his men were sent ashore, and, as prisoners, were escorted to the *Morro*. From his cell, Hobson was able to look down and see his short-lived command, partly out of the water. A month later, with the American victory imminent, their Spanish jailors released Hobson and the crew of *Merrimac* in a prisoner exchange.

The seven-man crew received the Medal of Honor, while Hobson, because naval officers were not then eligible for the medal, received a promotion.

Even more so, the eight men became heroes, especially Hobson, who toured the country, gave many speeches, and wrote a book, *The Sinking of the Merrimac*. Handsome and with a strong sense of self, Hobson became famous for stopping at every train station on his tour to kiss the young women who thronged the platform. Hobson, notes historian Bonnie M. Miller, gave Americans a whole new view of celebrity as the "hero with the merry smack." The man was for all intents and purposes a rock star of his age, a status he channeled into a successful run for a seat in Congress representing his home state of Alabama.

As for *Merrimac*, while an icon in its own right, with best-selling photographs of the wreckage of the ship that stuck up from the water, it slipped into obscurity when, after the war, efforts to clear the entrance dragged it into a deeper part of the channel and blasted down its bow. Even "Kissing Hobson" had faded from the popular view, though he finally did receive the Medal of Honor in 1934, and following his death was interred at

■ The sunken USS *Merrimac* in the channel at Santiago de Cuba (Naval History and Heritage Command)

Arlington. Our dive to study and film *Merrimac* would be the first visit to the wreck since Cuban divers had blasted more of the bow in 1976. The wreck lies in the main shipping channel, and diving is not allowed. Fidel Castro gave his personal permission for our dive and sent the governor of Santiago Province to dive with us.

Our dives found *Merrimac* upright, still filled with coal, and warped from heat. The coal has turned to clinker, and what we saw was that at the end, *Merrimac*'s coal had combusted, leaving decks and hatches contorted by the heat. The decks and the hull are also riddled with shot holes, some larger, others small. Some shot penetrated the ship at an angle, others ripped directly into the sides. The stern is a mangled mess, which Hobson had suspected when early in the run into the harbor, the crew lost control of the ship's steering. The steering gear is broken, the rudder partly shot away, and one propeller blade is missing. Hobson reported that after the battle, the captain of the Spanish picket boat that first opened fire "claimed that he shot away the rudder and the whole stern structure." I saw that not all of the stern was shot away, but I noted, 15 meters down in the dark waters of the channel, that the Spanish picket boat's gunners had done their job well, breaking the rudder head and leaving Osborn Deignan on the bridge with a dead helm.

The blasting by the Cubans took *Merrimac* down to the waterline forward of the bridge, but as I swam up to it, what struck me was how intact the bridge was, with a sheltered area to the starboard where the crew had huddled as their ship sank in the midst of what Captain Evans had aptly described as hell with the lid off. What also occurred to me then, as it does now, is the courage of those eight men. They steamed in on what by all rights was a suicide mission, intent on doing their duty. Caught in a deadly crossfire, their ship took tremendous punishment as they stood at their posts; Hobson wrote that a shell crashed through the bridge and Deignan, a 21-year-old from Iowa who had joined the navy just before the war broke out, never flinched and stayed at his post.

So, too, did the others. It is an amazing story that they lived through that night and the sinking, and rightly were awarded the country's highest honor. The battle scars of *Merrimac*, briefly lit up by our dive lights, are mute evidence of just how terrible a night that was. Ironically, the failure of *Merrimac's* mission did more than inspire the public. It allowed the Spanish fleet to escape a month later, only to die in an hours-long fight as the US Navy chased them along the coast and shot them down at close range.

THE BATTLE OF SANTIAGO AND ITS WRECKS

When news that Cervera's fleet had left Spain reached American newspapers, hysterical headlines warned of imminent attacks on "unguarded ports" and ships. The navy hastily recalled Civil War–era monitors to service, and the army rearmed old forts with Civil War–era guns retooled to fire modern projectiles. Theodore Roosevelt cynically noted in his autobiography that the fact that a monitor would not have been a "formidable foe to any antagonists of much more modern construction than the galleys of Alcibiades seemed to disturb nobody." When Cervera's fleet tucked into Santiago harbor, bottling it up had initially seemed the right tactic, hence the heroic but failed mission of USS *Merrimac*.

In the aftermath of that action, though, getting the Spanish to come out and fight was preferable, especially as hurricane season was coming, and battering into the harbor would have cost much blood. As for Cervera, he did not want to come out and fight, even as American troops pressed around Santiago and made his situation more untenable. Some of his ships were worn and weary, and his newest ship, *Cristobal Colon*, had left Spain without its main battery of guns because they had not yet been installed. He knew that his ships were doomed in the face of superior American naval power, and many of his men would die with them. Why fight, he argued in dispatches to his superiors, noting that he would be personally responsible "before God and history for the lives sacrificed on the altar of vanity, and not in the true defense of the country." Orders are orders, though, and when directly ordered, Cervera and his captains prepared to steam out of the harbor in a mad dash to evade the Americans and not fight it out.

On the morning of July 3, Cervera's fleet began streaming out of the harbor and into the open ocean. Cervera left behind his former flagship, the cruiser *Reina Mercedes*, after landing many of its guns to support Spanish troops ashore. Damaged from American bombardment and plagued with boiler problems, *Reina Mercedes* was in no shape to try to fight its way to sea. A day after the battle, *Reina Mercedes*'s crew scuttled it close to *Merrimac*'s wreck while under fire from American ships.

Cervera led his fleet out just past 9:30 in the morning in the cruiser *Infanta María Teresa*, now his flagship, followed by the cruisers *Vizcaya*, *Cristóbal Colón*, and *Almirante Oquendo*, and then the torpedo boat destroyers *Furor* and *Plutón*.

Outside, arrayed like "a group of huge gray cats watching a mouse hole," in the words of naval militia volunteer and author Russell Doubleday, the US fleet stood ready. The two officers who commanded the squadrons that day were William Sampson, who had ordered the ill-fated attempt of *Merrimac*, as the senior officer, and Commodore Winfield Scott Schley. In addition to their flagships, the armored cruisers *New York* and *Brooklyn*, were the steel battleships *Indiana*, *Iowa*, *Oregon*, and *Texas*. Two yachts converted into warships, *Gloucester* and *Vixen*, rounded out the American line of battle.

As the Spanish ships emerged shooting, they were met by heavy return fire from the American ships. Cervera had no intention of slugging it out. What followed, as the Spanish fleet raced southwest along the Cuban coast, was a spirited back and forth as an American column followed, and finally overcame the Spanish column and shot it down.

The cruiser *Infanta María Teresa* was the first to go down, little more than an hour after leaving harbor. Cervera had turned toward the enemy to hold them off as long as he could in order to let the other ships escape. Badly damaged, on fire, and with many dead and wounded, *Infanta María Teresa* was unable to keep fighting. Cervera ordered the crew to beach the cruiser a few miles outside the harbor entrance and flood the magazines before they exploded. As survivors swam toward shore, some were picked off by Cuban sharpshooters, but Cervera survived, remaining on the wreck with others until sailors from USS *Gloucester* rescued them. Mindful of his courtesies to Hobson and the crew of *Merrimac*, Cervera and the other survivors were treated with dignity and honor.

Next to die was *Almirante Oquendo*. The last ship in the battle line, it was targeted as *Infanta María Teresa* slowed and turned to shore. American shells hit *Oquendo* 57 times, one of which set off an unloaded 350-pound bag of powder being loaded into a gun in one of the turrets. The powder erupted in a flash of fire that vaporized the gun crew. Beached on the orders of its dying captain, *Oquendo* broke in two on the rocks close to the wreck of *Infanta María Teresa*. As the main line of American ships passed the wreck, chasing and shooting, the main magazine of *Oquendo* exploded. Out of 484 men on board, 127 men, including the captain, died with their ship.

The two destroyers also went down in a hail of shot and on fire. As the battleships opened fire, the crew of the armed yacht *Gloucester* engaged in a close duel with the destroyers as they exchanged shots with their rapid-fire guns. The Spanish destroyers outgunned *Gloucester*, but it was bigger and faster. *Plutón*, badly damaged, ran aground and exploded. Five minutes later *Furor* exploded offshore, taking more than half of its crew. Meanwhile, *Vizcaya*, now surrounded by the American battleships and cruisers, took heavy fire at close range until the armored cruiser was fully ablaze.

An explosion from a detonating torpedo tore off part of *Vizcaya*'s bow. Captain Juan Antonio Eulate, lying wounded in the sickbay, conferred with his surviving officers and decided to run *Vizcaya* aground. The fires on

■ The wreck of *Almirante Oquendo*, after the battle (Naval History and Heritage Command)

board were now out of control, and as the cruiser hit the rocks, men—some of them on fire—leaped into the sea screaming. Watching from the battleship *Texas*, some of the American sailors began to cheer, but were stopped by their captain, John Woodward Philip. "Don't cheer, boys, those poor fellows are dying."

As survivors struggled ashore, Cuban sharpshooters again opened up on them, striking down Spanish sailors struggling in the surf. The battleship USS *Iowa* approached, and its captain, Robley "Fighting Bob" Evans, incensed at the Cuban action, sent two boats ashore to warn the Cubans to stop shooting, or he would shell them. Among those rescued by *Iowa* was Captain Eulate, who refused to go below for treatment until he saluted his dying ship. As Eulate did, he shouted "Adios, *Vizcaya*," just as *Vizcaya*'s forward magazine erupted.

Last to die was *Cristóbal Colón*, the newest of Cervera's fleet. After an hours-long, 120-kilometer chase, the American ships began to catch up with *Colón* and hit it several times as it neared a section of coast that jutted offshore. The coast and the approaching enemy ships effectively blocked *Colón*, and so Captain Emilio Diaz Moreu y Quintana beached the cruiser ashore at the mouth of the Tarquino River. The Battle of Santiago was over. The cost to Spain was not only the destruction of Cervera's fleet. Spanish casualties stood at 323 dead and 151 wounded; the US Navy lost one man, and another was wounded. American ships had taken hits, but all remained serviceable.

In looking at the 120-kilometer-long landscape of the Battle of Santiago de Cuba, the coast is open, exposed to the sea, and Santiago is the only harbor. Whether you look at it from sea, where the narrow gap of the entrance easily disappears into the mass of the forested shoreline, or from space, Santiago harbor was indeed not just Cervera's refuge but also his trap. The centuries-old Spanish colonial fortress and gun batteries at the entrance helped keep the US Navy at bay, and even a sustained shore bombardment after the loss of *Merrimac* did not completely destroy the fortifications. The narrow gauntlet could only be guarded, and then through committing two separate squadrons of warships. *Merrimac*'s wreck, like that of *Reina Mercedes*, speaks not only to the heroic actions of their crews but also of the nonetheless difficult task of sealing the harbor entrance. Ultimately, the circumstances of the day led Cervera, against his wishes, to commit to a faint hope of escape that felt, and was, suicidal.

The close-in grim nature of the battle that followed reads both in print and in the landscape; this was a running fight, a chase in which an older, outmatched fleet was systematically destroyed, with the losers surrounded, cornered, and battered to death. Running the ships aground was a desperate last measure to save as many crew as the Spanish captains could. The violence of each ship's demise is dramatically evident, and unlike some battles on land, each warrior lies where they fell, exposed on the seabed to slowly deteriorate.

Cristóbal Colón rests in deeper water, with some damage, but for the most part an intact ghost ship. It rests in 30 meters of water, bow facing out to sea, because, after the battle, the Merritt & Chapman Wrecking Company, under contract to the US Navy, towed it off the beach in an attempt to refloat and salvage the cruiser. But the hull was too badly damaged and *Colón* went down for the last time.

The decks retain the secondary armament of *Colón*, a series of smaller-caliber guns, but the forward turret is empty. The 10-inch guns, each weighing 30 tons and capable of firing a 500-pound shell as much as 17 kilometers, were never installed in the rush to get *Colón* to Cuba. Instead, dummy guns made of wood and painted to look real were stuck into the turret.

After the war, Admiral Cervera was firm in his condemnation of the politicians who had sent his fleet and their crews to war. What made the struggle "hopeless," he wrote, was not only the lack of funding for maintaining the fleet, but not arming *Colón*, which was "sent to certain destruction." Just the same, they had to go. An article in a Spanish newspaper after the battle stated that the fleet steamed out of Santiago harbor knowing death was waiting, "but neither the men nor the officers could bear the thought of being stigmatized as cowards."

USS *MASSACHUSETTS*

Only one American warship from the pre-dreadnought era survives afloat. USS *Olympia*, Dewey's flagship at the Battle of Manila Bay, is a

National Historic Landmark moored off Philadelphia's riverfront as part of Independence Seaport. The wrecks of some of the American ships that served and fought in the Spanish-American War survive as stripped hulks used as targets for naval gunnery practice following their obsolescence in the post-dreadnought age. A handful continued to serve through World War I in lesser roles, relinquishing their names to new American battleships and assuming new ones—USS *New York* became USS *Saratoga*, and then USS *Rochester*, and USS *Texas* became USS *San Marcos*. *San Marcos* sank during target practice on Chesapeake Bay in 1911 and slowly settled into the bay mud. After a merchant ship collided with the submerged hulk and sank, explosives were used to clear as much of the wreck as could be blasted. The site is not one that gets visited or dived.

Halfway across the world, the USS *Rochester*, ex–*New York*, lies in 89 feet of water in Subic Bay. After a long career, the veteran of the Battle of Santiago went down when the navy scuttled it on December 24, 1941, as Japanese forces closed in during their conquest of the Philippines at the start of World War II. Lying on its side, the nearly intact warship is shrouded in murky, green water. In 1967, navy demolition teams placed charges to push the wreck deeper into the mud and mangled the stern. The massive guns remain in place in the forward turret, the stacks and masts lie off to one side, and it is a popular wreck dive, albeit a dive that has claimed the lives of some divers who became disoriented and died when trapped inside and ran out of air. The wreck has not been studied or documented archaeologically.

Archaeologists have studied two other warships from this period, one in the deep and one in the shallows. The former USS *Baltimore* is the deep-water wreck, lying in the darkness off Oahu. USS *Massachusetts* is the shallow wreck, lying in eight meters of water off Pensacola, Florida. Part of the expansion of the US Navy after decades of inactivity and decline following the Civil War, *Massachusetts* was an all-steel battleship laid down in 1890 as one of three sister ships along with USS *Indiana* and USS *Oregon*. These ships were the first heavy-caliber, heavily armored warships built by the United States. The construction and fitting out of the 106-meter-long, 10,000-ton battleship took six years. Powered by vertical triple expansion steam engines rated at 10,000 horsepower, and protected by armor as much as 45 centimeters thick, *Massachusetts* was armed with four 13-inch guns,

The U. S. Battleship " Massachusetts."
Copyright 1899 by J. F. Jarvis.

■ USS *Massachusetts* (Naval History and Heritage Command)

twin mounted in two turrets, and a secondary battery of eight 8-inch guns mounted in pairs in turrets. Those guns barked in anger, bombarding Santiago in 1898, but *Massachusetts* missed the naval battle because it was re-coaling at Guantánamo. It did fire on *Reina Mercedes* the next day as the crew of the Spanish ship scuttled it.

After the war, *Massachusetts* had a spotty career marked by accidents and a growing understanding that the battleship was obsolete. The rapid pace of the naval development had left *Massachusetts* behind. The US Navy laid up *Massachusetts* in 1906, but in 1910, the refitted battleship returned to service. Laid up again in 1914, *Massachusetts* returned to active duty in 1917 as a gunnery practice ship during World War I. It was then the oldest battle-ship in service for the US Navy.

In 1919, the navy loaned the obsolete *Massachusetts* to the War Department for use as a target ship for coastal artillery practice. In January 1921, the navy scuttled the battleship in shallow water off Pensacola, Florida, after stripping the ship of her guns. Once the latest word in warship design, *Massachusetts*'s armor and decks shook with the impact of more than 100 shells. A striking physical reminder of the nature of how rapidly ships became obsolete in the rapidly paced industrial push to create superior fleets before World War I, *Massachusetts* is also the last surviving battleship of her period. Archaeologists and volunteer divers, under the direction of

Florida State underwater archaeologist Roger C. Smith, mapped the wreck in its shallow grave in 1990; in 1993, their efforts resulted in the wreck's designation as a State Underwater Archaeological Preserve on the centennial of *Massachusetts*'s launch. The ship rests on a white sand seabed in eight to nine meters of water, now a dive spot enticing one to dive on "the worst battleship" in the navy, the wreck is a study in the slow decay and exposed internal works of a ship of its time as well as an artificial reef festooned with marine life.

THE RISE OF JAPAN

When forcibly "opened" to the rest of the world through gunboat diplomacy in 1853, Japan was a non-industrial, feudal power. Within two decades, the Japanese became a modern, industrial society. The age of the samurai gave way to a modern, European-styled army and navy. Instead of the samurai-backed shogun, the emperor, formerly a religious figurehead, now ruled. He had the backing of the rising industrial base and the military. That emperor, Meiji, used that backing and their power to expand his empire overseas and assert Japanese control in Asian waters. Until then, the last decades had seen European powers, and the United States, enter the region, controlling the seas with their navies, humiliating a weak China, and seizing territory in a naked display of colonial ambition. Japan had stood apart, safe in its feudal isolation, until American warships not only "opened" the country but also opened Japanese eyes to the reality of the new world order. Rather than be subjugated through war or trade, Japan took a page out of the West's playbook. Japan borrowed from its ostensible European rivals, both in strategy and technology, and only then did it openly challenge them. This included purchasing warships from England and training officers in the Royal Navy's strategies and tactics.

After two decades of naval expeditions and annexations of the smaller islands in the surrounding seas, and alarmed by increasing European incursions and colonial acquisitions in the region, Japan decided to strengthen its position by conquering neighboring Korea, nominally a vassal state of

China. China, belatedly modernizing its own navy with the purchase of German-built warships, was still weak and not an effective match for Japan's forces. Opposing Japan's plans, the Chinese landed troops near Seoul in the summer of 1894. But the Japanese were able to land their own expeditionary force, and by mid-September had defeated the Chinese army and taken the city of Pyongyang. As the Japanese army moved across the Korean peninsula toward the Yalu River and the border with China, the Chinese navy sailed with more troops to cut them off at the mouth of Yalu. The two fleets clashed on September 17, 1894, in the Battle of the Yalu River (sometimes called the Battle of the Yellow Sea), where a superior Japanese force sank five Chinese cruisers.

The surviving Chinese warships retreated to the naval base at Port Arthur. The Chinese ships, kept in port by a Japanese blockade of Port Arthur, managed to escape that port when it fell to Japan's troops in November. Fleeing to the naval base at Weihaiwei, the Chinese navy was quickly buttoned up by the Imperial Japanese Navy, who readied for an assault on Weihaiwei. It took the Japanese 23 days to take Weihaiwei. A series of forts, mounting 161 guns, many of them modern weapons of German and British manufacture, and 248 floating mines protected the harbor and the Chinese fleet. Japanese troops started the siege on January 20, 1895, ferrying ashore from their warships. A fierce storm on January 31 and February 1 forced both sides to fight in blinding snow, heavy winds, and freezing temperatures. The Chinese forts fell between January 30 and February 2, opening the way for a Japanese strike against the anchored Chinese fleet. The Japanese launched a surprise predawn attack on February 5 with a fleet of torpedo boats, hitting and damaging four Chinese warships. Within a week, the Chinese, boxed in, damaged and overwhelmed by superior Japanese forces, surrendered the remnants of its navy.

Japan's troops thrust into Manchuria, alarming the European powers, particularly Russia, which had designs of its own for that Chinese region. At the insistence of the West, Japan ended the war and its drive into China. The Treaty of Shimonoseki, signed by China and Japan in April 1895, however, forced China out of Korea, now recognized by that treaty as "independent," but in fact viewed by Japan as a vassal state, and also ceded

Taiwan and the Pescadores Islands to Japan. Japan was now the principal Asian power in the region, but faced a challenge from Russia. Eager to expand its own Far Eastern and Pacific power, Russia extorted a lease of Port Arthur from China after the Sino-Japanese War and occupied portions of Manchuria. Japan countered by exploiting Western rivalries and forging alliances with Britain and the United States, jointly patrolling the Yangtze River to "assist" the Chinese government and encouraging British and American warships to use Japanese naval bases.

A naval build-up of both Port Arthur and Vladivostok, Russia's naval base on Siberia's Pacific coast, and fear of a Russian advance into Korea finally induced the Japanese to attack the Russians. The Russo-Japanese War began with another surprise attack. Late on the evening of February 8, 1904, Japanese destroyers swept into Port Arthur, attacking the anchored Russian fleet with torpedoes. The next morning, the Japanese fleet bombarded the harbor, landed troops in Korea, and finally, on February 10, declared war on Russia. World opinion did not necessarily support the view that the Japanese would prevail against the power of the Russian empire, but in an amazingly adept display of strategy and tactics, the Imperial Japanese Navy defeated the Russian navy in two battles. The first fight, on the Yellow Sea in August 1904, defeated Russia's Pacific Squadron. The more decisive fight, in May 1905, was the first naval battle fought by "modern" big-gun battleships and cruisers.

To reinforce their fleet, the Russian navy dispatched a fleet of warships from the Baltic. After a difficult 27,358-kilometer, six-month voyage into the Pacific, the Russian fleet—a collection of both old and new warships—entered the Tsushima Straits between Japan and Korea on May 27. A Japanese fleet, commanded by Admiral Heihachiro Togo, was waiting there for them. Togo's ships engaged the Russians, cutting them off as they tried to flee north in the face of heavy fire and torpedo attack. When the battle ended on the morning of May 28, eighteen Russian ships had sunk with 4,830 casualties. Togo lost three of his torpedo boats and just over 100 men. The defeat of the Russians and the Treaty of Portsmouth in September 1905 confirmed Japan's new place as the pre-eminent Far Eastern power.

■ Japanese victory at Tsushima from a contemporary *ukiyo-e* (Author Collection)

Archaeologists have discovered the wrecks of some of the lost warships of these battles. In 2011, a joint Chinese-Russian expedition discovered the wreck of the Russian battleship *Petropavlovsk*, lost at Port Arthur in 1904. Port Arthur is now the city of Lyushun and a Chinese naval base. The locations of the ships lost at Tsushima are reportedly also known, most at a depth of some 90 meters. One of the Tsushima wrecks, the cruiser *Admiral Nakhimov*, was salvaged by a Japanese businessman who claimed he found a shipment of tsarist treasure, which the press at the time reported was 16 platinum and 48 gold bars and 5,000 pounds of British gold coins. It may have been a publicity stunt; the financier of the expedition, an ultranationalist Japanese businessman and politician, offered the enigmatic treasure in trade to the Soviet Union in exchange for the return of the Soviet-occupied Kurile Islands seized from Japan at the end of World War II.

What, if any, treasure was recovered remains shrouded in secrecy, leading some to suggest that perhaps none, or perhaps only some treasure was recovered from *Admiral Nakhimov*. A second Japanese expedition to the wreck in 1993 found no treasure. Inspired by the tale, which may have been a publicity stunt, South Korean salvagers discovered the wreck of the cruiser *Dmitrii Donskoi*, also lost at Tsushima, in 2000. In all of these cases, the former Soviet, and now the Russian, government protested salvage efforts because the sunken warships remain their legal property and are war graves. In the *Dmitrii Donskoi* case, reports of treasure were not only disputed, but the discoverers are under criminal investigation for fraud by the South Korean government.

The 4,380-man death toll at Tsushima shocked Russians, and I've visited monuments to the dead in St. Petersburg as well as the protected cruiser *Aurora*, which survived the battle of Tsushima and is now a museum ship. The argument over *Admiral Nahkimov*'s salvage as both a war grave and as Russian property despite 75 years on the bottom is considered by legal scholars as a key step in what in time became an international understanding among many nations that sunken warships remained the sovereign property of the nation whose flag they flew and served when they sank. That principle notwithstanding, salvage does continue. It has led to epic court battles. However, in recent years, as we will discuss later in regard to World War II ships, international law is being ignored with the unauthorized salvage and scrapping of Dutch, English, Australian, and American warships in Asia.

THE TORPEDO'S TRIUMPH

Perhaps the greatest irony of the race to build more, larger, and heavily armed battleships was that it was ultimately a wasted effort. The all-big-gun battleship's heyday was brief, if it ever really mattered at all other than as an exercise in military/political showmanship. The combination of two other 19th-century inventions, introduced at the end of the century, would pose the greatest threat to the world's navies by the start of World War I. Those inventions were the submarine and the self-propelled torpedo.

The advantages of the "automobile," ship-launched torpedo took a few years to catch on; Whitehead sold his first two torpedoes to the Royal Navy in 1870. But the potential of the weapon and Britain's adoption of it quickly inspired the navies of the world to follow suit. By the 1890s, flotillas of torpedo boats carrying the new weapon had joined the fleets of Great

Britain and other nations. Perceptive naval officers, like French Admiral Theophile Aube, argued that torpedo boats, in large enough numbers, could quickly swoop in, under the big guns of the battleships, and sink the huge ships with successive hits. Between 1890 and 1905, France built 435 first- and second-class torpedo boats, while Britain built 174. In response to this threat, navies adopted smaller-caliber, rapid-firing guns as part of a warship's armament, and a specific class of warship, the smaller, faster, and highly maneuverable "torpedo boat destroyers," which in time became known simply as "destroyers."

The ultimate success of the self-propelled torpedo came with its marriage with the submarine. Following the success of *H. L. Hunley*, various experiments with submarines resulted in a number of craft, among them the privately built *Resurgam* (Latin for "I shall rise again"), a 30-ton, steam-powered submarine invented by a British curate and launched in late November 1879. The short-lived *Resurgam* sank while under tow on February 26, 1880. While *Resurgam* was unsuccessful, across the Atlantic, in the United States, Irish-American inventor John Philip Holland was busy perfecting his submarine design. Holland launched his first submarine, a four-by-one-meter midget, in 1876 with funding from Irish rebels living in the United States.

The success of the small submarine in trials convinced the rebels of the "Fenian Brotherhood" to raise funds for a larger boat, the *Fenian Ram*. Launched in 1881, the 19-ton, nine-meter-long submarine was powered by a Brayton "petroleum engine" and armed with a pneumatic gun that used compressed air to fire a nearly two-meter-long projectile with a 100-pound explosive charge. It was a revolutionary piece of technology, a harbinger of the future. I will always remember the day when, thanks to the curators, I was sitting inside the submarine with fellow archaeologist Pete Capelotti, as it rested in the Paterson Museum in New Jersey. As we sat there, Pete remarked that the year this submarine was launched, Custer and the 7th Cavalry died at the Battle of the Little Bighorn. The advent of new technology and a new style of warfare came as men on horseback and foot fought and died, reminding us why it took decades for tactical and strategic thinking to adapt to this new weapon.

Fenian Ram was never used in combat; a falling-out between Holland and his backers in the Fenian Brotherhood laid her up. While other inventors in Europe tried various designs and propulsion systems, including electrically powered submarines, and successfully developed a torpedo-firing tube, finally merging the two weapons into a deadly instrument of war, Holland slowly persisted in developing his own submarine. The US Navy, meanwhile, alarmed at the progress of the various foreign submarine initiatives, held three open competitions for an American submarine design that could out-perform any European submarine. By 1895, Holland beat out his competitors, signing a contract to build a submarine for the US Navy. Not entirely satisfied with the government's specifications, Holland raised private support to build another submarine to his own design.

That boat, *Holland VI*, when launched in 1897, was the world's first completely successful submarine. It was armed with a single 18-inch-diameter torpedo tube, and powered by a 45-horsepower gasoline engine for running on the surface and a 50-horsepower, battery-powered motor to maneuver when submerged. The 74-ton boat was just under 16 meters long. *Holland VI* went on its sea trials in March 1898, just as the United States went to war with Spain. The performance of the sub impressed observers, including Assistant Secretary of the Navy (and future president) Theodore Roosevelt. Nonetheless, navy officials insisted on a number of changes to the submarine before they accepted *Holland VI*. It was not until April 11, 1900, that the navy purchased what newspapers called the "Monster War Fish" and commissioned it as USS *Holland* (SS-1).

The commissioning of USS *Holland* was more than the beginning of an American submarine fleet; it also inspired the Royal Navy to follow suit. While British admirals fumed about the submarine as "damned un-English" and a weapon "of a weaker power," they also realized the threat, and the need for their own. Negotiating with Holland, the Royal Navy purchased the rights to build five Holland boats, and in October 1901, the first, "HM Submarine Boat No. 1," slid down the ways of the Vickers Yard at Barrow-in-Furness. *No. 1*, also known as *Holland I*, was followed, first by other Holland boats, and later by other designs that gradually saw the submarine's size, number of torpedoes, and range of operations expand. Even as

■ US Navy crew on board USS *Holland* (Naval History and Heritage Command)

the various nations competed in a naval arms race to build larger, more powerful battleships, they also raced to build more, and better subs. Germany launched its first, U-1, in 1906, following France, the United States, and Britain's lead.

Ironically, it was the late-coming Germans who first demonstrated the potential of the submarine in warfare during World War I. By 1914, as German U-boats hit the Royal Navy along England's shores, the pioneering Holland boats were gone. *Holland 1*, after brief service, was already obsolete by 1913, and in November of that year was sold for scrap. Partially stripped, *Holland 1* sank off Plymouth while under tow to the scrapyard.

A Royal Navy minesweeper rediscovered the wreck of *Holland 1* in the Solent, not too far from where *Mary Rose* lay, in April 1981. No other Holland boat had survived, and so the Royal Navy Submarine Museum, under the direction of submarine expert Commander Richard Compton-Hall, raised *Holland 1* in September 1981. The boat was cleaned and treated

■ The torpedo tube of HMS *Holland*, after conservation and on display at the Royal Submarine Museum, Gosport (Geni/Wikipedia Commons)

to stop corrosion and placed on display at the museum, but in time the submarine began to suffer from additional corrosion and decay. Placed inside a tank and gradually soaked to free the steel of salt, and then to stop the rusting, *Holland 1* was reopened to the public inside a new, climate-controlled building in 2001. One other early Royal Navy Holland boat, HMS *Holland V*, was rediscovered in 2000 28 meters down off the English coast. A detailed survey by archaeologists Innes McCartney and Mark Beattie Edwards in 2005–2006 included opening the wreck site to divers. Unfortunately, sometime after 2008, someone cut off and stole the submarine's hatch, probably, according to British officials, for a private collector.

The recovery of *Holland I* did not add much to our knowledge of the Holland boats. But it did provide a later generation with something more than photographs and drawings that fail to give us a sense of just what these craft were and what it must have been like to serve in them. I've gone inside *Holland I* at Portsmouth thanks to the curators of the museum. It was a firsthand, personal opportunity to appreciate and experience both the sophisticated engineering and construction and the cramped, awful conditions of something otherwise only imagined. Like the wreck of CSS *H. L. Hunley, Holland 1* is a physical legacy of the beginnings of submarine warfare. The results of the 19th-century invention of the successful submarine and the torpedo, as seen in *Holland 1*, would be demonstrated before the world just a year after *Holland 1* was lost. The progeny of *Holland 1* would dramatically alter war at sea during World War I.

8

World War I

I must plough the seas of the world doing as much mischief as I can, until my
ammunition is exhausted, or a foe superior in power succeeds in catching me.
—Vice Admiral Maximilian Reichsgraf Von Spee

The war that erupted in Europe in 1914 spread to the Middle East, the
Mediterranean, East Africa, the Indian Ocean, the North Atlantic, to
the eastern shores of North America, and out into the Pacific. On both land
and sea, though, the four-year conflict was a bloody stalemate, marked on
land by horrific trench warfare, machine guns, tanks, barbed war, and
poison gas. At sea, the stalemate was highlighted by the kaiser's navy remaining out of reach of the Royal Navy except for a few encounters.

A Royal Navy raid with two light cruisers and two flotillas of destroyers
struck the Germans at Heligoland Bight, off the German coast in the North
Sea on August 28, 1914. The raiders sank two German torpedo boats, but
were then surprised and chased, and repeatedly hit by fire from reinforcing
German ships, including six light cruisers. The British commander called
for help from the Royal Navy's First Battlecruiser Squadron, 34 nautical

miles away. Racing to the scene, the British battlecruisers sank three of the German ships and forced them to withdraw.

The next fight, also in the North Sea at Dogger Bank, off Britain's northeast coast, took place on January 24, 1915. A German force of four battlecruisers and a number of light cruisers and torpedo boats sortied on the evening of January 23 to sink British patrols off Dogger Bank. Instead, thanks to naval intelligence, the Royal Navy ambushed the Germans, who turned and ran for home with the Royal Navy in pursuit. In a running fight, the German ships were hit repeatedly, with the big guns on the battlecruisers striking their targets at incredible ranges. For example, HMS *Lion*, the British flagship, made its first hit on the German battlecruiser *Blücher* at a range of nine nautical miles. The British then overwhelmed and sank *Blücher*, but the other German ships escaped. As many as 1,000 German seamen died with their battlecruiser.

Heligoland Bight and Dogger Bank did little to change the balance of naval power. Both the British and German fleets remained strong and capable. The German High Seas Fleet were effectively blockaded by the Royal Navy's Grand Fleet. To break that deadlock and destroy British sea power,

■ The German armored cruiser *Blücher* sinks during the battle of Dogger Bank, January 24, 1915. (Naval History and Heritage Command)

the Germans devised a plan to lure in the Royal Navy with a seemingly smaller force, and then smash them in an ambush in the North Sea off Denmark's Jutland peninsula. Instead, a two-day running fight between the two fleets, the last great sea fight between battleships, pitted 59 German ships and 99 British ships against one another in a series of actions that lasted from May 31 to June 1, 1916.

The two fleets hit each other hard. The British lost 14 ships and 6,784 men, while the Germans lost 12 ships and 3,099 men. The outcome of the battle was controversial. At the end of the battle, as the German battleships withdrew, the High Seas Fleet commander, Admiral Reinhard Scheer, ordered his destroyers and cruisers to launch a torpedo attack to cover the retreat. Admiral John Rushmore Jellicoe, commander of the Grand Fleet, did not pursue the Germans, fearing a trap and greater loss of life. His second-in-command, Admiral David Beatty, disagreed. Beatty urged Jellicoe to mop up the Germans, and make Jutland a "second Trafalgar." Beatty's detractors, meanwhile, criticized his actions in the battle. The Admiralty promoted Jellicoe to Sea Lord, a desk job, and placed Beatty in command of the Grand Fleet, leading to a protracted argument as supporters of Jellicoe and Beatty wrangled over the battle for well over a decade, with historians following suit for the next century.

Be that as it may, as a tactical draw, Jutland was a strategic victory for the Royal Navy. The High Seas Fleet never again effectively challenged British sea power. The consequence of that victory, however, was a successful argument that the German Navy rely on unrestricted submarine warfare, and what followed was an incredible slaughter on both sides.

THE ARCHAEOLOGY OF THE BATTLE OF JUTLAND

While searches for and dives on individual wrecks offered some sense of where a few of the Jutland ships had sunk and documented some of their battle damage, starting with Royal Navy dives on the wreck of HMS *Invincible* in 1919, it was not until 2001–2007 that dive expeditions found more of the wrecks, including HMS *Indefatigable*, HMS *Defence*, and HMS

Nomad. By 2007, historian, diver, and archaeologist Innes McCartney, aware of the advances in search and documentation technology, thanks to multibeam sonar and remotely operated vehicles (ROVs), proposed and organized an expedition to not only accurately map each wreck but also the entire naval battlefield, spread out over 3,000 square nautical miles.

Sponsored by the Sea War Museum Jutland of Thyborøn, Denmark, and working with a Danish marine exploration company, JD-Contractor AS, the expedition discovered and mapped 76 shipwrecks in the battlefield, 22 of which were Jutland losses. Aided by never-before-seen charts kept by the family of Admiral Jellicoe, and with the results of mapping the battlefield as defined by its still-fallen warriors on the seabed, McCartney notes these "have given us a better picture of what happened on 31 May and June 1, 1916. Ultimately, this is the true purpose of archaeology."

Combining 17 years of work, both through wreck diving and then the high-tech survey, McCartney has reconstructed the Battle of Jutland through the delineation of where each ship had sunk, in some cases in the midst of the fight, at other times after the action through progressive flooding or scuttling. He also compared the results of a physical study of the

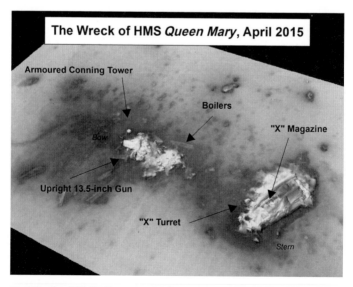

■ Wreck of HMS *Queen Mary*. (Innes McCartney/Image © Sea War Museum Jutland/JD-Contractor A/S)

wrecks with what was known before, and in some cases, adding much where there were no eyewitnesses or where a sense of the battle "resided only in books and on maps."

The physical record on the seabed is graphic. HMS *Indefatigable*, badly damaged, began to roll over as continued shelling detonated the forward magazines. HMS *Queen Mary* broke in two, and as the bow sank, the stern, unflooded and with engines still working, kept going for a while before sinking. However, *Queen Mary* did not explode as some witnesses had claimed. Another of the ships, HMS *Defence*, did explode. Both magazines, at the bow and stern, blew up and destroyed *Defence*, leaving it to sink in less than 12 seconds. HMS *Invincible*'s end came when a salvo of enemy fire blew the roof off turrets "Q," where extra cordite, the explosive used as a propellant for shells, had been stacked outside of the magazines where they should have been stored. The flash of the burning cordite set off the magazines below, where 50 tons of explosives sat. The resulting blast, calculated at 1,000 pounds per square inch, shot the turrets "P" and "Q" out of their mounts like bullets from a gun barrel, and *Invincible* broke in two, sinking in a few seconds.

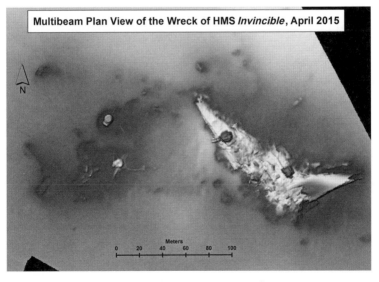

■ Multibeam plan of the wreck of HMS *Invincible*. (Innes McCartney/ Image © Sea War Museum Jutland/JD-Contractor A/S)

The positions of two of the British ships, HMS *Black Prince* and HMS *Turbulent,* showed that though damaged, they had turned away from the enemy when lost, while one of the German ships, SMS *Wiesbaden* was found where it had drifted, engines dead, but with its crew still fighting as British warships circled and pounded the ship until it was helpless. It is one thing to read, after a century has passed, of enmity and brutal fighting on the field of battle. It is something else to confront it, physically, at the bottom of the sea. Split guns and numerous shell holes match the account of the ship's sole survivor, who reported that when the shooting stopped, he was one of 22 men who made it off as their burning ship rolled over and sank in the darkness. Forty hours later, he alone was found, floating on a steel raft.

Many of the conclusions McCartney drew from the wrecks of Jutland beyond the course of the battle and the individual deaths of the ships—and in some cases, all of their crew—contained an intensely human connection. It came from finding exploded spare cordite charges in the turrets of HMS *Invincible,* despite standing orders and better judgment, a decision likely made in the face of an all-out running fight and the need to keep firing. On HMS *Black Prince,* McCartney found an isolated watertight hatch with only two clips of the six that were needed to seal it in their locked position and was reminded of an account from Robert Neale Lawson, captain of HMS *Chester.* The captain described, no doubt from personal observation at Jutland, when a watertight door was closed by only "one or two clips and a shell explodes in its vicinity," it would be "blown away bodily and will act as a very large splinter, being hurled the length of the compartment and killing everyone in its way." For McCartney, the *Black Prince* crew probably saw no need to completely seal the hatch, because the Royal Navy, "in the long calm lee" a century after Nelson's victory at Trafalgar had made it the world's most powerful force at sea, had become complacent. The wrecks of Jutland offered a variety of examples of "human agency," as McCartney terms it.

McCartney's study of the submerged battlefield of Jutland included a look at the effects of the ocean environment on the wrecks, noting that over the next century the ships will no longer be either identifiable, and in some cases, even there. This is due in part to corrosion and current, but also to large-scale salvage that has included blasting, grappling, and tearing open most of the ships for their metal. This ongoing salvage, as well as looting of artifacts from the wrecks for individual collections, is not confined to the Jutland wrecks alone: it is a worldwide issue. In some cases, artifacts have made it into museums and the Laboe Naval Memorial at Kiel. For the most part, however, this has not been the case. McCartney argues for more archaeological work at Jutland, noting that there are some wrecks, such as HMS *Warrior*, which, resting upside down and settled into soft mud, remains an undisturbed time capsule. This is the time, he says, "to use it or lose it." Already beyond living human memory, the ships of Jutland will in time be "beyond our sight. Jutland will have returned to the virtual world of the archive and that [which] we could have learned will have been lost for all time."

THE TRIUMPH OF THE SUBMARINE

Germany's principal success at sea during the war was the demonstration of the submarine as a potent new force in naval warfare. In the 50 years since *H. L. Hunley* sank USS *Housatonic* during the American Civil War, no other submarine had been successful in combat. Initial German U-boat sorties were not successful. The first submarine war patrol in history, by 10 German submarines, sailed from Heligoland on August 6, 1914. Two of the subs were lost, one in a minefield, the other rammed and sunk by the British cruiser *Birmingham* after it was caught on the surface, unable to dive because of mechanical problems. Success finally came on September 5, 1914, when U-21, under the command of Lieutenant Otto Hersing, caught the light cruiser HMS *Pathfinder* 48 kilometers off the Scottish coast and sank it. *Pathfinder* went down with 259 of the crew in four minutes.

The abilities of the submarine in warfare were again demonstrated, this time by the submarine U-9's commander, Lieutenant Otto Weddigen, and his crew on September 22 when they encountered the light cruisers HMS *Aboukir*, HMS *Hogue*, and HMS *Cressy* in the North Sea. Hitting *Aboukir* with a single torpedo, Weddigen was delighted to see the other two British ships come to its aid in the mistaken belief *Aboukir* had struck a mine. Firing two more torpedoes, U-9 hit *Hogue* and then *Cressy* as its captain tried to flee. With five torpedoes and in less than an hour, Weddigen and U-9 sank three light cruisers, killing 1,460 British seamen. Three weeks later, Weddigen repeated his feat when he ambushed and sank the cruiser HMS *Hawke* on October 15. The submarine was definitely a weapon to be feared, a lesson that was demonstrated to the world when U-20 sank the liner *Lusitania* in May 1915.

In face of international condemnation and the possibility that the previously neutral United States might enter the conflict, Germany stopped unrestricted submarine warfare on October 5, 1915. In the aftermath of Jutland, and the realization that the High Seas Fleet was effectively blocked in, while Germany and its allies' armies were bogged down in a protracted, bloody war of attrition in the trenches, the Germany Navy resumed unrestricted submarine warfare on February 1, 1917. German naval strategists estimated that the renewed U-boat assault would end the war in six months as Britain's overseas lifeline was severed.

■ An unnamed British transport sinking at an unknown location after a U-boat attack. (Naval History and Heritage Command)

The ensuing battle was exceptionally brutal, on both sides, with no holds barred, including sinking well-lit hospital ships. The Allies responded with Q-ships, which were disguised warships masquerading as merchant vessels and serving as decoys. Out of 200 Q-ships, 27 were lost to enemy action, while only sinking 11 U-boats. The U-boat onslaught inspired a series of inventions, including underwater hydrophones to listen for and to locate subs, and the depth charge. Massive undersea barricades of undersea mines and active anti-submarine patrols attempted to pen in the German submarine fleet. A number of U-boats were lost as a result of these countermeasures.

The theater of war expanded after the United States entered the war on April 6, 1917, in large measure as a result of Germany's U-boat campaign and the loss of American ships and lives. In response, in 1918, the German Navy sent long-range U-boats to the eastern seaboard of the United States. U-boats were already operating off Canada's east coast. Laying mines off ports and torpedoing merchant ships, German U-boats attacked shipping

DEPTH BOMBS DEAL DEATH TO U-BOATS

FOR THIS HUN THE WAR IS OVER, BLOWN TO BITS BY A DEPTH BOMB PLANTED AT THE RIGHT TIME. IT IS THE MERRY LITTLE DEPTH BOMB—IN DESTROYER LINGO, "THE ASH CAN" WHICH UPENDS THE KAISER'S SUBS AND PUTS THEM TO SLEEP ON THE OCEAN BED. CONTAINING A HEAVY CHARGE OF EXPLOSIVE, THE BOMB IS DROPPED AND EXPLODES AT A SET DEPTH. IN THIS CASE THE EXPLODING BOMB MUST HAVE BEEN DROPPED BEFORE THE U.BOAT DOVE OVER IT.

British depth charges sink a German U-boat. (Naval History and Heritage Command)

off Boston, Philadelphia, New York, and North Carolina's Outer Banks. Among their victims was the Coast Guard lightship off Cape Hatteras at Diamond Shoals when it radioed a warning to shipping in the area. U-boats also struck Canadian shipping and laid mines off Halifax.

The single greatest American casualty loss at sea in the war came with the sinking of the USS *Tampa*, a Coast Guard revenue cutter turned over to naval command. After escorting a convoy across the Atlantic, *Tampa* fell victim to the U-boat UB-91 in Bristol Channel on September 26, 1918. There were no survivors out of the 131 men on board. The wreck has not yet been found; it lies in a field of hundreds of shipwrecks that cover the seabed off the British Isles, the legacy of two world wars.

In all, 15 US Navy ships were either sunk or damaged by enemy torpedoes, bombs, or naval gunfire in World War I, and another four were either sunk or damaged by enemy-laid mines. One of them, the veteran cruiser USS *San Diego*, formerly the USS *California*, sank 10 miles off the Fire Island lightship on the approaches to New York Harbor on July 19, 1918. Six of the crew died.

■ USS *San Diego* sinking off Long Island, July 19, 1918. Painting by Francis Muller. (Naval History and Heritage Command)

The German U-boats came close to winning the Battle of the Atlantic, and, with it, likely the war. The success of German submarines was the major naval demonstration of the war, inspiring other nations to send increasing numbers of submarines into combat. British submarines in the Baltic, Mediterranean, and the Black Seas were able to challenge the Germans and their allies, the Ottoman Turks, but the submarine successes in the Mediterranean were German and Austrian, as a number of ships, including many older British battlecruisers, were lost to torpedoes and submarine-laid mines.

The sinking of old warships had less effect, though, than the sinking of incredible numbers of merchant ships with valuable supplies, ordnance, armament, and troops. In just eight months, between May 1916 and January 1917, for example, German submarines sank 1,152 ships. In the end, Germany's war against its enemies' commerce proved to be as effective as the beleaguered Confederacy's raids against Yankee shipping—striking economic blows as opposed to initiating warship-to-warship encounters. Ultimately, the toll of the German U-boat campaign in the war was 6,927 allied ships, accounting for nearly 12 million tons of shipping along with 202 U-boats and some 5,000 men lost. The lessons of the submarine war of 1914–1918 would be remembered and carried to even greater lengths by both sides in the next world conflict.

THE ENGLISH CHANNEL AS BATTLEFIELD

Wreck diver-explorers in Great Britain and from nearby countries have pinpointed, dived, and in some cases recovered artifacts from a number of U-boat wrecks in the English Channel, the North Sea, and the Atlantic. Others have joined in the quest. The survey crews of adventure author and explorer Clive Cussler's not-for-profit National Underwater Maritime Agency (NUMA) have found several U-boats, including U-20, which sank *Lusitania*, and U-21, which sank HMS *Pathfinder*.

Under the leadership of Antony Firth, Wessex Archaeology, a private cultural resources firm, has done much work, and Firth has been a powerful practitioner and advocate for looking at the larger landscape of World War I losses as a collection. Some of his more recent work with his new company, Fjordr, has assessed the East Coast War Channels (a key part of the World War I naval battlefield marked by mines and "safe" channels) through the lens of battlefield archaeology as opposed to individual sites.

A number of the wrecks had been identified in a 1919 British survey. Not all of those identifications were accurate; as it would be seen, only two-thirds of them were, and there were a number of additional "mystery" wrecks. McCartney's work decisively identified a number of these U-boats, a matter of importance not only for historians and archaeologists but also for the families of the lost, for whom the events a century ago remain personal, and important. Not only were locations accurately plotted, but as in the case with McCartney's work at Jutland, the circumstances of the losses also came into focus as the result of investigating each wreck. At least 40 percent of them were lost in the Dover minefield, and Innes's work is the first clear archaeological documentation of the success of the mines as a tactic at least in that sector of the larger undersea battlefield.

One submarine identification reported by McCartney revealed the wartime cover-up of an erroneous report on the sinking of the German U-boat UC-79. The Admiralty tasked its Anti-Submarine Division (ASD) with the creation and maintenance of a list of confirmed U-boat kills and where they had been lost as part of their overall task of determining Britain's best means of countering Germany's submarine offensive. In his study, McCartney found that ASD's work in determining the what, who, and where of German U-boat losses was only 48 percent correct.

According to ASD, the British submarine E-45 sank UC-79 in the southern North Sea on October 19, 1917. McCartney notes that the evidence was flimsy at best, with E-45's battle report noting that after their attack, all they had seen was a "great disturbance of water." ASD nonetheless credited E-45 with the kill and marked the location on their charts. At the same time, British intelligence was intercepting and reading German naval messages. In February 1918, intelligence learned that UC-79 was still in action. This was relayed to ASD, who ignored it. UC-79 departed on what would be its last patrol on March 20, 1918, but never returned.

On June 12, a British aerial reconnaissance of the minefields at Dover spotted an oil slick, which suggested a submarine had struck a mine and sunk. It took until August 7 before a Royal Navy diving and salvage team reached the site and discovered that it was indeed a U-boat that had hit a mine and sank after being blown apart. The wreck was UC-79. Again, intelligence notified ASD, and once again, the report was ignored. In 1919, ASD released a final report on German U-boat losses, and in it, continued the fiction that E-45 had sunk UC-79 in October 1917, and as would later be revealed, far away from where the wreck lay.

French divers, acting on the report of a fisherman who had snagged a wreck, rediscovered UC-79 in 2000. Scraping propellers free of marine growth revealed the stamped number of the U-boat. In this case, one was stamped UC-77, and the other UC-79. Historian Michael Lowery discovered the British report of the oil patch seen by the spotting plane on June 12, and with further digging in the archives, the report of the August 1918 dive on UC-79 also emerged. With the forensic evidence on the seabed and in the archives, the question of what actually happened to UC-79 was revealed.

As to why ASD had never corrected the erroneous report of UC-79's loss, McCartney points to an unpublished memoir of one of the British intelligence officers who noted that ASD in order "to boost their own efforts" had "insisted on the success of many attacks that we…knew to have been abortive and many officers had received decorations in consequence." The final question, says McCartney, is "how many other cases, similar to this, still lie in the historical lists" of both lost U-boats and all the ships reported as sunk by U-boats?

GALLIPOLI

Archaeologists, historians, naval architects, and technical divers have also focused on another naval battlefield of World War I at Gallipoli. The Gelibolou (Gallipoli) Peninsula guards one side of the narrow sea passage from the Aegean Sea into the Sea of Marmara, and thence to Istanbul, formerly known as Constantinople. From there, the Bosporus connects to the Black Sea. This strategic waterway, which cuts through Turkey, has been navigated since antiquity as a highway of both trade and war.

In 1914, Turkey was the heart of the Ottoman Empire, a once-mighty entity now politically and militarily weak. Both Britain and Germany had vied for the favor of the "Sick Man of Europe," especially with a mind to the international waterway that passed through its heart. Keeping Turkey as a non-combatant in World War I was key to maintaining maritime access for trade and military supplies to allied Russia's Black Sea ports. British politicians blundered, however, when they reneged on a contract to build two modern warships for the Ottoman Empire in British shipyards and instead returned the money and took the ships for use by the Royal Navy with the looming prospect of war.

The loss of the ships *Sultan Osman I* and *Rashadieh*, now respectively HMS *Agincourt* and HMS *Erin*, was more than an affront to Turkish pride. It played into the hands of pro-German Turkish officials who believed that joining Germany in the coming war would help stave off any Russian designs on Ottoman territory. It was also an opening for the German kaiser, who promptly made a gift of two of his ships, the cruiser *Goeben* and the light cruiser *Breslau*, as replacements. Shadowed by the Royal Navy, *Goeben* and *Breslau* gave the British the slip, and the two, still manned by their German crews, joined the Ottoman Navy as *Yavuz Sultan Selim* and *Midilli*.

Initially, the kaiser had planned to keep the Ottoman Empire out of the war, but as the first battles bogged down the armies of Germany and the Central Powers, those plans changed. Still under German officers and with all-German crews, the two nominally Ottoman warships ventured into the Black Sea to shell Russian ports in a surprise attack on October 29. Russia declared war on November 2, and with this, the Ottoman Empire entered World War I on Germany's side. The Black Sea once again became a naval battlefield, with the Russians at an advantage. The next Ottoman action was to close the Dardanelles to shipping in January 1915, effectively blockading Russia's Black Sea ports.

The stage was set for what would be one of the bloodiest and most futile engagements of World War I. Firm in a belief that the weak Ottoman

Empire would surrender in the face of an Allied fleet arriving at Istanbul, the British government approved a naval expedition proposed by Winston Churchill, First Lord of the Admiralty, to send a fleet of obsolete old battleships and cruisers to the Dardanelles. They would run the gauntlet of Turkish defenses, now also manned by the Germans.

The strait's entrance, off the site of ancient Troy, was two and a quarter miles wide and defended by fortresses. Fourteen miles up the strait it narrowed at Çanakkale, spanning less than a mile. This was also fortified. To force through it, a large naval force would be needed. Heavy capital ships would silence the forts, allowing minesweepers to come in and clear the minefields that closed the channel. Having taken that, the next step would be to do the same at Çanakkale, and then push into the Sea of Marmara, and from there, on to Istanbul.

The combined force, largely made up of older battleships and cruisers drawn from the Royal Navy and the French Navy, assembled off the entrance to the strait in mid-February, and commenced bombarding the Turkish forts. After silencing the forts, minesweepers cleared the first leg of the gauntlet by February 25. Eager to push on, Churchill urged the commanders to mount the second attack at Çanakkale. The admiral in charge cabled that he expected the fleet to be in Istanbul in just two weeks' time.

The attack commenced on March 18 as the first of three waves of battleships swarmed the entrance. The Turks were ready, having laid more mines, and with mobile batteries of howitzers in position. The assault waves faltered and broke as the French battleship *Bouvet* strayed into a minefield and sank. Mines also sank the British battleships *Irresistible* and *Ocean*. The mines and gunfire damaged other ships, including the battleships *Inflexible*, *Galois*, and *Suffren*, and so the fleet withdrew. As they waited for reinforcements, with more ships to come, the plan of attack shifted. Only after the war did the British learn that the Turkish defenders were low on ammunition, and an immediate, renewed naval assault likely would have pushed through.

Instead of trying to force the narrows by ship, the plan now was to land an army to march up the peninsula and take out the forts, opening the door for the fleet, while submarines would be used to slip into the Sea of

Marmara and attack Turkish ships. The first troops, largely comprising Australian and New Zealand volunteers, hit the peninsula on April 25. The Turkish response, led by an impassioned junior commander, Kemal Mustafa (the future Attaturk, founder of the modern Turkish state), was to dig in and fight. Heavy losses during the landings, and the pushback by the Turks, led to a stalemate that defined the Gallipoli Campaign.

When the invading troops finally evacuated on January 8–9, 1916, close to a half-million casualties and more than 130,000 dead had piled up on both sides. While most of these were lost on land, the totals included thousands of men who were the crews of the ships and submarines. The battleship *Goliath*, anchored in Morto Bay inside the entrance to the strait, had wreaked havoc as it shelled Turkish positions. A daring nighttime attack on May 12 by the Turkish destroyer *Muâvenet-i Millîye* sank the battleship with three torpedoes that capsized and quickly sank *Goliath*. The fast-moving waters of the strait swept survivors out to sea and away from rescue. Out of 750 men, only 180 lived. On the other side of the peninsula, the German U-boat U-21, under command of Otto Hersing, sank the British battleships *Triumph* and *Majestic* on May 25 and May 27, killing 127 men. The shock of the sinkings led to the withdrawal of the big ships, making the situation on land for the troops even more untenable.

The exploits of the Allied submarines were heroic and drew blood. The undersea defenses of the straits were formidable, with the minefields and anti-submarine nets and patrol boats making passage at best difficult. Nonetheless, the British submarine B-11 sank the Turkish battleship *Mesudiye* on December 13, 1914, ahead of the naval attack. The French submarine *Saphir* and the British E-15 were less lucky; *Saphir* struck a mine and sank, while E15 ran aground and was lost. The Australian submarine AE2 finally threaded the defenses on April 24–25, and proceeded to the Sea of Marmara. Plagued by mechanical problems, AE2 had a short run, alarming the Turks but not sinking any ships. While lining up to sink the torpedo boat *Sultanhiser* on April 30, AE2 popped to the surface. *Sultanhiser* opened fire, and the Australians abandoned their craft before it sank.

The British submarine E-14, following AE2's lead, was already in the Sea of Marmara, having arrived on April 27. When E-14 was finished and returned through the straits to safety, its captain and crew had sunk the Turkish gunboat *Nur-el Bahr* and torpedoed and damaged a troop ship and a minelayer. The submarine E-11 made the next successful entrance on May 18. E-11 ran amok, sinking ships and arriving off Istanbul, where it sank a transport ship as shore batteries opened up on it, though it escaped. E-11's daring attack struck fear in the Turkish capital; an enemy vessel had successfully run the gauntlet and struck a blow. In all E-11 made three successful sorties into the Sea of Marmara, sinking 80 vessels ranging from small boats and transports to the battleship *Barbaros Hayreddin*.

THE WRECKS OF GALLIPOLI

The sunken ships and submarines of the Gallipoli campaign lie on a vast undersea battlefield that has slowly been mapped and better understood thanks to the efforts of Turkish naval scholars, archaeologists, and divers, most notably Selçuk Kolay and Savas Karakas. Kolay began diving on known wrecks and searching for others in 1974. At that time, the Turks had salvaged some of the wrecks, blasting into hulls to recover machinery and propellers. Kolay saved artifacts that would have otherwise been lost in his role as director of Istanbul's Rahmi Koç Museum. In time, Kolay joined with others to form the Turkish Institute of Nautical Archaeology (TINA) and also served on the board of the US-founded, Turkish-based Institute of Nautical Archaeology. He also expanded his dives into a comprehensive project to define the undersea landscape and the extended battlefield of the Dardanelles and the Sea of Marmara.

A certain number of the wrecks were already known to the Turks because they lay close to military bases and had been in part salvaged. Other wrecks had not been discovered. Between 1993 and 2011, Kolay and his partners located and documented the wrecks of four merchant vessels sunk by the British submarines, as well as the gunboat *Nur-el Bahr*, the French submarine *Joule*, and the Australian submarine AE2. The discovery of AE2 in July 1998 after a quiet three-year search made headlines in Australia, for whom Gallipoli holds special meaning as an altar upon which the

318 ■ WAR AT SEA

former colony had laid so precious a sacrifice during World War I. AE2 and its sister submarine AE1, also lost during the war, were Australia's first submarines.

Australian and Turkish divers, supported by the Turkish Navy, dived on the wreck, which lies in 72 meters of water, and surveyed it in October 1998. A return expedition in September 2007, again a joint Turkish-Australian operation with archaeologists Mark Spencer and Tim Smith, enabled the team to lower a camera into AE2's control room, providing a view last seen by human eyes on April 30, 1915. Because the submarine's wreck, when found, was very well preserved, the idea was proposed to raise and display it ashore in a tank of water for more study. Another idea involved moving the wreck into shallower water to allow better access to divers, but by 2008, concerns over the fragility of the wreck, an unexploded torpedo inside it, costs, and the advent of new technology, which allowed for virtual display, led to the decision to leave AE2 in its grave.

A remotely operated vehicle (ROV) survey of the wreck in June 2014 reinforced the fact that the latest technology adds to our understanding of sites like this, with a clear and complete survey of the entire site and the discovery of new features such as the submarine's portable wireless antenna, something historians had known the submarine carried, but which had not been seen on the previous dives. One hundred years after its loss, AE2 is yet another wreck not forgotten. As Tim Smith has noted, "No other E-class submarine wreck site has been the focus of controlled archaeological survey and rigorous scientific analysis."

Many of the Gallipoli campaign wrecks lie in water in excess of 60 meters, and so Kolay also made use of the increasingly sharp definition of what lies below through the use of multibeam sonar. At the same time, as already seen with the 2008 dive on AE2 with a Seabotix ROV, that technology has also opened new doors. ROVs are robotic workhorses on which we attach a variety of scientific instruments and cameras. Thanks to satellites, we can stream what we are seeing and what the instruments tell us to a global audience of scientists, but also to anyone and everyone with an interest. The practice of "telepresence," as I've said before and will repeat again with more emphasis in the discussion on World War II and Cold War wrecks, has opened the door of exploration and learning at an unparalleled level in the age of the Internet.

Two separate missions to Gallipoli by Dr. Robert Ballard's Ocean Exploration Trust (OET) in 2009 and 2010 underscored the promise and premise of telepresence. The E/V *Nautilus* and its dual ROVs *Argus* and *Hercules*, dived on the wrecks of HMS *Irresistible*, HMS *Triumph*, AE2, *Midilli*, and landing craft in Anzac Cove, both live-streamed and filmed for another National Geographic special. Among the dives were a series of circular rings clustered around the wreck of *Triumph*. Archaeologist Michael Brennan, who coordinated the dives for OET, notes that the circles appear to have come as a result of the explosive forces of shells fired across the peninsula by British ships in the early stages of the battle as they shelled Turkish positions in advance of the landings by the Commonwealth troops.

By the time of the centennial of the battles, in 2015–2016, much of the sea floor at Gallipoli had been mapped, and with it, high-resolution sonar maps of the various wrecks delineated them and the damage of their sinking as well as subsequent damage. The Turkish national park at Gallipoli, with its manicured monuments, is a unique mix of monuments and restored trenches, as well as other reminders. I will always remember walking through a freshly plowed field with Savas Karakas and looking into the furrows, as we walked, seeing shrapnel, spent bullets, and fragments of human bone.

The work of Selçuk Kolay and his team has now revealed what was once out of sight in their documentation of the wrecks of the Ottoman warships *Mesudiye, Nur-el Bahr, Barbaros Hayrettin*, and *Midilli*; the submarines *Saphir, Joule, Mariotte*, AE2, E-7, E-14, and E-15; and the battleships *Bouvet, Irresistible, Ocean, Goliath, Triumph*, and *Majestic*; landing craft; and merchant ships lost during the campaign. Their work has also illuminated other aspects of the battle.

The French battleship *Bouvet* capsized and sank in less than a minute when it strayed into the minefield, taking 603 of its 639-man crew with it. The explosion came as Turkish shore batteries were firing on *Bouvet*, and Turkish accounts stressed how a hit with a massive 12-inch shell had caused *Bouvet* to swerve into the minefield. Other accounts suggested the battleship simply came too close and hit a mine or mines that opened it up to the sea. Working with forensic naval architects Larrie Ferreiro and Sean Kery, the team found clear evidence of both the shell hit midships, near the waterline, and punched into the hull. The damage to the bow from the mine hit was not large enough to catastrophically flood *Bouvet*, but the hole from the shell, into the boiler compartments, introduced enough instability, combined with flooding from the bow, to capsize the battleship.

There is a statue of conscripted woodcutter Corporal Seyit Ali Çabuk at the battery that fired the fatal shot that took out HMS *Ocean*. It honors the woodcutter as the hero who "sank" the battleship. At a critical point in the battle, the battery's ammunition lift, damaged by shelling, failed. The burly Seyit, no doubt spurred by adrenalin, bodily picked up a 12-inch shell weighing more than 800 pounds, and hoisted it into the gun. He then hoisted two more. Today a statue of the corporal stands by his gun, which is part of the national park. Those guns, and the men who manned them on one side, as well as those who fought in their ships on the other, have left to us the material evidence of their deeds at this battlefield, both on land and beneath the sea.

THE DESTRUCTION OF GERMANY'S EAST ASIATIC SQUADRON

Far from the battlefields of Europe and the Near East, the Pacific was host to a series of naval actions. They were both a response to Germany's presence in the Pacific and because Japan joined the war as an ally of Britain. Coincidentally, both Germany and Japan had started their rise to naval and colonial power at roughly the same time between the 1870s and 1890s. The creation of the German Empire in 1871, at the end of the Franco-Prussian War, combined not only a vast territory in the heart of Europe, but it also concentrated considerable industrial resources under the control of the kaiser and his "iron chancellor," Otto von Bismarck. Bismarck's military strategy relied on the creation of a strong army. A large navy was not needed, as Germany's potential enemies were its neighbors. This policy changed after 1888 when a new kaiser, Wilhelm II, ascended the throne. Under Wilhelm's influence, the German navy expanded, but without a consistent direction as naval construction and deployment wavered between the creation of a large, home-based battle fleet to confront European foes and a diverse, scattered force of cruisers and raiders.

Germany's acquisition of far-flung colonies in the Pacific included the forced lease of the Chinese harbor of Tsingtao as a German naval base. The presence of the Germans in the region was a problem for the Japanese as well as the Chinese. When World War I commenced, Japan allied itself with the European powers opposed to Germany. Germany's naval forces in the Pacific were small, antiquated, and no match for Japan's. With the coming of war in 1914 and Japan's entry into the conflict, German officials realized that the Pacific colonies would be lost, and the more effective battle to be fought was not in those waters. The German East Asiatic Squadron, under the command of Admiral von Spee, consisted of two heavy cruisers, three light cruisers, and a few armed merchant ships.

Leaving the light cruiser *Emden* and the converted merchant cruiser *Cormoran* behind to harass British shipping while avoiding the Japanese, Spee headed for the west coast of South America. *Emden* waged a successful, but brief campaign in the Indian Ocean, sinking 23 ships and bombarding Madras, India, before the Australian light cruiser HMAS *Sydney* caught up with it on November 9, 1914, when *Emden* stopped at remote Cocos Islands to destroy a British wireless station there. As *Emden* pulled into range, the wireless station broadcast that an unidentified ship was approaching. *Sydney* was only about 52 nautical miles away. While the German shore party was still on the island, destroying the station, *Sydney* hove into view and *Emden*'s crew opened fire.

In a brief, but bloody engagement, *Sydney* stood out of range of *Emden*'s guns and blasted the German raider until it was a complete wreck and the captain surrendered after running his badly damaged command ashore on the reef of North Keeling Island. Partially salvaged by the Australians and a Japanese salvage company, the battered remains of *Emden* lie in the shallows of North Keeling, now a national park, and Australian archaeologists have documented the site, with one account describing the wreckage as scattered in "chunks." *Emden*'s actions and last fight became the stuff of

■ The shell-ravaged deck of the cruiser SMS *Emden*, aground on Cocos Reef. (Naval History and Heritage Command)

legend on both sides during the war. A number of relics taken off the cruiser within the first months and years of the battle are held by the Australian War Memorial, including the warped, shot-up bell of *Emden*, graphic evidence of the ferocity of the fight that battered the ship into surrender and killed 131 of its crew.

THE WRECK OF SMS *CORMORAN*

After von Spee sent off the raiders, *Cormoran* engaged in a short cruise, hiding from the Japanese, until, finally, low on coal and provisions, it put into Guam on December 14, 1914. An American territory, Guam was a neutral port because the United States had not yet entered the war. Unable to gain enough coal or food for a voyage to German East Africa, the captain of

Cormoran agreed to intern his ship in Guam. There the ship and crew sat, not quite prisoners, but unable to fight, and out of the war. The officers and crew of *Cormoran* could not leave the island, but they did integrate into the community, some through marriage.

The friendly status of their enforced visit changed three years later with the US entry into the war on April 7, 1917. Ordered to surrender the ship, *Cormoran*'s captain gave the order to scuttle the ship. As the crew shouted "*Cormoran! Cormoran!*" and leaped into the sea, explosive charges set deep in the hull exploded. Settling by the stern and then rolling over to starboard, *Cormoran* sank in 56 meters of water as men struggled in the debris-filled water. Seven of the crew were lost, and their graves are a visible reminder of the ship, and of the close association the people of Apra, Guam, had with interned guests turned "enemies."

After the sinking, the US Navy sent hard-hat divers down to *Cormoran*, recovering its guns, ammunition, the anchors and chain, deck winches, and its bell, which is now displayed at the United States Naval Academy Museum in Annapolis. After that, *Cormoran* was left to the sea until after World War II and the advent of sport diving. The intact wreck of *Cormoran* lies on its port side on the bottom of Apra Harbor. The water is usually clear and as you hover over the wreck, much of it is visible. Guam's Department of Parks and Recreation first surveyed the wreck in 1978, and in 1983, while on Guam doing a comprehensive survey for what was then War in the Pacific National Historical Park, the National Park Service's Submerged Cultural Resources Unit (now the Submerged Resources Center) dived and documented the wreck, and completed a detailed map of it in 1988–1989.

A contributing factor in the coming world war was Japan's seizure of Germany's Pacific colonies. Japan used its superior navy, the largest in the Pacific, to occupy Germany's colonies in Micronesia, including the Palaus, Marianas, Carolines, and the Marshalls. The Treaty of Versailles confirmed Japan's seizures at the end of the war, expanding the Empire of Japan well out into the Pacific and providing a series of island bases that Japan wasted little time fortifying, in defiance of the treaty. Emboldened by its role in the war, and the elimination of a European colonial power in a sphere Japan regarded as its own, Japan was now in a position to dominate the Pacific and Asia, much to the chagrin of its wartime allies who were eager to retain their own Far Eastern and Pacific possessions.

THE SPECTACULAR RUN OF THE GERMAN EAST ASIATIC SQUADRON

By the time *Cormoran* pulled into Guam, German sea power in the Pacific was no more. Admiral von Spee was dead and his squadron was on the bottom of the ocean. After leaving the Far East, Spee's squadron steamed west, alarming officials in Canada who thought the Germans were headed for Esquimalt, near Victoria, British Columbia. At the same time, the cruiser *Leipzig*, which had been off Mexico's west coast when the war began, moved into position off San Francisco. Esquimalt, the British Empire's principal naval base on the Pacific Coast, was not the target though. Instead, the Germans headed for South America. Stopping at Easter Island in mid-October, Spee met up with the German light cruiser *Dresden*, which had begun the war in Mexico's Gulf waters. Unable to head for Germany, *Dresden* instead embarked on a voyage around the top of South America to rendezvous with the East Asiatic Squadron. They also met up with *Leipzig* and the raider *Prinz Eitel Friederich*.

At Valparaíso, Chile, von Spee learned that a smaller, weaker British squadron was 200 miles away, intent on finding and engaging the German squadron. Primarily composed of older, obsolete ships commanded by Rear Admiral Sir Christopher Cradock and an experienced group of officers, the British squadron of four ships was not only outmatched in numbers to Spee's five ships, but the German ships were more modern, and outgunned their foes in both range and firepower. The two fleets met off the Chilean coast near the city of Coronel in the late afternoon of November 1. Cradock pushed forward to close the range, and as he did, the Germans, firing every 20 seconds, repeatedly hit *Good Hope*, Cradock's flagship, and the cruiser *Monmouth* with an accurate and deadly fire that set the British ships ablaze. As darkness fell, the light of the burning ships allowed the

Germans to keep shelling as the British ships struggled to fire at an enemy delineated solely by muzzle flashes.

Good Hope exploded when its bow magazines ignited and quickly sank in the dark, while *Monmouth*, burning and nearly dead in the water, tried to withdraw in the hope of beaching the cruiser. Instead, the cruiser *Nürnberg*, drawn to the burning ship, signaled the British to surrender, and when they did not, sank *Monmouth*. There were no survivors from either of the British cruisers. In total, 1,570 men died. The Germans suffered no major damage or losses, with only three men wounded. The Battle of Coronel shocked Great Britain when the news reached the country through German news sources. The first loss by the Royal Navy in a century, and coming on the heels of the torpedoing and loss of *Aboukir*, *Cressy*, and *Hogue*, was an insult to be avenged, and quickly.

Aware that the British would seek revenge by sending more ships after him, Spee headed into the Atlantic and back home to Germany. The regular sea route through the South Atlantic passed the British colony of the Falkland Islands, off the coast of Argentina. On his way home, lured by a false message sent by British intelligence, Spee decided to attack its only port, Stanley. It was there that a larger, more modern British fleet, the battlecruisers *Invincible* and *Inflexible*; armored cruisers *Carnarvon*, *Cornwall*, and *Kent*; the light cruisers *Bristol* and *Glasgow* (a veteran of the Coronel fight); and the armed merchant cruiser *Macedonia* lay in wait under the command of Vice Admiral Doveton Sturdee.

When Spee's ships arrived on the morning of December 8 and approached to attack Stanley, they were met with gunfire and quickly turned away as Spee realized he was outmatched. Sturdee ordered his fleet to follow, and as they steamed out of Stanley Harbor, the Germans were 24 kilometers ahead on the open sea. Three hours later, the newer, faster British ships had caught up with the Germans, and the fight began. Spee put his heavier ships between his smaller light cruisers, to give them a chance to get away, but Sturdee detached some of his ships to go after and sink them. Methodically and mercilessly, the British fleet overwhelmed and sank Spee's squadron, firing into the enemy ships even as they sank.

The waters of the South Atlantic off the Falklands are very deep. To this day, despite searches, the East Asiatic Squadron of the Graf Spee remain undiscovered, slumbering in the eternal darkness of that ocean.

THE ODYSSEY AND DEATH OF SMS *DRESDEN*

On March 14, 1914, the 21,000-nautical-mile odyssey of the Imperial German Navy cruiser *Dresden* came to an end in the harbor of Isla Juan Fernández (Robinson Crusoe Island) in the Pacific. After an arduous if not heroically brief career that had drawn first blood from the British Royal Navy at Coronel, followed by a decisive victory against *Dresden's* squadron mates off the Falklands, the German cruiser had escaped British retribution. Following a protracted chase and hunt, the Royal Navy caught and cornered *Dresden* in a remote bay, and quickly sank it. Despite the drama of the final battle, the end of *Dresden* was portrayed by the victors as anticlimactic, noting the cruiser "put up a half-hearted fight" that lasted five minutes before the Germans surrendered, struck their flag, and abandoned

■ SMS *Dresden* cornered and under fire at Isla Juan Fernández. (Royal Museums Greenwich/Wikimedia Commons)

ship. "Shortly after the crew had left their ship her magazine exploded and she disappeared."

Thus wrote naval historian Harold F. B. Wheeler in *The Story of the British Navy* in 1922. In doing so, Wheeler echoed the official line of the Royal Navy. He also drew a rather pointed and clear distinction in regard to the German crew and ship. Cornered on a distant island, they had acted less than honorably in requiting themselves. This Wheeler implied in a brief comment: "A pig from the *Dresden* became the mascot of one of the British warships, and was duly decorated with a cardboard replica of the Iron Cross." The British tars named the pig "Tirpitz." To stress the point further, Wheeler noted that the German ship, abusing Chilean neutrality and international law by staying more than 24 hours, was about to be interned by Chilean officials. "At this juncture the British ships arrived, and when she was ordered to surrender the crew blew up the magazine."

In the face of the incident being a "subject of protest" of the Chilean government, Wheeler noted the official Royal Navy view that the armed and dangerous *Dresden* was "only awaiting a favorable opportunity to sally out and attack British commerce again," and so the arrival of the British ships had been fortuitous in forcing the Germans' hand. Nonetheless, the British government "offered a full and ample apology," even though "it was afterward stated officially that the action took place about twelve miles off Robinson Crusoe's Island." Simple enough and case closed, one might think. However, as the old saying goes, history is written by the victors.

The facts that have emerged in the century since the action indicate that the British account is not only wrong, but intentionally misleading. Even at the time of the action, the then-neutral US press noted that the reports from both sides were "in conflict." *The New York Times*, in March 1915, reported that the Germans asserted that *Dresden* had been at anchor in Cumberland Bay, in neutral waters, and that the British ships had fired on it in this defenseless position, also striking other non-combatant ships in the harbor, with shells going ashore and killing a woman and child. The *Times* cited British authorities in reporting the action 16 kilometers from shore. A German survivor of the action, also quoted in the *Times*, stated that his ship was about a third of a mile from the beach, and that the British ships kept up continuous fire at *Dresden* even as the Germans abandoned ship.

After the war, German veterans of the battle, among them *Oberleutnant zur See* Wilhelm Canaris (who later gained fame as an admiral in command of the *Abwehr* in World War II, and when found to be secretly opposed to Hitler, was executed) reported that their ship had been anchored, out of fuel, desperately calling over the telegraph for any ships with coal to come to the harbor and sell it to them. The British Navy had intercepted the transmissions, and, closing in on *Dresden*, commenced firing when entering the bay at 8:40 in the morning.

As *Kapitan zur See* Fritz Emil von Lüdecke hoisted a signal to cease fire and commence negotiations, he dispatched his adjutant Canaris by boat to the lead British ship to protest the illegality of the action. On board HMS *Glasgow*, Captain John Luce, a veteran of the British defeat at Coronel, and none too sympathetic, listened to the German officer's protests over the violation of Chilean sovereignty and replied that his orders were to sink *Dresden*, and leave the rest to the diplomats. With that, Canaris reported, the British took up positions and at nearly point-blank range continued firing into *Dresden*. As heavy gunfire forced the German crew from their guns, von Lüdecke raised the white flag and ordered all to abandon ship. *Glasgow, Kent*, and *Orama* continued to shoot, however, until a scuttling charge set in *Dresden*'s bow erupted at 10:45. As *Dresden* slipped beneath the bay at 11:15, a second charge detonated in the engine room. *Dresden*'s survivors, crowded on the beach, cheered for their ship and comrades, eight of whom had died in the action.

With divergent views on what happened on that March morning, a joint Canadian-Chilean team headed to Isla Juan Fernández in 2002 with German archaeologist Willii Kramer, who was there on behalf of the German government, and me. We were there to document the wreck archaeologically for the first time and to capture its imagery and its story for National Geographic Television. What we found, at 70 meters, was that the German accounts seemed right. Indeed, while the victors write the history, in this case they did so to gloss over their violation of the law, and unfairly maligned their opponents.

The German accounts reported that *Dresden* went down heavily by the bow as the first scuttling charge went off. The severed end of the bow, with its steel ram, rests upright on the bottom. This area of the ship is badly mangled, and the detailed examination of the damage clearly showed that it was *Dresden's* death wound. The crew set a scuttling charge in the forward or number-one magazine of the ship where ammunition was stored. This resulted in a massive and catastrophic internal explosion. As diver Mike Fletcher dropped to the bottom to inspect the bow, he found that a long string of anchor chain trails off the bow and heads off into the gloom of deeper water, where the anchor that held *Dresden* in place when the cruiser sank remains dug into the bottom. *Dresden* was not underway, not ready to flee. The Germans reported the ship had only 80 tons of coal left on board, barely enough to keep up steam for the generators to broadcast the cruiser's futile calls for fuel.

I monitored Mike's dive as he swam, tethered to the surface by a long line through which breathing gas and communications flowed; we explored together thanks to "hard hat" dive technology. We found a deck gun, possibly

■ Mike Fletcher at the stern of the wreck of *Dresden*. (Author Photo)

■ *Dresden's* helm. (Author Photo)

■ *Dresden's* wreck still mounts its guns. (Author Photo)

hit by British shellfire, angling inward and pointing straight down at *Dresden's* deck. Close by are three perfectly spaced shell holes, one after the other, that showed how gunfire moved smoothly along the ship's hull toward the casemate. The armored casemate or compartment is partially collapsed. Its partner, the forward casemate on the port side, however, was gone—gun, thick armor, and all. It likely disintegrated thanks to a solid hit, or was destroyed by the scuttling explosion. The level of damage does not agree with the British accounts of the fight. British reports stressed that after a few hits on the stern and on the deck guns, *Dresden* sank intact when the crew set off a scuttling charge deep in the hull. Instead, the forensic evidence shows a sustained shelling and evidence of the two scuttling charges the Germans mentioned. This was no five-minute encounter marked by a white flag and an ignominious scuttling.

The British commanders had orders to sink *Dresden*, and they made sure they did just that. The question of where the British ships were firing from was also answered. While British accounts and maps of the battle show *Glasgow*, *Kent*, and *Orama* outside of Cumberland Bay, firing at *Dresden* from a distance, the wreck offers clear, forensic evidence of point-blank shooting. This was less a battle and more a punishing execution of a cornered foe. Shell holes on the cliffs ashore show that *Dresden* was subjected to a deadly crossfire, as well, as the ship or ships circled the wounded cruiser and pumped lethal rounds into it. It was a brilliant but brutal tactical maneuver. Captain Luce of *Glasgow*, in command of the British force, had orders to sink *Dresden*, and he took no chances. The British approached the crippled and burning ship, firing at point-blank range after the last Germans abandoned their ship and before the scuttling charges detonated inside the hull. The archaeological evidence at the battlefield above and below the surface is irrefutable.

After a century, should we care about confirming the German accounts of the battle? Accuracy in history is important, especially when one side is denigrated or proposed to posterity as cowardly, as Wheeler and other writers of his time did for the crew of *Dresden*. This was no short action, nor just a scuttling. Despite the violation of international law and Chilean sovereignty, the actions of John Luce and the other commanders on Cumberland Bay that March morning in their time faced only official praise and approbation for their actions, white-washed with an official apology to Chile and half-truths. *Dresden* had overstayed its legal limit in a neutral port, British officials argued. Sir Julian Corbett, writing in his epic history of naval operations during the war in 1922, wrote that the Chileans "were glad enough to be rid of the obnoxious cruiser, but their honour was touched."

But *Dresden* was flying a flag of truce in Chile's neutral waters when attacked. It must be remembered that after a shocking loss of 1,570 men and two British cruisers at Coronel, in which *Dresden* had participated, both the retribution repaid to *Dresden*'s squadron mates at the December 1914 Battle of the Falklands, and then the execution of *Dresden* were seen as fair compensation for Britain and the Royal Navy. Then again, Coronel and the Falklands were both open sea battles, not three ships against one anchored in a small harbor.

A century after the battle, and two world wars later, the one-time foes are now friends. Both as civilized nations rightly insist on the rule of law. Therein lies the answer as to why we now turn to the truth. Truth should be, and likely will be, revealed in time thanks to forensic analysis. Not all history remains hidden or forgotten. This fact was also made clear on *Dresden* as the team discovered heavy damage to its stern, which had been blasted clear to the deck. The images of the cruiser sinking show it to be intact. On inquiry into what had happened, a Chilean officer, out of camera range, shrugged his shoulders and raised his arm into a Nazi salute. Checking in German archives after the expedition, Willi Kramer found documents that showed that *Dresden* had been carrying a cargo of gold coin from German bank accounts in Tsingtao, China.

The coins had been transferred to *Dresden* by Admiral Graf Maximilian von Spee, whose East Asiatic Squadron had fled those waters with the gold and had then rendezvoused with *Dresden* on the west coast of South America. Before the fatal battle of the Falklands, Spee had the gold transferred to *Dresden*, which was then ordered to sail behind the other warships—and when the fighting erupted, *Dresden* had orders to flee, which is what von Lüdecke did. Years later, the archives showed, as Germany geared up for another war, a secret expedition by German and Chilean hard-hat divers blasted open von Lüdecke's stern cabin and retrieved the gold for Hitler. Sometimes, if not often, history is as colorful as a Clive Cussler novel.

THE GRAND SCUTTLE

When the war finally ended in November 1918, Germany's navy was intact, but bottled up not only by the Royal Navy but also by mutiny. The sailors rebelled against the orders of High Seas Fleet commander Admiral Franz von Hipper, who called for a last, desperate, perhaps suicidal sortie against the British. Allied successes on land and sea, and a Communist revolution in Germany, forced the kaiser to abdicate on November 9, and two days later Germany signed an armistice. Under its terms, the High Seas Fleet was ordered to disarm and turn itself over to the Royal Navy.

Rendezvousing on November 21, 1918, with the British Grand Fleet, the still-powerful German Navy steamed into Scapa Flow in the Orkney Islands for internment, its crews virtually imprisoned aboard, as negotiators thrashed out a treaty to conclude hostilities. On June 21, 1919, responding to rumors that the British would seize his ships, the German commander, Rear Admiral Ludwig von Reuter, gave the command to scuttle the fleet. While the British managed to beach some of the ships, 59 of 74 German warships sank that morning, granting at last von Hipper's wishes for a suicidal end for the fleet, even if not by fire and torn steel.

A concerted salvage effort after World War I scrapped nearly every one of the scuttled German High Seas Fleet from Scapa Flow. Starting in 1923 and continuing until 1939, divers raised the wrecks, which were towed away to ship-breaking yards. Today, only seven of the scuttled fleet remain on the bottom. The battleships *Konig, Kronprinz Wilhelm,* and *Markgraf,* and the cruisers *Brummer, Karlsruhe, Köln,* and a new *Dresden*—many of them veterans of Jutland—are also one of the last great collections of pre-dreadnought warships and an unparalleled and popular dive site. In 2017, archaeologist Innes McCartney conducted an overall, landscape-based survey of Scapa Flow with Gerd Normann Anderson and his firm JD-Contractor AS from the ship M/S *Vina,* which had conducted the Battle of Jutland survey. The goals were the same with a detailed multibeam sonar survey of 39 square kilometers of seabed and the sites of the scrapped and partially salvaged wrecks as well as intact ships, followed by ROV inspection of several of them.

■ The scuttled SMS *Hindenburg*'s upper works rise above the waters of ship Scapa Flow. (Royal Navy/Imperial War Museum Sp 1635)

The results of the war's end—a ravaged Europe, the increased Pacific empire of Japan, the failure of the battleship to actively contribute to the naval war, the success of the submarine, and the development of aircraft as weapons—were portents of the future. This was perhaps also obvious, at least to some observers, in Germany's humiliation over the final collapse and surrender underscored by the scuttling of the High Seas Fleet. Germany's simmering anger would lead to the rise of Hitler and a new war within two decades. A continued emphasis on the battleship and a renewed naval arms race, Japan's fortification of its new Pacific empire, and the failure of politicians and some military leaders to assess the potential of both the submarine and the airplane led to a difficult, if not near-disastrous start to World War II when Germany and Japan struck their first blows.

9

World War II

Writhing in agony on the surface of the water, this unsinkable giant ship is now an ideal target for bombs, nothing more.

           —Yoshida Mitsuru, aboard the battleship *Yamato*, April 7, 1945

The brief 21-year period between the first and second world wars witnessed an amazing denial by some powers, notably the United States and Japan, of the failure of the battleship to substantially deliver on its promise as an effective weapon. The battles between the German and British fleets had not altered the progress or the outcome of the last war. The United States and Japan, both winners in World War I, now jockeyed for domination of their respective spheres, in the case of Japan, the western Pacific and the Far East, and in the case of the United States, the Pacific, Atlantic, and Caribbean shores of the country. Both nations built large numbers of battleships, with the Japanese slowly outpacing American forces in the Pacific. At the same time, the Japanese also introduced heavier armor and bigger guns. In 1920–1921 they launched the battleships *Nagato* and *Mutsu*, the first battleships to carry 16-inch naval guns, capable of firing a shell well over the horizon at approaching ships.

The more significant naval development of the period was the steady adoption of submarines and aircraft into the naval arsenal. While condemning the German U-boat war, the victorious powers built up their own submarine forces. At the same time, the world's navies began to experiment with landing aircraft on ships as opposed to seaplanes, which were introduced just before the war and could land on the water. Seaplanes successfully attacked targets during the war with torpedoes and bombs, but they were merchant ships, not warships, and naval strategists considered the airplane an auxiliary at best, with the capital ships—the strength of any navy—to be battleships. That view was challenged, as early as the end of World War I, by US Army Brigadier-General William "Billy" Mitchell. In 1921, using captured German warships as targets to demonstrate the vulnerability of the battleship, Mitchell sent squadrons of aircraft to attack. They quickly sank the cruiser *Frankfurt* and the battleship *Ostfriesland*, the latter in 22 minutes.

While US naval officers were furious with Mitchell's staged tests, and the US Navy itself concluded, as late as 1925, that "airplanes cannot...exercise control of the sea," it did launch its first aircraft carrier, the converted collier USS *Langley*, in 1922. The next two American carriers, and their Japanese counterparts, were the result of naval arms limitation treaties. Laid down as gunships, the cruisers *Lexington* and *Saratoga*, the battlecruiser *Akagi*, and the battleship *Kaga* were completed as aircraft carriers between 1927 and 1928. Over the next decade, both countries, as well as Britain, built more carriers, although when the war in the Pacific started in 1941, Japan held the lead.

But even with these developments, the battleship still reigned supreme. When the naval arms treaties negotiated between the world's naval powers (Britain, the United States, Japan, France, and Italy) finally expired and were not renewed in 1934, each country placed most of its assets into building more battleships. The United States took the lead, although most of its ships were not ready when it entered the war in 1941. The Germans and the Japanese built some of the world's most powerful ships of their time in the late 1930s, launching the powerful *Scharnhorst* in 1939, *Bismarck* in 1940, and *Musashi* in 1942. The Japanese battleships were, on paper at least, the

most powerful warships in the world, mounting huge 18-inch naval guns—
the largest ever carried on a ship and the culmination of the age of the gun
afloat. But each of these ships, as well as many other battleships and cruisers, fell victim to the yet-scorned submarine and airplane in the conflict
that erupted between 1939 and 1941.

THE BATTLE OF THE ATLANTIC

It was no irony that the naval part of World War II commenced in September
1939 with the return of German U-boats to the Atlantic. Submarine warfare
against the enemy's commercial enterprises had nearly led to German victory in World War I. Mindful of this, with the outbreak of war in September
1939, Britain and France created a naval blockade of Germany, the British
reinstituted the convoy system of the last war to escort merchant shipping,
and in a repeat of the last submarine war, U-30, commanded by Fritz-Julius
Lemp, attacked and sank the liner *Athenia* just hours after the declaration of
war. With 1,418 people on board, the loss could have been worse than the
98 passengers and 19 crew who died. Widespread international outrage followed, including from the United States, which lost 28 citizens in the sinking. Nazi officials denied the attack and claimed the British had deliberately
sunk *Athenia*. German officials finally confessed that U-30 had sunk the
liner during the Nuremberg trials.

Thus began what would become the largest and longest battle of World
War II, on land or sea, the "Battle of the Atlantic," which is a misnomer. It
was a global battle waged by and against submarines. A new Allied naval
blockade of Germany and the second German U-boat offensive against
Allied shipping was more than a replay of World War I's U-boat war. The
1939–1945 battle was global, with U-boat attacks and anti-submarine warfare expanding beyond the waters off the British Isles; into the South
Atlantic, the Arctic, and off the Americas; in the Gulf of St. Lawrence, the
Eastern Seaboard, Carolinas, and the Gulf Coast of the United States; the
Caribbean; and beyond those "Atlantic" theaters, into the Mediterranean,
the Black Sea, and the Indian Ocean. The toll was massive, with some 3,500

merchant ships, 175 Allied warships, and 765 U-boats lost, and over 100,000 deaths on both sides.

After the war, salvagers such as the famous Risdon-Beazley marine salvage company made a fortune in recovering lost cargoes and scrapping wartime losses from water as deep as 300 meters. In all, they raised more than 56,000 tons of metal from the sea from the end of the war through the 1960s. Having documented a torpedoed Liberty Ship, SS *Alexander Macomb*, which lies off Georges Bank in the North Atlantic, I can attest to the thoroughness of Risdon-Beazley's crew. Beazley's ship *Droxford* salvaged *Macomb* in 1965, leaving a scattered field of broken plates, loose ammunition, and the broken remains of a few tanks where once an entire ship had sat on the seabed.

The locations of many of the ships lost in the battle, however, were never precisely marked. It was not until late 2017, for example, that oceanographer and wreck searcher David L. Mearns announced that a wreck that lies off Ireland—one of many on a seabed littered with broken ships from both world wars—was likely *Athenia*. A number of wrecks lie very deep in the North Atlantic, where they will remain undiscovered until a comprehensive sonar map of the seafloor is made.

That is not to say that casualties of the Battle of the Atlantic have not been found, dived, or studied. Wreck divers have located a number of warships, merchant vessels, and U-boats off European and American shores, and deep-water surveys have located others. The U-boat U-166, lost in the Gulf of Mexico on July 30, 1942, was discovered by Robert Church and Daniel Warren in 2001 during an archaeological survey. It rests in more than 1,500 meters of water. The U-boat and its final victim, the passenger steamer *Robert E. Lee*, lie within three kilometers of one another, with U-166 largely buried in mud.

NOAA's Office of National Marine Sanctuaries, with the archaeological team of the Monitor National Marine Sanctuary leading the effort, teamed with the Bureau of Ocean Energy Management, the National Park Service, East Carolina University, the University of North Carolina's Coastal Studies Institute, and the State of North Carolina to take a comprehensive look at the wrecks of "Torpedo Junction," the area off North Carolina's Cape

Hatteras, and a busy part of the battlefield of the Battle of the Atlantic. The project was also dedicated to raising awareness of the war that was fought so close to the American coastline, but was in danger of being forgotten as the wartime generation is passing, and to documenting the ongoing changes to the wrecks from natural and human factors, as well as how a number of them had become artificial reefs. Another key partner in the study was the Battle of the Atlantic Research Group, private citizens and volunteers who dived, mapped, and made many important contributions.

The study, which lasted from 2008 to 2014, was comprehensive, looking at American, British, and German naval vessels, as well as merchant vessels of various nationalities lost in that section of ocean also known to this day as the Graveyard of the Atlantic. The products have been more than scholarly reports, images, and films. They have included detailed underwater dive slates to help explain to some divers what they are seeing on the bottom, all part of encouraging underwater tourism.

Among the wrecks surveyed were the U-boats U-85, sunk April 14, 1942 by USS *Roper*, with all 46 of its crew; U-352, sunk May 9, 1942, by the Coast Guard cutter *Icarus*, with 15 of the 48-man crew lost; and U-701, sunk by an aerial attack on July 7, 1942, with only seven survivors from the 46-man crew, and not discovered until 1989. The team also surveyed Allied combatants. They were the British Armed Trawler *Bedfordshire*, sunk on May 12, 1943 by U-558 killing the entire 37-man crew, and USS YP-389, a New England fishing trawler converted into a navy patrol vessel for anti-submarine warfare. YP-389 went down in the best traditions of the service in an hour-and-a-half-long gunfight in the dark with U-701 in the predawn hours of June 19, 1942. The U-boat sank the patrol boat, and the crew took to the water in their lifebelts with six of them dead and 12 injured, several of them seriously. That individual fight's outcome notwithstanding, these were dangerous waters for both sides. Two weeks later, army aircraft spotted and sank U-701 in the same area.

The project also discovered, explored, and documented merchant ships lost to U-boat attack. The total number of ships lost off Cape Hatteras within the first months of the war alone is staggering. The rampage of the U-boats was not widely broadcast during the war because "loose lips sink ships."

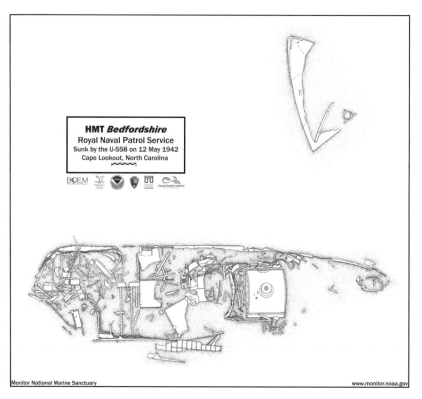

HMT *Bedfordshire*
Royal Naval Patrol Service
Sunk by the U-558 on 12 May 1942
Cape Lookout, North Carolina

■ Site plan for the wreck of HMT *Bedfordshire*. (NOAA/Office of National Marine Sanctuaries)

The scope of the battle was apparent to the residents of North Carolina's Outer Banks, with older residents still recalling ships burning offshore in the night so brightly that it seemed like daylight, and mothers walking the beaches in the morning to make sure that their children would not encounter the bodies of dead sailors who washed ashore.

Some of the wrecks surveyed by the Battle of the Atlantic project include the tanker *Ashkhabad*, sunk by U-402 but without loss of life on April 29, 1942; the tanker *Dixie Arrow*, sunk by U-71 on March 26, 1942, with 11 dead; the tanker *E. M. Clark*, sunk on March 18, 1942, by I-124, with one man lost; the tanker *Empire Gem*, sunk January 24, 1942, by U-66, with only two survivors out of a crew of 51 men; and the tanker *Lancing*, sunk April 7, 1942, with one dead. One aspect of this was closure for some families, especially those from the merchant ships whose lost fathers, uncles,

■ The grave of an unknown sailor from HMT *Bedfordshire*. (National Park Service)

brothers, and sons were not officially considered combatants for many years, and as the "unsung heroes," ferried the bullets, tanks, planes, fuel, and troops across the ocean to the theaters of war. Their service and their status as veterans was not granted by Congress until 1988.

The team connected with Jean Revels, who lost her father, Captain Anders Johnson, when *Dixie Arrow* sank. She was only 13 at the time, and with his death, her mother and the children were evicted from company-owned housing and went to live with relatives. Told she could not talk about what her father had been doing, or how he had died, she kept quiet in school when other children asked if her father was fighting in the war and was mercilessly teased. He also never had a funeral. During the survey, the NOAA team took the then-87-year-old Jean and her family out to the wreck site, and the divers unfurled a US flag on the wreck while the service above took place. They photographed the flag in place as it flew over her father's grave and then returned with it for the Revels family.

The most recent work on the Battle of the Atlantic wrecks was a focused look at the battlefield associated with U-576's attack off Cape Hatteras on Convoy KS-520, a group of 19 merchant ships being escorted by three US

Navy and two Coast Guard vessels from Norfolk, Virginia, to Key West, Florida on July 15, 1942. U-576 sank the freighter *Bluefields* and severely damaged the ships *J. A. Mowinckel* and *Chilore*. At that point, U-576 suddenly popped to the surface. Two days earlier, U-576's commander, Kapitänleutnant Hans-Dieter Heinicke, had radioed a report that the submarine had suffered damage to its #5 ballast tank during an aerial depth charge attack. The damage likely had not been repaired, or the repairs had not held. Just before the attack on KS-520, one of the escorting cutters picked up a sonar contact and dropped eight depth charges over the next several minutes. All of these factors may have led, after the firing of four torpedoes, to the submarine's abrupt rise. The Naval Armed Guard on the ship *Unicoi*, alerted by the torpedo hits on the ships around them, opened up on U-576 and hit it. US Navy Kingfisher aircraft, providing the convoy's air cover, bombed U-576, which quickly sank, taking all 45 of its crew with it.

Meanwhile, the damaged *J. A. Mowinckel* and *Chilore* limped away from the convoy and entered a minefield laid to define and defend the edges of the channel used by convoys. Both hit mines, but did not sink. Two days later, the navy tug *Keshena*, coming in to tow out the ships, struck a mine and sank on July 19, 1942, killing two of its crew. *Chilore*, under tow, also sank while entering Chesapeake Bay. The wrecks of *Chilore* and *Keshena*, both known and dived sites, marked two of the victims of the attack on KS-520, but to better understand the battle, and to find U-576 and *Bluefields*, NOAA archaeologist Joe Hoyt and his colleagues studied the records, using military battle analysis as well as archaeology, and surveyed the area with sonar. In early 2014, the NOAA ship *Okeanos Explorer*, passing through the area, conducted a multibeam sonar survey to assess a possible target for *Bluefields* at 228 meters. As they mapped it, the sonar delineated another target, lying in 210 meters and a few hundred meters away. Those targets, dived by Hoyt and team in August 2014, proved to be the U-boat and its victim, lying in close proximity to each other.

The study of KS-520 took place while across the Atlantic, archaeologist Innes McCartney studied World War I naval battlefields and resolved the fates and locations of U-boats from both world wars. In this, again using multibeam sonar, as we've seen on other wrecks and projects discussed, the

■ The deep-water wreck of U-576 off North Carolina, as first seen since it sank in combat. (NOAA/Office of National Marine Sanctuaries)

emphasis has shifted from one ship or submarine at a time to a larger picture that includes the forensics of battles as well as battle damage, but also looks at the human story. Before the discovery of U-576 and *Bluefields*, historians believed that the damaged U-boat and its crew had encountered the convoy on their way home. The position Kapitänleutnant Hans-Dieter Heinicke radioed from, two days earlier, was 193 kilometers in the opposite direction. Why had Heinicke reversed course and returned to the hunting grounds of the convoy routes?

Joe Hoyt and his colleagues believe that it is because on this, his fifth U-boat cruise, Heinicke had sunk no ships on his first two patrols, only one on his third patrol, and two on his fourth. Empty-handed, and damaged, he risked his boat and the lives of his crew to return home with a kill or kills. The gamble did not pay off, and the sad fate of U-576 and its crew is not a solitary one. What we have also learned, decades after the passions of war fade, is more about the men, or in most cases, the boys who went off to fight on both sides. That process began with the book and film *Das Boot*, which humanized a crew of a U-boat, and through the discovery of combat-lost submarines and meetings with families.

Those who find these lost ships and connect with families speak powerfully of how loss was felt on both sides, and how discoveries bring closure to former enemies. I will always remember an email I received from the

nephew of a German submariner, after being part of a team that discovered
the U-215, sunk off Nova Scotia, Canada, on July 3, 1942. His uncle, a 19-year-
old engineer, had never come home, and the family's grief remained profound. He thanked us, because now they knew exactly where he lay. He also
wanted to tell me that his uncle was no Nazi, just a boy who went off to war
to fight for his country.

Eight decades after World War II and the Battle of the Atlantic began, the
work of wreck divers, historians, and archaeologists are better defining the
fates, locating the lost, and adding a human dimension to a campaign that is
overwhelming, if not numbing, in its numbers. The repository for much of
this data is online, at Uboat.net, which is the definitive site. It documents
the postwar discovery of 67 U-boats, nine of which were subsequently
raised, 43 that are dive sites, and 14 that have been found but are too deep
to be dived. Most lie off the United Kingdom, and the remainder off the
United States and Turkey, Brazil, Denmark, Estonia, France, Norway, Poland,
Portugal, and Spain. Even where a U-boat's wreck was known, through
access to new sources of data, including the discovery of wrecks, Uboat.
net's webmasters have revised the fates of 165 U-boats. The fates of many of
their victims, noted in logbooks, have not yet been confirmed, revised, or
added to by underwater surveys and discoveries.

THE WRECK OF *GRAF SPEE*

Laid down at Wilhelmshaven in 1932, the pocket battleship *Admiral Graf
Spee* was named for the German admiral who had died in the Battle of the
Falklands in December 1914. Part of a new German naval strategy that emphasized a fast, movable force that could strike an enemy's commerce and
outrun heavy battleships, *Graf Spee* was known as a *panzerschiff*, or "panther
ship." Launched in June 1934, *Graf Spee* was a unique result of the naval
arms limitation treaties and the German Navy's desire to secretly circumvent the terms of those agreements. Limited to just 10,000 tons in weight
by the treaties, the new *panzerschiff* actually displaced 12,000 tons. The long,
sleek hull was welded, not riveted, which saved weight, as did aluminum

in the ship's interior and superstructure. Instead of heavy steam turbines, *Graf Spee*'s engines were lighter diesels. The weight saved by these changes allowed the Germans to add more armor to protect the ship. It also packed quite a punch: six 280-mm guns, mounted in two turrets; eight 150-mm guns; six 105-mm heavy antiaircraft guns; eight 37-mm light antiaircraft guns; and twelve 20-mm guns; as well as eight torpedo tubes.

With the outbreak of war, Germany's *Kriegsmarine* was not as prepared as the *Wermacht* on land or the *Luftwaffe* in the air. The commander of the *Kriegsmarine*, Admiral Erich Raeder, had a force of two battleships, six cruisers, 17 destroyers, and 57 U-boats in 1939. This was not enough to challenge Britain and France at sea and win a decisive battle. Instead, as Germany prepared for war, Raeder stepped up the construction of more U-boats and also dispatched *Graf Spee*, under the command of Kapitan zur See Hans Langsdorff, to the South Atlantic, where it took up station as a commerce raider just as Hitler's troops crossed into Poland. On August 26, Langsdorff received instructions from Berlin to attack. Four days later, *Graf Spee* made the first of nine kills, sinking all of those British merchant ships without loss of life on either side. Langsdorff was an honorable warrior of the old school.

Alarmed by the depredations of the raider, the British Admiralty ultimately dispatched 23 ships to find and sink *Graf Spee*. On December 13, 1939, the cruisers *Exeter, Ajax*, and *Achilles* found the Germans off the mouth of the River Plate on the Uruguayan coast as it waited to attack a British convoy. Commodore Henry Harwood, in command of the three British cruisers, had gambled on Langsdorff attacking the convoy. The running fight began early in the morning. *Graf Spee*'s guns hit *Exeter* hard, killing scores of men, smashing the bridge, and knocking one turret out of action. As its captain and crew fought to return fire and keep moving, more shells hit them, putting *Exeter* out of the fight with more than 50 casualties and the ship listing and on fire. Shells also hit *Ajax*, and it looked as if *Graf Spee* would finish off its attackers.

But British shells had also hit the German raider, damaging it. Nineteen British shells rained down and into *Graf Spee*, and Langsdorff decided to run for neutral Montevideo for repairs. Far from home, he could not risk further damage. The decision proved fatal for both captain and ship. Blockaded in port by the wounded, but still capable British cruisers, and with more ships arriving to reinforce Harwood, Langsdorff buried his dead, rushed through some emergency repairs, and faced the reality of being trapped in a port that while neutral had no desire to shelter him except as an interned, near-prisoner. Instead, on December 17, Langsdorff sailed at 6:30 P.M. and when just three miles out of Uruguayan waters, scuttled his ship at the mouth of the Plate. As explosions ripped through *Graf Spee*, it sank into the shallows, burning through the night. Three days later, in his hotel room in Buenos Aires, Langsdorff lay down on a flag of the old German Imperial Navy, lifted his revolver to his head, and shot himself.

Archaeologists under the direction of Mensun Bound surveyed the wreck of *Admiral Graf Spee* in 1997, feeling their way around the shattered hulk in near-zero visibility in the muddy waters. Bound's survey documented a number of holes and missing portions of the ship, which he believes were not caused by battle damage or the scuttling, but from a clandestine British salvage of the wreck that recovered 50 tons of material including rangefinders and the ship's primitive radar on a mission that is still classified.

Hundimiento del Acorazado "Admiral Graf Spee".

■ The German pocket battleship *Graf Spee* burns and settles into the water. (Naval History and Heritage Command)

But the surveys also showed that the scuttling blasts had torn off the ship's stern and destroyed the aft turret, which the crew had packed with shells and other explosives. Bound, working with the Uruguayan Navy, raised one of *Graf Spee*'s 150-mm guns, which has been restored and is now on display along with other artifacts raised from the wreck.

Ongoing salvage of *Graf Spee* has been controversial. In February 2006, when salvagers raised the ship's stern ornament, a large bronze eagle clutching a swastika, the German government expressed concern over the ongoing recovery of pieces of the ship and a proposed auction, and the Uruguayan government stopped the salvage and confiscated the bronze eagle. Late in 2017, the Uruguayan government announced a plan to sell the eagle at auction and share the sale price with the salvagers.

HMAS *SYDNEY* AND KMS *KORMORAN*

The loss of HMAS *Sydney* in November 1941 was a shocking event in Australia's naval history, and a decades-long controversy with many unanswered questions until the 2008 discovery of the wreck, and close by, its opponent, the German raider *Kormoran*. A 2015 expedition provided more definitive answers.

The Australian government purchased the light cruiser HMS *Phaeton* prior to its September 1934 launch and renamed it for the original HMAS *Sydney* of World War I fame. When World War II began, the Royal Australian Navy sent *Sydney* on convoy escort on the Indian Ocean, and then to the Mediterranean. There the cruiser operated in tandem with British and French forces and gained battle honors in engagements with Italian naval forces, sinking the cruiser *Bartolomeo Colleoni*. When *Sydney* returned home to Fremantle in February 1941, the city greeted the ship and crew as heroes, as did the Australian nation.

After a refit, *Sydney* resumed escorting convoys and was returning to Fremantle after a cruise toward Singapore and turning the convoy over to HMS *Durban* on November 17, 1941. *Sydney* never reached home. A search for the ship initially proved unsuccessful but the discovery of boats with

318 German sailors, some landing on the beaches of Western Australia, revealed what had happened.

On November 19, *Sydney* approached the disguised German raider KMS *Kormoran* and drew close to examine the ship, which apparently seemed suspicious. After being challenged, *Kormoran*'s crew attacked, opening fire on *Sydney*. The Germans hit the cruiser with repeated gunfire and torpedoes, badly damaging *Sydney* while taking damage of their own in a brief but intense half-hour fight. *Sydney* drew off and disappeared in the darkness, on fire, until it disappeared before midnight. *Kormoran*, on fire and engines disabled, was unsafe to remain on, and so the Germans abandoned ship and set explosive charges among the hundreds of mines stored on board. These exploded early on the morning of November 20. German casualties numbered 62 men, but all of *Sydney*'s 645 men were lost. Continued searching by the RAN found only a lifebelt and a battered life raft. Eighteen months after the battle, another Carley float drifted ashore, northwest of Australia at Christmas Island in the Indian Ocean, with a badly decomposed body of a sailor.

The Australian government initially kept the loss of all of *Sydney*'s crew a secret, aggravating families who even at war's end were told nothing. The actions of the government and the lack of official news fed conspiracy theories. The fact that the battle-tested crew of *Sydney* had been bested by a single ship was not believed, with some suggesting that another enemy vessel, perhaps a submarine, had teamed up with *Kormoran* and that the German survivors were lying. The controversy over what happened to *Sydney* and its crew continued through the 1990s, despite the declassification of Australia's wartime archives in 1975.

The Western Australian Museum, which had established a national reputation for its landmark work with historic shipwrecks, became the steward for the as-then-undiscovered wrecks of *Sydney* and *Kormoran* in 1976, and over the next decades, conducted research, convened seminars to examine the evidence, and sought partners to survey the seabed to find the wrecks. They, and later, the Finding *Sydney* Foundation (FSF), a private group, identified a likely area to search; it was a large, 400-square-mile box in deep water. The survey that followed came through a partnership with David L. Mearns, who agreed with other researchers that a likely place to start was where the captain of *Kormoran* said the battle took place and where his ship had sunk. Find *Kormoran*, said Mearns, and then use it to find *Sydney*. After factoring in wind and currents and where the German lifeboats had come ashore, a survey box was drawn on the chart, and the drive to raise money for the search began. With government and private funds, the FSF raised A$5.3 million, and Mearns and team went to sea in late February 2008. With side-scan sonar, they found *Kormoran* on March 12, and *Sydney* four days later, just over 12 nautical miles away. The German survivors of the battle had told the truth.

ROV dives on the two wrecks followed in early April. The ROV team's inspection was guided by David Mearns, assisted by the RAN's chief historical officer, Lt. John Perryman. The Western Australian Museum's Dr. Michael "Mack" McCarthy was the observer for the Commonwealth government. A series of invaluable observations were made that led to a separate study and a substantial report combining historical, archaeological, and forensic naval architectural evidence. Many longstanding questions were answered, but a key question, why the captain of HMAS *Sydney* chose to come close enough to *Kormoran* to be in an "almost suicidal position nearly abeam," as McCarthy has noted, remained a mystery.

Both ships lie in just over 2,400 meters of water, *Sydney* upright, its bow blasted off and lying distant and inverted in a 488-meter-long debris field. *Kormoran* is also upright, but half of the ship is gone from the bridge to the stern, with scattered debris including the bridge in the wreckage field. Lying on a hard substrate, both wrecks are not buried deep in sediment, leaving much of their hulls exposed. The images of the two ships as first found offered powerful, compelling physical testimony about the battle and the damage each ship suffered. Both ships as found did not have much corrosion or marine growth and were still painted. Shell holes in the hulls, a torpedo hole in *Sydney*'s port side, guns still in firing position, an exploded turret with its roof and one wall peeled away, and a wooden lifeboat resting upright on the seabed were mute testimony to the events of November 19–20, 1941.

After the 2008 expedition, a second, detailed study of the wrecks, with three-dimensional mapping and an assessment on ongoing corrosion, took place in May 2015 with Curtin University, the Western Australian Museum, the FSF, and government officials. The return expedition not only gathered thousands of images allowing three-dimensional models of each wreck but also additional details not seen in 2008. A key piece of evidence is a single, nearly six-inch shell hole into the bridge of *Sydney*. That shot, which the Germans said came early, demolished the bridge and killed *Sydney's* senior officers. With the command center and key officers gone, others obviously stepped in from auxiliary stations, but from the onset, *Kormoran* dealt *Sydney* a crippling blow by that shot. The peeled-open turret's gun breeches, exposed to the open sea, offer more than mute testimony to the effects of another hit. One of the breeches is open. Was it being loaded when the German shell punched into the turret, leading to a larger explosion?

In the midst of the forensic, scientific analysis, the human story remains paramount. For the *Sydney* families, there is a measure of closure now. No one appears to have survived the end, for the gunfire was so extensive that the life floats and boats were shot through and sank with *Sydney*. A badly ruptured Carley float lying on the seabed photographed and mapped in 2015 is evidence of that. On fire, sinking, *Sydney* either took its crew with it, or left survivors struggling in the open water to then follow their ship down. Scattered boots on the site are one sign of those men, whether the shoes fell on their own or came to rest with the bodies of their owners. Another human side of the story came from the damaged but amazingly intact *Kormoran*. The 2015 expedition team found, on the still-painted hull, a roster of the ships sunk by *Kormoran*—a "kill board" tally kept by a proud crew who also painted the gun shields on *Kormoran's* hidden gun deck with names and skull-and-crossbones motifs.

BISMARCK AND HMS HOOD

The heavy battleship *Bismarck* lies far deeper than the shallow grave of *Admiral Graf Spee*. Laid down in 1936 to counter the threat of France's battleships, *Bismarck* was one of the first post-naval arms treaty battleships to break the 35,000-ton limit for a battleship. When launched in February 1939, the massive *Bismarck* displaced 44,734 tons. Armed with eight 330-mm turret-mounted guns, 12 150-mm guns, and 16 105-mm guns,

Bismarck was a formidable and much-feared foe. Commissioned in August 1940, *Bismarck* finally sortied in May 1941 with its smaller "little brother," the heavy cruiser *Prinz Eugen*, a smaller near-copy of the huge battleship. Sent into the North Sea to attack British convoys, the two ships were spotted "breaking out" of the Baltic and intercepted by a British battle force off Iceland on May 24, 1941.

As the cruisers *Suffolk* and *Norfolk* spotted the German ships, the veteran battle cruiser *Hood* and the newer *Prince of Wales* moved to intercept them. *Prinz Eugen* opened fire, followed by *Bismarck*. Shells from *Prinz Eugen* hit *Hood*, and as it turned to port to bring more of its own guns to bear, a shell from *Bismarck* came in high and plunged through the decks, deep into the British battle cruiser. The shell exploded inside a magazine, and then, in an instant, *Hood* exploded, breaking in two, its bow and stern rising out of the sea before it sank in a fireball and pillar of black smoke. Only three of the 1,418-man crew survived.

■ Sinking of HMS *Hood*, May 24, 1941, painting by J. C. Schmitz-Westerholt (Naval History and Heritage Command)

Prince of Wales, hit several times by the Germans, withdrew with heavy damage. *Bismarck*, also hit and partially flooded, did not pursue. Instead, Admiral Gunther Lutjens and Kapitan Ernst Lindemann decided to run to Nazi-occupied St. Nazaire, France, for repairs and separate from *Prinz Eugen*. The Royal Navy, however, had other plans. The brief 16-minute battle and the loss of *Hood* was a stunning blow to British morale and pride. Prime Minister Winston Churchill, an astute politician, decided that the Royal Navy had to sink *Bismarck* at any cost. The Admiralty dispatched more ships, including the battleship *King George V*, the battle cruiser *Repulse*, and the aircraft carrier *Victorious* to pursue the Germans.

While the heavy gunships stayed clear, shadowing *Bismarck*, *Victorious* launched eight torpedo-carrying Swordfish aircraft in a late-afternoon attack on May 24. A hit from a torpedo jarred open temporarily patched holes, but *Bismarck* shook off its pursuers and continued on. Thirty-two hours later, on May 26, a patrolling seaplane spotted the German battleship and the Royal Navy again raced to the scene to pick up the fight. Another torpedo bomber attack, from the carrier *Ark Royal*, hit *Bismarck's* stern, damaging the steering gear and jamming the rudders. Damaged, not fully maneuverable, and leaking oil, *Bismarck*, crippled but still a deadly foe, continued to race for France.

The Royal Navy caught up with *Bismarck* on the morning of May 27. *King George V*, the battleship *Rodney*, and a force of cruisers and destroyers engaged the German battleship and within an hour had blasted *Bismarck* so heavily that the ship was a blazing shambles. Closing and firing almost point blank into *Bismarck*, the British warships shot off 2,876 rounds. As many as 400 of these shells actually hit *Bismarck*. Then, burning fiercely as the crew abandoned ship, *Bismarck* began to roll over as the cruiser *Dorsetshire* fired a torpedo into it. *Bismarck* slipped beneath the waves at 10:36 A.M. The crew, struggling in the cold, oil-thick water, called for help as the British ships closed in to pull them out of the sea. But a submarine alarm called off the rescue, and with just 110 German sailors on their decks, the British pulled away to leave *Bismarck's* survivors to the Atlantic. Only three of them reached home, plucked off a raft by a passing U-boat after drifting on a now-empty sea.

Doctor Robert D. Ballard and his team of scientists discovered the wreck of *Bismarck* some 648 kilometers off Brest, France, in 4,572 meters of water in June 1989. Using cameras towed over the wreck, Ballard's team extensively photographed and surveyed the battered hulk, which capsized as it sank. The heavy turrets, with the 330-mm guns, tore free of the ship and sank as *Bismarck* righted and then hit the slopes of an undersea mountain. An avalanche of mud carried the sunken battleship and its turrets deeper, where the ship now lies, half-buried, with any battle wounds below the waterline obscured by the mud.

The survey allowed naval architects and battleship historians William H. Garzke Jr. and Robert O. Dulin Jr. to conduct a detailed forensic analysis of *Bismarck's* battle damage. Torpedo holes in the hull did not play a major role in the sinking, despite the fact that the ship took 300 to 400 hits from gunfire. Punched holes and plowed furrows in armored deck steel show where huge shells hit, as does the near complete destruction of the battleship's superstructure. When it sank, *Bismarck* was heavily damaged, sinking, and yet demonstrated to Garzke and Dulin the ship's "damage resistant" construction "absorbed a remarkable amount of punishment before succumbing to overwhelming damage."

The discovery team was surprised, given the accounts of how many shells hit *Bismarck*, to find it relatively intact. The stern is gone, having torn free, probably as it hit the bottom and the torpedo-damaged area gave way. But the evidence also points to the fact that while British shellfire had started *Bismarck* on her way to the bottom, German scuttling charges finished the job. The testimony of *Bismarck* survivors that they had set off the charges is seen in the fact that when the ship went under, it was completely flooded. Otherwise, the pressure of the depths would have crushed a partially flooded hull, and perhaps broken up the ship. Instead, it glided down to rest in eternal darkness, the secondary armament still pointing out and up at long-gone foes, with traces of the painted swastika deck identification marking a symbol of resurgent German militarism as well as the Nazi regime that sent the ship and its crew to sea to die.

The wreck of HMS *Hood* was discovered by David Mearns on July 19, 2001, at a depth of 2,845 meters, 434 kilometers southwest of Reykjavik,

Iceland. Using an ROV, the Mearns team made four dives and found the wreck in three sections with the bow, midships, and stern lying apart with two large debris fields. Lying on its port side, a battered, partly crushed, 31-meter-long section of the bow lies in one debris field 76 meters from the stern. The stern sticks out of the seabed at a 45-degree angle, with the rudder still in place and locked in position for what the survey team believes was a 20-degree turn to port, with the innermost propellers also still in place. Damaged by the explosion that destroyed *Hood*, the wreckage nonetheless retains traces of paint, teak decking, and deck fittings, as well as the base of the ensign staff, where *Hood*'s flag would have fluttered from the stern. In between the bow and stern is a dense field of wreckage and debris, intermixed with the boots of the lost crew, some of them closely spaced to indicate that a body came to rest in the midst of the wreckage at that spot.

The main part of the wreck, the midsection of *Hood*, lies at an angle inside the impact crater some 700 meters from the bow. Battered, it retains the mount for the A and B turret, but no trace of the superstructure was seen. Identifiable sections and areas of the superstructure lie at the site in the debris fields. Analyzing the evidence, Mearns and his forensic team believe that a hit from *Bismarck* set off the after magazines, blowing off the stern, and as *Hood* started to go down, bow in the air, a spreading conflagration of burning cordite set off the forward magazines. The second explosion blew off the bow, with pieces of the ship coming off and out of the ship as the midsection glided at an angle, hitting the seabed some distance from the rest of the ship. Pulled down rapidly, the three pieces of the ship dragged down the crew, with a bubble of released air pushing the three survivors to the surface.

Mearns worked very closely with the families of *Hood*'s lost crew, and Ted Briggs, at that time the only one of the three survivors left alive, participated in the mission. On July 25, as the ROV moved into position off the bow, Mearns turned the controls over to Ted Briggs, and he dropped a cast bronze "roll of honor" memorial plaque on the wreck to remember the sacrifice of his 1,415 shipmates who died with the ship. It was fitting and serves as a reminder that this broken hull is freighted with memory and sadness for the families who otherwise have no grave to visit and lay flowers on.

The HMS *Hood* Association notes, and rightly so, that they now have a proper grave marker.

While no disturbance or recovery is the general rule, the families and the Royal Navy agreed that *Hood*'s bell should be recovered, preserved, and placed in the National Museum of the Royal Navy in Portsmouth. In August 2015, co-founder of Microsoft, philanthropist, and shipwreck explorer Paul Allen raised the bell. The archaeological conservators of Mary Rose Archaeological Services X-rayed, cleaned, and prepared it for display. The bell is a powerful memorial not only to *Hood* but also to Rear Admiral Sir Horace Hood who died on HMS *Inflexible* at Jutland. Admiral Hood's widow presented this bell to the ship when it was launched in 1918. The bell links both wrecks and underscores the irony that while *Hood* is a revered grave site, untrammeled by salvage, Admiral Hood's grave, and that of his crew, HMS *Inflexible*, has been despoiled by salvagers. Salvage, as we will see in the rest of this chapter, is an all-too-common fate for the lost warships of the last century. The difficulty of reaching *Hood*, not propriety, is likely what protects it.

HMS *ARK ROYAL*

The veteran British aircraft carrier, and avenger of HMS *Hood*, the *Ark Royal*, did not last long after the sinking of *Bismarck*. *Ark Royal* sank off Gibraltar on November 13, 1941, after U-81 fired four torpedoes, and one hit amidships, tearing a huge hole in the carrier's bottom on the starboard side. The torpedo's damage also took out half the ship's power, and as *Ark Royal* began to list, the crew fought to stabilize the ship and get power back. As they fought, the Royal Navy dispatched the tug *Thames*. The flooding continued to pull the carrier over, and when the list reached 27 degrees, the captain ordered the crew to abandon ship. Everyone evacuated safely, except one man who had died when the torpedo hit. When *Ark Royal* rolled to 45 degrees, the carrier capsized, broke in two, and sank at 6:19 in the morning of November 14.

The story of *Ark Royal*, which had fought in many of the early naval battles of the war, including the sinking of *Bismarck*, inspired documentary filmmaker Mike Rossiter, who felt that to find, film, and share the story offered "not only…the chance to see again this imposing ship, but … the opportunity it would present to tell a different story about the Royal Navy and the early years of the Second World War." The wreck lay deep, and Rossiter not only had to convince the BBC to hire him to do a film but he also had to find enough money and the right people to do the survey. Working with Louisiana-based survey company C&C Technologies, he and C&C's Rick Davey pulled together a survey team, hired a vessel that was available, R/V *Odin Finder*, and discovered the probable wreck of *Ark Royal* after surveying 289 square nautical miles of seabed.

To better understand the target, Rossiter and Davey took a second ship, R/V *Big Supporter*, back to the site in 2002, this time with a C&C–supplied autonomous underwater vehicle (AUV). My colleagues Dan Warren and Robert Church were the archaeologists on the mission. With the AUV flying close to the seabed, its sonar provided higher-resolution images, and with that, the wreck emerged, albeit as a reflection of sound that on a screen looks like a shadow. One of the shadow images was particularly exciting for the team, for it was the outline of an aircraft. What the C&C survey dramatically showed was the vast area of the wreck, beginning with the bow, which broke off as the carrier capsized. As that massive piece plummeted to the seabed, the rest of *Ark Royal* began a long, spiraling dive to the bottom, leaving a trail of debris before it plowed into the mud, burying part of the ship.

There was no money available to dive the wreck, but Paul Allen and the E/V *Octopus* came to the rescue in October 2004. After an ROV dive that confirmed that the wreck was *Ark Royal, Octopus* returned to Gibraltar and embarked four *Ark Royal* veterans—John Moffat, Ron Skinner, Bill Morrison, and John Richardson. On station again, the ROV descended nearly 1,524 meters, and those four men, all in their eighties, had the rare privilege of seeing their old ship again as the lights of the ROV illuminated the decks, guns, and even a Swordfish aircraft—the one seen on the sonar earlier, and the type of plane that John Moffat had flown off that same deck to attack the mighty *Bismarck*. They shared their stories, as they shared their ship, which lies upright, its bow broken off and laying at a distance, with a field of debris that includes the island, aircraft, and machinery, all evidence of the final moments when the carrier rolled over, broke open, and spilled its contents into the sea.

USS *ARIZONA* AND USS *UTAH*

World War II witnessed the death of more than individual battleships. It was the last war fought by battleships. The war was a triumph for both the submarine and the aircraft carrier. There were plenty of hints from before the war, like Billy Mitchell's aerial bombing demonstrations. Early in the war, on the evening of November 11–12, 1940, Swordfish torpedo bombers from HMS *Illustrious* swept in from the Mediterranean to attack the Italian fleet at Taranto, sinking the battleships *Littorio, Conte de Cavour*, and *Caio Duilio*, as well as two fleet auxiliaries. The lesson of Taranto was not lost on some officers in the Imperial Japanese Navy, particularly Isoroku Yamamoto, newly appointed commander-in-chief of the Combined Fleet. Yamamoto and his staff officers, particularly a talented young commander named Minoru Genda, began to plan for a surprise attack on the United States Pacific Fleet at its base at Pearl Harbor, Hawai'i.

Tensions between the United States and Japan had grown in the 1930s, particularly following Japan's invasion of China in 1937 and the bloody war it waged there. When, in December 1937, Japanese aircraft "accidentally" sank the gunboat USS *Panay*, part of the international patrol on the Yalu River, both sides avoided war. But the United States's outrage grew as the Japanese occupied Hainan Island in the Gulf of Tonkin, and signed a pact with Nazi Germany and fascist Italy to form the Axis Powers. President Franklin D. Roosevelt relocated the United States Pacific Fleet from its base at San Diego to Pearl Harbor to counter Japanese plans. The Japanese felt the implicit threat and accelerated their war plans. In the summer of 1941, they seized French Indochina. When Roosevelt halted oil sales to Japan in response to this, Japan's war cabinet decided to strike throughout Southeast Asia. The army and navy made preparations to seize the Dutch East Indies, British Malaya, and the American Philippines after neutralizing the US Pacific Fleet.

To sink the American fleet's battleships and carriers, Yamamoto and Genda planned to send in waves of carrier-launched torpedo, dive, and high-altitude bombers. Even as negotiations with the US government continued, the Japanese task force of 33 ships sailed from northern Japan in late November. The carriers *Akagi, Hiryu, Sōryū, Kaga, Zuikaku*, and *Shōkaku* reached their launch position, 321 kilometers north of Oahu, early in the morning on December 7, 1941. Two waves of fighters, high-altitude and dive-bombers, took off just before dawn. At 7:55 A.M., Hawai'i Time, the first wave, under the command of Cmdr. Mitsuo Fuchida, hit Pearl Harbor and surrounding US Army, Navy, and Marine Corps bases, destroying aircraft on the ground and attacking Battleship Row. A second wave, under the command of Lt. Cmdr. Shigekazu Shimazaki, struck again an hour later. Japanese torpedoes, bombs, and projectiles slammed into ships, aircraft, and men, wreaking a terrible toll. When the attack ended, eight battleships, three light cruisers, three destroyers, and four auxiliary craft had either sunk or capsized, or were damaged; 188 aircraft were lost and 159 were damaged; and 2,403 were killed or missing and 1,178 sailors, marines, and soldiers were wounded.

In a morning filled with explosions, fire, and death, the most traumatic event was the destruction of the battleship *Arizona*. By 8:10, the ship was on fire from several hits as the crew fought both the flames and incoming aircraft. Then the ship exploded. The blast from *Arizona* blew men off the decks of surrounding ships and threw tons of debris, including parts of bodies, all over the harbor. The fury of the attack continued unabated, with *Arizona* reportedly receiving eight bomb hits as it sank. Abandoned at 10:32 A.M., *Arizona*'s burning superstructure and canted masts loomed through the smoke that blanketed the harbor. Of the approximately 1,177 men aboard, less than 200 of *Arizona*'s crew survived.

The battle-scarred and submerged remains of *Arizona* are the focal point of a shrine erected by the people of the United States to honor and commemorate all American servicemen killed on December 7, 1941, particularly *Arizona*'s crew. *Arizona*'s burning bridge and listing masts and superstructure, photographed in the aftermath of the attack with the image of the sinking vessel emblazoned on the front pages of newspapers across the land, epitomized to the nation the words "Pearl Harbor" and form one of the best-known images of World War II in the Pacific. *Arizona* and the *Arizona* Memorial have become the major shrine and point of remembrance for both Americans and foreign visitors, including large numbers of Japanese.

The burned out, sunken wreck of USS *Arizona*, in the days following the Pearl Harbor attack. (Naval History and Heritage Command)

The USS *Arizona* Memorial. (National Park Service)

National Park Service archaeologists from the Submerged Cultural Resources Unit began to survey and study the wreck of *Arizona* in 1983. More or less continual work since then has examined both the exterior of the sunken battleship and most recently the interior compartments in the aft sections. Slightly listed to port, *Arizona*'s decks lie just beneath the surface, with portions of the ship rising above the water. The hull just aft of the bow is distorted and cracked from gunwale to keel on the port side and nearly so on the starboard side, indicating the bow was either nearly blown off or has since settled and cracked. The armored deck forward was blown both upward and forward by the force of tons of powder blasting from deep within the battleship's twisted portions of the deck, folding it together near the bow. But the wooden decks in this area are intact, with snaking lines of fire hoses still in place. They lie exactly where they were dropped when the final, fatal blast swept the decks and killed the ship's crew.

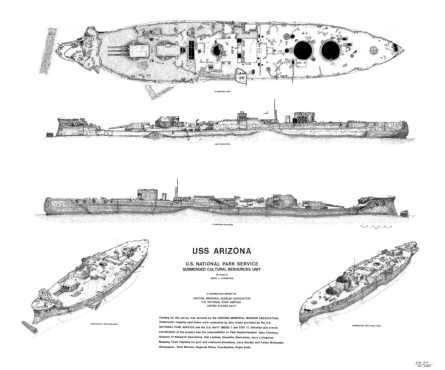

■ The wreck of USS *Arizona* as mapped by the National Park Service and the US Navy. (Submerged Resources Center, National Park Service)

■ The guns in the No. 1 turret of USS *Arizona*. (National Park Service Photograph by Brett Seymour)

Near there, the ship's No. 1 turret, with its gun barrels pointed down, rests inside a collapsed crater formed by the explosion. Archaeologists were surprised to find it when they made the first dives in 1983, since historical accounts suggested that every bit of *Arizona*'s armament was salvaged in 1942. Popular belief, beginning during the war, also suggested that a bomb going down the stack and into the boilers sank *Arizona*. But the stack gratings are intact. The fatal shell hit, like *Bismarck*'s hit on *Hood*, went through the deck. Based on the archaeological analysis and historical research in Japan, it became clear that a huge aerial bomb, modified from a Japanese 16-inch shell, hit the deck near the No. 2 turret and plunged down to erupt in the forward magazine.

Recent dives inside the wreck, using a small remotely operated vehicle developed by Marine Imaging Technologies and the Advanced Imaging and Visualization Laboratory at Woods Hole Oceanographic Institution, have moved through silt-clogged corridors and into compartments and cabins and discovered furniture lying on decks, uniforms on hangars, a telephone still cradled and on a desk, and unbroken light bulbs. That work is part of the ongoing documentation of *Arizona* by the National Park

Service's Submerged Resources Center (SRC), which has included scientific studies of the corrosion of the battleship and the possibilities for the release of the fuel oil trapped inside *Arizona*'s bunkers.

Thanks to the robotic penetration deep inside the ship, where human divers would face too much risk, we now know from measuring low levels of dissolved oxygen in the water that the conditions inside the wreck have led to exceptional preservation of artifacts inside the hull. Brett Seymour, the current deputy chief of the SRC, told *National Geographic* reporter Jeremy Berlin in December 2016 that for all the science, "this ship has a soul. It's the only shipwreck I've been on in 20-plus years and 400 dives where you feel a personal, emotional connection. You get engaged in the science you're doing, but then you find a jacket hanging in a locker. Or a shoe sole. Or a shaving kit."

A key part of the National Park Service mission has been to share *Arizona*'s story, especially that of the crew and of that day. An early effort was drawing the wreck to give the public a view of what the waters of Pearl Harbor hide from view, followed by an impressive large-scale model of *Arizona*, and a painting of the wreck by artist Tom Freeman. An active oral history program captured the stories of survivors, not just from *Arizona*, but from other ships and bases, and the island community. I participated in several of those interviews in 1991, during the 50th anniversary commemoration, and was again powerfully and emotionally reminded that when I work as an archaeologist or historian, it is not the wreck, but the story of the people associated with it that I am drawn to and work to share.

Modern science is also providing closure for some of the families. Bodies recovered from the sunken USS *Oklahoma* after the attack, unidentifiable with the technology of 1941 and buried anonymously, are now regaining their names. The Defense POW/MIA Accounting Agency (DPAA) of the Department of Defense is tasked with finding and repatriating more than 80,000 missing service members from World War II, Korea, and Vietnam. In answer to the petitions of USS *Oklahoma* families, in 2015 the Department of Defense authorized exhuming the graves of the "*Oklahoma* unknowns" for modern forensic analysis, including DNA matches. It is slow, careful work, but by December 2017, DPAA had identified 100 men, some of whom were returned to their hometowns for burials, while others, like 27-year-old USS *Oklahoma* radioman 3rd class Howard W. Bean, have been interred at Arlington.

The National Park Service archaeological effort, initially co-directed by Daniel Lenihan and Larry Murphy, and later by David Conlin, Matthew Russell, and Brett Seymour, has also examined and documented the wreck of the battleship USS *Utah*. Like *Arizona*, *Utah* was a World War I battleship that remained in service for 25 years. But unlike *Arizona*, which was modernized to remain a potent, fighting capital ship, *Utah* was stripped of its big guns and turned into a floating platform to test antiaircraft weapons. Unfortunately for *Utah*, those guns, including experimental types just being adopted by the US Navy, were unmanned on December 7 when Japanese torpedoes bored into the hull and sank it along with more than 50 of the crew. Though not as visible, and less visited, *Utah* has not been forgotten. The same level of documentation now helps share *Utah* with a larger audience.

Ultimately, the archaeology of USS *Arizona* and USS *Utah* is part of a larger story, and one that the National Park Service also assessed through a larger survey of the battlefield of December 7, 1941. That battlefield, as NOAA archaeologist Hans Van Tilburg notes, encompassed all of Oahu, on land, in the air, and on and under the sea. We surveyed for Japanese aircraft shot down on December 7, for evidence of ships sunk and later salvaged on Battleship Row, and out to sea, for a Japanese midget submarine sunk an hour before the aerial assault as it tried to penetrate Pearl Harbor's defenses. That work continues, both by the NPS and by NOAA, with ongoing deep-sea dives on not one but two of the midget submarines, and with work by Van Tilburg and colleagues at the University of Hawai'i on a navy PBY Catalina aircraft strafed and sunk at Kaneohe Bay along with others during the first wave of the Japanese attack.

JAPAN'S MIDGET SUBMARINES

Prior to World War II, Japan developed a class of small, two-man "midget" submarines for use on the high seas. Battery-powered, and armed with two torpedoes, they were designed in 1939–1940 as top-secret weapons. Seaplane tenders converted into mother ships were to carry 36 of the *ko-hyoteki*, as they were known. In the middle of an all-out sea battle, the mother ships would launch swarms of the midget subs, which would dart in, fire their torpedoes at enemy ships, and then retreat. As the Imperial Japanese Navy completed the first *ko-hyoteki* and trained a class of young officers and enlisted men to crew them, plans for Pearl Harbor changed the fate of both the subs and their crews. At the insistence of some of the more diehard midget submariners, the navy agreed to modify them to be used as stealth weapons launched from the back deck of a larger submarine.

The first target was Pearl Harbor, where five *ko-hyoteki* were to enter the inner harbor, wait for the aerial assault to begin, and then surface and fire their torpedoes into the sides of American battleships. The plan did not succeed. Only one of the submarines, commanded by the leader of the initial class of midget submariners, made it inside Pearl Harbor, and when it surfaced, was quickly sunk. Four other submarines never made it inside. One, caught at sea off the entrance, sank after being hit by gunfire from the destroyer USS *Ward* an hour before the main attack began. Two others were also caught but avoided sinking by hugging the bottom close to the entrance and were later scuttled by their crews. The fifth drifted ashore, and its commander, captured, became America's first POW. His sub, dismantled and studied by the US Navy, then toured the United States in order to promote the sales of war bonds.

Despite the failure of the *ko-hyoteki* at Pearl Harbor, the Imperial Japanese Navy allowed continued use of the midget submarines crewed by eager young men. The navy sent *ko-hyoteki* into battle at Guadalcanal, the Aleutians, Rabaul, the Philippines, Madagascar, and a daring raid into Sydney, Australia's harbor. While ships were damaged by *ko-hyoteki* torpedoes at Guadalcanal, Sydney, and Madagascar, the results were minimal and came at high cost. Ultimately, the frustrated young men of the *ko-hyoteki* corps demanded a change and were granted their wish to pilot one-man suicide weapons known as *kaiten*. *Kaiten* sorties also met with minimal success, sinking only the fleet oiler USS *Mississinewa* and the destroyer USS *Underhill*. Hundreds of *ko-hyoteki* and *kaiten* crew members lost their lives, many in training accidents.

Only a handful of these craft survive, some taken for study or as trophies at war's end, others as archaeological sites. Archaeologists have studied the wrecks of *ko-hyoteki* at Guadalcanal and in the Aleutians, where a midget submarine base survives on the island of Kiska. They have studied them in Australia, where the remains of two of the three *ko-hyoteki* involved in the May 31, 1942, Sydney attack, raised and studied during the war, are on display, and the third, missing after the attack, was discovered by Australian divers in 2006. The Australian government, in cooperation with Japan, has studied the site and manages it as a war grave.

I was involved in the initial 1990 survey for the midget submarine sunk by USS *Ward*. It remained lost until the team at the University of Hawai'i discovered it in August 2002. Terry Kerby, Steve Price, Max Cremer, and the rest of the team discovered and documented three separate sections of another *ko-hyoteki*, also off Pearl Harbor, and over time proved it was also from the December 7 attack. It had been scuttled, rediscovered after the war, cut into its three component sections, and dumped in deeper water. Working with the Hawai'i Undersea Research Laboratory (HURL) team and fellow NOAA archaeologist Van Tilburg, and with naval historian Russ

▪ The conning tower of the Japanese midget submarine sunk by USS *Ward* on December 7, 1941, off Pearl Harbor. The hole in the conning tower resulted from the first shot fired by US forces in the Pacific war. (NOAA/Office of Ocean Exploration and Research)

Matthews, I was part of a team that continued to document the two *ko-hyoteki*, building on an archaeological project I'd started to study as many of these craft as we could find after we did not find the *Ward*-sunk midget. Another key part was using archaeology to virtually reassemble and operate these craft based on preserved examples and wrecks.

In doing so, I was reminded again, as an archaeologist, that what you really study is people through the things they build and what they do. The *ko-hyoteki*, despite post-war US propaganda, were not failed weapons. They were highly sophisticated, designed and built for one use, and then employed in a role they were not suited for. The leaders of the Imperial Japanese Navy exploited the patriotism and zeal of the midget submarine corps, who, inspired by the lies spread after the Pearl Harbor mission, went where they should not have. The minimal successes they achieved came only through exceptional actions in the face of death.

There was also another human factor that wartime propaganda on both sides masked. The *ko-hyoteki* and *kaiten* corps were not all fanatics, nor were they crazy. Before his death, I became friends with then-81-year-old *kaiten* pilot Toshiharu Konada. A submarine officer early in the war, he found himself toward the end at a naval base where he stood at attention with others as a senior officer harangued them and asked them all to step forward to use the *kaiten* in a last-ditch effort not just to win the war, but to save their families, and their country, from a war they knew was coming to their own shores soon. "Have you ever been caught up in something bigger than yourself?" he asked me when we talked about that experience. He was willing to die to save his parents and siblings, as well as his shipmates, and so he volunteered.

In my work on these wrecks of the Pacific war, I often think of Konada-san, who became a dear friend, and I think of my friend Mike Mair's dad, John A. "Jack" Mair Jr., who was a sailor aboard USS *Mississinewa*. Mike's dad lived through the *kaiten* attack that sank his ship on November 20, 1944. Sixty-four men died that morning. The *kaiten* pilot was a friend of Toshiharu Konada's, and in time, with the passions of that war faded, when he met Mike and me, he became our friend as well. I saw the same process at Pearl Harbor as I worked on its wrecks; while some still bore both the scars and the anger, others, even the scarred, no longer felt anger. I watched old men who had decades earlier fought a brutal, fierce war, embrace as friends, share experiences, and, together on that day, remember their friends and comrades who now sleep forever in steel tombs beneath the sea.

MIDWAY: USS *YORKTOWN* AND HIJMS *KAGA*

Following the Battle of the Coral Sea, in which the US and Australian naval forces took a pounding, and lost the carrier USS *Lexington* in May 1942, while diverting a Japanese assault on Australian-held Port Morseby, in Papua New Guinea, US naval intelligence learned of a planned Japanese naval attack on Midway. Midway, a small atoll in the northwestern Hawaiian archipelago, was a vital base. The Japanese attack was a ruse to lure the surviving American aircraft carriers into an all-out naval battle, destroy them, and leave the US vulnerable.

Learning the Japanese plan, Admiral Chester Nimitz sent three carriers, including the battle-damaged, hastily (and partially) repaired USS *Yorktown* to intercept the Japanese fleet of four carriers, both fleets accompanied by escort ships, and the Japanese also sailing with ships to bombard and take Midway. In all, three American carriers—*Enterprise, Hornet*, and *Yorktown*—escorted by seven heavy cruisers, one light cruiser, 15 destroyers, and 16 submarines, steamed for Midway. They would contend against a force of four Japanese carriers, two battleships, two heavy and one light cruiser, and 12 destroyers, but the confrontation came in waves of aerial attacks as 460 American planes and 248 Japanese aircraft went into battle.

As ships and Midway itself came under attack, losses were heavy, among them the famous sortie of *Hornet*'s Torpedo Squadron 8, led by Commander John C. Waldron, all shot down by Japanese fire without making a hit, and leaving but one survivor, Ensign George Gay, floating in the water. Torpedo Squadron 6 from *Enterprise* lost 10 of 14 planes, and Torpedo Squadron 3 from *Yorktown* lost 10 of 12 despite the incredible bravery of their pilots. They did distract the Japanese, and that opened the door for a group of dive bombers from the three US carriers to attack as the Japanese were refueling their planes on their carrier flight decks. In quick progression, they hit the carrier *Kaga* and left it a burning wreck, then the carrier *Akagi*, and then the carrier *Sōryū*. The Japanese carrier *Hiryu*, undamaged, launched a counter-attack that badly damaged USS *Yorktown*. The next US attack took out *Hiryu*, effectively ending the battle. After a tremendous effort to save *Yorktown*, the carrier was lost when a Japanese submarine, I-168, torpedoed it and its escorting destroyer USS *Hammann*. Despite the loss of 307 men, the ships, and some 150 aircraft, the United States had won a tremendous victory. The Japanese lost four carriers, a heavy cruiser, 248 aircraft, and 3,057 men, among them irreplaceable veteran naval aviators, senior naval officers, and seamen. The ultimate price for Japan was the loss of forward momentum in the war. Midway was the crucial turning point, and while the war continued for three more years, Japan was increasingly on the defensive.

As the pivotal battle of the Pacific, Midway was a priority target for Robert Ballard as he sought to locate the iconic wrecks of the war. Surveying in waters more than 16,000 feet deep, Ballard sought the carriers *Yorktown*, *Kaga*, *Akagi*, *Hiryu*, and *Sōryū* and the destroyer *Hammann*. The scale of Midway was vast in terms of hundreds of square kilometers. Undersea technology was not sufficiently advanced in 1998 to systematically survey that much seabed to find every ship, as well as every aircraft where they had fallen. That is a goal I'd like to see achieved now, in the second decade of the 21st century, now that we have deep-diving autonomous underwater vehicles and high-resolution sonar that can do the job. The level of detail from such a survey would reveal the intricacies of the action as ships dodged, aircraft dived and flew low to launch bombs or torpedoes, and, in the follow-up, likely indicate the position of each warrior who fell from the sky and into the sea in this decisive carrier battle. The 26-day survey of 1998 focused on finding larger targets in the form of the sunken aircraft carriers, which while large would still be very small sonar signatures at depths three miles down. Ultimately, the wreck that Bob Ballard's team found was the intact USS *Yorktown*.

Damaged at the Battle of the Coral Sea, *Yorktown* had been hastily returned to combat for Midway after a 48-hour turnaround in the shipyard at

Pearl Harbor. The air group took casualties, but sank the Japanese carrier *Sōryū* before a counterattack in which *Yorktown* took a pounding from Japanese aircraft with three bomb and two torpedo hits. Dead in the water and listing, *Yorktown* was unable to recover or launch planes. The captain ordered the crew to abandon ship. The following day, with the carrier still afloat, the captain and small salvage party returned to Yorktown and worked to save the ship only to lose *Yorktown* and the screening destroyer USS *Hammann* to torpedoes launched from I-168. On the morning of June 7, 1942, *Yorktown* capsized to port and sank by the stern, carrying with it the bodies of 141 crew.

The robotic exploration of *Yorktown* in May 1998 revealed it lying intact, upright, and listing to starboard. Antiaircraft guns still pointed skyward, and torpedo blast holes, probably from aerial torpedoes, sent into the hull and bomb holes in the flight deck remained visible as the scars of Midway. Amazingly well preserved, the lost carrier's wooden decks were intact, and the paint on the hull, except where it was scarred by fire, looked fresh. The letters spelling YORKTOWN remained visible at the ship's stern. Examining images of *Yorktown*, it was easy to imagine that the carrier had sunk recently. The return to *Yorktown* was particularly emotional for William F. Surgi Jr., a former aviation machinist's mate who survived the sinking, and who joined Bob's team. He told *Washington Post* reporter Mike Ruane that "it was home. I was coming home, in a way," when they found *Yorktown*.

While there is an intense American interest to find the lost ships of World War II, there has been until very recently little interest in Japan. There are a variety of reasons, stemming from a post-war rejection of Japan's pre-war and wartime militarism, and a sense, as I have been told, that the ships and the men on them were buried at sea, and best left alone. Hence, while Americans sought the lost ships from the Battle of Midway, Japanese did not. The quest to find the Japanese carriers, initially part of Robert Ballard's plan, was carried forward by David Jourdan, retired US Navy submarine officer, deep-sea explorer, historian, and CEO of the Nauticos Corporation. Dave and his team made significant deep-sea discoveries of the Japanese submarine I-52 in 1995, the Israeli submarine *Dakar* in 1999, and immediately following that, went to Midway in May of the same year.

The Nauticos team partnered with the US Navy for the search, working with coordinates from the log of the submarine USS *Nautilus*, which had observed the burning, sinking Japanese carrier. They "re-navigated" *Nautilus*'s course, plotted a search area, which a navy ship then surveyed with a new acoustic mapping system, SEAMAP. The Nauticos team, analyzing the sonar, found promising targets that looked to be ship debris. That led to a second trip in September on the USNS *Sumner* to lower cameras to photograph what lay in the darkness. The cameras revealed twisted steel and identifiable artifacts like a sailor's boot, and wreckage that they turned to naval historians Tony Tully, Jon Parshall, and David Dickson to analyze.

They identified one more substantial piece of wreckage as two 25mm antiaircraft gun tubs, with a landing light from the side of the carrier *Kaga*. Another piece of wreckage was the ship's bell. There is a trail of debris 17,500 feet long that will in time lead to the main body of the wreck, but there was not enough time to do so in 1999. A planned return in 2016 was thwarted by bad weather, but the time will come, and I am confident that not only *Kaga* but the entire battlefield, scattered over hundreds of kilometers, will be mapped, documented, and studied.

THE LOST SHIPS OF GUADALCANAL

The end of the battleship was again underscored when Japanese aircraft sank the British battle cruisers *Repulse* and *Prince of Wales* off Malaya on December 10, 1941. Japan's early victories in the Pacific War, including Pearl Harbor, the fall of the Philippines, and the fall of Hong Kong and Singapore expanded the Japanese Empire to what proved to be untenable limits. The high-water mark was reached by mid-1942. In June of that year, Japanese troops began construction of an airfield on Guadalcanal, in the recently occupied British Solomon Islands Protectorate in what would be Japan's farthest south-eastward expansion in the Pacific. The Japanese thrust was met by the United States, Australia, and New Zealand in a bloody six-month campaign on the island, in the skies, and on the sea.

The campaign was critical. Up until then, the Allies had fought a losing, defensive war in the Pacific. When the Japanese took the Solomons, leaving Australia vulnerable, the time had come for more than a stand. The battles in the Solomons, especially at Guadalcanal, marked the beginning of the Allied offensive against the Japanese. The result was a brutal campaign, fought in the air, in the jungle, and at sea. I will never forget Ed Bearss, my former boss and a Marine Raider veteran of that campaign, telling me how the clashes in the jungle that he participated in were rifle to rifle, knife to knife, and then fist to fist. Nearly 20,000 men died, and several thousand more were wounded, some of them, like Ed, grievously. Ed took several bullets, ending his war. Other losses included more than 1,000 aircraft, many with their crews, and a large number of ships of various types and sizes, some with most or all of their crews. When the battles ended after six months of combat, Japan's forces in the islands had been defeated at Guadalcanal, and Allied troops, planes, and ships began the long push toward Tokyo, starting in the other islands of the Solomons and then heading north, bypassing some heavily fortified bases, taking others in keeping with General Douglas MacArthur's "island-hopping" strategy.

A number of naval engagements, skirmishes, and battles sank nearly 50 ships off Guadalcanal and nearby islands. The two most famous engagements took place on August 8–9, 1942 (the Battle of Savo Island) and November 12–16, 1942 (the Battle of Guadalcanal). The waters surrounding the islands were named "Iron Bottom Sound" because of the many ships sent to the bottom during these battles.

The naval battle on the evening of November 13, 1942, was one of the most ferocious. American cruisers and Japanese battleships, joined by destroyers, pounded each other, with tremendous cost in lives. In all, over 2,100 sailors and marines were killed, and nearly 4,500 tons of steel went to the bottom of the ocean. The fighting was wild, and in some ways, according to historian James Grace, reminiscent of an earlier age as technological advantages, such as radar, were abandoned. A planned American ambush of the Japanese force went awry as both fleets stumbled into each other in the dark. The battle that followed, argues Grace, exemplified Nelson's adage that "no captain can do very wrong if he places his ship alongside that of an enemy." Facing battleships that outgunned them, and at considerable cost, the captains of the US cruisers and destroyers forced the Japanese to withdraw by engaging the enemy at point-blank range. In this way, says Grace "the Americans won a fight that, by all odds, they should have lost."

In the fall of 1991, Dr. Robert D. Ballard led a team of scientists; US Navy technicians and specialists; and American, Japanese, and Australian veterans of the battles to survey the waters of Iron Bottom Sound. They found 10 wrecks and returned in the summer of 1992 to look for more and photographically document them with robotic cameras and the submersible Sea Cliff. Warship specialist Charles Haberlein of the Naval History and Heritage Command in Washington, DC, made the identifications of the sunken ships.

In all, 13 wrecks were studied. They included the Australian heavy cruiser HMAS *Canberra*, and the US cruiser *Quincy*—both sunk in the Battle of Savo Island—and the Japanese battleship *Kirishima*, the US cruiser *Atlanta*, the Japanese destroyers *Ayanami* and *Yudachi*, and the US destroyers *Laffey*, *Cushing*, *Barton*, *Monssen*, and a wreck that was either the destroyer *Little* or *Gregory*, but unidentified—all sunk during the Battle of Guadalcanal. Ballard also rediscovered the wreck of the US cruiser *Northampton*, sunk during the Battle of Tassafaronga on November 30, 1942, and the US destroyer *DeHaven*, sunk by Japanese bombers with 167 of the crew lost on February 1, 1943, another blow just as the campaign for Guadalcanal ended.

The survey pinpointed where the lost warships had sunk, oftentimes at great distances from where naval records had placed the ships, as would be expected when ships sink in fierce battle, at times in the dark, and with great confusion. Like the work on *Bismarck* and *Arizona*, the Guadalcanal surveys also gained a more detailed understanding of battle damage, including shell hits, torpedo damage, and evidence of magazine explosions that tore some huge ships apart. USS *Quincy* had its bow blown off, and its stern area has partially collapsed. USS *Monssen*, hit by at least 33 shells, lost its superstructure, and USS *Barton* was blown in half by a torpedo hit. The survey only discovered the destroyer's bow. The Japanese *Kirishima* lies in pieces and upside down, the bow torn apart by a catastrophic magazine explosion.

The majority of the wrecks lay in waters ranging from 300 to 1,109 meters deep. Other wrecks lie in shallower waters, like the cruiser *Atlanta* in 129 meters of water. A joint US and Australian technical dive team led by Terrence Tysall and Kevin Denlay photographed several wrecks in November 1995, focusing on *Atlanta*, and the US destroyer *Aaron Ward*, sunk on April 7, 1943, in 74 meters of water and rediscovered by divers Brian Bailey and Ewan Stevenson in September 1994. They also visited the US oiler *Kanawa*; the bow of the US battleship *Minneapolis*, blown off by a torpedo (the battleship survived); the US attack transports *Calhoun* and *John Penn*; the Japanese transports *Asumassan Maru*, *Sasako Maru*, and *Ruaniu*; the Japanese submarine I-123; the New Zealand corvette *Moa*; the US tug *Seminole*; landing barges; submerged aircraft, including a B-17 "Flying Fortress"; and Japanese and American fighters and Kawanishi flying boats.

The dedication of wreck divers and naval historians to find the wrecks and study the physical evidence of the Solomons campaign also includes the decades-long work of Ewan Stevenson and his Archaehistoria Expeditions, whose work in shallow and deep water, as well as wrecks in the intertidal zone, has discovered and documented submarines, including Japanese two-man "midget" craft, airplane wrecks, and landing craft based on historical research and analysis of ongoing sonar surveys. In this work, a more comprehensive understanding of the physical evidence of the battlefield that encompasses the various islands and the waters surrounding them is emerging.

Utilizing the latest technology, Paul Allen financed a detailed, AUV survey of Iron Bottom Sound in January 2015. Under the direction of Robert Kraft, veteran sonar expert and wreck hunter Garry Kozak conducted the survey from Mr. Allen's yacht and research vessel *Octopus*. The comprehensive, detailed map of 725 square kilometers of seabed, mapped by the underwater drone and processed by Kozak revealed 29 wreck locations, including reacquiring some of the wrecks discovered in 1992 during the Ballard expedition. One of those was the destroyer *Little*, which had not been definitively identified in 1992.

Among the new discoveries in 2015 were the heavy cruiser USS *Astoria*, sunk with the loss of 219 crew in the battle of Savo Island after taking more than 65 hits on August 9, 1942; the destroyer USS *Preston*, sunk in a naval engagement with a Japanese force on the night of November 14, 1942, with a loss of 116 men; and the destroyer USS *Walke*, lost in the Battle of Guadalcanal on November 15. In addition, the 2015 survey discovered the Japanese destroyer HIJMS *Fubuki*, sunk in the Battle of Cape Esperance on October 11, 1942, with only 109 survivors. Twelve wrecks could not be identified without further work, and seven debris fields were indistinct and also required dives. Not all of the sites were dived, but *Octopus's* ROV provided much new footage and information about those which were explored, adding to the record from 1992.

Paul Allen's team returned to the Solomons in 2018, where they discovered, dived on, and confirmed the identity of two famous ships lost in the battles off Guadalcanal. The light cruiser USS *Juneau*, one of the more tragic losses in the battle, had long been sought. Allen's team found the wreck lying in water 4,206 meters deep. Badly mangled, it is a garden of twisted steel that speaks to its violent end. The ship's name is visible on the stern, partly covered by crumpled hull plating. *Juneau* was lost in a nighttime fight with a superior Japanese force during the evening of November 12–13, 1942. The US fleet turned back the Japanese with heavy losses both on ships left afloat as well as those sunk. The heavy cruiser *San Francisco*, caught in a deadly crossfire, remained afloat despite taking 45 hits and losing 77 men, among them the senior commanders of the task force and the ship's captain.

The losses from *Juneau* totaled 687 men, among them five brothers serving together on the ship: George, Francis, Joseph, Madison, and Albert Sullivan. Only 10 of *Juneau's* crew survived after more than 100 survivors of the sinking drifted for several days before the navy, thinking all had died when the ship exploded, finally launched a belated rescue mission in a response to a misfiled report from a B-17 bomber that had spotted the men in the water. The "Fighting Sullivan" brothers' loss became a rallying cry in the United States and spurred enlistments, with their parents touring the country selling war bonds, stating they did so so that their sons would not have died in vain. A 1944 Hollywood film and the destroyer USS *The Sullivans*, launched and christened by their mother on April 4, 1943, kept the memory of the Sullivans alive. Finding the shattered hulk of USS *Juneau* led to numerous stories that once again told the story of the men of the ship and the five Sullivan brothers. The massive damage documented by Paul Allen's team offered mute testimony to why the cruiser sank in less than a minute.

The Allen team also discovered and documented the broken remains of the light cruiser USS *Helena*, which lies in 859 meters of water. Not much footage was released, but the stern of *Helena*, with propellers attached, was filmed lying upright with a 20mm antiaircraft gun in place in its gun tub. The cruiser's number, "50," is still painted on the stern. The team also found and filmed the intact forward turret. A survivor of the Pearl Harbor attack, where it took a single torpedo hit, *Helena* returned to sea after repairs and joined Task Forces heading to Guadalcanal. A participant in the night battle that claimed Juneau, *Helena* survived the battle with minor damage. After providing shore bombardment, the cruiser was part of a battle group that once again intercepted a Japanese naval force on the night of July 5–6, 1943. Illuminated by the flash of its own guns, *Helena* took one and then two more torpedo hits in rapid succession. In an epic rescue operation, as the crew took to the water, a number of them also found shelter when the bow tore free of the ship and bobbed on the surface. Nearby destroyers saved some men, while the cruiser's crew took their own small boats and ferried men ashore to a nearby island. The men on the bow were saved when a navy plane dropped lifejackets and four rubber rafts. Of the 900 men on *Helena*, only 168 were lost. The discovery of the wreck provided, yet again, a sense of immediacy and connected generations not born when the ship was lost.

The discoveries from the Allen team, along with those of Ballard's team, show that Iron Bottom Sound is an untouched underwater battlefield where the lost warriors lie exactly where they fell. For Ballard, it was "the literal evidence of war—shell holes in blasted metal, guns and torpedo tubes still trained as if to fire or pointing crazily askew, the wrecked bridge where a captain or an admiral breathed his last" that makes these lost warships special. The emerging map of the undersea terrain and every fallen warrior, be it a ship or an aircraft, provides a more detailed understanding of the larger picture as well as the intimate details of the ships and their crews in their last moments.

THE PACIFIC WAR AFTER GUADALCANAL

After Guadalcanal, a concerted campaign to eliminate some island bastions held by the Japanese while bypassing others, known as "island-hopping," left the US Navy, rapidly expanding as America's industrial might poured more ships and aircraft into the war, to take out Japan's merchant fleet and navy. American submarines literally "swept the sea clean" of merchant shipping over the next three years, also sinking troop transports and inflicting losses on the Imperial Japanese Navy. Japanese industry worked to turn out replacement ships, as well as aircraft, but could not keep pace. By 1944, when Japan had launched and sent three new aircraft carriers into battle, the United States had surpassed that with more than two dozen carriers of the large *Essex* class as well as smaller *Independence*-class light carriers and various classed escort carriers. The Battle of the Philippine Sea from June 19–20 1944, ended Japan's ability to fight with carriers, losing the carriers *Taihō*, *Shōkaku*, and *Hiyō* and more than 600 aircraft in what one American pilot's quip led it to be called: the "Great Marianas Turkey Shoot."

That was followed by Leyte Gulf, the largest naval battle not only of World War II but in human history. For three days, nearly 400 ships and more than 1,800 aircraft met in a raging battle off the Philippine Island of Leyte. When it was over, a decisive American victory came with the cost of six ships— three carriers and three destroyers—as well as more than 200 planes and 3,000 lives. The Japanese lost 28 ships, among them four carriers, three battleships, 10 cruisers, and 11 destroyers, but also more than 300 planes and more than 12,000 men. Leyte Gulf was effectively the end of the Imperial Japanese Navy as a major fighting force. Desperate measures followed— kamikaze aircraft, manned *kaiten* torpedoes, midget submarine sorties, and the final suicidal dash of the super battleship *Yamato* in April 1945.

Leyte secured the American beachhead in the Philippines, while the Battle of the Philippine Sea opened the way for the successful retaking of

Guam and the invasion of Saipan. What followed in the final stages of the war were the amphibious invasions of Iwo Jima, in February 1945, the invasion of Okinawa in April—both in the face of intense kamikaze attack—and bloody battles on land with heavy casualties. The taking of the islands close to Japan allowed American bombers to commence a punishing aerial bombardment of Japan, culminating in massive fire-bombing raids and finally in the atomic bombing of Hiroshima and Nagasaki in August, ending the war.

The scale of World War II at sea is so vast, and the losses so great, that a separate volume just on the lost warships of that conflict could be written. The rate of discovery of the lost ships of World War II has grown exponentially as technology has improved, and in particular as advanced deep-sea technology, once classified, reaches the civilian world. In shallow and deep waters, wreck divers, historians, and archaeologists have discovered World War II ships and downed aircraft throughout the world, with solitary finds as well as battlefield discoveries. It is impossible to name them all, but among those not already mentioned are the ongoing work to find all 52 US Navy submarines lost during the war and still on "eternal patrol," with recent discoveries of USS *Perch*, USS *Lagarto*, USS *Flier*, USS *Wahoo*, USS *Grunion* (discovered by the sons of its captain), R-12, and S-28, off Hawai'i. The discoveries provide more than closure; they offer details on the losses of the submarines, such as the catastrophic damage suffered by *Flier* when it hit a mine and sank in 100 meters of water on August 12, 1944; only eight men survived the sinking.

The Allen team's work in the Pacific has revealed the Japanese battleship *Musashi*, sunk by a US aircraft carrier during the Battle of Leyte Gulf on October 24, 1944, with nearly 1,000 of its crew, and the battleship *Yamashiro*, sunk at the Battle of Surigao Strait on October 25, 1944, with nearly all of its 1,636-man crew. Other finds in the strait were other Battle of Leyte Gulf losses: the battleship *Fuso*, and the destroyers *Michishio*, *Asagumo* and *Yamagumo*. All told, Japanese casualties at Leyte stood at over 4,000 men. Another Allen find in Philippine waters is USS *Ward*, the destroyer that fired the first shot of World War II in the Pacific off Pearl Harbor on December 7, 1941, and subsequently lost on December 7, 1944, after being hit by a kamikaze during the landings at Leyte, and then sunk by gunfire from the destroyer *O'Brien*, commanded by the captain who had skippered *Ward* four years earlier to the day. Other R/V *Petrel* discoveries made by the Robert Kraft and the Paul Allen team were the Japanese destroyer *Shimakaze*, sunk in Ormoc Bay on November 11, 1944; another probable, but as yet unidentified Japanese destroyer; and three Japanese merchant ships. At the same time, the team also discovered the destroyer USS *Cooper*, which sank with 191 of its crew in Ormoc Bay on December 3, 1944, after being hit by a torpedo fired by the Japanese destroyer *Take*.

The greatest discovery by the Allen team culminated years of unsuccessful searches by others in the very deep, rugged undersea terrain off the Philippines for the most tragic American naval loss at the end of the war. The cruiser USS *Indianapolis*, after it had delivered the components for the atomic bomb, was sunk by the Japanese submarine I-58 on July 30, 1945, with the loss of some 300 of the crew in the sinking and several hundred more in subsequent shark attacks as the survivors drifted—many of them in the water without lifebelts—for three and a half days before rescue. Working with the US Naval History and Heritage Command, the crew on R/V *Petrel* systematically surveyed a 1,199-square-kilometer area to discover the wreck in 5,486 meters of water on August 19, 2017. Despite the bow and forward turret laying separate from the main part of the wreck, which sits inside an impact crater, *Indianapolis* was remarkably well preserved, with its identification number painted on the bow.

With the announcement of the discovery of *Indianapolis*, Paul Allen spoke in a press release to the importance of this find. "To be able to honor the brave men of the USS *Indianapolis* and their families through the discovery of a ship that played such a significant role during World War II is truly humbling....As Americans, we all owe a debt of gratitude to the crew for their courage, persistence, and sacrifice in the face of horrendous circumstances....I hope everyone connected to this historic ship will feel some measure of closure at this discovery so long in coming."

In February 2018, Allen's team followed the discovery of *Indianapolis* with a survey in the Coral Sea that found the broken wreck of the carrier

USS *Lexington*. Lost after its clash with a Japanese force in May 1942, the torpedo- and bomb-damaged *Lexington* burned and suffered a series of secondary explosions that threw aircraft and wreckage high into the air. After rescuing more than 2,700 survivors, the carrier's escorting destroyers stood by as the destroyer USS *Phelps* scuttled *Lexington* with a spread of torpedoes. After the ship sank, a massive underwater explosion was heard. With *Lexington* went 216 members of the crew killed in the battle.

The team on R/V *Petrel* located *Lexington* after analyzing the logs of the ships engaged in the battle, which resulted in a search "box" that lay in a complex undersea terrain. *Lexington*, broken into three sections with the bridge superstructure detached from the hull, is still painted, and the carrier's name is on the hull. The scattered aircraft that sank with *Lexington* lay close by, also brightly painted, a reminder that the dark, oxygen-free depths often result in incredible preservation of these deep-sea wrecks.

In shallower waters, archaeologists and diver/historians have discovered and surveyed lost Japanese warships and transports in the Marshalls, particularly at Kwajalein, in Palau, Rabaul, Saipan, and Guam, and recently turned to the study of invasion beaches and landing craft. In Hawai'i, Hans Van Tilburg has worked for the past few years assessing the wrecks and lost equipment from the beaches where the US Navy and Marine Corps trained for Pacific Island landings.

In the Pacific, a variety of Japanese and American ships are being discovered, including the work from the University of Hawai'i Undersea Research Laboratory, whose World War II finds include aircraft; the two Japanese midget submarines from the December 7 attack that lay off the entrance to Pearl Harbor; the postwar scuttled Japanese submarines I-14, I-201, I-400, and I-401; and the net tender USS *Kailua*, I-400 and I-401, the latter being the largest submarines built by Japan during World War II. The submarines—captured, taken to Pearl Harbor for study, and then sunk to keep them out of sight of the Soviets—are amazing craft. The only other sub of their type, I-402, was scuttled by the US Navy off Nagasaki along with 22 other Imperial Japanese Navy submarines after the war. In 2004, Brett Phaneuf, along with sonar expert Bob Asplin from Simrad Mesotech, found the submarine graveyard 64 kilometers off Nagasaki in 182 meters of water and conducted an ROV inspection of them. Among those lying in the dark was I-58, the submarine that torpedoed and sank USS *Indianapolis*.

Other NOAA maritime heritage dives have included work with Robert Ballard and the Ocean Exploration Trust, with a dive off the Pacific Coast of Canada in June 2016 to identify and survey a target we suspected and proved was SS *Coast Trader*, a US Army–chartered merchant ship torpedoed and sunk by the Japanese submarine I-26 on June 7, 1942. NOAA deep-sea discoveries and dives in 2016 also included the Japanese water tanker *Amakusa Maru*, sunk by the USS *Triton* off Wake Island on December 24, 1942. The year ended with the detailed mapping and assessment, culminating in a live Internet broadcast on December 7, 2016, from *Okeanos Explorer* as we explored the two Japanese midget submarines discovered by the University of Hawai'i Undersea Research Laboratory.

THE WRECKS OF CHUUK LAGOON

The best-known collection of World War II wrecks in the Pacific lies in Chuuk (Truk) Lagoon, a 40-mile-diameter atoll comprising 245 islands in the Central Pacific, with an exceptional natural anchorage. Chuuk, a German colony, was ceded to Japan after World War I and developed as a base for the Imperial Japanese Navy's Fourth Fleet. Known as the "Japanese Pearl Harbor," Japan fortified Chuuk after 1940, when small repair and refueling facilities and a seaplane base were built. Additional fortifications were added after January 1944 in anticipation of an Allied invasion, and Imperial Japanese Army troops arrived to garrison the islands. During the war, American radio broadcasts referred to Chuuk as the "impregnable bastion of the Pacific."

The US Navy attacked Chuuk on February 16–17, and April 29–30, 1944, as did the Royal Navy on June 16, 1945. US bombing raids by B-24 and B-29 aircraft also hit Chuuk. In 1944, US military planners also considered dropping the atomic bomb, then under development, on Chuuk's anchorage, but the plan was never acted on.

After the war, the US Strategic Bombing Survey concluded that the strikes against Chuuk had destroyed more than 416 aircraft and sunk at least 43 major ships, including three light cruisers, four destroyers, a sea-plane tender, a patrol vessel, and numerous small craft. Many of the atoll's airstrips and naval facilities were crippled or destroyed. Chuuk had been neutralized as an extension of Japanese military power in the Pacific.

The carrier raids and bombing of Chuuk left a substantial submerged material record in the form of sunken vessels, aircraft, and equipment. Chuuk Lagoon is today considered one of the world's top diving attractions because of its large number of World War II shipwrecks. Some of the wrecks protrude above the water, while others lie deep in the lagoon. The deep-water wrecks have an incredible array of untouched material, including cargoes, armament, and ordnance, and human remains, although a concerted effort by Japanese groups has resulted in the recovery of many remains for cremation in funeral services ashore.

Surveys and photographic documentation of the wrecks at Chuuk have been undertaken by diving researchers and historians, and a more recent survey by Australian archaeologist Bill Jeffrey and other experts to assess the ongoing changes to the wrecks and to develop a preservation plan has added more to our understanding of this undersea battlefield.

REDISCOVERING THE LOST SHIPS OF WORLD WAR II IN THE ATLANTIC AND THE MEDITERRANEAN

Active work by diver-historians and archaeologists in Europe and off the coast of Africa have resulted in the discovery of a large number of wartime wrecks of Italian, German, British, and American ships and planes off the Mediterranean coasts of France, Italy, Greece, Albania, Croatia, Tunisia, and Malta. Others have done amazing work in the darkness of the Baltic, including documenting the ghastly aftermath of the sinking of the German ships *Wilhelm Gustloff*, sunk by the Soviet submarine S-13 on the evening of January 30, 1945, off Poland while evacuating more than 10,000 Germans fleeing the advancing Soviets. More than 9,000 of the people on board, more than half of them children, died. It is the largest loss of life in a shipwreck. In 2004, researchers discovered the wreck of *Steuben*, another liner torpedoed off Poland on February 9, 1945, again by S-13, with a loss of nearly 5,000 people. I know one of the divers who has visited the wreck, located in deep, pitch-black water. The cargo holds are filled with human bones. He took no photos; *Steuben* is a wreck that most would rather not visit.

The work of Paul Allen's teams on his ships *Octopus* and *Petrel*, in addition to the previously mentioned work on HMS *Hood* and the survey off Guadalcanal, include the discovery of the Italian destroyer *Artigliere*, sunk off Capo Passero in the Mediterranean on October 13, 1940, with the loss of 132 men. This work is important, and the discoveries have provided closure and resolved (and posed) questions, and collectively have added to an inventory of ships once lost and now found. Most have not been studied by archaeologists; Innes McCartney, well known for his work on World War I wrecks and submarines, has continued to work on World War II submarines off the United Kingdom.

French divers and historians have discovered and documented the lost ships of the Normandy landings off the French coast. That coast and its

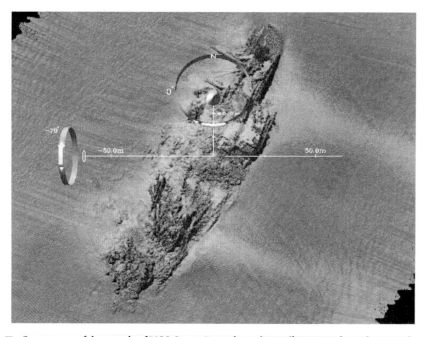

■ Sonar map of the wreck of USS *Susan B. Anthony*, lost off Normandy and mapped during a US Navy History and Heritage Command survey of the D-Day invasion beaches that took place from 2000 to 2003. (US Navy)

beaches were the battlefield that marked the beginning of the end for Hitler's *Festung Europa*, or "Fortress Europe." Comprehensive surveys using sonar have mapped the offshore areas and the remains of D-Day and the landings that followed.

At the same time, diving into that vast battlefield has documented wrecks, aircraft, tanks, and a variety of things lost as well as the sunken hulks and concrete structures of the Mulberry Harbour—the temporary, sheltered harbors sunk into place off the beaches of Normandy and used to land two-and-a-half million troops, a half million vehicles, and millions of tons of supplies. Archaeological studies of D-Day have included work done by the US Navy History and Heritage Command, and most recently by France's Department of Underwater and Submarine Archaeological Research (DRASSM). The French have merged the study of the underwater sites with those on land—the vestiges of the Atlantic Wall, foxholes, logistical structures, prison camps, casualties not recovered after the battles, and the "small traces" to bring new perspectives to our understanding of D-Day and the subsequent invasion of occupied Europe.

THE LESSONS AND THE PERILS OF THE UNDERSEA MUSEUM OF WORLD WAR II

When war came in September 1939, following Hitler's invasion of Poland, Britain and its allies were ill-equipped to deal with the well-prepared Nazi military juggernaut that swept across Europe, taking most of the continent, including France. British expeditionary forces, trapped at Dunkirk, were saved only by a massive evacuation, under fire, by a flotilla of hastily assembled craft, including private yachts. By 1940, Britain was an island nation besieged, its continental allies gone, and its tenuous positions in the Mediterranean under attack from the Germans and their Italian allies. The situation was not good at sea; while the Royal Navy still possessed a better navy than its enemies, the German navy once again turned to its best naval weapon, the submarine, to strike at British warships and merchant shipping. Assisted by its colonial allies, particularly Canada, as well as the

United States, which, while officially neutral, "loaned" warships and supplies, Britain grimly held on.

The naval battle that followed lasted the entirety of the war, and it is important to remember that of all battles fought, that "Battle of the Atlantic" was the most decisive, for had the Germans prevailed, Britain would have fallen, and likely so, too, the Soviet Union. Keeping the lines of supply open meant delivering the men, equipment, armament, supplies, and ammunition that were critical to defeating the Nazis.

The war expanded globally at the end of 1941, when Japan entered the conflict, striking at American, British, and Dutch holdings and military bases in the Far East and in the Pacific. During the next four years, as war raged on nearly every continent and every sea, the scale of the fighting was unprecedented in human history. In the Pacific, it was a war decided by projecting sea power underwater as US submarines devastated Japanese shipping and disrupted supply lines, on the surface in all-out battles, and also in the air, as this was a war in which the aircraft carrier emerged, as did the submarine, as the ultimate naval weapons. Naval warfare as defined by World War II was truly three-dimensional, as forces contended with foes in front of, behind, above, and below them.

The naval war was ultimately won, as was the conflict on land, by superior force, industrial output, and the development of new technologies and weapons. The technologies developed by the Axis, while impressive, did not change the outcome of the war, but aspects of it, especially in rocket and missile technology, radar, and submarine developments, would all be carefully studied by the victorious allies and used in the next generation of ships, subs, and weapons that served during the Cold War.

As several decades have passed, and so too many of the generation who fought in it, there has been an increased interest in the history and archaeology of World War II. This has extended underwater. There are a vast number of sites to study. The global scale of the conflict and the vastness of the oceanic battlefields have left the largest single group of shipwrecks tied to one event—World War II—on the planet. These wrecks reflect more than the scale of the conflict but also its nature. War at sea became more effective, and in that deadlier.

In all, 1,454 warships were lost in World War II. The greatest number, 402, were Japanese, followed by the ships of the royal navies (359), Germany (244), and the United States (167). The greatest numbers of ships sunk were destroyers—545 were lost—followed by 110 cruisers, 78 battleships and battlecruisers, and 47 aircraft carriers. The global nature, and the ferocity of the conflict in some theaters, is illustrated by where most of these lost warships went down—332 sank in the Mediterranean, 227 were lost in Southeast Asia, 163 went down off Japan. In the South Pacific, 105 warships were lost; while 108 sank in the Atlantic. These rusting hulks represent the greatest number of lost warships in history, and hold the bones of over 100,000 drowned sailors and marines.

A growing sense of the importance of these wrecks, as undersea memorials, as historic places, and as sites worthy of study by forensic naval architects, archaeologists, and historians seeking answers about their final moments, or simply just to find them, regardless of depth, led to a number of expeditions in the late 20th and early 21st centuries. As a result, the last decade has witnessed a rapid increase in the number of World War II shipwrecks discovered and documented. These discoveries have provided families with closure, spurred the last survivors of the generation that fought in that conflict to share their memories, answered some questions, and also sparked hard questions about what is to happen to these wrecks. Some of them hold vast amounts of oil—some of it fuel, some of it cargo. In the case of the fleet oiler USS *Mississinewa*, sunk at Ulithi Atoll in the Pacific, concern over the environmental impact of its leaking oil led to a multimillion-dollar cleanup.

While many of the World War II wrecks pose a peril to the environment, a number of them are also in peril. More modern wrecks, especially those from World War II, are increasingly at risk from salvagers who come not for artifacts or souvenirs, but for the entire ship. The problem is increasingly global, with salvage off Europe in the North Sea, and in Asian waters, including areas off the coasts of Vietnam, Malaysia, and Indonesia. What has happened has outraged families, alarmed government officials and archaeologists, and frustrated tourism officials and wreck divers who seek to pay respectful visits and take only photographs. In some of these cases, the ships that have vanished have been massive vessels, displacing thousands of tons. Among the wrecks to have been hit hard are those from the Battle of the Java Sea, an early war action on February 27, 1942, and the follow-up action, the Battle of Sunda Strait, on February 28 between the Imperial Japanese Navy, and British, Dutch, Australian, and American ships. While essentially equally matched in gun power, the allied naval force had never fought as a unit before, and communications were hampered by different languages. They also fought without air support. In all, 10 allied ships and over 2,000 men were lost.

A number of the wrecks had been discovered through the first decade of the 21st century, but by the time the 75th anniversary of the battles came in 2017, the divers who led the discoveries were shocked to find that for the most part, only craters remained even a few hundred meters deep. HNMLS *DeRuyter*, HNMLS *Java*, HNMLS *Kortenaer*, HMS *Encounter*, HMS *Exeter*, HMS *Electra*, and the submarine USS *Perch*, scuttled on March 3, 1942, were either completely or largely gone. Meanwhile, in 2014, in response to reports of illegal salvage, the US Navy sent divers and archaeologist Alexis

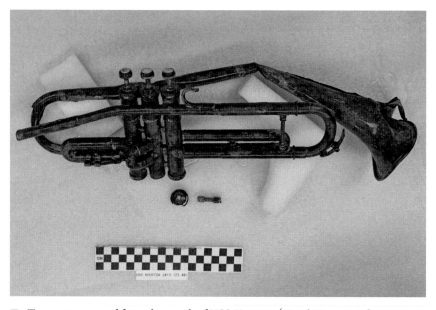

■ Trumpet recovered from the wreck of USS *Houston*. (Naval History and Heritage Command)

Catsambis to Sunda Strait to assess USS *Houston*, sunk with several hundred of the crew. They found the wreck partly stripped, with plates cut off and a diver's air hose from a surface-supplied diving rig draped across the hull.

Australian archaeological colleagues Kieran Hosty and James Hunter and Indonesian colleague Shinatria Adhityatama have found even worse with the wreck of HMAS *Perth*, also sunk in the Battle of Sunda Strait with 353 dead lost with their ship. Their 2017 survey, a joint effort between the Australian National Maritime Museum and Indonesia's *Pusat Penelitian Arkeologi Nasional* (ARKENAS), documented that ongoing salvage and souvenir hunting had taken place since the 1967 discovery of *Perth*, but that starting around 2015, more industrial-level salvage was taking place. The 2017 survey found that 60 percent of the starboard hull plating and the armor belt had been stripped off since the last survey in 2013.

For the families of the dead inside these ships, as I've already noted, the news of the discovery of the salvage work, both complete and partial, has been devastating. The 2017 archaeological report from Australia took pains to note that while they did not see any human remains, there was the strong potential for them inside the ship, especially if buried in silt. I know from firsthand reports of remains inside other World War II ships, and there are well-known, published images of skulls and long bones inside the wrecks at Chuuk. The 2017 survey team "observed significant, complex and deep deposits of artefact material... uniform buttons, buckles, a pair of spectacles, leather shoes, rubber boots, cotton clothing fragments" during their dives on *Perth*.

There is no definitive assertion as to what those deposits represent. The general practice of most nations is not to disturb the places in sunken warships that are thought to hold the remains of the crew, and with *Perth*, the project focused on documenting what was found, without recovery. To do so on any warship wreck requires permissions and permits, and then a careful scientific approach. What was found by the team to me suggests that the ongoing salvage of *Perth* is literally ripping open a grave that is not a metaphorical construct, but a formerly sealed tomb.

In other cases, the salvagers of some of the warships have reportedly hauled large sections ashore, where workers broke the wreckage into small

■ Sailors from USS *George H. W. Bush* (CVN 77) place a wreath on the USS *Houston* Memorial in 2012. (US Navy Photo by Mass Communications Specialist 1st Class Chris Laurent)

pieces. According to a January 2018 story in the *Guardian*, workers found "skulls, jawbones, feet and hand bones, hips and ribs" that were "dumped in an anonymous grave." When our team from *The Sea Hunters* dived the wrecks of HMS *Prince of Wales* and HMS *Repulse* off Malaysia, they found, and did not film, a large number of human bones. As I said, images from early dives at Chuuk on its World War II Japanese wrecks show skulls and long bones. In short, we know what rests inside these ships. Some care; others, like the salvagers, do not

What's in it for the salvagers? Using explosives and grappling the bottom with giant claws, they tear apart the ships and pull the chunks onto barges. Those barges either then take wreckage to shore facilities for the type of processing reported by the *Guardian*, or go directly to China, where the scrap steel fetches $150 a ton, while more valuable metal, like bronze from propellers, sells for more. In addition to the Allied wrecks, Japanese wartime wrecks are also stripped or have disappeared. A February 2018 article in Malaysia's the *Star* reported as many as 19 warships have now been salvaged illegally, including *Repulse* and *Prince of Wales*. Reporter Eddie Chua, speaking to an unnamed informant, explained that the metal is now a highly sought after commodity in China, as it predates the atomic era, and without post-1945 radioactive contamination from decades of nuclear testing, the steel is used to make medical and scientific instruments and equipment. The source also claimed that while seemingly an operation with a number of small operators, the salvage effort is the work of an unnamed Chinese company operating subsidiaries as part of a syndicate.

What is the appropriate thing to do with the wrecks of World War II? Some do create a risk of pollution because of oil trapped inside of them. Some of them are graves, and important to families of the lost. For others, they are historic sites, and as we've seen, offer archaeological insights into the events, the ships, and their crews. Is there a legitimate place for salvage? Bear in mind that for salvage to take place, legally, permission is needed, because all of these sunken warships, under international law, remain the property of the governments under whose flags they sailed, fought, and died. None of them have sanctioned what is happening, and those of us who care about these ships fear that what has taken place will spread globally.

10

The Cold War and Beyond

The *Sturgeon* class submarine...has been consigned to the scrap heap of history as a direct result of the end of the cold war.

—Captain Alfred S. McLaren, USN (Ret.)

The aftermath of World War II left the United States as the major naval power in the world. The era of the battleship was over, even though the United States had built a group of powerful *Iowa*-class battleships armed with 16-inch guns—and accepted the Japanese surrender on the deck of one of them, the battleship *Missouri*. But as the new global power, the United States faced a series of challenges. The first was the role of nuclear weapons. Did the atomic bomb make navies obsolete? Was there a role for the US Navy in the age of aircraft and missile-delivered nuclear weapons? When those questions were answered, the next steps were to place as many nuclear weapons, of different types, on ships. In time, that led to the development of the ballistic missile submarine as the ultimate weapon and hopefully ultimate deterrent for a global nuclear exchange.

The second challenge came from a wartime ally, the Soviet Union. The "Cold War" that lasted from 1946 until 1990 witnessed a series of regional conflicts throughout the world. The development of the nuclear-powered submarine in the late 1950s and the capability of those submarines to deliver massive nuclear strikes made them the ultimate naval weapon, surpassing even the aircraft carrier as the new capital ships. While the Soviet Union posed little strategic threat immediately after World War II, with its navy largely restricted to coastal operations in the expanded Soviet empire, that changed after 1953 with the rise of a new commander of the Soviet Navy, Admiral of the Fleet Sergei Gorshkov, who, under Nikita Khrushchev and Leonid Brezhnev, built the Soviet Navy into a global force that challenged the United States and its allies on the high seas in his nearly four-decade-long career.

Lost warships from the last half of the 20th century now join other naval wrecks of the past four millennia. They include the Korean War, Vietnam War, Arab-Israeli conflict wrecks, and British and Argentine combat losses—including the Exocet missile–devastated HMS *Sheffield* and the former American cruiser *Admiral Belgrano*, lost to submarine attack. There are also a handful of nuclear submarine losses, ranging from early American fleet boats like USS *Thresher* and *Scorpion*, the Soviet *Komsomolets*, and the Russian submarine *Kursk* among others.

In addition to Cold War losses in service, the undersea legacy of the era includes the oceanic sites of nuclear testing, beginning at Bikini Atoll in the Marshall Islands and extending to nearby atolls and islands of Enewetak in the Pacific Proving Ground, Britain's test site at Western Australia's Montebello Islands, and France's Moruroa and Fangataufa atolls in French Polynesia. There are also ocean dumping sites for atomic waste, chemical and conventional weapons, lost Cold War–era aircraft, some with weapons, and a large fleet of ships sunk post-service in weapons tests and naval training exercises. Next to the sunken legacy of World War II, the Cold War has left the greatest undersea legacy.

Another undersea legacy is the issue of derelict and abandoned Soviet submarines, some awaiting or undergoing dismantling, and discarded reactors that lie in Russia's coastal waters, especially in the Arctic and the North Pacific. The archaeological signature of war at sea over the last several decades offers more than opportunities for learning about the past and answering historical questions. The naval archaeological legacy of the Cold

War, when one considers discarded and lost reactors and weapons, is one of ongoing concern.

HMS *VOLAGE*'S BOW

The first naval casualty of the Cold War lies off the Albanian city of Sarandë. Sarandë lies at one end of the Corfu Channel, a three-nautical-mile-wide strait between the Greek mainland and the island of Corfu that then follows the northeastern end of the island and the Albanian coast. On October 22, 1946, the first naval incident of the Cold War came when British warships challenged then-Communist Albania's contention that the channel was an internal waterway that they could defend. Two Royal Navy ships struck mines laid by the Albanians that killed 44 men and nearly sank the ships. The bow of the destroyer HMS *Volage* was blown off the ship and sank, carrying many of the dead with it.

With the end of World War II, Britain regained use of its former naval base on Corfu. The base was key, as the Corfu Channel is a strategic waterway that for thousands of years has been the means by which ships transit to and from the Adriatic. Not everyone wanted the British back, among them Enver Hoxha, the communist leader of Albania. Despite Allied assistance to Hoxha's partisan-led opposition to Nazi occupation, Hoxha was no friend. In postwar elections, Hoxha and his party claimed victory, exiled the prewar ruler, King Zog, and formed a Communist government.

Hoxha was paranoid and viewed foreign powers, particularly Britain and the United States, but also neighboring Greece, as Albania's principal enemies. In response to increased tensions and Hoxha's anti-Western actions, Britain withdrew its diplomats and a military mission from Albania in April 1946. Hoxha, meanwhile, began to jealously guard his borders. This in time led to the imposition of an Albanian iron curtain, and intensive fortification of its borders after 1967. A striking example of this is more than 173,000 bunkers and pillboxes the People's Republic of Albania built along its borders. I've seen them along the beaches, positioned so that if one border guard decided to make a run for it, the guards in the other bunkers had a clear shot at him.

In 1946, Albanian military forces were on high alert, manning coastal gun batteries overlooking Corfu Channel. Hoxha was worried that Greek and British warships and merchant vessels were coming too close, especially to Sarandë. Hoxha was right, because the geography of the strait makes it impossible for larger ships to make the turn to go into the channel from the south without crossing Albania's maritime border.

The stage was set for conflict, especially as Britain was eager to regain their naval base, but also reassert the traditional British view of freedom of the seas. In May 1946, the first of what would be a series of incidents, now collectively known as the Corfu Channel Incident, took place. On May 15, two British cruisers, HMS *Orion* and HMS *Superb*, transited the Channel and headed toward Corfu. They were the first British warships to use the Channel since the end of World War II. As they passed Sarandë, the Albanians sent as many as twelve shots their way. They missed, but the Royal Navy was, to say the least, displeased, as was His Majesty's government. Diplomatic cables went back and forth, but without any satisfaction for Britain, who demanded free, open passage through the channel. The Albanians answered that *Orion* and *Superb* had intruded into Albanian waters, but shooting at them had been a mistake. That was not good enough.

The Royal Navy ordered its ships not to use the channel while discussions continued not only on the right of passage but the larger question of resuming diplomatic relations. By the fall, the opportunity to "test" Albania's position came with a decision by the Royal Navy to once again send ships through the Corfu Channel, with a mind to determine, according to a navy cable to the commander-in-chief of naval forces at Corfu, "whether the Albanian Government have learned to behave themselves." The means of determining that was sending four ships—the cruisers HMS *Mauritius* and HMS *Leander*, and the destroyers HMS *Saumarez* and HMS *Volage*—through the channel on October 22, 1946.

That afternoon, after entering the channel, the ships set course for Kepi Denta (Denta Point) at the southern edge of the Bay of Sarandë. *Mauritius* was in the lead, and as the small fleet made its turn, HMS *Saumarez* hit a mine.

Thirty-six men died as a hole was torn from keel to deck on the destroyer's starboard side. Badly damaged and on fire, *Saumarez* drifted helplessly toward shore. HMS *Volage* approached the burning *Saumarez* to attach a tow line. As *Volage* began to pull *Suamarez* from the beach, the tow line parted. Quickly rigging a second line, *Volage* began to slowly tow the wounded *Suamarez*, when, 36 minutes later, it also struck a mine, head-on.

Historian Eric Leggett, an eyewitness, wrote that "in a split second forty feet of the destroyer, from the fore peak to just in front of 'A' gun turret, had vanished. Mess decks, store rooms, the paint shop, the cable locker containing tons of anchor cable, the anchors themselves, literally dissolved in the air." Eight men also died in the blast, seven of them never accounted for. To keep from sinking, *Volage*'s crew threw heavy items including shells, depth charges, and deck equipment overboard until the mangled bow, still hanging by scraps of steel, tore free and sank. With that, *Volage* righted onto its keel.

Amazingly, *Volage* not only remained afloat, but the destroyer was able to raise steam and Commander Reginald Paul once again laid out a tow line to *Saumarez*. Finding that his blast-damaged bulkheads would likely buckle if he steamed forward, in an amazing show of seamanship, Paul backed *Volage* and *Saumarez* to Corfu. The two badly damaged destroyers reached safe harbor at 3:00 the following morning, nearly twelve hours after departing on the ill-fated cruise.

Britain's response was relatively quick. In November, a British fleet steamed into the channel and then into Albania's waters, and cleared it of the World War II German-manufactured mines they had recently painted and laid. Albania publicly denied having laid them, but recently released documents show that they did. Britain, arguing that the presence of the mines, and the lack of a warning about a minefield, constituted a breach of international law, ultimately brought suit against Albania in what would be the first case of the International Court at The Hague. What was key, the British argued, was that the court not only sanction Albania but also note that Britain had a right to transit the channel and that their exercise had not been a belligerent action but rather an "exercise of the right of innocent passage."

Albania argued in return that Britain had broken international law, and that the cruise of the British warships was a provocation. This had not been an "innocent passage." The case dragged on for three years. The Hague decided for Britain, but noted with disapproval that Britain had violated Albania's sovereignty by going into their waters to remove the mines. The Hague ordered Albania to pay Britain £843,947 in compensation. Hoxha refused, and Britain seized Albanian gold held in the vaults of the Bank of London. It was not until 1991 that the two countries resumed regular diplomatic relations.

In 2009, I joined an ongoing survey of Albania's coastal waters by the non-profit RPM Nautical Foundation intended to find and document the country's underwater cultural heritage. Working from the research vessel *Hercules* with RPM's founder, George Robb, RPM archaeologist Jeff Royal, and Albanian archaeologist Adrian Anastasi, I asked if any of the targets they had found off Sarandë were small enough to be the bow of *Volage*. George, Jeff, and Adrian, with a list of ancient Greek and Roman ships, had found two World War II wrecks and 14 unidentified modern wrecks, one of them very small. As I talked about *Volage*, George decided we needed to dive that target with *Hercules*'s remotely operated vehicle.

It was the bow of *Volage*. A 15-by-9–meter expanse of blast-damaged, welded steel, tangled electrical wiring site lay shrouded in mud. Among the wreckage was a British military canteen, shoes, what looked like a human long bone, an ammunition locker, loose clips of .303 ammunition, and stacked dishware that clearly showed we were in the midst of the forward berthing and messing spaces where men had lived, slept, ate, and died.

The discovery was announced three months later in cooperation with Albanian officials. Our dive coincided with the 1990 publication of a book by Albanian naval captain and historian Artur Meçollari. I met him after the dive as he was then the commanding officer of Albania's naval flotilla in the Corfu Channel region. He gave me a copy of his book and showed where his research, based on Albanian archives, showed *Suamarez* and *Volage* had been hit. His position was different than the one provided by Britain to The Hague. He was not surprised to learn that we had found *Volage*'s bow where we did; the positions matched, just a few hundred meters off Sarandë's waterfront. Captain Meçollari had argued in his book that all other histories were wrong, and that the British ships had come into the bay before turning. They were not in the channel. One could argue that the "innocent passage" was in fact a defiant act by the Royal Navy that dared the Albanians to shoot and never considered whether the area just offshore was mined. The bow of *Volage*, a war grave, is another reminder of how archaeology can help correct the record and rewrite the recent past.

THE SUNKEN FLEET OF BIKINI ATOLL

In July 1946, another early shot in the Cold War came with not one but two atomic blasts. The United States conducted the first nuclear weapons tests in the world in the middle of the Pacific Ocean. Bikini Atoll, 4,500 miles west of San Francisco, was the setting for "Operation Crossroads," a massive military effort to assess the effects of the atomic bomb on warships less than a year after Hiroshima. In all, a fleet of 242 ships—95 of them floating targets—220 tons of test equipment, several thousand test animals, and 43,000 military personnel and scientists were assembled within a matter of months at a cost of hundreds of millions of dollars.

In a spectacular display, two "nominal yield" 20-kiloton atomic bombs were detonated at Bikini, sinking 22 ships, and irradiating 73 others. Bikini, with its 167-person native population evacuated for the tests, was contaminated with fallout. Several decades later, the Bikinians are still not able to come home permanently. They are known as the nuclear nomads of the Pacific. The United States used the atoll between 1946 and 1958 for dozens of more powerful nuclear tests, including a 15-megaton hydrogen bomb blast, "Castle Bravo," in March 1954. Bikini is now abandoned, its shores littered with rusting machinery and cables, its islands covered by thick concrete bunkers. The bottom of Bikini's lagoon was left alone at last, its reefs scarred by oil, the seabed pocked with nuclear blast craters and littered with the sunken legacy of Operation Crossroads.

In 1989 and 1990, I was part of a small team of archaeologists from the National Park Service's Submerged Cultural Resources Unit (now the

■ Test Able bomb detonation over the fleet at Bikini. (Naval History and Heritage Command)

Submerged Resources Center) who went to Bikini with the US Navy to relocate the sunken fleet of Operation Crossroads and conduct a detailed study of the ships. The project included a survey of the condition of the vessels and their nuclear blast damage, documenting them through still and video photography and baseline trilateration, and assessing Bikini's potential for designation and use as a national park area by the Bikini Council. We were accompanied by a scientist and radiation measuring devices, as contamination was known to be a problem on the atoll, but no one was certain what the risks were with the sunken ships. That was important, not only for our own safety, but because our work at Bikini not only examined the potential of the wrecks to be heritage dive attractions but was also the first major archaeological assessment of a nuclear test site. As it was, none of the wrecks was "hot."

We surveyed 11 vessels during two field seasons, including the wreck of the former German cruiser *Prinz Eugen*, a Crossroads target vessel, at nearby Kwajalein Atoll. The majority of the fieldwork at Bikini focused on the aircraft carrier *Saratoga*. Other vessels surveyed to varying degrees were the battleships *Arkansas* and *Nagato*; the attack transports *Gilliam* and *Carlisle*; the submarines *Apogon* and *Pilotfish*; the yard oiler YO-160; the floating drydock ARDC-13; and a landing craft, LCT-1175.

The surveys documented extensive nuclear damage to the vessels. Formerly classified accounts from 1946 report that the second atomic test, "Baker," on July 25, placed the target ships around a bomb lowered 27 meters below the surface. When "Baker" erupted from the lagoon, a mass of steam and water mounded up into a "spray dome" that climbed at a rate of 2,762 meters per second into a gigantic column. The center of the 297-meter-thick column was a nearly hollow void of superheated steam that rose faster than the more solid 91-meter-thick water sides, climbing 3,350 meters per second and acting as a chimney for the hot gases of the fireball. The gases,

■ The Test Baker bomb erupts from Bikini Lagoon, July 25, 1946. (Naval History and Heritage Command)

mixed with excavated lagoon bottom and radioactive materials, formed a mushroom cloud atop the column. When the column collapsed, two million tons of irradiated water and sand fell back onto the target ships.

The battleship *Arkansas*, caught in the upward blast, was crushed and capsized and sank in less than a second. Navy divers in 1946 sank into thick, radioactive mud and could not see much. In 1989–1990, that mud was gone, and we documented how two-thirds of the breadth of the hull was crushed nearly flat, leaving only a deformed, but intact port side. The superstructure and turrets above the main deck were hammered into the coral bottom, leaving only a 2-meter gap between deck and seabed.

The "Baker" blast also created atomic tidal waves that smashed into the ships. The first wave, a 29-meter-tall wall of radioactive water, lifted and pummeled *Saratoga*. The carrier's hull was twisted, and the flight deck partially collapsed. *Saratoga* sank within seven and a half hours, slowly settling by the stern. Our dives documented a six-meter-deep, two-meter-wide,

■ USS *Saratoga* sinks after Test Baker at Bikini Lagoon, July 25, 1946. (Naval History and Heritage Command)

61-meter-long dent in the flight deck, heavy "washboarding" along the starboard side, which faced the blast, and the rupture and twisting of every starboard hatch and deadlight. The attack transport *Gilliam*, lost in the first "Able" test (July 1, 1946), was caught in the incandescent fireball and battered down into the water by the bomb's shock wave, sinking in 79 seconds. The blast swept away *Gilliam's* superstructure, and the intense heat softened and warped the hull into a collapsed, twisted wreck that looks like a child's plastic model left out in the sun.

In addition to documenting gross physical damage to the ships, we also measured residual radiation, which was negligible (less than a dental X-ray); assessed unexploded convention (non-nuclear) ordnance left aboard the ships for the tests; and documented the presence of test instruments for measuring blast, heat, and radiation effects. We found some instruments that had not previously been recovered despite post-test salvage dives on the ships. I believe that the presence of these instruments speaks to fears of radioactive contamination immediately after the tests.

During the "Baker" test, a boiling mass of radioactive water and steam penetrated nearly every target ship left afloat and contaminated the lagoon water. Radioactive material adhered to wooden decks and paint, rust and grease. For weeks, the navy tried to wash the fallout off with water and lye, and sent crews aboard contaminated ships to scrub off paint, rust, and scale with long-handled brushes, holystones, and any other "available means," but they could not remove the radiation. In August, it was clear there was no way to get rid of the contamination. The military abandoned Bikini, sinking some of the more badly damaged, contaminated ships that were still afloat. Less damaged, but still "hot" ships were towed away to Kwajalein, Pearl Harbor, and San Francisco. Ultimately, all but a handful of the Crossroads target ships were scuttled after being placed "off-limits" at various naval bases. *Prinz Eugen* capsized and sank at Kwajalein Atoll under these circumstances in December 1946.

The sunken ships of Bikini Atoll represent more than historic vessels whose physical survival on the ocean bottom are reminders of Operation Crossroads. Our reasons for diving the shipwrecks of Bikini Atoll were not merely to satisfy historical curiosity about these vessels and their fate. Rather, we emphasized how these ships are artifacts that speak beyond the written record. For example, the presence of two badly battered Japanese ships on the bottom is a material statement of domination and power. These ships, seized by the victorious United States at the end of World War II, were taken to Bikini for symbolic reasons and deliberately placed in close proximity to each test detonation to ensure that they sank. The selection of the battleship *Nagato* was particularly significant, inasmuch as it was the former flagship of the Imperial Japanese Navy and the site of that navy's planning for the attack on the United States Pacific Fleet at Pearl Harbor.

In the case of most of the wrecks, we documented what the bombs had done, especially with *Saratoga*, where our dives provided a detailed blast damage assessment, something that had not been possible in 1946 due to radiation and other priorities. As we did the dives, I had access to then-recently declassified damage assessments, which included drawings showing blast-induced deformation of steel, broken equipment, and missing gear. What struck me, as we mapped *Saratoga*, was how the work we were doing would have been a top-secret mission not long before we arrived at Bikini in 1989. We were then one year away from the "end" of the Cold War.

Another fascinating aspect of the dives was examining the abandoned test instruments, some of them primitive tools for determining pressure and heat with means as simple as rupturing disks of tin foil, or crushed tin cans on a string, as well as metal plates appearing as if scratched by a stylus as nuclear waves bucked and tossed ships. In addition to documenting abandonment due to fear of contamination, I see in them evocative physical statements of a very human need to try to understand, and perhaps harness, the unfathomable power and effects of a nuclear detonation.

After our 1989–1990 dives, Bikini was opened to wreck-diving tourists who possessed advanced skills. Over the course of the next few decades, all of the major ships sunk at Bikini have been found. This included the Japanese cruiser *Sakawa*, which in 1990 I suspected lay in the crater of the Baker blast, perhaps mangled or pounded into scrap. That's where the divers found *Sakawa*, with a mangled stern, and a flattened superstructure giving evidence of an atomic detonation 27 meters above the wreck. The other two wrecks we had not found, the destroyers *Anderson* and *Lamson*, were also pinpointed and dived. I returned to Bikini in 1999 and dived

Anderson, which lies on its side in 54 meters of water, lying on white coral sand, with a rack of depth charges still at its stern, and its forward naval gun twisted nearly straight back toward the ship's bridge by the force of the Able blast.

One aspect of the ghost fleet at Bikini that is perhaps the most striking is the incredible and vast physical record of Operation Crossroads that lies on the lagoon floor. It is the world's first nuclear naval battlefield, albeit a simulated one. The target arrays were laid out to simulate a fleet with adjustments made to ensure that a maximum amount of quantifiable information would be recorded by the ships, the equipment, instruments, and test animals on board them; this played out with ships anchored in curving spokes on a wheel so no one ship provided a "blast shadow" for another. While the sunken ships are in essence the fallen soldiers on that simulated battlefield, massive concrete mooring blocks still in place down there show where every other "soldier" was standing. Surrounding the ships are items blown off the decks of those target vessels. We've seen naval aircraft, tanks, trailers, and isolated and scattered items that together are a detailed record of two atomic "attacks," one from above and another from below, on the fleet at Bikini.

While we were conducting our work at Bikini, a National Park Service colleague, Doug Scott, was reassessing the site of Custer's Last Stand at the Little Bighorn by mapping every discharged cartridge, and other dropped items—and some human remains—that lay close to the surface. The Little Bighorn project rewrote the concept of battlefield archaeology. If we were able to go back to Bikini, with robotic vehicles using high-resolution sonar to map, and Doug's approach, we could map not just individual ships but that first, and hopefully last, nuclear battlefield as it rests in the gloom of Bikini Lagoon.

USS *INDEPENDENCE*

The end of Operation Crossroads in August 1946 came as military officials and scientists realized that the Baker blast had heavily contaminated almost all of the target ships left afloat. The lagoon itself was irradiated, and the support ships were taking in radioactive saltwater that contaminated the ship's plumbing and boilers, both of which drew water from the sea. It was bad enough that nervous scientists passed Geiger counters over ships' seawater-fed heads (toilets) before sitting down. Marine growth on the hulls was radioactive, and men were not allowed to sleep in bunks close to the sides of ships. Rather than shift work to repositioning target ships for a third test, the military tried without success to decontaminate ships, and then cancelled Crossroads. The navy steamed out of Bikini, sinking a few badly damaged target ships as they reached deep water, and towing others to Kwajalein or Pearl Harbor. From there, navy tugs towed other ships to the West Coast, most of them to San Francisco's Hunters Point or Mare Island, another naval base farther north on San Francisco Bay.

The navy continued to work on decontaminating ships, and reduced radiation readings to "tolerable levels" on many, some of this in part due to natural decay of short-lived radioactive byproducts of the blasts. However, citing blast-damage, no longer needing to maintain a large wartime navy, and the fact that some ships were obsolete, as well as their not wanting to scrap, melt, and reuse steel exposed to radiation, the navy towed almost all of the surviving target ships to sea and sank them between 1947 and 1951. The navy scuttled the largest group, including the battleship USS *Pennsylvania*, in deep water outside of Kwajalein lagoon. Navy tugs towed the battleships USS *Nevada* and USS *New York* 161 kilometers out to sea from Pearl Harbor, and sank them with shells and aerial torpedoes. Naval gunnery, rocket, and torpedo exercises sank the cruisers USS *Salt Lake* City and USS *Pensacola*; the submarines USS *Skipjack*, USS *Searaven*, USS *Tuna*, and USS *Skate*; and a host of destroyers, attack transports, and LSTs off the California coast, and in the case of *Pensacola*, off the coast of Washington State.

The last target ship sunk was the aircraft carrier USS *Independence*. The "Mighty I," badly damaged during the Able test, and irradiated by Baker, stayed afloat longer than the others because the navy made it their first radiological laboratory. The navy also used *Independence*, tied up at the dock at Hunters Point, to train sailors in how to respond to an atomic attack on their ships, complete with monitoring radiation and working to reactivate blast- and heat-damaged systems. By 1950, the navy began loading *Independence* with contaminated pieces from other target ships and laboratory equipment, much of it packed into 55-gallon steel barrels capped with concrete and then stowed deep inside the carrier.

On January 25, 1951, two navy tugs pulled the carrier past the Golden Gate Bridge. Thirty miles out to sea, a demolition team placed two experimental torpedo warheads inside *Independence*. The blast ripped open the hull, and *Independence* quickly capsized and then sank by the stern, disappearing from the surface in 14 minutes. While gone, the "Mighty I" was not forgotten. By the 1970s, concern grew that a "highly radioactive" ship filled with "nuclear waste," as well as the realization that the government had dumped more than 40,000 barrels of other "waste" off San Francisco's shores alarmed environmentalists and residents alike. A sonar survey of the seabed picked up the likely site of the wreck in 1990, but it was not until we conducted a deep-sea sonar survey of that target in 2016 that scientists were able to see that it was *Independence*, upright and seemingly intact in 823 meters of water.

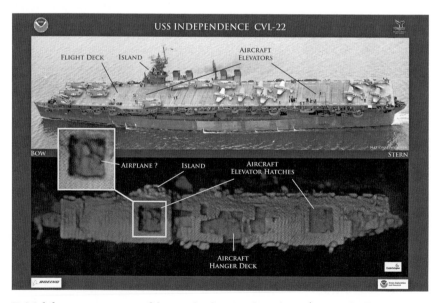

■ Multibeam sonar image of the wreck of USS *Independence*. (NOAA/Office of National Marine Sanctuaries)

In 2017, with Robert Ballard's Ocean Exploration Trust, on board E/V *Nautilus*, we returned to *Independence* for the first dives to the wreck, using the ROVs *Argus* and *Hercules*. Having dived at Bikini extensively, I was excited to see what condition the carrier was in, and what examining it might tell us about Operation Crossroads, and *Independence* as an atomic laboratory. I also wanted to look into the question of the "nuclear waste." We spent more than 30 hours exploring *Independence*, and where there were big enough holes, as well as the carrier's two open elevator pits, we dropped into the hangar deck.

Independence sits upright, slightly to one side, with its bow deeply dug into the seabed. After sinking by the stern, the carrier apparently righted, and then angled down, plowing into the bottom with enough force to bend the steel bow, which flexed and tore open as the thick mud stopped *Independence*'s slide into the seabed. The impact tore off two gun tubs alongside the flight deck at the bow. We found the tubs, with their 20mm antiaircraft guns still inside, lying next to the wreck. There were other traces of the sinking and subsequent changes to *Independence* after six decades in the

■ Science team on board E/V *Nautilus* during the USS *Independence* archaeological reconnaissance mission. (Ocean Exploration Trust, Photo by Julye Newlin)

■ Preparing for a nighttime deployment of the ROV *Hercules* from E/V *Nautilus*. (Ocean Exploration Trust, Photo by Julye Newlin)

ocean: snagged trawl nets, holes in the flight deck where rust had worn through the steel, and fallen pieces from the galleries that ran alongside both sides of the flight deck that tumbled from the impact of hitting bottom had been freed by the nets, or had succumbed to rust. Large white sponges have begun to dot the hull and decks, making the wreck look like a vast alien garden. A huge blast hole in the center of the flight deck and damage to the hull on one side showed where the torpedo warheads used to sink *Independence* had punched through the carrier in January 1951.

Deep-sea shipwrecks, resting in cold, pitch-black water, are often very well preserved, with slow rates of corrosion and biological colonization. As we explored *Independence*, we found that the hull was still painted. Along each side of the carrier, at its waterline, numbers painted for Crossroads as an easy guidepost for damage control reports to show exactly where along the ship's hull damage had happened were still visible. At the stern, raised

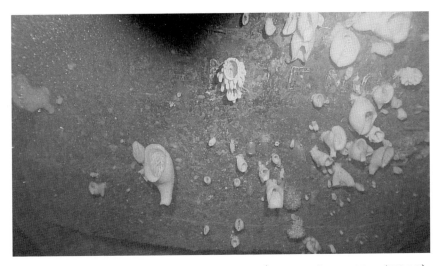

▪ USS *Independence*'s name on the stern of the wreck. (Ocean Exploration Trust/NOAA)

steel letters picked out with white paint still read INDEPENDENCE. On the small "island" superstructure, a faint patchwork quilt of white squares and bands delineated where the carrier's crew had painted their "kill board" of small enemy flags.

Our inspection inside the elevators and hangars made an unexpected set of discoveries. Two battered aircraft remained inside *Independence*. One was a Navy Hellcat fighter aircraft, one wing twisted up the side of the elevator pit, its fuselage laid out, cockpit open to the sea and partly filled with silt. The white star that clearly showed these as American planes was still there, but none of the darker red or blue paint. That is because the plane had been exposed to the atomic blast, and the flash and heat, reflected by the white paint, had removed the darker colors. The other plane, badly mangled, was a navy Helldiver bomber. Both planes had been used as test equipment on *Independence*, and while historical records from the tests clearly stated the Helldiver had been damaged and then disposed over the side after the Able test, there it was, still on the carrier in 2016.

As the ROV slowly moved along the hull and over the decks, the damage of the Able blast was powerfully apparent. While it was clear that time had passed, *Independence*, unlike the ships at Bikini, which are coated with rust, coral, and silt, still powerfully resembled the ship it had been that we had

■ Twin 40-mm antiaircraft guns on the wreck of USS *Independence*. (Ocean Exploration Trust/NOAA)

studied from newsreel footage and photographs from 1946, as well as a handful from 1947 to 1951. As I've said, while time doesn't stand still down there, it seems to move more slowly. Seventy years after Operation Crossroads, in an almost eerie way we were seeing the almost-fresh results of the bomb as if we were there. Working with scientists from the University of California and the US government's Lawrence Berkeley Lab, we removed a number of the sponges growing on the wreck to measure them, as living organisms, for residual radiation. There was no trace of the bomb in them. Why? After seventy years, the half-lives of the residues of Able and Baker's bombs had declined. Declassified radiation readings taken in 1950 showed that decline was well on its way even then.

Our questions about "nuclear waste" were not completely answered. We did not find the carrier sitting in a field of scattered 55-gallon barrels, and formerly top-secret reports on placing "waste" inside *Independence* showed that the navy had emptied an engine room of its machinery to use it as the repository. Deep inside and at the bottom of the hull, that space is beyond reach, sealed behind tons of steel. We did, however, find three 55-gallon barrels in the forward elevator pit next to the plane. One had fallen over, broken apart, and exposed a pile of rubber gloves. Once contaminated from laboratory work, they confirmed what we had read about the nature of much of the "waste."

Like the target ships sunk at Bikini, *Independence* is more than a relic of World War II and Operation Crossroads. It, like other Cold War sites, speaks to the feelings, emotions, and actions of that time in response to an undeclared conflict that had the potential to end all life on earth through nuclear war. Getting rid of no-longer-needed, obsolete "contaminated" target ships unusable for scrap was only one reason for sinking the target ships that made it out of Bikini. The other reason was to keep these ships, and what they could tell spies about the bomb—how powerful the blasts had been, what the nature of their atomic cores had been based on residues and the contamination—away from prying eyes.

By the time *Independence*, the last of the target ships sent down, was readied for scuttling, the US government knew, from intercepted Soviet transmissions, that there was an active network of spies in America, some of them working from within the government. Now declassified, the "Venona" intercepts show more than 300 Americans spied for the USSR. As we decry the hysteria and reputation-ruining witch hunts of the McCarthy era, there was a grain of truth behind them. The intercepts, as well as Soviet archives, show that some of these people, despite denials, were guilty. In this atmosphere, *Independence* was vulnerable. When the navy sank it in 1951, press reports were deliberately misleading about where it was sunk because the intention was to get it not only out of sight, but, the US government hoped, beyond reach. The carrier rests 161 kilometers away from where it was said to have been sunk. We found the same for the location of the Japanese super-sub I-400, also sunk to keep it safe from Soviet spies. Unlike the simulated nuclear battlefield at Bikini, and its sunken warships, *Independence* speaks powerfully to us as an archaeological relic of the Cold War.

THE COLD WAR OPENS THE DOOR TO FIND DEEP-WATER SHIPWRECKS

Robert Ballard has noted that during the Cold War, the US Navy sponsored missions to find their own lost warships as well as those of the Soviet Navy but "these efforts remain classified and far from the public view," driven by the need to deny the Soviets intelligence that could be gathered from our wrecks while learning all we could from theirs. Developing the capability to search for and find ships, aircraft, and weapons that had been lost in the ocean was one goal. Finding them was not the only goal; there was also recovery. Submersibles that could dive deep and tap into undersea communications cables, and undersea sound surveillance systems known as SOSUS extended the Cold War into the deepest depths of the ocean. Some aspects were well publicized, some of them as cover for other classified purposes. Others remained closely held secrets for a long time, and some remain so to this day.

Ballard's discovery of *Titanic* in 1985 came after a secret mission to map the scattered wreckage of the US nuclear submarine *Scorpion* in 3,505 meters of water off the Azores. The *Titanic* search, funded by the US Navy, was perfect cover when Ballard's team announced their discovery on September 1 of that year. The news of the discovery and the first images broadcast to the world captured global attention. To those of us in the maritime archaeological community, it was electrifying. It meant that given enough money and time (which the money would buy), the technology existed to find anything lost in the ocean, seemingly no matter the depth. From discovery, many of us felt, we could follow with accurate documentation and in time archaeological excavation and recovery.

Little did we know that then, in 1985, more discoveries than anyone ever knew had already been made. The world knew of some, like the hair-raising tale of the deep-water searches and recovery of a lost hydrogen bomb that fell into the Mediterranean in 1966 when a B52G bomber collided in midair with its KC-135 tanker while refueling. The bomb was found, after two and a half months, on a steep undersea slope in 777 meters of water. The submersible *Alvin* lost the bomb in the first attempt to raise it. *Alvin* relocated the bomb nearly 120 meters deeper. A subsequent attempt with the unmanned vehicle CURV-1 to attach a recovery line fouled CURV in the bomb's parachute, leading to a risky recovery in which CURV was raised too close to the surface with the bomb and the parachute. The story was widely reported because the world needed to know that all missing bombs were accounted for.

Other missions and other craft were less known, and only emerged into the public eye as the Cold War waned and then ended. The nuclear-powered oceanographic submarine NR-1, which the navy used for a variety of missions that still remain classified, also took scientists on dives that helped provide some measure of cover, albeit while doing serious work. But, as Robert Ballard has noted, even the basic features of NR-1 were classified, which "severely limited its usefulness to science." One unclassified mission was the mapping and recovery of parts of the space shuttle *Challenger* in 1986. NR-1 was also used for archaeological and shipwreck missions, notably by Ballard. Among his NR-1 missions was a slow survey of the maritime route plied by Roman ships between Carthage and Rome in 1995.

Public acknowledgment of the navy's "secret subs" for deep-sea work, long-rumored, emerged from Cold War secrecy in 1994 in a *New York Times* article by William J. Broad. Broad's article laid out the names of leading figures like the navy's John P. Craven, and early missions. Broad quoted Bob Ballard, saying that "the genie's out of the bag," not only in terms of no-longer-classified stories, but in terms of the navy itself opening the door to commercial applications, with more than 100 companies, he noted, then selling remotely operated vehicles capable of deep-sea work. Like a handful of other archaeological colleagues, I've been able to use those systems, now advanced beyond the 1980s and 1990s, to find and document lost warships, including some featured in this book.

USS *THRESHER*

The first of a new class of fast-attack submarines, USS *Thresher* was described by Vice Admiral E. W. Grenfell as the "result of the quantum technological advances coming from the technological revolution of the last decade" in what essentially was the US Navy's obituary for the sub and its crew. *Thresher* was, he said, "without question the most advanced operational attack submarine in the world...the fastest, deepest-diving, quietest and best-armed submarine ever delivered as an operating warship to any fleet."

■ Bow view of USS *Thresher* at sea, July 24, 1961 (Naval History and Heritage Command)

Two years into its shakedown after launching, *Thresher* sank, fresh out of a nine-month refit, on April 10, 1963, while undergoing sea tests 354 kilometers east of Boston. With *Thresher* went 129 crew under the command of Lt. Commander John W. Harvey. The loss of *Thresher* in some 2,598 meters of water meant that there was no chance of survival, but the navy wanted to know why the submarine had sunk.

The only initial clues were light floating debris on the surface, mostly plastic, and a few garbled messages to the surface ship monitoring the test dives. One was "minor difficulties, have positive up-angle, attempting to blow" the ballast tanks to bring *Thresher* to the surface, and four minutes later "exceeding test depths." Two minutes later came the muffled sounds of the sub's hull imploding under pressure. Surveys by the navy oceanographic research vessel USNS *Mizar* discovered the broken wreck near Corsair Canyon off Georges Bank. The navy's bathyscaphe *Trieste II* then dived, photographed wreckage for clues, and recovered small pieces of debris.

The 1964 mission, followed up by Robert Ballard in 1985, discovered that *Thresher* imploded after leaving the surface at about 478 meters, but perhaps deeper at 731 meters. *Thresher* disintegrated in a tenth of a second, leaving a trail of wreckage on the sea floor with big pieces lying in impact craters in the soft mud but lighter wreckage trailing off for over a kilometer. As to what went wrong, there were a few theories. One was that a brazed seam on a saltwater pipe failed, filling the engine room with high-pressure salt spray that shorted out electrical systems. The engines stopped, and as *Thresher* fell, freezing temperatures at depth clogged the ballast tanks with ice, making it impossible to blow them free and rise to the surface. Another theory is that an electrical bus failure in the engine room shut down the main coolant pumps that kept the reactor safe. It scrambled and shut down, leaving *Thresher* to fall beyond crush depth.

■ The crushed sonar dome of USS *Thresher*, photographed at the wreck site by the submersible *Alvin* (Naval History and Heritage Command)

Captain Joseph F. Yurso, who at the time of the loss was the shipyard watch officer at Portsmouth Naval Shipyard, where *Thresher* underwent its final maintenance prior to the cruise, reminisced in late 2017 about the loss and his trying to understand "the whys and wherefores of this terrible loss." He believed it was a joint failure. As an attack submarine, and at a time when missile submarines received top priority in the yard, *Thresher* did not get the proper attention or the best shipwrights. He pointed to the need to inspect all brazed seams on the saltwater pipes, which did not happen. There was a push to get the sub to sea, said Captain Yurso, and the Navy sent it out on trials after shock damage tests that were not followed up by a detailed inspection.

Whichever theory one chooses, what is clear is that the most advanced operational attack submarine in the world was lost through the failure of some of its simplest technology. In the aftermath of the loss, notes Captain Yurso, the Navy established its Submarine Safety (SubSafe) Program after *Thresher*'s loss, created a Submarine Safety Center, and learned from the loss. Today, notes Captain Yurso, submarines "are much improved and safer. The 129 men on *Thresher* did not die in vain."

USS *SCORPION*

The second US nuclear submarine lost during the Cold War sank five years after *Thresher*. After departing Rota, Spain, the *Skipjack*-class attack submarine USS *Scorpion*, under the command of Commander Francis Slattery, headed for the United States and its home port of Norfolk, Virginia. A classified message diverted *Scorpion* to an area near the Canary Islands, where a Soviet taskforce was operating in close proximity to a SOSUS array. After this diversion, *Scorpion* resumed its course to Norfolk. When it failed to arrive at Norfolk on May 27, the navy launched a search. SOSUS had picked up the sounds of *Scorpion* imploding and hitting the seabed. There have been unconfirmed stories that the navy launched a search for the sub within 24 hours of the loss, perhaps because SOSUS hydrophones recorded the death of *Scorpion* and the 99 men on board.

■ USS *Scorpion*, as seen from USS *Tallahatchie County* (AVB 2) outside of Naples, Italy, on April 10, 1968. (Naval History and Heritage Command)

Ultimately, in October, the USNS *Mizar*, veteran of the *Thresher* search, located the wreckage of *Scorpion* in 3,505 meters of water 240 nautical miles southwest of the Azores near the Mid-Atlantic Ridge by towing an underwater sled with a camera. The deep-diving submersible *Trieste II* then conducted dives and recovered material. There is not much detail, as much of the mission remains classified. Robert Ballard completed a detailed map of the wreck site on his secret mission to the site, but this has not been released, and only a series of individual images of *Scorpion* wreckage are in the public domain. As to the loss, the navy's Court of Inquiry blamed mechanical failure.

There has been much speculation, as well as misinformation regarding the loss of USS *Scorpion*. Theories of the accidental arming (known as a "hot run"), and detonation of one of the sub's torpedoes, the failure of a trash disposal unit (which would have flooded the hull), the loss of the propeller

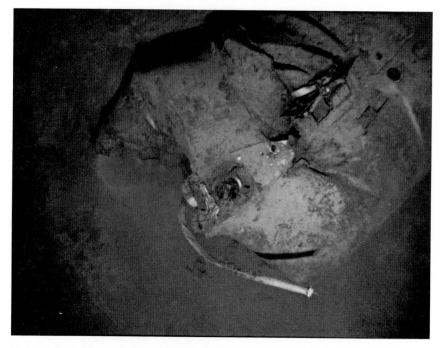

■ A portion of the periscope protrudes from the hull of the wreck of USS *Scorpion*, from images captured during the August 1986 secret mission to the wreck. (Naval History and Heritage Command)

shaft (leading to catastrophic flooding), the explosion of hydrogen gas leaking from a battery, or an outright attack by a trailing Soviet submarine have been proposed. In a time when conspiracy theories abound, one school of thought suggests that the Soviets sank *Scorpion* in retaliation for an ostensible US Navy sinking of the Soviet submarine K-129 in the Pacific.

In 2012, the US Submarine Veterans petitioned the navy to allow them to mount a privately funded assessment of the wreck in an effort to determine if the propeller shaft seals had indeed failed. The navy did not allow the mission to proceed.

The SOSUS recordings show that at 6:22 P.M. (Greenwich Time) on May 22, *Scorpion* had stopped, and then imploded somewhere around 457 to 609 meters down. One hundred eleven seconds later, *Scorpion*'s hull sections hit bottom in a rain of debris. Sub veterans believe that *Scorpion*, with a host of mechanical issues (so much so that a crewmember allegedly wrote home that they had started referring to their boat as "USS Scrap-Iron") flooded through a failure of propeller shaft seas, the valves that flooded the torpedo tubes. Flooding and unable to stop the leaks or surface, *Scorpion* began to fall, pressure building until the hull began to collapse and tear apart.

The navy returned to the wreck of *Scorpion*, and also *Thresher*, on several occasions, including Robert Ballard's mapping mission. The last "monitoring" mission was in 1998. The focus of the missions reportedly has been to determine if radiation is being released into the environment by the two subs' reactors, which apparently remain inside their containment vessels despite the break-up of both hulls. Another reason was to determine if *Scorpion*'s two nuclear-tipped Mark 45 ASTOR torpedoes with their 11-kiloton warheads remained intact. *Scorpion*'s bow, as shown in photographs released by the navy, is intact, and the navy notes the torpedoes are inside. While no archaeological work is planned for *Scorpion* or *Thresher*, both in their own way contributed to deep-sea archaeology, as the lessons learned in mapping their scattered wrecks guided Robert Ballard in his successful search for *Titanic*, and subsequently on a variety of other deep-wreck projects including some of World War II's most famous battle losses.

NUKES AT SEA: NUCLEAR-POWERED AND NUCLEAR ARMED

All told, seven nuclear submarines have been lost at sea, four of these during the Cold War. These were two US (USS *Thresher* and USS *Scorpion*) and five Soviet/Russian submarines (K-8, K-159, K-219, K-278 *Komsomolets*, *Kursk*, and K-429). Additionally, non-nuclear-powered submarines have also been lost, notably the Soviet Golf II-class boat K-129, which sank in 1968 with three nuclear weapons. One of the US submarines, *Scorpion*, also sank with nuclear weapons on board. None of these weapons, as far as is known, has not been recovered. What lies below in these lost warships are humanity's deadliest weapons, and with a half-life of a quarter million years for weapons-grade plutonium, as well as the nuclear cores of their reactors, the nuclear legacy of these Cold War–era submarines will likely be among the longest-lasting artifacts of human existence, as well as reminders of 20th-century war at sea.

Working from declassified US Defense Department documents released in February 2015, Robert Norris and Hans Kristensen found that the US Navy carried thousands of nuclear weapons to sea from 1954 to 1991, starting with 91 in 1954, growing to 1,516 in 1960, 3,826 in 1970, and a peak of 6,191 warheads in 1975—a total that represented 23 percent of the US nuclear arsenal. After that, the numbers dropped to an average of some 5,000 weapons per year, or 20 percent of the nation's nuclear stockpile. These included nuclear ballistic missiles, torpedoes, aircraft carrier–delivered bombs, and shells—including the once top-secret "Katie" W23 atomic shell for *Iowa*-class battleships' 16-inch guns. Each Katie shell reportedly had the same yield as the bomb dropped on Hiroshima. Since 1991, when President George H. W. Bush ordered the removal of tactical nuclear weapons from naval ships, only strategic missiles on submarines have gone to sea.

While the information remains classified, Norris and Kristensen estimate that the number of warheads increased to 33 percent of the total arsenal, and, as of 2015, it stood at about 22 percent, meaning thousands of warheads remain out there just on American submarines alone. The number of warheads put to sea by the Soviets and later the Russians is less known, but Norris and Kristensen estimate that as of 2017, some 768 warheads are in Russia's submarine missile arsenal.

K-129

The Soviet diesel-electric ballistic missile submarine K-129 was lost while on patrol in the North Pacific in March 1968 some 1,600 miles northwest of Pearl Harbor. When the submarine failed to make two radio check-in reports, and did not respond to open calls from Soviet naval authorities, the Soviets launched a large air-sea search that failed to find any trace of K-129. It had vanished with 98 crew and three R-21 nuclear missiles, each of them capable of an 800-kiloton burst and a several-hundred-mile range. That's the same as 800,000 tons of TNT. The detonation of one of these bombs would have created a mile-wide fireball 4,000 times hotter than the sun, even underwater, and 1,200-kilometer-per-hour blast wave that would lay waste to more than 259 square kilometers in a resulting firestorm, according to Stanford University emeritus scientist Lynne Eden, whose compelling book *Whole World on Fire*, without embellishment, lays out what nuclear weapons would do in real-life settings.

SOSUS technicians heard the loss of K-129, and analysis of the acoustic signal, which was picked up by several Pacific arrays, allowed intelligence experts to pinpoint a general location of the loss, which was more than the Soviets had. I had the privilege of hearing this story firsthand from retired navy commander Edward Ettner, whose team did the analysis. I met Commander Ettner while conducting a robotic deep dive on the wreck of his Cold War command, the submarine *Bugara*.

In August 1968, the navy's deep-water survey submarine USS *Halibut* located the wreck of K-129 in 4,876 meters feet of water and allegedly did a very complete photographic survey of it. While crushed, key areas of K-129 were more or less "intact," at least enough for the navy to realize that the missiles, as well as codes and other material greatly desired by the United States, remained on board. That led to a CIA-organized effort, Project Azorian, which used Howard Hughes's *Glomar Explorer* to raise some—if not all, according to some accounts—of K-129. Most of the details of Azorian remain classified; it was a "heavy lift" operation that used a grapnel to retrieve some, or all, of the submarine. With them came six bodies of K-129 crewmembers, which the CIA reburied at sea in a formal, respectful ceremony.

The subject of K-129 remains a source of much speculation, contention, and some controversy. It has been suggested in popular forums that a collision with a US submarine sank it, that it was deliberately sunk by a fail-safe when a rogue crew attempted to launch a nuclear strike on Pearl Harbor, or a mechanical failure. Perhaps most controversial is another publicly discussed theory that in response to what they saw as the US Navy's complicity in sinking K-129, the Soviets lured and sank the US Navy submarine *Scorpion*. They further argue that both countries agreed to cover up the incidents. Other arguments swirl over how much was recovered, with some stating only the forward portion was raised, with *Glomar Explorer* losing the command and missile compartment areas and all the valuable intelligence they held.

K-129's saga, and even the exact location of the wreck, remain a closely guarded secret, and unless there is a declassification of the CIA's files, the world will never know the complete story. Having worked on Cold War naval sites, I would argue here that in order for the story to be known in as complete a fashion as we can, a project that merges the classified historical record, an archaeological survey, and a forensic naval architectural study needs to be done. Given the recent nature of the Cold War, and the fact that families of the lost are still alive, such a project might not take place for decades, and perhaps longer. Given the conditions of deep-sea wrecks, I am sure that even a 22nd-century archaeological study of K-129 would rewrite the history books.

For now, the archaeology of war at sea is confined solely to the dawn of the atomic age, and the wrecks associated with Operation Crossroads at Bikini Atoll. Anything after that is too soon, still classified, ever sensitive, and as we appear to be entering a new Cold War, perhaps the most important thing we can do is assess the past. The record of our achievements must be measured by the scale of their cost. Resting in the depths, and spanning more than a millennium, the lost warships and their crews speak to many things including service and sacrifice. They also offer a grim sum of the costs of war. As stated at the start, the sea is our greatest battlefield, and our largest cemetery. As we use archaeology to try to understand the past, we confront more than sites, ships, and technologies from those times. We confront the human face and the costs of our conflict-driven nature.

GLOSSARY

Aft: Toward and at the rear of a ship. In naval and nautical use, it is an adverb (to go aft) as well as an adjective (the aft cabin).

Aground: When a vessel is resting hard on the land at the bottom of a body of water and in contact with it.

Aircraft carrier: A major surface vessel whose primary weapons are aircraft.

All hands: Everyone on board a ship.

Aloft: Up high, as high up on a mast; when sailors went aloft in the days of sail, they were climbing up a mast.

Armor: Iron or steel used to protect a ship against projectiles.

Astern: Toward the back, or the aft end of a ship. It also can mean when a vessel is following, or is moored behind another ship.

Atoll: A ring-shaped coral reef, usually associated with low-lying sand islands, with a lagoon in the center.

AUV: An Autonomous Underwater Vehicle is an untethered (not connected to a ship or another system) vehicle used in underwater survey. AUVs (also known as UUVs in the military) are battery powered and can carry a variety of systems such as sensors, cameras, and sonar.

Ballast: Weight added inside a hull to stabilize a ship; in earlier times, ballast was usually stone or gravel. Military ships of the 18th and 19th centuries carried iron pigs known as kentledge as ballast. In modern vessels, water and fuel stowed in tanks are also used as ballast.

Ballista: A catapult used to hurl stones; also used to fire a large crossbolt.

Barbette: A circular or semi-circular track on which a gun carriage can rotate while firing.

Bark (Barque): A three-masted ship with the first two masts square-rigged, and the foremast fore-and-aft rigged.

Barkentine (Barquentine): A three-masted ship with the first mast square-rigged and the aft two masts fore-and-aft rigged.

Battery: The main armament of a ship of war, usually its main and secondary guns, each classified by their caliber or weight. The main battery, therefore, would be the same type of gun, as in 32-pdr. guns in older ships, or 16-inch guns on a World War II battleship.

Battle group: A main offensive unit of a fleet.

Beam: The extreme width of a ship.

Berth: Both an anchorage or mooring place as well as where a sailor sleeps.

Bilge(s): The inside bottom of a ship.

Bireme(s): Two-decked rowed warships of antiquity.

Blockade: A naval action that bars other ships from entering certain ports or ocean areas.

Boat: A small craft capable of being hoisted and carried on board a ship.

Boom: A horizontal spar hinged at the forward end of a mast.

Bosun: The boatswain (pronounced and now often spelled *bosun*) is a warrant officer whose duties are related to the deck and boat seamanship.

Breech: The end of a gun opposite of the muzzle.

Breech-loading (also see *muzzle loading*): A gun loaded from the aft or breech end.

Bridge: Usually an elevated portion of a ship dedicated to the command and control of the vessel.

Brig: A two-masted square-rigged vessel.

Brigantine: A two-masted vessel with the fore mast square-rigged and the aft mast fore-and-aft rigged.

Bulkhead: A wall or partition inside a ship.

Bulwark: A section of a ship's side carried up beyond the main deck to protect the decks from heavy weather.

Cabin: Quarters on board a ship for officers.

Caliber: The diameter of a gun's bore measured in inches or centimeters.

Caravel: A small, fast Iberian ship of the 15th and 16th centuries with a high stern castle and a gently sloping bow.

Carley float: An invertible, life raft made of an oval copper or steel tube covered with kapok and waterproof, painted canvas, it was the standard type used by warships through World War II.

Carrack: A large, three- to four-masted sailing ship commonly used by European powers in the 15th through 16th centuries as both merchant vessels and warships.

Carriage: The part of a gun that supports the gun itself.

Carvel: In wooden shipbuilding, planks laid on hull with the edges abutting one another to make a smooth side.

Casemate: An armored enclosure on a ship for a gun or guns.

Ceiling: Planking inside a ship's hull.

Clinker: Both partially burned coal and in wooden shipbuilding, a term used to describe planks laid on a hull with overlapping edges.

Clipper: A fast sailing ship of the 19th century.

Cofferdam: A waterproof compartment or walled area.

Cog: An early ship with a round shape, developed in the 10th century and the common European ship of medieval times.

Collier: A ship that carries coal; usually this is a purpose-built vessel.

Concretion: A solid mass that forms around metal objects and artifacts, composed of corrosion byproducts and the surrounding sand or silt.

Conning tower: An armored control station on a ship as well as the command-and-control compartment on World War II submarines.

Conservator: A scientist trained in the treatment of artifacts to stabilize, stop ongoing corrosion within, and restore artifacts.

Convoy: A group of merchant ships escorted by naval ships and also by aircraft in modern times.

Cordage: Rope and line of all kinds on board a ship.

Davit: A fixed or movable crane on the side of a ship used to raise and lower boats.

Dead in the water: A vessel that has completely stopped and is not maneuvering, as opposed to a vessel tied up to a pier or anchored.

Deadlight: A hinged metal cover for a port; also a heavy glass set flush with a deck to let light in below.

Displacement: The weight of water displaced by a ship and the standard means of expressing the size of a warship.

Draft: The depth of a ship below the waterline.

Editor: An indispensable guide and friend to authors.

Fathom: A maritime measure of depth equivalent to six feet.

Fighting Top: A platform on a mast where marines and sailors took position with muskets during close ship-to-ship actions.

Flagship: A ship from an admiral or other commander that controls the actions of a squadron, flotilla, or a fleet.

Fleet: An organization of ships in the past; in modern times a fleet encompasses air and shore-side services and units.

Flotilla: A group of ships consisting of two or more squadrons commanded by a flagship.

Fore: The front or forward end of a ship.

Forecastle: The forward section of a ship's hull; the term originated with elevated wooden fighting stages, hence a "castle" with another aft, thus the "stern castle." The term later came to mean an area forward where the crew berthed and ate.

Frame: A structural element that forms the hull; known colloquially as a ship's "rib." On more modern naval vessels, frames are numbered, running fore and aft, to assist in designating positions for damage and damage control.

Frigate: A sailing warship with a single gun deck as well as on the forecastle and poop deck; that is, with two decks carrying guns. Modern frigates are warships smaller and slower than destroyers.

Galley: The area of a ship where meals are prepared; in ancient to Renaissance times, the term for rowed (oared) warships.

General quarters: The call for all hands to go to their battle stations.

Gig: A ship's boat designated for the use of the commanding officer.

Grapnel or **Grappling iron**: A small, four-armed anchor used in the days of sailing warships to snag onto and fasten alongside another vessel; also used to drag and recover objects in the water.

Gunport: An aperture or hole cut through a hull or superstructure through which guns would project and fire.

Gunwale: The upper edge of a boat's side.

Halbard: A hand weapon that was a combination of a spear and a battle ax.

Hatch: An aperture cut through the deck of a ship for access. They are sealed by hatch covers.

Hawsepipe(s): Apertures where the anchor chain or cable runs from the ship to the anchors.

Helm: The steering position on a ship. The helmsman steers the ship from the helm.

Hoist: To raise aloft, as in hoisting a flag.

Hulk: In modern times a worn-out, stripped vessel. In medieval times, a hulk or hulc was a specific type of ship.

Hydrophones: Underwater microphones.

IFF: "Identification, Friend or Foe" is a term that describes an electronic system that allows ships and aircraft to exchange identification.

Inboard: Toward the center of a ship.

Jackstaff: A flagpole at the bow of a ship.

Jettison: To throw something over the side of a ship.

Keel: The central beam or timber on a ship that forms its backbone.

Keelson: A longitudinal beam or timber bolted on top of a keel to form additional support for the hull.

Kentledge: Cast-iron pigs of the 18th and 19th centuries employed as a more permanent ballast.

Kiloton: An explosion equal to the detonation of a thousand tons of TNT. Early nuclear detonations were measured in kilotons.

Knees: Curved timbers, later iron and steel structural members, used to support deck beams and to reinforce the edges of hatches.

Knot: Both a knob in a line or rope, or the nautical unit of speed, equivalent to one nautical mile (6.076 feet) per hour.

Ladders: A sailor's term for stairways on a ship.

Langrage: Shot used to destroy sails, rigging, and enemy personnel. Composed of metal junk—chain links, nails, small shot—it was deadly and effective.

League: A now rare measurement of distance at sea measured at three nautical miles.

Lee: The direction away from the wind.

Magazine: A compartment on board a ship and ashore specially fitted to store ammunition.

Mainmast: The second mast of a ship with two or more masts, aft of the foremast and forward of the mizzenmast.

Mangonel: A medieval catapult used to hurl heavy stones.

Man-of-war: A warship.

Marines: An elite, sea-going soldier corps assigned to ships and also used in shore actions.

Mark (MK): A term used to identify a specific type of weapon, followed by a Model (MOD) number, such as "Torpedo MK46, MOD 1."

Megaton: A very high-yield nuclear explosion equivalent to the detonation of a million tons of TNT.

Mess: To eat on board ship, also where the crew gathers to eat; that is, the crew's mess.

Mess Decks: Where the crew dines on board ship in modern (20th- and 21st-century) times.

Mine: A submerged charge set to detonate against or beneath a ship. Originally known as torpedoes, the term was transferred when the "automobile," or "maneuverable torpedo," came into use.

Moor: To secure alongside a pier.

Mount: A system of gun-supporting parts that include mechanisms to elevate and train a weapon and to deal with recoil and counter-recoil.

Muster roll: A list of all crew aboard a ship; when the crew musters, they assemble for roll call. When a sailor leaves a ship, they are mustered out.

Mutiny: A crime committed against the constituted authority on a ship, which traditionally is expressed as refusal to do duty, and, at the extreme, an armed seizure of a vessel.

Muzzle-loading: A gun that loads from the front of the barrel as opposed to a breech-loading weapon.

Nautical mile: A measurement of distance at sea measured at a one-minute arc of the great circle of the earth, or 6,076 feet (1,851 meters). A statute mile is 5,280 feet (1,609 meters).

Navigation: The means by which, using a variety of methods, sailors take a ship or aircraft from one position to another.

Oarlock: A device that holds oars in place on a boat when it is being pulled (rowed). Also known as rowlock.

Octant: An obsolete navigational device replaced by the sextant that measured the angular distance between two objects, usually the horizon and a celestial body (stars or the sun).

Ordinary: A ship in ordinary was not in commission but was standing by in a navy yard and maintained by a skeleton crew.

Orlop Deck: A partial deck below the lowest deck in a ship.

Outboard: Any distance away from the center line of a ship and the opposite of inboard.

Outrigger: A counter-balancing spar or float rigged to one side of a canoe or boat to prevent it from capsizing.

Passageway: A corridor or hallway in a ship.

Petty officer: A noncommissioned officer on board a naval vessel, also known in later times as chiefs. They run most navies.

Pinnace: A large double-banked (oared) boat used as a tender for naval and merchant vessels. Also used as a term for single-decked, square-stern warships and vessels employed by early explorers in the 16th through 20th centuries.

Polyreme(s): Multi-decked rowed warships of antiquity.

Pontoons: Floating, watertight structures fastened together to float something, such as a bridge.

Poop: The aft deck on a ship and the command position on ships in the days of sail and early steam.

Port: The left side of the ship and anything in that direction; that is, "ship off the port bow."

Pressure hull: The central core of a submarine; it is pressure-resistant and houses the machinery, crew, and weapons.

Projectile: A missile fired by a gun.

Q-ship: A disguised man-of-war generally used to attack an enemy's commercial shipping, but also used during World War I to lure submarines into close range.

Quadrireme(s): Four-decked rowed warships of antiquity.

Quarter: The aft end of a ship near the stern; there is a port and starboard quarter.

Quarterdeck: A ceremonial area on the main deck, commanded by the officer of the deck when a vessel is docked or moored as it is where personnel and guests come aboard.

Quinquereme(s): Five-decked rowed warships of antiquity.

RADAR: The acronym for "radio detection and ranging."

Rail: An open fence on a ship made of pipe or other immovable materials.

Recoil: The force of a gun driven back when it is fired.

Rigging: The lines, in the past cordage, and later wires, used to support and manage the masts, yards, and sails, as well as funnels and other structures above deck. Standing rigging is more or less permanently fixed, while running rigging is adjustable, as in the lines used to sail.

ROV: A Remotely Operated Vehicle, or ROV, is a pressure-resistant robot, connected to a ship by a cable, which can carry a variety of instruments into the deep on missions.

Rowlock: See "Oarlock."

Sailor: A person who has spent time at sea who is accustomed to ways of the sea and ships. It is a term to be earned.

Schooner: A two- or more masted vessel rigged fore-and-aft.

Screw: Another term for a propeller.

Scuppers: Fittings on deck that act as troughs and feed water on deck to scupper pipes that allow the water to drain off the deck.

Ship of the Line: A battleship in the days of sail.

Sloop: A single-masted, fore-and-aft rigged vessel.

Sloop-of-War: A warship from the days of sail and steam mounting its main battery on a single deck.

Spar: A long, round stick of wood, iron, or steel; spars were employed as yards or booms on ships.

Squadron: A naval division consisting of two or more divisions of ships.

Stack: A pipe extending from the main deck to exhaust smoke and gas. On merchant ships, they are also called funnels.

Starboard: The right side of a ship and a direction; that is, "torpedo off the starboard quarter!"

Stern: The aftermost section of a ship.

Superstructure: All structure above the main deck of a ship.

Telepresence: The means by which, using an ROV and satellite broadcast, exploration is shared with a live audience ashore.

Thwarts: Cross seats or planks in a boat below the gunwale. Oarsmen sat on thwarts to propel the boat.

Transom: Planks or metal plates that form the upper part of the stern of a ship. The name of a ship can usually be found on the transom.

Treenail (Trunnel): A wooden fastener used in ship construction.

Trials: Tests of a ship after it is launched.

Trireme(s): Three-decked rowed warships of antiquity.

Turbine: A multi-bladed rotor in an engine, driven by steam or hot air, which in turn drives a propeller or a compressor.

Turret: An armored enclosure on a deck that protects the heavy guns of a man-of-war.

'Tween deck: Any deck in a ship below the main deck.

Van: The forward part of a formation of ships.

Vessel: Any craft that carries people or goods by water.

Warrant officer: An officer senior to all petty officers.

Watch: A seagoing period of duty, normally four hours long.

Waterline: The line to which a vessel settles in the water, and designated by a painted line on the hull that indicates when a vessel is properly trimmed and not listing or sinking.

Weather deck: The topmost deck of a ship, and the one exposed to weather, hence the name.

Windlass: A mechanism used to handle the anchor chain.

Wire rope: Rope made of wire strands twisted together.

Yard: A spar attached to the middle of a mast and used to carry sail.

Yardarm: The end of a yard.

Sources

De Kerchove, René. *International Maritime Dictionary*, 2nd ed. (New York: Van Nostrand Reinhold Company, 1961).

Noel, John V., Jr., and Edward L. Beach. *Naval Terms Dictionary*, 5th ed. (Annapolis, MD: Naval Institute Press, 1988).

BIBLIOGRAPHY

A separate book could be filled with a bibliography of books on warships, naval war and articles from various archaeological journals and dive magazines about surveys and excavations of warship wrecks. Listed below are the sources that I have read and consulted in the preparation of this book. In addition, a number of web sites were very helpful, particularly those for museums and archaeological sites and projects.

Books
Ahlberg, Gudrun. *Fighting on Land and Sea in Greek Geometric Art.* Athens: Svenska Institut, 1971.

Ahlstrom, Christian. *Looking for Leads: Shipwrecks of the Past Revealed by Contemporary Documents and the Archaeological Record.* Helsinki: The Finnish Academy of Science and Letters, 1997.

Akerlund, Harald. *Nydamskeppen: En Studie Tidig Skandinavisk Skeppsbyggnadskonst.* Goteborg: Elanders Boktryckeri Aktiebolag, 1963.

ARKA. *Informe de Peritaje Arqueológico Subacuático Monumento Histórico Corbeta Esmeralda.* Valparaíso: ARKA—Arqueología Marítima, 2013.

Atauz, Ayse Devrim. *Eight Thousand Years of Maltese Maritime History: Trade, Piracy and Naval Warfare.* Gainesville: University Press of Florida, 2008.

Bailey, Dan E. *World War II Wrecks of Palau.* Redding, CA: North Valley Diver Publications, 1991.

———. *World War II Wrecks of the Truk Lagoon.* Redding, CA: North Valley Diver Publications, 2000.

———. *WWII Wrecks of the Kwajalein and Truk Lagoons.* Redding, CA: North Valley Diver Publications, 1989.

Ballard, Robert D., ed. *Archaeological Oceanography.* Princeton and Oxford: Princeton University Press, 2008.

Ballard, Robert D., and Rick Archbold. *The Discovery of the Bismarck.* New York: Madison Press, 1990.

Ballard, Robert D., and Rick Archbold. *The Lost Ships of Guadalcanal.* New York: Madison Press, 1993.

Ballard, Robert D., and Rick Archbold. *Return to Midway.* Washington, DC and Toronto: National Geographic Books/Madison Press, 1999.

Barnes, Gina L. *The Rise of Civilization in East Asia: The Archaeology of China, Korea and Japan.* London: Thames and Hudson, 1999.

Bass, George F., ed. *A History of Seafaring Based on Underwater Archaeology*. New York: Walker and Company, 1972.

Bass, George F., ed. *Ships and Shipwrecks of the Americas*. London and New York: Thames and Hudson, 1988.

Bearss, Edwin C. *Hardluck Ironclad: The Sinking and Salvage of the Cairo*. Revised edition. Baton Rouge: Louisiana University Press, 1980.

Beeching, Jack. *The Galleys at Lepanto*. London: Hutchinson & Company, 1982.

Beltrame, Carlo, and Renato Gianni Ridella, eds. *Ships and Guns: The Sea Ordnance in Venicle and in Europe between the 15th and the 17th Centuries*. Oxford: Oxbow Books, 2011.

Bender, James. *Dutch Warships in the Age of Sail, 1600–1714: Design, Construction, Careers and Fates*. Barnsley, Yorkshire: Seaforth Publishing, 2014.

Blow, Michael. *A Ship to Remember: The Maine and the Spanish-American War*. New York: William Morrow & Co., 1992.

Bound, Mensun, ed. *The Archaeology of Ships of War*. Oswestry, Shropshire, England: Anthony Nelson Ltd., 1995.

———, ed. *Excavating Ships of War*. Oswestry, Shropshire, England: Anthony Nelson Ltd., 1998.

Bound, Mensun. *Lost Ships: The Discovery and Exploration of the Ocean's Sunken Treasures*. New York: Simon & Schuster, 1998.

Bratten, John R. *The Gondola Philadelphia and the Battle of Lake Champlain*. College Station: Texas A&M University Press, 2002.

Broadwater, John D. *USS Monitor: A Historic Ship Completes Its Final Voyage*. College Station: Texas A&M University Press, 2012.

Brogger, A. W., and Haakon Shetelig. *The Viking Ships*. Oslo: Dreyers Forlag, 1971.

Brown, David. *Warship Losses of World War II*. London: Arms and Armour Press, 1990.

Bruce, Anthony, and William Cogar. *An Encyclopedia of Naval History*. New York: Checkmark Books, 1999.

Bruseth, James E., Amy A. Borgens, Bradford M. Jones, and Eric D. Ray. *LaBelle: The Archaeology of a Seventeenth Century Ship of New World Colonization*. College Station: Texas A&M University Press, 2017.

Bruseth, James E., and Toni S. Turner. *From a Watery Grave: The Discovery and Excavation of La Salle's Shipwreck, La Belle*. College Station: Texas A&M University Press, 2005.

Cain, Emily. *Ghost Ships: Hamilton and Scourge, Historical Treasures from the War of 1812*. New York and Toronto: Olympic Marketing Company, 1983.

Capponi, Niccolò. *Victory of the West: The Great Christian-Muslim Clash at the Battle of Lepanto*. Cambridge: Da Capo Press, 2007.

Casson, Lionel. *The Ancient Mariners: Seafarers and Seafighters of the Mediterranean in Ancient Times*. Princeton, NJ: Princeton University Press, 1991.

Casson, Lionel. *Ships and Seafaring in Ancient Times*. London: British Museum Press, 1994.

Casson, Lionel, and J. Richard Steffy. *The Athlit Ram*. College Station: Texas A&M University Press, 1991.

Cederlund, Carl Olof, and Frederick M. Hocker. *Vasa 1: The Archaeology of a Swedish Royal Ship of 1628*. Stockholm: Vasamuseet, 2006.

Compton-Hall, Richard. *The Submarine Pioneers*. Phoenix Mill, Gloucestershire: Sutton Publishing Ltd., 1999.

Crisman, Kevin, ed. *Coffins of the Brave: Lake Shipwrecks of the War of 1812*. College Station: Texas A&M University Press, 2014.

———. *The Eagle: An American Brig on Lake Champlain during the War of 1812*. Annapolis, MD and Shelburne, VT: Naval Institute Press, 1987.

Crumlin-Pedersen, Ole. *Viking Age Ships and Shipbuilding in Hedeby/Haithabu and Schleswig*. Shleswig & Roskilde: The Viking Ship Museum, 1997.

Crumlin-Pedersen, Ole, and Olaf Olsen. *The Skuldelev Ships I: Topography, Archaeology, History, Conservation and Display*. Roskilde: Vikingskibmuseeet, 2002.

Cussler, Clive, and Craig Dirgo. *The Sea Hunters: True Adventures with Famous Shipwrecks*. New York: Simon & Schuster, 1996.

De Bassi, Parker, Maria Teresa. *Kreuzer Dresden: Odyssee ohne Wiederkehr*. Herford: Koehlers Verlagsgesellschaft mbH, 1993.

Delgado, James P. *Encyclopedia of Underwater and Maritime Archaeology*. New Haven and London: Yale University Press, 1998.

———. *Ghost Fleet: The Sunken Ships of Bikini Atoll*. Honolulu: University of Hawaii Press, 1996.

———. *Khubilai Khan's Lost Fleet: In Search of a Legendary Armada*. Berkeley and Los Angeles: University of California Press, 2009.

———. *Lost Warships: An Archaeological Tour of War at Sea*. Vancouver and Toronto: Douglas and McIntyre/New York: Facts on File/London: Conway Maritime Press, 2001.

———. *Misadventures of a Civil War Submarine: Iron, Guns and Pearls*. College Station: Texas A&M University Press, 2012.

———. *Nuclear Dawn: The Atomic Bomb from the Manhattan Project to the Cold War*. Oxford and New York: Osprey Publishing, 2009.

———. *Silent Killers: The History and Archaeology of the Submarine*. Oxford and New York: Osprey Publishing, 2011.

Delgado, James P., Tomás Mendizábal, Frederick H. Hanselmann, and Dominique Rissolo. *The Maritime Landscape of the Isthmus of Panamá*. Gainesville: University Press of Florida, 2016.

Delgado, James P., Terry Kerby, Steven Price, Hans K. Van Tilburg, and Russell Matthews. *The Lost Submarines of Pearl Harbor*. College Station: Texas A&M University Press, 2016.

Doubleday, Russell. *A Gunner aboard the "Yankee": From the Diary of Number Five of the After Port Gun*. New York: Doubleday & McClure Company, 1898.

Doumas, Christos. *The Wall-Paintings of Thera*. Athens: The Thera Foundation—Petros M. Nomikos, 1992.

Dubbs, Chris. *America's U-Boats: Terror Trophies of World War I*. Lincoln and London: University of Nebraska Press, 2014.

Dunmore, Spencer. *Lost Subs: From the Hunley to the Kursk, The Greatest Submarines Ever Lost*. Cambridge: Da Capo Press, 2002.

During, E. *De Dog På Vasa: Skelettfynden Och Vad de Berättar*. Stockholm: Vasamuseet, 1994.

Eden, Lynne. *Whole World on Fire: Organizations, Knowledge, and Nuclear Weapons Devastation*. Ithaca: Cornell University Press, 2004.

Elkin, Dolores, Cristian Murray, Ricardo Bastida, and Mónica Grosso. *El Naufragio de la HMS Swift, 1770: Arquelogía Marítíma en la Patagonia*. Buenos Aires: Vazquez Mazzini, 2011.

Forward, Laura, and Ellen Blue Phillips. *Napoleon's Lost Fleet: Bonaparte, Nelson and the Battle of the Nile*. New York: Roundtable Press, Inc., 1999.

Franke, Herbert, and Denis Twitchett, eds. *The Cambridge History of China*. Vol. 6 of *Alien Regimes and Border States, 907–1368*. Cambridge: Cambridge University Press, 1994.

Friel, Ian. *The Good Ship: Ships, Shipbuilding and Technology in England, 1200–1520*. Baltimore: Johns Hopkins University Press, 1995.

Gardiner, Julie, ed. *Before the Mast: Life and Death aboard the Mary Rose*. Portsmouth: Mary Rose Trust, 2005.

Gardiner, Leslie. *The Eagle Spreads Its Claws: A History of the Corfu Channel Incident and of Albania's Relations with the West, 1945–1966*. Edinburgh: William Blackwood, 1966.

Gardiner, Robert, ed. *The Line of Battle: The Sailing Warship, 1650–1840*. London: Conway Maritime Press, 1992.

Geoghagen, John J. *Operation Storm: Japan's Top Secret Submarines and Its Plan to Change the Course of World War II*. New York: Broadway Books, 2013.

George, James L. *History of Warships: From Ancient Times to the Twenty-First Century*. Annapolis, MD: Naval Institute Press, 1998.

George, S. G. *Jutland to Junkyard*. Edinburgh: Birlinn Ltd., 1999.

Gesner, Peter. *Pandora: An Archaeological Perspective*. Queensland, South Brisbane: Queensland Museum, 1991.

Glete, Jan. *Warfare at Sea, 1500–1650: Maritime Conflicts and the Transformation of Europe*. New York: Routledge, 2000.

Gould, Richard A. *Archaeology and the Social History of Ships*. Cambridge: Cambridge University Press, 2000.

———, ed. *Shipwreck Anthropology*. Albuquerque: University of New Mexico Press/ School of American Research, 1983.

Greenhill, Basil, and John Morrison. *The Archaeology of Boats and Ships: An Introduction*. London: Conway Maritime Press, 1995.

Griffith, Paddy. *The Viking Art of War*. London: Greenhill Books, 1998.

Guilmartin, John F. *Galleons and Galleys*. London: Cassell, 2002.

Guilmartin, John F. *Gunpowder and Galleys: Changing Technology and Mediterranean Warfare at Sea in the Sixteenth Century*. Cambridge: Cambridge University Press, 1974.

Hale, John R. *Lords of the Sea: The Epic Story of the Athenian Navy and the Birth of Democracy*. New York: Viking, 2009.

Harding, Richard. *Seapower and Naval Warfare: 1650–1830*. London: UCL Press, Ltd., 1999.

Haywood, John. *Dark Age Naval Power: A Reassessment of Frankish and Anglo-Saxon Seafaring Activity*. 2nd ed. Norfolk, England: Anglo-Saxon Books, 1999.

Head, David. *Privateers of the Americas: Spanish American Privateering from the United States in the Early Republic*. Athens and London: University of Georgia Press, 2015.

Herodotus. *The Histories*. Translated by Aubrey de Selincourt. Revised by John A. Marincola. London: Penguin Books, 1996.

Hien, Le Nang. *Three Victories on the Bạch Đằng River*. Hanoi: Nha xuat ban Van hoa-thong tin, 2003.

Hildred, Alexandra, ed. *Weapons of Warre: The Armaments of Mary Rose*. 2 vols. Portsmouth: David K. Brown Book Company, 2011.

Hill, Richard. *War at Sea in the Ironclad Age*. London: Cassel, 2000.

Hobson, Richmond Pearson. *The Sinking of the "Merrimac": A Personal Narrative*. New York: Century Company, 1899.

Hurst, Henry R. *The Circular Harbour, North Side: The Site and Finds Other Than Pottery*. Vol. 2, 1 of *Excavations at Carthage: The British Mission*. Oxford: British Academy and Oxford University, 1994.

Hutchinson, Gillian. *Medieval Ships and Shipping*. London: Leicester University Press, 1994.

Ireland, Bernard. *War at Sea, 1914–45*. London: Cassell, 2002.

Jane, Frederick T. *The Imperial Russian Navy: Its Past, Present and Future*. London: W. Thacker & Co., 1899.

Jasper, Joy, James P. Delgado, and Jim Adams. *USS Arizona: Ship and Symbol*. New York: St. Martin's Press, 2001.

Johnstone, Paul. *The Sea-Craft of Prehistory*. London and Henley: Routledge & Kegan Paul Ltd., 1980.

Jones, Mark. *For Future Generations: Conservation of a Tudor Maritime Collection*. Portsmouth: The Mary Rose Trust, 2003.

Jourdan, David W. *The Search for the Japanese Fleet: USS Nautilus and the Battle of Midway*. Lincoln, NE: Potomac Books, 2015.

Keatts, Henry C., and George C. Farr. *U-Boats*. Vol. 3 of *Dive into History*. Houston: Pisces Books, 1994.

———. *Warships*. Vol. 1 of *Dive into History*. Houston: Pisces Books, 1990.

Keegan, John. *Battle at Sea: From Man-of-War to Submarine*. London: Pimlico, 1993.

Kemp, Paul. *The Admiralty Regrets: British Warship Losses of the 20th Century*. Phoenix Mill: Sutton Publishing Ltd., 1999.

Kierman, Frank A., Jr., and John K. Fairbank. *Chinese Ways in Warfare*. Cambridge, MA: Harvard University Press, 1974.

Kimura, Jun. *Archaeology of East Asian Shipbuilding*. Gainesville: University Press of Florida, 2016.

Kirsch, Peter. *The Galleon: The Great Ships of the Armada Era*. Annapolis, MD: Naval Institute Press, 1990.

Kocabaş, Ufuk, ed. *Yenikapı Shipwrecks: The "Old Ships" of the "New Gate"* (Yenikapı Batıkları). Istanbul: Yenikapı'nın Eski Gemileri, 2008.

Kolay, Selçuk, Okan Taktak, and Savas Karakas. *Echoes from the Deep: Wrecks of the Dardanelles Campaign*. Istanbul: Vehbu Koc Foundation—Ayhan Sahenk Foundation, 2013.

Kvarning, Lars-Ake, and Bengt Ohrelius. *The Vasa: The Royal Ship*. Translated by Joan Tate. Stockholm: Bokforlaget Atlantis, 1998.

Lavery, Brian. *The Arming and Fitting of English Ships of War, 1600–1815*. Annapolis, MD: Naval Institute Press, 1987.

———, ed. *Line of Battle: The Sailing Warship, 1650–1840*. London: Conway Maritime Press, 1992.

———. *The Royal Navy's First Invincible*. Portsmouth: Invincible Conservations, 1988.

———. *The Ship of the Line*. 2 vols. London: Conway Maritime Press, 1983.

Leeke, Jim. *Manila and Santiago: The New Steel Navy in the Spanish American War*. Annapolis, MD: Naval Institute Pres, 2009.

Leggett, Eric. *The Corfu Channel Incident*. London: New English Library, 1976.

Lenihan, Daniel J., ed. *USS Arizona Memorial and Pearl Harbor National Historic Landmark: Submerged Cultural Resources Assessment*. Santa Fe: National Park Service, 1989.

Levathes, Louise. *When China Ruled the Seas: The Treasure Fleet of the Dragon Throne, 1405–1433*. New York: Simon & Schuster, 1994.

Lewis, Archibald R. *Naval Power and Trade in the Mediterranean, A.D. 500–1100*. Princeton, NJ: Princeton University Press, 1951.

Lewis, Archibald R., and Timothy J. Runyan. *European Naval and Maritime History, 300–1500*. Bloomington: Indiana University Press, 1985.

Lewis, Flora. *One of Our H-Bombs Is Missing*. New York: Bantam, 1967.

Lindemann, Klaus P. *Hailstorm over Truk Lagoon*. Singapore: Maruzen Asia, 1982.

Lunderberg, Philip K., Arthur B. Cohn, and Jennifer L. Jones. *A Tale of Three Gunboats: Lake Champlain's Revolutionary War Heritage*. Vergennes, VT and Washington, DC: Lake Champlain Maritime Museum and the National Museum of American History, Smithsonian Institution, Basin Harbor, 2017.

MacDonald, Rod. *Dive Scapa Flow*. Edinburgh: Mainstream Publishing Company, 1990.

———. *Force Z Shipwrecks of the South Sea: HMS Prince of Wales and HMS Repulse*. Dunbeath, Caithness, Scotland: Whittles Publishing, Ltd., 2013.

Mallett, M. E., and J. R. Hale. *The Military Organization of a Renaissance State: Venice c. 1400 to 1617*. Cambridge: Cambridge University Press, 2006.

Marsden, E. W. *Greek and Roman Artillery: Historical Development*. London: Oxford University Press, 1969.

Marsden, Peter. *English Heritage Book of Ships and Shipwrecks*. London: B. T. Batsford Ltd. and English Heritage, 1997.

———. *Sealed by Time: The Loss and Recovery of the Mary Rose*. Portsmouth: Mary Rose Trust, 2003.

———, ed. *Mary Rose: Your Noblest Shippe*. Portsmouth: Mary Rose Trust, 2009.

Martin, Colin. *Full Fathom Five: The Wrecks of the Spanish Armada*. New York: Viking Press, 1975.

———. *Scotland's Historic Shipwrecks*. London: B. T. Batsford Ltd. and Scottish Heritage, 1998.

Maydew, Randall C. *America's Lost H-Bomb: Palomares, Spain, 1966*. Manhattan, KS: Sunflower University Press, 1997.

McCartney, Innes. *Jutland 1916: The Archaeology of a Naval Battlefield*. London and New York: Conway, 2016.

———. *Lost Patrols: Submarine Wrecks of the English Channel*. Penzance, Cornwall: Periscope Publishing, Ltd., 2002.

———. *The Maritime Archaeology of a Modern Conflict: Comparing the Archaeology of German Submarine Wrecks to the Historical Text*. New York and London: Routledge, 2015.

McKee, Alexander. *King Henry VIII's Mary Rose*. London: Souvenir Press, 1973.

Mearns, David L. *The Search for the Sydney*. Pymble, New South Wales: HarperCollins, 2009.

Mearns, David L. *The Shipwreck Hunter: A Lifetime of Extraordinary Discoveries on the Ocean Floor*. Crows Nest, Australia: Allen & Unwin, 2017.

Mearns, David L., and Rob White. *Hood and Bismarck: The Deep-Sea Discovery of an Epic Battle*. London: Channel Four Press, 2001.

Meçollari, Artur. *Incidenti I Kanalit Të Korfuzit: Dresjtësi e Annuar*. Vlorë, Albania: Triptik, 2009.

Miller, Bonnie M. *From Liberation to Conquest: The Visual and Popular Cultures of the Spanish-American War*. Amherst: University of Massachusetts Press, 2011.

Miller, Edward M. *USS Monitor: The Ship That Launched a Modern Navy*. Annapolis, MD: Leeward Press, 1978.

Molaug, Svein, and Rolf Scheen. *Fregatan Lössen: Et Kulturhistorisk Skattkammer*. Oslo: Norsk Sjofartsmuseum, 1983.

Morrison, J. S., and J. F. Coates. *The Athenian Trireme: The History and Reconstruction of an Ancient Greek Warship*. Cambridge: Cambridge University Press, 1986.

———. *Greek and Roman Oared Warships: 339–30 BC* Oxford: Oxbow Books, 1996.

Murphey, Rhoads. *Ottoman Warfare: 1500–1700*. New Brunswick, NJ: Rutgers University Press, 1999.

Murray, William M. *The Age of Titans: The Rise and Fall of the Great Hellenistic Navies*. New York: Oxford University Press, 2012.

Musicant, Ivan. *Divided Waters: The Naval History of the Civil War*. New York: HarperCollins, 1995.

Noppen, Ryan K. *Ottoman Navy Warships, 1914–18*. Oxford: Osprey Publishing, 2015.

Offley, E. *Scorpion Down: Sunk by the Soviets, Buried by the Pentagon: The Untold Story of USS Scorpion*. New York: Basic Books, 2007.

Oliver, Dave. *Against the Tide*. Annapolis, MD: Naval Institute Press, 2014.

Ormerod, H. A. *Piracy in the Ancient World*. New York: Dorset Press, 1987.

Owen, Olwyn, and Magnar Dalland. *Scar: A Viking Boat Burial on Sanday, Orkney*. Phantassie, East Linton, Scotland: Tuckwell Press, 1999.

Palmer, Roy, ed. *The Oxford Book of Sea Songs*. New York: Oxford University Press, 1986.

Parshall, Jonathan, and Anthony Tully. *Shattered Sword: The Untold Story of the Battle of Midway*. Dulles, VA: Potomac Books, 2005.

Partington, J. R. *A History of Greek Fire and Gunpowder*. Cambridge: Cambridge University Press, 1960.

Peers, Chris. *Warlords of China, 700 BC to AD 1662*. London: Arms and Armour Press, 1998.

Pitassi, Michael. *Roman Warships*. Woodbridge, Suffolk: Boydell Press, 2011.

Pleshakov, Constantine. *The Tsar's Last Armada: The Epic Voyage to the Battle of Tsushima*. New York: Basic Books, 2002.

Plutarch. *The Rise and Fall of Athens: Nine Greek Lives*. Translated by Ian Scott-Kilvert. London: Penguin Books, 1960.

Polmar, Norman. *The Death of the USS Thresher: The Story behind History's Deadliest Submarine Disaster*. Lanham, MD: Rowman & Littlefield, 2004.

Price, T. Douglas. *Ancient Scandinavia: An Archaeological History from the First Humans to the Vikings*. Oxford and New York: Oxford University Press, 2015.

Raoul, Bénédicte Hénon, ed. *Vestiges of War: The Archaeology of the Battle of Normandy, 6 June–25 August 1944*. Normandy: INRAP and Regional Cultural Affairs Department, 2014.

Ravn, Morten. *Viking Age War Fleets: Shipbuilding, Resource Management and Maritime Warfare in 11th-Century Denmark*. Roskilde: Viking Ship Museum, 2016.

Read, George H. *The Last Cruise of the Saginaw*. Boston: Houghton-Mifflin, 1912.

Redknap, Mark, ed. *Artefacts from Wrecks: Dated Assemblages from the Late Middle Ages to the Industrial Revolution*. Oxbow Monograph 84. Oxford: Oxbow Books, 1997.

Reynolds, Clark G. *Navies in History*. Annapolis, MD: Naval Institute Press, 1998.

Rickover, Hyman G. *How the Battleship Maine Was Destroyed*. Annapolis, MD: Naval Institute Press, 1976.

Rodgers, W. L. *Greek and Roman Naval Warfare: A Study of Strategy, Tactics, and Ship Design from Salamis (480 B.C.) to Actium (31 B.C.)*. Annapolis, MD: United States Naval Institute, 1937.

———. *Naval Warfare under Oars, 4th to 16th Centuries: A Study of Strategy, Tactics, and Ship Design*. Annapolis, MD: United States Naval Institute, 1940.

Rodríguez O., Jaime E. *The Independence of Spanish America*. Cambridge: Cambridge University Press, 1998.

Rose, Susan. *England's Medieval Navy, 1066–1509: Ships, Men and Warfare*. Barnsley: Seaforth Books, 2013.

———, ed. *The Navy of the Lancastrian Kings: Accounts and Inventories of William Soper, Keeper of the King's Ships, 1422–1427*. London: George Allen & Unwin for the Navy Records Society, 1982.

Rossiter, Mike. *Ark Royal: The Life, Death and Rediscovery of the Legendary Second World War Aircraft Carrier*. London: Corgi Books, 2007.

Roy, Martin, and Lyle Craigie-Halkett. *Risdon Beazley, Marine Salvor*. Southampton: Martin & Craigie-Halkett, 2007.

Rule, Bruce. *Why the USS Scorpion (SSN 589) Was Lost: The Death of a Submarine in the North Atlantic*. Ann Arbor, MI: Nimble Books, 2011.

Rule, Margaret. *The Mary Rose: The Excavation and Raising of Henry VIII's Flagship*. Annapolis, MD: Naval Institute Press, 1982.

Samuels, Peggy, and Harold Samuels. *Remembering the Maine*. Washington, DC and London: Smithsonian Institution Press, 1995.

Sanderson, Michael. *Sea Battles: A Reference Guide*. Middletown, CT: Wesleyan University Press, 1975.

Sands, John O. *Yorktown's Captive Fleet*. Charlottesville: University Press of Virginia and the Mariner's Museum, 1983.

Sasaki, Randall J. *The Origins of the Lost Fleet of the Mongol Empire*. College Station: Texas A&M University Press, 2015.

Scheina, Robert L. *Latin America: A Naval History, 1810–1987*. Annapolis, MD: Naval Institute Press, 1987.

Sewell, Kenneth, and Jerome Preisler. *All Hands Down: The True Story of the Soviet Attack on the USS* Scorpion. New York: Simon & Schuster, 2008.

Sharp, David. *The CIA's Greatest Covert Operation: Inside the Daring Mission to Recover a Nuclear-Armed Soviet Sub*. Lawrence: University Press of Kansas, 2012.

Shomette, Donald G. *Flotilla: The Battle for the Patuxent*. Solomons, MD: Calvert Marine Museum, 1981.

Skowronek, Russell K., and George R. Fischer, *HMS* Fowey *Lost and Found: Being the Discovery, Excavation, and Identification of a British Man-of-War Lost off the Cape of Florida in 1748*. Gainesville: University Press of Florida, 2009.

Smith, Peter L. *The Naval Wrecks of Scapa Flow*. St. Ola, Kirkwall: Orkney Press, 1989.

Smith, Roger C. *Vanguard of Empire: Ships of Exploration in the Age of Columbus*. New York: Oxford University Press, 1993.

So, Kwan-wai. *Japanese Piracy in Ming China during the 16th Century*. Lansing: Michigan State University Press, 1975.

Starr, Chester G. *The Influence of Sea Power on Ancient History*. Oxford and New York: Oxford University Press, 1989.

———. *The Roman Imperial Navy*. Cambridge: Heffer, 1960.

Steffy, J. Richard. *Wooden Ship Building and the Interpretation of Shipwrecks*. College Station: Texas A&M University Press, 1994.

Steinby, Christa. *Rome Versus Carthage: The War at Sea*. Barnsley, South Yorkshire: Pen & Sword Maritime, 2014.

Stenuit, Robert. *Treasures of the Armada*. Newton Abbot: Devon, 1972.

Stevens, Peter E. *Fatal Dive: Solving the World War II Mystery of the USS Grunion*. Washington, DC: Regenery History, 2012.

Stewart, William H. *Ghost Fleet of the Truk Lagoon*. Missoula, MT: Pictorial Histories, 1985.

Stillwell, Paul. *Battleship Arizona: An Illustrated History*. Annapolis, MD: Naval Institute Press, 1991.

Stirland, A. J. *The Men of the Mary Rose: Raising the Dead*. Stroud, Gloucestershire: Sutton Publishing Ltd., 2005.

Sturma, Michael. *The USS Flier: Death and Survival on a World War II Submarine*. Lexington: University Press of Kentucky, 2008.

Swanson, Bruce. *Eighth Voyage of the Dragon: A History of China's Quest for Seapower*. Annapolis, MD: Naval Institute Press, 1982.

Tarling, Nicholas, ed. *From Early Times to c. 1500*. Vol. 1, part 1 of *The Cambridge History of Southeast Asia*. Cambridge: Cambridge University Press, 1999.

Tucker, Spencer C. *The Jeffersonian Gunboat Navy*. Columbia: University of South Carolina Press, 1993.

Unger, Richard W., ed. *Cogs, Caravels and Galleons: The Sailing Ship, 1000–1650.* London: Conway Maritime Press, 1994.

U.S. House of Representatives. 63rd Congress, 2nd Session, *Final Report on Removing Wreck of Battleship "Maine" From Harbor of Havana, Cuba: Letter from the Secretary of War, Transmitting with a Letter from the Chief of Engineers Final Report of a Special Board of Engineers Officers on Raising and Removing the Wreck of the U.S. Battleship "Maine" from the Harbor of Havana, Cuba.* Washington, DC: Congressional Printing Office, 1914.

Van der Vat, Dan. *The Grand Scuttle: The Sinking of the German Fleet at Scapa Flow in 1919.* Annapolis, MD: Naval Institute Press, 1986.

Van Tilburg, Hans K. *A Civil War Gunboat in Pacific Waters: Life on Board USS* Saginaw. Gainesville: University Press of Florida, 2010.

Vegetius, Publius Flavius. *Epitome of Military Science.* Translated and edited by N. P. Milner. Liverpool: Liverpool University Press, 1993.

Veronico, Nicholas A. *Hidden Warships: Finding World War II's Abandoned, Sunk, and Preserved Warships.* Minneapolis, MN: Zenith/Quarto, 2015.

Wachsmann, Shelley. *Seagoing Ships and Seamanship in the Bronze Age Levant.* College Station: Texas A&M University Press, 1998.

Wallinga, Herman Tammo. *The Boarding Bridge of the Romans.* Groningen: J. B. Wolters, 1956.

Weisgall, Jonathan M. *Operation Crossroads: The Atomic Tests at Bikini Atoll.* Annapolis, MD: Naval Institute Press, 1994.

Winter, Harold A. *Battling the Elements: Weather and Terrain in the Conduct of War.* Baltimore: Johns Hopkins University Press, 1998.

Worcester, G. R. G. *Sail and Sweep in China: The History and Development of the Chinese Junk as Illustrated by the Collection of Junk Models in the Science Museum.* London: Her Majesty's Stationary Office, 1966.

Yamada, Nakaba. *Ghenko: The Mongol Invasion of Japan.* London: Smith Elder, 1916.

Yamamura, Kozo. *Medieval Japan.* Vol. 3 of *The Cambridge History of Japan.* Cambridge: Cambridge University Press, 1990.

Yoshida, Mitsuru. *Requiem for Battleship Yamato.* Annapolis, MD: Naval Institute Press, 1999.

Zarzynski, Joseph W., and Bob Benway. *Lake George Shipwrecks and Sunken History.* Charleston, SC: The History Press, 2011.

Articles

Abbass, D. K. "Newport and Captain Cook's Ships." *The Great Circle* 23, no. 1 (2001): 3–20.

Abbass, D. K. "Underwater Archaeology in Rhode Island." In *International Handbook of Underwater Archaeology*, edited by Carol V. Ruppé and Jan F. Barstead, 89–100. New York: Springer Science+Business Media, 2002.

Adams, Jonathan R., Annita Antoniadou, Christopher O. Hunt, Paul Bennett, Ian W. Croudace, Rex. N. Taylor, Richard B. Pearce, Graeme P. Earle, Nicholas C. Flemming, John Moggeridge, Timothy Whiteside, Kenneth Oliver, and Anthony J. Parker. "The Belgammel Ram: A Hellenistic-Roman Bronze *Proembolion* Found Off the Coast of Libya: Test Analysis of Function, Date and Metallurgy, with a Digital Reference Archive." *International Journal of Nautical Archaeology* 42, no. 1 (2013): 60–75.

Allmae, Raili. "Human Bones in Salma 1 Boat-Grave, The Island of Saaremma, Estonia." *Papers on Anthropology* 20 (2011): 24–37.

Allmae, Raili, Liina Maldre, and Teresa Tomek. "The Salme 1 Ship Burial: An Osteological View of a Unique Viking Boat Burial in Northern Europe." *Interdisciplaria Archaeologica: Natural Sciences in Archaeology* 11, no. 89 (2012): 109–124.

Auer, Jens. "Fregatten *Mynden*: A 17th-Century Danish Frigate Found in Northern Germany." *International Journal of Nautical Archaeology* 33, no. 2 (2004): 264–280.
———. "*Prinsessen Hedwig Sophia*: Fieldwork Report 2010." *International Journal of Nautical Archaeology* 41, no. 2 (2012): 456–457.

Averdung, Denise, and Ralph K. Pederson. "The Marsala Punic Warships: Reconsidering Their Nature and the Function of the 'Ram.'" *Skyllis* 2 (2012): 125–131.

Barker, R. "The Size of the 'Treasure Ships' and Other Chinese Vessels." *The Mariner's Mirror* 75, no. 3 (1989): 273–275.

Basch, Lucien. "Another Punic Wreck in Sicily: Its Ram." *International Journal of Nautical Archaeology* 4, no. 2 (1975): 201–218.
———. "When Is a Ram Not a Ram: The Case of the Punic Ship." *The Mariner's Mirror* 69, no. 2 (1983): 129–142.

Batchvarov, Kroum. "Archaeology of a 17th Century Naval Battle: The First Two Seasons of the Rockley Bay Research Project in Tobago." *International Journal of Nautical Archaeology* 45 no. 1 (2016): 105–118.

Beattie-Edwards, Mark, Peter Le Fever, and Frank Fox. "The Norman's Bay Shipwreck, East Sussex, UK: A Possible 17th Century Dutch Ship from the Battle of Beachy Head." *International Journal of Nautical Archaeology* 40 (2017).

Bell, L. S., J. A. Lee Thorp, and A. Elkerton. "The Sinking of the *Mary Rose* Warship: A Medieval Mystery Solved?" *Journal of Archaeological Science* 36, no. 1 (January 2009): 166–173.

Birch, Steven, and D. M. McElvogue. "*La Lavia, La Juliana* and the *Santa María de Vison*: Three Spanish Armada Transports Lost Off Streedagh Strand, Co Sligo: An Interim Report." *International Journal of Nautical Archaeology* 28, no. 3 (1999): 265–276.

Blaufarb, Rafe. "The Western Question: The Geopolitics of Latin American Independence." *The American Historical Review* 112, no. 3 (June 2007): 742–763.

Borgens, Amy A. "Artillery and Arms from the Mardi Gras Shipwreck." *Historical Archaeology* 51 no. 3 (September 2017): 392–408.
———. "Small Arms and Munitions from a Texas Coastal Shipwreck." *Historical Archaeology* 50, no. 2 (2016): 127–151.

Brennan, Michael L., Dwight Coleman, Christopher N. Roman, Tufan Turanli, Dan Davis, Alexis Catsambis, James Moore, Maureen Merrigan, Brennan Bajdek, Daniel Whitesell, and Robert D. Ballard. "Maritime History of Anzac Cove." In *New Frontiers in Ocean Exploration: The E/V Nautilus 2010 Field Season*, edited by Katie Croff Bell and S. A. Fuller. Supplement, *Oceanography* 24, no. 1 (2011): 20–21.

Broadwater, John D. "Naval Battlefields as Cultural Landscapes: The Siege of Yorktown." In *Historical Archaeology of Military Sites: Method and Topic*, edited by Clarence R. Geier, Lawrence E. Babits, Douglas D. Scott, and David G. Orr, 177–187. College Station: Texas A&M University Press, 2010.

Buccellato, Cecilia, and Sebastiano Tusa. "The Acqualdroni Ram Recovered near the Strait of Messina: Dimensions, Timbers, Iconography and Historical Context." *International Journal of Nautical Archaeology* 42, no. 1 (March 2013): 76–86.

Buckland, M. G. Gamble, M. Skeen, and L. de Yong. "The Identification of the Battle Damage to HMAS *Sydney II*." In *International Maritime Conference 2010: Maritime Industry—Challenges, Opportunities and Imperatives, 27–29 January 2010, Sydney, Australia*, 186–195. Sydney: Engineers Australia, 2010.

Calomina, D. "Sea Rams from Sicily," *Minerva* 22, no. 6 (November/December 2011): 32–34.

Catsambis, Alexis. "Before Antikythera: The First Underwater Archaeological Survey in Greece." *International Journal of Nautical Archaeology* 35, no. 1 (2006): 104–107.

Clark, Paul, and Zhang Wei. "A Preliminary Survey of Wreck Sites in the Dinghai Area, Fujian Province, China." *International Journal of Nautical Archaeology* 19, no. 3 (1990): 239–241.

Clarke, Richard, Martin Dean, Gillian Hutchinson, Sean McGrail, and Jane Squirrell. "Recent Work on the R. Hamble Wreck near Bursledon, Hampshire." *International Journal of Nautical Archaeology* 22, no. 1 (1993): 21–44.

Clarkson, Christopher, Ben Marwick, and Sue O'Connor. "Early Modern Human Lithic Technology from Jerimalai, East Timor." *Journal of Human Evolution* 101 (2016): 45–64.

Cofila, Barbara. "Ramses III and the Sea People: A Structural Analysis of the Medinet Habu Inscriptions." *Orientalia* 57, no. 3 (1988): 275–306.

Conlin, David L., and Matthew A. Russell. "Archaeology of a Naval Battlefield: *H. L. Hunley* and USS *Housatonic*." *International Journal of Nautical Archaeology* 35, no. 1 (2006): 20–40.

Curry, Andrew. "The First Vikings." *Archaeology* 66, no. 4 (July/August 2013): 24–29

Delgado, James P. "Archeological Reconnaissance of the 1865 American-Built *Sub Marine Explorer* at Isla SanTelmo, Archipielago de las PerlasPanama." *International Journal of Nautical Archaeology* 35, no. 2 (June 2006).

Delgado, James P. "Letter from Bermuda: Secrets of a Civil War Shipwreck." *Archaeology Magazine* 64, no. 6 (November/December 2011): 48–62.

Delgado, James P., Michael L. Brennan, Jan Roletto, Frank Cantelas, Russell Mathews, Kelly Elliott, Kai Vetter, Christopher Figueroa, Megan Lickliter-Mundon, Robert V. Schwemmer. "Exploration and Mapping of USS *Independence*." Supplement, *Oceanography* 30, no. 1. (March 2017): 34–35.

Delgado, James P., Kelley Elliott, Frank Cantelas, and Robert V. Schwemmer. "Initial Archaeological Survey of the Ex-USS *Independence* (CVL-22)." *Journal of Maritime Archaeology* 11, no. 1 (Spring 2016): 9–24.

Delgado, James P., Jeffery Royal, and Adrian Anastasi. "Revisiting an Early Naval Incident of the Cold War: Archaeological Identification of the Bow of HMS *Volage*

Sunk During the Corfu Channel Incident of October 22, 1946." *The INA Annual* 3 (2010): 54–60.

Denlay, Kevin. "Solomon Islands/Guadalcanal." *Immersed: The International Technical Diving Magazine* 2 (Summer 1996): 44–51.

De Yong, L, R. Neill, and S. M. Cannon. "The Interpretation of the Evidence and Visualisation of the Sinking of HMAS *Sydney* II." In *International Maritime Conference 2010: Maritime Industry—Challenges, Opportunities and Imperatives, 27–29 January 2010, Sydney, Australia*, 196–205. Sydney: Engineers Australia, 2010.

Dreyer, Edward L. "The Poyang Campaign, 1363: Inland Naval Warfare in the Founding of the Ming Dynasty." In *Chinese Ways in Warfare*, edited by Frank A. Kierman Jr. and John K. Fairbank, 202–242. Cambridge, MA: Harvard University Press, 1974.

Eden, Lynn. "City on Fire." *Bulletin of the Atomic Scientists* 60, no. 1 (2004): 32–43.

Einarsson, Lars. "*Kronan*—Underwater Archaeological Investigations of a 17th Century Man-of-War: The Nature, Aims and Development of a Maritime Cultural Project." In *International Journal of Nautical Archaeology* 19, no. 4 (1990): 279–297.

Emanuel, Jeffrey P. "The Sea Peoples, Egypt, and the Aegean: Transference of Maritime Technology in the Late Bronze—Early Iron Transition." *Aegean Studies* 135, no. 1 (2014): 21–56.

Eriksson, Niklas. "The Edesö Wreck: The Hull of a Small, Armed Ship Wrecked in the Stockholm Archipelago in the Latter Half of the Seventeenth Century." *International Journal of Nautical Archaeology* 43, no. 1 (2014): 103–114.

Eriksson, Niklas, and Johan Rönnby. "*Mars* (1564): The Initial Archaeological Investigations of a Great 16th-Century Swedish Warship." *International Journal of Nautical Archaeology* 46, no. 1 (March 2017): 92–107.

Firth, Antony. "East Coast War Channels: A Landscape Approach to Battlefield Archaeology in the North Sea." *International Journal of Nautical Archaeology* 44, no. 2 (2015): 438–446.

Firth, Antony. "A Thousand Wrecks: The First World War on England's East Coast." *Soundings* 65 (2015): 28–29.

Ford, Ben, Amy Borgens, and Peter Hitchcock. "The 'Mardi Gras' Shipwreck: Results of a Deep-Water Excavation, Gulf of Mexico, USA." *International Journal of Nautical Archaeology* 39, no. 1 (2010): 76–98.

Friel, Ian. "Henry V's *Grace Dieu* and the Wreck in the R. Hamble, near Bursledon, Hampshire." *International Journal of Nautical Archaeology* 22, no. 1 (1993): 3–19.

Frost, Honor. "The Discovery of a Punic Ram: Four Campaigns of Excavation and a 'Mini-Museum' at Marsala." *The Mariner's Mirror* 61 no. 91 (1975): 23–25.

Garside, Paul, and Paul Wyeth. "Assessing the Physical State of the Fore-topsail of HMS *Victory*." In *Postprints First Annual Conference of the AHRC Research Centre for Textile Conservation and Textile Studies, Scientific Analysis of Ancient and Historic Textiles: Informing Preservation, Display and Interpretation*, edited by R. Janaway and Paul Wyeth, 118–125.

Garzke, William H., Jr., and Robert O. Dulin Jr. "Who Sank the *Bismarck*?" United States Naval Institute *Proceedings* 117, no. 6 (June 1991): 48–57.

Giesecke, Heinz-Eberhard. "The Akrotiri Ship Fresco." *International Journal of Nautical Archaeology* 12, no. 2 (1983): 123–143.

Gould, Richard A. "The Archaeology of HMS *Vixen*, an Early Ironclad Ram in Bermuda." *International Journal of Nautical Archaeology* 20, no. 2 (1991): 141–153.

Green, Jeremy "The Song Dynasty Shipwreck at Quanzhou, Fujian Province, People's Republic of China." *International Journal of Nautical Archaeology* 12, no. 3 (1983): 253–261.

Green, Jeremy, Nick Burningham, and the Museum of Overseas Communication History. "The Ship from Quanzhou, Fujian Province, People's Republic of China." *International Journal of Nautical Archaeology* 27, no. 4 (1998): 277–301.

Green, Jeremy, and Zae Guen Kim. "The Shinan and Wando Sites, Korea: Further Information." *International Journal of Nautical Archaeology* 18, no. 1 (1989): 33–41.

Hockmann, Olaf. "Late Roman Rhine Vessels from Mainz, Germany." *International Journal of Nautical Archaeology* 22, no. 2 (1993): 125–135.

Hockmann, Olaf. "The Liburnian: Some Observations and Insights." *International Journal of Nautical Archaeology* 26, no. 3 (1997): 192–216.

Höglund, Patrik. "*Mars* 1564: The History and Archaeology of a Legendary Warship." *Skyllis* 2 (2012): 142–146.

Hoppe, Jonathan L. "Ghosts of Operation Drumbeat." *Naval History* 30, no. 6 (December 2016): 44–47.

Hornell, James. "Constructional Parallels in Scandinavian and Oceanic Boat Construction." *The Mariner's Mirror* 21, no. 4 (1935): 411–427.

Horrell, Christopher E., and Amy A. Borgens. "The Mardi Gras Shipwreck Project: A Final Overview with New Perspectives." *Historical Archaeology* 51, no. 3 (September 2017): 433–540.

Hunter, James William, III. "The Phinney Site: The Remains of an American Armed Vessel Scuttled During the Penobscot Expedition of 1779." *International Journal of Nautical Archaeology* 33, no. 1 (2004): 67–78.

Hurst, Henry. "Exceptions Rather Than the Rule: The Shipshed Complexes of Carthage and Athens." In *Riveri per navi military nei porti del Mediterraneo antico e medieval, Atti del Workshop, Ravello, 4–5 novembre 2005*, edited by D. J. Blackman and M. C. Lentini, 27–36.

Hurst, Henry, and Lawrence E. Steger. "A Metropolitan Landscape: The Late Punic Port of Carthage." *World Archaeology* 9, no. 3 (1977): 334–346.

James, Simon. "The Roman Galley Slave: Ben-Hur and the Birth of a Factoid." *Public Archaeology* 2, no. 1 (2001): 35–49.

Jeffery, Bill. "World War II Underwater Cultural Heritage Sites in Truk Lagoon: Considering a Case for World Heritage Listing." *International Journal of Nautical Archaeology* 33, no. 1 (2004): 106–121.

Johnston, Paul F., John O. Sands, and J. Richard Steffy. "The Cornwallis Cave Shipwreck, Yorktown, Virginia Preliminary Report." *International Journal of Nautical Archaeology* 17, no. 3 (1978): 205–226.

Kahanov, Yaacov, and Eliezer Stern. "Ship Graffiti from Akko (Acre)." *The Mariner's Mirror* 94, no. 1 (February 2008): 21–35.

Kapitan, Gerhard. "Ancient Two-Armed Stone-Stocked Wooden Anchors—Chinese and Greek." *International Journal of Nautical Archaeology* 19, no. 3 (1990): 243–245.

Keith, Donald H., and Christian J. Buys. "New Light on Medieval Chinese Seagoing Ship Construction." *International Journal of Nautical Archaeology* 10, no. 2 (1981): 119–132.

Kelleher, Connie. "*La Trinidad Valencera*—1588 Spanish Armada Wreck: Results of the Underwater Archaeology Unit's Work at the Site, 2004–6." *The Journal of Irish Archaeology* 20 (2011): 123–139.

Kimura, Jun, Mark Staniforth, Lê Thi Lien, and Randall Sasaki. "Naval Battlefield Archaeology of the Lost Kublai Khan Fleets." *International Journal of Nautical Archaeology* 43, no. 1 (2013): 76–86.

Konsa, M., R. Allmäe, L. Maldre, J. Vassiljev. "Rescue Excavations of a Vendel Era Boat-grave in Salme, Saaremaa." *Archaeological Fieldworks in Estonia* (2008): 53–64.

Lahr, Marta Mirazón, Frances Rivera, and Robert A. Foley. "Inter-group Violence among Early Holocene Hunter-gatherers of West Turkana, Kenya." *Nature* 529 (January 21, 2016): 394–398.

Li, Guiqing. "Ancient Chinese Anchors: Their Rigging and Conservation." *International Journal of Nautical Archaeology* 27, no. 4 (1998): 307–312.

Ling, Johan. "War Canoes or Social Units? Human Representation in Rock Art Ships." *European Journal of Archaeology* 15, no. 3 (2012): 465–485.

Lo, Jung-Pang. "The Decline of the Early Ming Navy." *Oriens Extremus* 5 (1958): 149–168.

———. "The Emergence of China as a Sea Power during the Late Sung and Early Yuan Periods." *Far Eastern Quarterly* 14 (1954–1955): 489–503.

———. "Maritime Commerce and Its Relation to the Sung Navy." *Journal of the Economic and Social History of the Orient* 12, no. 1 (1969): 57–101.

Marsden, Peter. "A Hydrostatic Study of a Reconstruction of Mainz Roman Ship 9." *International Journal of Nautical Archaeology* 22, no. 2 (1993): 137–141.

Marsden, Peter, and David Lyon. "A Wreck Believed to Be the Warship *Anne*, Lost in 1690." *International Journal of Nautical Archaeology* 6, no. 1 (1977): 9–20.

Martin, Colin J. M. "Incendiary Weapons from the Spanish Armada *Wreck La Trinidad Valencera* 1588." *International Journal of Nautical Archaeology* 23, no. 3 (1994): 207–217.

McCarthy, Michael. "Archaeology and the HMAS *Sydney*." *The Journal of the Australasian Institute for Maritime Archaeology* 35 (2011): 18–27.

McCartney, Innes. "The Battle of Jutland's Heritage under Threat: Commercial Salvage on the Shipwrecks as Observed 2000 to 2016." *The Mariner's Mirror* 103, no. 2 (May 2017): 196–204.

McGrath, H. Thomas, Jr. "The Eventual Preservation and Stabilization of the USS *Cairo*." *The International Journal of Nautical Archaeology and Underwater Exploration* 10, no. 2 (1981): 79–94.

Meide, Chuck, and John de Bry. "The Lost French Fleet of 1565: Collision of Empires." In *2014 Underwater Archaeology Proceedings*, edited by Charles Dagneau and Karolyn Gauvin, 79–92. Rockville: Advisory Council on Underwater Archaeology, 2014.

Merwin, Douglas, ed. "A Brief Report on the Excavation of a Sung Dynasty Seagoing Vessel at Ch'uan-chou Bay," "Geographical Permutations of Ch'uan-chou Harbor and the Overseas Contacts During the Song-Yuan Period," "The Shipbuilding Industry in the Sung Dynasty," and "Preliminary Attempts at Restoration of the Sung Dynasty Seagoing Vessel in Ch'uan-chou Bay." *Chinese Sociology and Anthropology* 9, no. 3 (1977): 6–53, 54–71, 72–87, 88–106.

Mitchell, David. "Predatory Warfare, Social Status, and the North Pacific Slave Trade." *Ethnology* 23, no. 1 (1984): 39–48.

Moll, F. "The Navy of the Province of Fukien." *The Mariner's Mirror* 9, no. 12 (1923): 360–377.

Moreno, Eduardo. "The 'Out of Africa Tribe.'" *Communicative and Integrative Biology* 6, no. 3 (2013): e24145. Accessed December 17, 2017. https://doi: 10.4161/cib.24145.
———. "The Society of Our 'Out of Africa' Ancestors." *Communicative and Integrative Biology* 4, no. 2 (2011): 163–170.

Morneau, Daniel. "The Punic Warship." *Aramco World Magazine* 37, no. 6 (November/December 1986): 2–9.

Mott, Lawrence V. "Ships of the 13th Century Catalan Navy." *International Journal of Nautical Archaeology* 19, no. 2 (1990): 101–112.

Murray, William M., Larrie D. Ferreiro, John Vardelas, and Jeffrey G. Royal. "Cutwaters before Rams": An Experimental Investigation into the Origins and Development of the Waterline Ram." *International Journal of Nautical Archaeology* 46, no. 1 (2017): 72–82.

Murray, William M., and M. Petsas. "Octavian's Campsite Memorial for the Actian War." *Transactions of the American Philosophical Association* 79, no. 4 (1989): 1–172
———. "The Spoils of Actium." *Archaeology* 41, no. 5 (1988): 28–35.

Nelson, Harold H. "The Naval Battle Pictured at Medinet Habu." *Journal of Near Eastern Studies* 2, no. 1 (1943): 40–55.

Neyland, Robert S. "The Archaeology of Navies: Establishing a Theoretical Approach and Setting Goals." In *Underwater Archaeology, 1998*, edited by Lawrence E. Babits, Catherine Fach, and Ryan Harris. (Tucson, AZ: Society for Historical Archaeology, 1998), 14–19.
———. "Preserving and Interpreting the Archaeology of the United States Navy." In *International Handbook of Underwater Archaeology*, edited by Carol V. Ruppé and Jan F. Barstead, 765–782. New York: Springer Science+Business Media, 2002.

Neyland, Robert S., and Jeffrey M. Enright. "Archaeology of the Chesapeake Bay Flotilla." In *Archaeology of the War of 1812*, edited by Michael T. Lucas and Julie M. Schablitsky, 121–143. London and New York: Routledge, 2014.

Norris, Robert S., and Hans M. Kristensen. "Declassified: US Nuclear Weapons at Sea during the Cold War." *Bulletin of the Atomic Scientists* 72, no. 1 (2016): 58–61.

O'Connor, Susan, Rintaro Ono, and Christopher Clarkson. "Pelagic Fishing at 42,000 Years before the Present and the Maritime Skills of Modern Humans." *Science* 334 (2011): 1117–1121.

Oliveri, Francesca. "Bronze Rams of the Egadi Battle: Epigraphic Evidences on the Rams Egadi 4 and 6." *Skyllis* 2 (2012): 117–124.

Papatheodorou, George, Maria Geraga, and George Ferentinos. "The Navarino Naval Battle Site, Greece—An Integrated Remote-Sensing Survey and a Rational Management Approach." *International Journal of Nautical Archaeology* 34, no. 1 (2005): 95–109.

Pascoe, Daniel, and Robert Peacock. "The Wreck of the Warship *Northumberland* on the Goodwin Sands, England, 1703: An Interim Report." *International Journal of Nautical Archaeology* 44, no. 1 (2015): 132–144.

Peets, J., R. Allmäe, L. Maldre. "Pre-Viking Age Complex of Burial Boats in Salme Village: Archaeological Investigations in 2010." *Archaeological Fieldwork in Estonia* (2012): 29–48.

Prytulak, M. George. "Weapons on the Thera Ships?" *International Journal of Nautical Archaeology* 11, no. 1 (1982): 3–6.

Pulak, Cemal, Rebecca Ingram, and Michael Jones. "Eight Byzantine Shipwrecks from the Theodosian Harbour Excavations at Yenikapi in Istanbul, Turkey: An Introduction." *International Journal of Nautical Archaeology* 44, no. 1 (March 2015): 39–73.

Raban, Avner. "The Medinet Habu Ships: Another Interpretation." *International Journal of Nautical Archaeology* 18, no 2 (1989): 163–171.

———. "The Thera Ships: Another Interpretation." *American Journal of Archaeology* 88, no. 1 (1984): 11–19.

Rankov, Boris. "Roman Shipsheds and Roman Ships." *Memoirs of the American Academy in Rome: Supplementary Volumes* 6 (2008): 51–67.

Reynolds, Winston A. "The Burning Ships of Hernán Cortés." *Hispania* 42, no. 3 (September 1959): 317–324.

Rodríguez Mariscal, E. Nuria, Eric Rieth, and M. Izaguirre. "Investigaciones en el pecio de Camposoto: Hacia La Identificación del Navío Francés *Fougueux*." *Revista H Instituto Andaluz del Patrimonio Histórico* 75 (2010): 94–107.

Royal, Jeffrey G., and John M. McManamon. "At the Transition from Late Medieval to Early Modern: The Archaeology of Three Wrecks from Turkey." *International Journal of Nautical Archaeology* 39, no. 2 (2010): 327–344.

———. "Three Renaissance Wrecks from Turkey and Their Implications for Maritime History in the Eastern Mediterranean." *Journal of Maritime Archaeology* 4 (2009): 103–129.

Shinmin, Liu, Du Genqi, and Jeremy Green. "Waterfront Excavations at Dongmenkou, Ningbo, Zhe Jiang Province, PRC." *International Journal of Nautical Archaeology* 20, no. 4 (1991): 299–311.

Skowronek, Russell K., Richard F. Johnson, Richard H. Vernon, and George R. Fischer. "The Legare Anchorage Shipwreck Site—Grave of HMS *Fowey*, Biscayne National Park, Florida." *International Journal of Nautical Archaeology* 16, no. 4 (1987): 313–324.

Smith, Robert. "The Canoe in West African History." *The Journal of African History* 11, no. 4 (1970): 515–533.

Spirek, James D. "The Archaeology of Civil War Naval Operations in Charleston Harbor, 1861–1865." *Legacy* 16, no. 2 (2012): 4–9.

Tilley, A. F., and Paul Johnstone. "A Minoan Naval Triumph?" *International Journal of Nautical Archaeology* 5, no. 4 (1976): 285–292.

Tusa, Sebastiano, and Jeffrey Royal. "The Landscape of the Naval Battle of the Egadi Islands (241 B.C.)." *Journal of Roman Archaeology* 25 (2012): 7–48.

Van Doorninck, Frederick H., Jr. "Did Tenth-Century Dromons Have a Waterline Ram? Another Look at Leo, *Tactica*, XIX.69." *Mariner's Mirror* 79 (1993): 387–392.

———. "Protogeometric Longships and the Introduction of the Ram." *International Journal of Nautical Archaeology* 11, no. 4 (November 1982): 277–286.

Ward, Cheryl. "Building Pharaoh's Ships: Cedar, Incense and Sailing the Great Green." *British Museum Studies in Ancient Egypt and Sudan* 18 (2011): 217–232.

———. "Super-Sized Egyptian Ships." *International Journal of Nautical Archaeology* 39, no. 2 (2010): 387–435.

Ward, Cheryl, and Chiara Zazzaro. "Evidence for Pharaonic Seagoing Ships at Mersa/ Wadi Gawasis, Egypt." *International Journal of Nautical Archaeology* 39, no. 1 (2010): 27–43.

Watts, Gordon P. "The Location and Identification of the Ironclad USS *Monitor*." *International Journal of Nautical Archaeology* 4, no. 2 (1975): 301–329.

Woodward, Robyn P. "USS *Saranac* and USS *Suwanee*: The Forgotten Naval Gunboats along British Columbia's Inside Passage." In, *Underwater Archaeology, 1998*, edited by Lawrence E. Babits, Catherine Fach, and Ryan Harris, 67–73. Tucson, AZ: Society for Historical Archaeology, 1998.

Yang, Qin Zhang. "South-Song Stone Anchors in China, Korea and Japan." *International Journal of Nautical Archaeology* 19, no. 2 (1990): 113–121.

Yurso, Joseph F. "Unraveling the *Thresher*'s Story." *Proceedings* 143, no. 10 (October 2017): 38–43.

INDEX